Cultural Diversity in Family Life Education

First Edition

Written and Edited by

Kimmery Newsom, PhD, CFLE, LMFT

Lover Chancler, BSW, PhD

Keondria McClish, PhD, CFLE

University of Wisconsin – Stout | *University of Central Missouri*

Bassim Hamadeh, CEO and Publisher
Amy Smith, Senior Project Editor
Abbey Hastings, Associate Production Editor
Emely Villavicencio, Senior Graphic Designer
Stephanie Kohl, Licensing Coordinator
Natalie Piccotti, Director of Marketing
Kassie Graves, Vice President of Editorial
Jamie Giganti, Director of Academic Publishing

cognella® | ACADEMIC PUBLISHING
3970 Sorrento Valley Blvd., Ste. 500, San Diego, CA 92121

Contents

Acknowledgments

Thanks to our families both biological and God-given for always supporting the dreams of these little brown girls … Without the help of this village we surely would have fallen short of our goal.

To the colleagues and students who have called for a comprehensive book on diversity and intersectionality to help better prepare for working with diverse families: thank you for your relentless efforts to increase cultural competence.

Thanks to our universities for supporting and encouraging scholarship.

Thanks Dr. Lorenza Lockett for his contributions.

Much respect, appreciation, and admiration to all of the trailblazers who paved the way and gave themselves, their thoughts, and their words for the betterment of others; to the present leaders who continue to inspire and rouse critical analysis, and to the future trailblazers who will use little nuggets taken from this text to make their mark on the world.

Introduction

I N THE LAST few years, there has been an increased focus on diversity and cultural competence in American society due in large part to questions of racial equality. We believe focusing on our role as family scholars in this rejuvenated movement is extremely important. The mission of this book is to ensure diversity courses in family science programs meet the needs of our field by providing information about the unique experiences of families. Our goal is to prepare our students to be competent practitioners in the field by addressing the question, "What is diversity and why is it important in family science undergraduate programs?" According to the National Council on Family Relations (NCFR, 1987), family science is a discipline of study in which "the primary goals are the discovery, verification and application of knowledge about the family" (p. 49). NCFR (2018) goes on to describe diversity as dynamic and continuing to evolve over time: "Diversity provides a lens for understanding (a) disparities of power, privilege, and access as well as the (b) exclusion of marginalized groups" (p. 1).

An increase in "diversity" has become a goal for many institutions across the country. As family scientists, it is of the utmost importance that we are able to serve individuals and families by meeting their needs in their current environment. Underlying the ability to effectively serve any given population is a proficient level of cultural competence—understanding the specific cultural, language, and social and economic nuances of particular people and families (National Association of Social Workers, 2015). Continued education and training are available for family scientists/family life educators (Wiley & Ebata, 2004), but what does this education look like for students who will go on to serve families?

Need for Textbook on Diversity for Family Science

In the field of family science, the family as a unit of analysis is a unique approach to diversity courses. Students learning about diverse families in their distinctive context adds value to any family science program. Previous research indicates that diversity is beneficial for education in general (Clark, 2004; Gurin et al., 2002; Misra & McMahon, 2006) and has positive, immediate, and long-term effects on academic, personal, and professional growth for the student (Gurin et al., 2002; Hu & Kuh, 2003; McTighe et al., 1999). Those positive effects foster students' academic and social growth, promoting active thinking skills and perspective-taking while engaging in intellectual and meaningful conversation with peers to actively engage and understand racial and cultural affinity among different groups (Gurin et. al., 2002). Furthermore, family diversity courses construct a more culturally sensitive student, which will ultimately benefit the families served as well as the student's professional future while adding value to the university's undergraduate program.

The contemporary family is characterized by a wide variety and combination of individuals who are closely or not closely associated with one another (Hanson & Lynch, 1992). Media and television have changed the way family is viewed in society. While levels of cohesion and intimacy have always varied, today our images of this social group include all types of family structures. For example, LGBTQIA+ and stepparent families are prevalent in the media.

The changing nature of the "family" and how it has been affected by the media, culture, and diversity needs to be considered. What we want to provide for family life education programs is a textbook that informs educators in the family field about the diverse needs of the various types of family systems that exist in the world. Our textbook aims to provide materials and resources that will assist educators and students as they learn about diversity in the context of family relationships and interactions with their physical, political, and cultural environments. Facilitation of conversations about race, class, gender, sexual orientation, religion and aging may stir emotions and biases, which could impede the learning process (Beitin et al., 2008). These reactions are not limited to students in classroom settings. Instructors and professors are also susceptible to the emotional reactivity that may be evoked by these specific topics. Although we have the intention to present the information objectively, it is important to acknowledge that subjectivities inform our perspectives and affect the lens through which information is processed and disseminated. Without such exploration, however, these responses might go unexamined.

Family, Diversity, Culture, and the Classroom

Before White settlers came to the continent, some Native people viewed family in a broad sense within larger tribal or kinship support. Since then, society has moved to the "nuclear family" and now to a more "modern" family, as the percentage of nuclear families in the United States has decreased and therefore the diversity of family units has increased (Hanson & Lynch, 1992). Because of the recognition of this shift, family life educators need to be prepared to work with students and parents from different cultures and family structures. As a result, learning that is personal and meaningful must take place in a culturally responsive environment, one that incorporates students' cultural and historical frames of reference to make their learning more relevant (Tanner et al., 2017). Educators who are culturally competent are more likely to teach students how to be culturally aware and responsive to those around them.

The foci of family science include the diverse nature of the family. Additionally, the examination of the effects of race, culture, and diversity on the family structure needs to be a significant part of the focus. "From a cultural competence perspective, social scientists need to understand the cultures of families of color for research studies and in developing effective interventions for them" (McBride Murry et al., 2001, p. 912). Cultural awareness and cultural competency are essential for helping professionals, in this case family life educators, to have as they navigate the work that needs to be done with families. We must strengthen students' understanding of the centrality of diversity to family processes that exist within all populations.

Class discussions about diversity, especially race, gender, sexual orientation, religion, and spirituality tend to create emotional responses in students and professors. These emotions can range from shame to anger (Beitin et al., 2008). Since they are social constructs, emotional responses and the habit of expression can be broken, making room for the development of new ones (Schueths et al., 2013). These emotional responses are linked to values and feelings such as pride and shame and "involve value judgments about the act or situation that evokes these emotions for both students and instructors" (Schueths et al., 2013, p. 1262). These may be the result of their personal experiences with the subject matter, what it means to them, and how they have viewed it juxtaposed with their own lives.

Why Diversity Isn't Enough

TRANS THEORIST SAYS FEMINIST DOORS NOT OPEN TO ALL

By Mandy Van Deven

In her 2007 book *Whipping Girl: A Transsexual Woman on Sexism and the Scapegoating of Femininity*, transsexual theorist Julia Serano made the case that transphobia is rooted in sexism and that transgender activism is a feminist movement.

In her new book, *Excluded: Making Feminist and Queer Movements More Inclusive*, Serano issues a challenge to feminist and queer leaders. She argues that "gender policing" and "sexuality shaming" in the feminist and queer movements have created double standards and hierarchies that prevent these movements from being truly trans-inclusive. Rejecting the notion that everyone is, or should be, the same, Serano argues that movements must learn how to value the strength of difference.

Herizons: How does feminist and queer activism exclude trans people?

JULIA SERANO: Sometimes trans issues are left out unintentionally and other times they are purposefully excluded. There's a particular tendency within feminist and queer movements to challenge sexism and homophobia, while also creating their own hierarchies with regard to ways

American trans writer and spoken word performer Julia Serano argues that diversity is a limiting word that focuses too much on how people look and not enough on how they think.

of being gendered. I call these double standards "sexism-based exclusion." There's a long history in these movements of not just excluding trans people, but of arguing that trans people somehow reinforce traditional gender roles. These allegations aren't just wrong; they actually hurt the movements.

How so?

JULIA SERANO: It's a recurring problem for these movements to create standards that everyone is expected to meet in order to participate. This ignores human diversity more generally, but it also ignores the fact that there's variation within the spectrums of gender and sexuality. It's unrealistic to expect everyone who identifies as a feminist or queer activist to act the same or perform their genders and sexualities in similar ways. And having that expectation creates hierarchies for people to live up to within the movements.

What are some of those hierarchies?

JULIA SERANO: Many feminist women who rightfully complain about being viewed as inferior because of their gender will ignore—or even engage in—instances where transgender people are dismissed because of our genders. And lesbian and gay folks who passionately critique heterosexism in society will dismiss bisexual folks because of sexual orientation.

There is also a tendency among feminists to look down on women who are feminine. This tendency not only excludes people with a more feminine gender expression, but also reinforces the idea that we should all act the same and do the same things.

Historically, feminist and queer movements have emphasized the similarities of people who face gender and sexuality discrimination in order to bring them together. Have we reached a point where these movements need to dispose of this strategy?

JULIA SERANO: It tends to work when a bunch of people with some identity in common get together because of an injustice they all face, and fight for their rights. Those movements tend to be successful at getting traction in society at large. But within those movements, there are all these stereotypes and assumptions about what you have to do to qualify as a legitimate member of the group. That's where a lot of exclusion comes from.

It's important to talk about trans people as a group, and to fight for trans people's basic human rights, but I think we can have a more heterogeneous idea of what those things mean.

Instead of focusing on identity labels, we can think in more umbrella terms and recognize that within any group, people are going to be marginalized in different ways. We can get beyond the idea that certain acts or ways of being are always right or wrong, always righteous or immoral. Understanding that different things have different meanings in different contexts will help to move beyond the problems that exist within our movements.

Have you seen changes that reflect this understanding?

JULIA SERANO: I think progress is being made, but in a very piecemeal fashion. When groups petition for their own inclusion, it can lead to being more accepted over time. Trans people are being included in feminism and queer activism more than we used to be, so that kind of progress is happening. But I don't think we're learning basic, fundamental lessons about why it's important to challenge all double standards and stop creating hierarchies.

There are parallels between the exclusions in our society and the exclusions in our movements, and we can use that knowledge as a tool to challenge marginalization when it is happening in our movements. It has been my experience that people who are familiar with one form of marginalization often fail to recognize other forms of marginalization when they occur.

I've seen a lot of feminists and queer folks give lip service to the need to challenge exclusions in their own movements, but continue to dismiss the needs of the excluded. When the excluded groups point out that hypocrisy, they're accused of being divisive and derailing progress. How do we sort out this gridlock?

JULIA SERANO: We should expect heterogeneity both within our movements and in the population overall. I intentionally use the word "heterogeneous" rather than "diverse" because when we talk about diversity, we're usually only talking about a handful of things: gender, sexual orientation, race, class and age. Maybe there are a few more, but then it stops there. But we don't talk about wanting a diversity of opinions or being interested in many different issues. We talk about diversity as though it's a picture in which everyone looks different from one another, but they all think and act the same. Thinking about our movements as heterogeneous and expecting differences of opinion and priorities is a very good starting point for creating truly inclusive movements.

What are some critical qualities and competencies that effective trans allies have?

JULIA SERANO: Basically, they are the same principles that work for being a good ally to any other excluded group. It's important to listen to people's concerns and accept the fact that we're going to have different views and face different issues. I want to make it really clear that the fact that trans people are talked about as being outsiders who are trying to get into feminist and queer spaces is actually a part of the problem.

Do you find it difficult to communicate the complexity of these ideas?

JULIA SERANO: Yes, it is very hard. A lot of the time, I use terms that audiences aren't familiar with—like heterogeneous, trans-misogyny and intersectionality—which are useful and describe very real phenomena. At the same time, I don't want to alienate anyone. As a person who writes about feminism, gender and sexuality, the writers who have been most influential to me are people like bell hooks, Audre Lorde, Riki Wilchins and Patrick Califia. These are writers whose work is clear and persuasive, which is what I strive for.

It's interesting that you bring up intersectionality—the study of intersections between different disenfranchised groups or groups of minorities—because when I read your chapter on using "holistic feminism" to overcome exclusion, I was wondering how this concept is different from intersectionality.

JULIA SERANO: Holistic feminism starts from the premise of intersectionality and evolved to provide a complementary way of looking at issues that will do a great deal to reduce the exclusions that happen within our movements. I use the word "holistic" to talk about the fact that we each have different perspectives and that we need to move beyond assuming that our own perspective applies to other people. That definitely ties in with what is known as intersectionality.

A new idea that I haven't seen articulated before—or, at least, not to the same extent I talk about it when I describe holistic feminism—is to use an approach that challenges *all* double standards, rather than having the standpoint of challenging this issue or that issue. I'm describing a bottom-up approach that looks at the parallels between different forms of sexism and marginalization and learns to recognize the signs that double standards are occurring or people are being invalidated.

Can you give an example of how this bottom-up approach might work?

JULIA SERANO: The traditional way to challenge discrimination is for each group to petition for their own inclusion. So, transgender people teach others about what transphobia looks like, and bisexuals teach about what biphobia looks like. This is important work, but it's limited in scope. After all, learning how to recognize transphobia doesn't necessarily help you to understand biphobia, or racism, or ableism.

Holistic feminism starts with recognizing the common tactics that are used to delegitimize people, like being depicted as mentally incompetent or unintelligent. Once you learn to see the tropes working to delegitimize people, you can start to take a complementary approach to advocacy.

"It has been my experience that people who are familiar with one form of marginalization often fail to recognize other forms of marginalization when they occur."—Julia Serano

---

Intersectionality

Intersectionality has been characterized as "the belief that no one category is sufficient to account for individual experience or behavior" (Levon, 2015, p. 295). Harrison (2017) said that "social identities intersect in a distinctive way that each identity can only be defined through the intersection with other identities" (p. 1022). According to Carbado et al. (2013), intersectionality is rooted in Black feminism and critical race theory. Also, according to Harrison (2017), "Intersectionality is not simply used to explain how intersecting marginalized identities operate, but rather it has a political undertone that highlights how the intersection of identities can leave particular groups oppressed" (p. 1026). The belief that social identities intersect in a way that each one can only be defined through the intersection of the other identities is fundamental to the intersectionality theory (Harrison, 2017). Thus, in order to understand the depth and breadth of culture and diversity, we must teach our students to examine the ways that these concepts intersect, the meaning of these intersections, and how understanding them can be used to serve families. As we examine family relationships, we must teach our students that relationships are complex and dynamic, particularly due to the nature of private (within) and public family pressures, which can make it difficult to identify the layers of meanings, challenges, influences, and strengths that tend to shape family experiences (Pitre & Kushner, 2015).

Ferree (2010) examined intersectionality and family from two models: locational and relational intersectionality: "A focus on intersectional location emphasizes the identity categories and social positions that are found when multiple forms of subordination co-occur" (p. 428). This makes efforts to bring the experiences of marginalized family types to the forefront of study and research. For example, research studies targeting families in poverty have shown "what these socially devalued individuals face, but also their standpoint theoretically to gain insights into the workings of the intersectional systems of disadvantage" (Ferree, 2010, p. 28).

The locational emphasis on giving a voice to those who have been marginalized and oppressed has contributed to what is called "content specialization" (Hancock, 2007). This interpretation of intersectionality creates a focus on the study of many marginalized groups in isolation from broader systems (Ferree, 2010). As family scientists, creating an understanding of the social location and how that intersects with the larger systems in society to formulate the family experience will be imperative as we work to develop family professionals who are culturally sensitive.

The other model from Ferree (2010) is relational intersectionality. The framing of intersectionality in terms of relations must begin by identifying processes that create complex patterns of inequality for everyone, not just those who are the most disadvantaged. The relational approach has placed importance on the ways that individuals deal with institutionalized practices and cultural discourses. In fact, relational models of intersectionality have been able to include and emphasize institutions with an active power in families through researchers' focus on specific struggles. Some researchers, for example, have studied how state support and women's childcare labor is negotiated by caseworkers and their clients in welfare offices (Ferree, 2010).

The relational and locational models of intersectionality apply to the scientific study of the family. They suggest that in order to understand how the various entities the family intersects with, we must understand the context of their social positions and locations (e.g., poor, Black, LBGTQIA+) and the relations (e.g., social services, the welfare system, school system) to the community. Family science students' exposure to such systems of thinking needs to occur before they are in the field working with families where these models need to be taken into consideration. This textbook aims to advance the process of providing the necessary exposure for students as they embark on the educational journey in the study of the family.

Race, Class, and Gender in Boys' Education
REPOSITIONING INTERSECTIONALITY THEORY

By Joseph Derrick Nelson, Garth Stahl, and Derron Wallace

Boys' identities are distinctly gendered, racialized, and classed across disparate social and cultural contexts. Scholarship exploring these identity processes has focused on them in isolation, honoring the assumption that race, class, and gender are autonomous social categories. Omi and Winant (1994) posit that "race, class, and gender are not fixed and discrete categories.... They overlap, intersect, and infuse with others in countless ways" (p. 68). While acknowledging how boys' education scholarship has engaged analytically with class, race/ethnicity, sexuality, and disability, and has identified connections across these identity categories, our concern is with what we call a "light touch" approach to intersectionality theory that stops short of fully engaging it. Thorough engagement of intersectionality has the capacity to complicate isolated representations of boys' schooling experiences, and unearth new or overlooked dimensions of boys' identities. Amid a so-called "crisis" in boys' education, below we spotlight what we consider underutilized analytic approaches, while asserting that a more robust engagement with intersectionality theory is essential for future scholarship.

Boys' Intersectional Identities at School

Schools are mired with contingencies, confusions, and contradictions linked to the discursive and cultural production of competing forms of masculinity, and boys must continuously negotiate these strenuous environments to learn. Seminal research has illustrated how supporting boys' identities across home, neighborhood, and school contexts, may foster both positive and negative school and life outcomes (Fordham & Ogbu, 1986; Smalls, White, Chavous, & Sellers, 2007; Willis, 1977). Kenway and Willis (1998) already contend that: "A number of studies which show how the masculinities associated with class, ethnic, race, and sexuality groupings; and friendship, family, neighborhood, and other sub-groupings; intersect with the dominant discourses and micro politics of schooling." (p. 511). While these studies hold value, we illuminate the limited attention given to intersectionality, and that, when engaged, this is done tepidly.

Our critiques related to the use of intersectionality are threefold. First, analytic approaches often prove reductive. A focus on race or class or gender tends to operate in silos, rather than in tandem, and without theoretical frameworks addressing their intersections, significant gaps emerge in the scholarly literature on identity. Exploring intersections of class, race/ethnicity, and gender throughout boys' identities holds the potential to reveal more expansive theoretical insights than currently available. We value current efforts by scholars to employ intersectionality within scholarship on boys' schooling and identities, for instance by J.E. Davis, L. McCready, T.E. Dancy, and E. Brockenbrough. However, our reservations lie with the extent such scholarship accounts for key debates in the field of boys' education. Below we offer a balanced critique of intesectionality's use within recent scholarship on boys, and to compel boys' education scholars to more fully leverage the history, constructs, and epistemologies of intersectionality theory.

Second, intertwined with what we consider a "light touch" approach to intersectional theorizing of boys' schooling, is a tendency among intersectionality theorists to cling to theory (Cho, Crenshaw, & McCall, 2013; Crenshaw, 1991; Hill-Collins, 2000), with few examples of intersectional theory being rigorously applied to data capturing boys' schooling experiences (Núñez, 2014). As the "social identities of class, race, gender, and sexuality continue to rub up uncomfortably against learner identities within much educational research" (Reay, 2010, p. 281), we contend there is a need among educational research on boys to explore methods of applying intersectionality to empirical data. Close scrutiny of the trends within boys' education scholarship, and insufficient engagement of intersectionality with a rich theoretical knowledge-base, has arguably led educational research on boys' social and learner identities and schooling experiences to become static, operating too often in separate inquiry communities.

Third, we argue there is a need for interpretative tools with the multi-dimensionality necessary to explore the interplay of boys' schooling and intersectional identity processes. Some researchers have indeed drawn attention to boys' intersectionality within studies of gender, sexuality, race, disability, nationality, and age, but these efforts can be characterized as a "tipping of the hat," or "glossing over" of intersectionality, rather than using the theoretical construct to rigorously interrogate data (compare Hill-Collins, 2015; Rollock et al., 2012). Given its dynamic theorizing of race, class, and gender (Crenshaw, 1991; Hill-Collins, 2000), intersectionality theory provides a valuable logic of interpretation for scholars concerned with boys at school. By pointing this out, we seek to inspire educational researchers of boys to both employ and extend intersectionality theory, particularly when investigating distressing school issues.

Evolving from a moral panic tied to boys' underachievement (Griffin, 2000; Smith, 2003), more specifically to underachieving working-class males (Epstein et al., 1998), a so-called global "crisis" in boys' education has widely animated policy reports and social commentary. Such a "crisis" has informed up-scaled investments in research on boys' schooling (e.g. targeted strategies, programs, and interventions) from the late 1990s to present-day. Scholarly debates over "failing boys" and boys' persistent "underachievement" (Epstein et al., 1998) tend to focus heavily on a so-called "crisis of masculinity." Not only do we view such theorizing skeptically, we draw attention to its repetitive, reductive nature. Furthermore, the "crisis" discourse has a tendency to represent boys in a masculinity vacuum, without consistently accounting for the role class, race/ethnicity, and sexuality plays in masculine identity construction. While considering intersectionality theory a promising hermeneutic, and integral to the future of educational research on boys, we showcase the potential of intersectionality to garner nuanced insights related to identity and education. As social researchers, we acknowledge a responsibility to more fully engage with intersectional frameworks to understand the experience of boys' schooling.

In the following section, we explicate how the "boy crisis" in education has been theorized in academia—depicting debates and trends. To frame the discussion of intersectionality's utility for investigating critical issues in boys' education, we then examine intersectionality theory—its history, constructs, and epistemologies; how it has been operationalized and criticized; as well as its core processes and dynamics. We proceed with a brief critique of the boys-and-schooling literature, followed by case studies of seminal research on the use of intersectionality to illuminate what intersectional approaches can offer scholarship exploring boys' schooling, engagement, and identity. We conclude with implications of intersectional inquiry for educational research on, and with, boys.

Background: "Boy Crisis" in Education

Boys' low educational outcomes globally have sparked unprecedented concern among parents, school professionals, activists, and policymakers (Francis, 1999; Harper, 2004; Sewell, 1997; Swain, 2005; Younger & Warrington, 1996). In the United States, particularly, educational researchers have identified a set of academic issues associated with what is popularly known as a *boy crisis* (Kimmel, 2010; Eckholm, 2006). In *The Problem with Boys: Beyond the Backlash* (Martino, Kehler, & Weaver-Hightower, 2009), contributors provided empirical studies of boys' education in various countries, but with a focus on the sociopolitical, economic, and cultural context of the United States. The purpose of this seminal volume was to identify which factors impeded educational gains for boys, with careful attention to social policy. School and community-based interventions have been employed internationally.

Weaver-Hightower (cited in Martino et al., 2009) has recently interrogated why efforts to address boys' issues in U.S. schools have been less successful and far removed from public consciousness. The boys' schooling literature is fraught with debate regarding factors that contribute to a *gender gap* in education (Sadker, Sadker, & Zittleman, 2009), and boys' educational outcomes specifically. Explanatory frameworks have been rooted in either structural or cultural perspectives. Structuralists consider boys to be passive recipients of debilitating policies and practices within schools, and leave little or no room for boys' individual agency (Bowles & Gintis, 1976; Carnoy & Lavin, 1985). Culturalists deemphasize environmental factors and suggest that boys' behavior is emblematic of their values, beliefs, norms, and socialization, and originates in their neighborhoods and families (Glazer & Moynihan, 1963; Lewis, 1966). Synthesizing elements from both frameworks, individual agency emerges as shaped not only by structural forces, but also by values, beliefs, and norms embedded within cultural milieus (MacLeod, 1987; Willis, 1977). Structural and cultural forces are intertwined and facilitate choice, but neither exert the requisite power to be the sole determinant of boys' schooling, engagement, and achievement (Connell, 1995; Foster, Kimmel, & Skelton, 2001; Noguera, 2008). Our interest is with scholarship employing intersectional approaches that engage both structural and cultural perspectives, and therefore has the potential to disrupt narrow, binary conceptions of structural or cultural approaches to boys' identities, and offer critical insights into boys' schooling.

Research suggests for boys generally, and even more so for boys of color and boys from low-income backgrounds, that their distressing educational outcomes mostly fall within the discrete categories of literacy, retention, special education, school discipline, and postsecondary education. Weaver-Hightower (2009) makes a number of prominent claims in a review of debates and educational research centered on boys' schooling. First, parents of boys were at the forefront of making their issues more public through formal complaints, and not overprotective middle class parents with the time, knowledge, and resources to advocate on behalf of their sons. Second, school systems, specifically teachers' inattentiveness to boys' needs, were deemed a root cause of boys' disengagement from school. Instructional strategies were considered less hands-on, failed to tap into boys' interests, and emphasized emotional intelligence rather than cognition. Teachers were labeled disciplinarians, and harshly criticized for lacking the ability to harness boys' boisterous energy. There was a public outcry among parents, which was motivated by exasperation with a general lack of urgency to address boys' academic issues, especially with recent amendments to the Elementary and Secondary Education Act (*No Child Left Behind*, 2001). Parents acknowledged efforts by teachers and administrators to help boys at school, but usually felt placated or perceived the efforts piecemeal, and thus enabled the issues to persist. Under the G.W. Bush administration, and its promotion of neoliberalism, teacher accountability, equity, and high-stakes testing, each factor contributed to further shaping debates surrounding the "boy crisis."

In light of prominent trends characteristic of the global "crisis" surrounding boys' schooling, the attention given to the adverse behavior of boys cannot be discounted (Martino, 1999). Empirical scholarship on boys has often associated their school misconduct with various learning disabilities, whereby, for example, in the United States, boys represent two-thirds of students who receive special education services (Office of Special Education and Rehabilitation Services, 2005; Skiba et al., 2008).[1] Boys' disengagement from school can have a significant impact on life outcomes, and this trend is compounded for boys from low socioeconomic backgrounds. Boys in the U.S. repeat grades at a higher frequency than girls, and a larger percentage drop out of high school (Bae et al., 2000). Graduation rates are also correlated with disciplinary infractions; for instance, boys' high rates of suspension and expulsion often predict their matriculation toward a secondary diploma or postsecondary degree (Bae et al., 2000).

Although the aforementioned scholarship holds considerable value, the concern lies with the narrow focus on misconduct, and other distressing issues relating to boys' education. The future task of sociological and educational research on boys' education is to consider the multiplicity of all boys' schooling experiences. This renders intersectional approaches indispensible.[2]

Intersectionality Theory: History, Constructs, and Epistemology

Intersectionality has its historical roots in empirical studies where identity processes were considered fragmented, discursive, hybridized, and global (Wetherall & Mohanty, 2010). More broadly, intersectionality "refers to the interaction between gender, race, and other categories of difference ... social practices, institutional arrangements, cultural ideologies, and the outcomes of these interactions" (Davis, 1992, p. 223). Concerned with inequality, intersectionality explores the dynamics of power in relation to the interplay of race, class, and gender. Intersectionality thus entails the elucidation of the intertwining of these identity categories, which constitute multiple axes of intragroup and intergroup difference and elicit multilayered narratives embedded within and across critical social and cultural contexts (Crenshaw, 1991; Hill-Collins, 2000; Phoenix, 2009).

Beginning with feminist theory, specifically Crenshaw's (1991) and Hill-Collins' (2000) scholarship investigating societal oppression and women of color, intersectionality has sought to address how theorists identify *categories of difference*, or power differentials, and illustrate how these categories and differentials interact or become entangled. Intersectionality explores social structures and how power is distributed in absolute and asymmetrical terms, whereby human subjects, and the embodied categories and identities that come to pertain to them, are primarily constituted by systems of domination and marginalization (Prins, 2006). Anthias and Yuval-Davis (1983) as well as Skeggs (2002, 2004) situate identities, and the experience of these identities, within interrelated and overlapping identity categories, where "gender is always lived in the modalities of ethnicity and class, nationality in the modalities of gender and race, and class in the modalities of gender and nationality" (Prins, 2006, p. 278). Social positions are treated as inherently relational, and their identification is aimed at making "visible the multiple positioning that constitutes everyday life and the power relations that are central to it" (Phoenix, 2004 p. 187). For those social theorists who engage in intersectional analysis, critical engagement with power differentials among social categories is essential and required to fully appreciate the complexities of how these inequities not only function in the real world, but are also resisted/subverted by individuals. Such theoretical scholarship attempts to show identity processes as complex and is more compelling than persistent, reductive, and polemical arguments that would show that "boys struggle to read" or that "all boys disengage."

Intersectionality refers to a burgeoning epistemological stance with close ties to post-structuralism, performativity, and queer theory (Wetherall & Mohanty, 2010). A noteworthy portion of critical epistemologies construct subjects as highly discursive, multiple, nonessential, and subject to change, which aligns them with post-structural approaches to theorizing identities, subjectivities, and social positions. Intersectionality, considered both a social theory of knowledge and approach to analysis, is focused on people occupying not just different social categories, but also different social positions, as well as possessing different and multiple forms of knowledge. Judged from intersectional perspectives, knowledge is always partial, dynamic, and subject to the interplay of multiple social forces. Intersectionality is an inductive, *bottom-up* concept, derived from the everyday observation and analysis of routine practices and social positioning, rather than imposed *top-down* at the cue of a single discipline or theorist (Phoenix, 2010). Intersectionality has the capacity to be employed across disciplines and fields, but historically, and in light of this capacity, it has been treated with suspicion and cynicism, and often remains underdeveloped by social scientists, including those exploring boys' education.

Intersectionality: Operationalizing, Criticisms, and Dynamics

A chief barrier that prevents more robust engagement of intersectionality is the lack of consensus regarding its definition. Whether a researcher considers intersectionality a theory, a construct, a heuristic device, or an analytic strategy (Davis, 1992), it often remains relatively vague, and "clarity about what it means, and how to use it, can be as problematic, as productive" (Ali, 2010, p. 3). Stuart Hall (1995) noted that, "When separating out the advantages and disadvantages of using intersectionality in research, it becomes apparent that its strengths and weaknesses—as with any theory or methodology [*sic*]—are deeply intertwined" (p. 5). Intersectionality generally raises two prominent concerns for researchers. The first is precisely its greatest indelible strength—the lack of fixed definition, its vagueness (Davis, 1992), or *elasticity* (Phoenix, 2009). Crenshaw (1991), for instance, defines an intersection as a *crossroads*, while Yuval-Davis (2011) terms it an "axis of difference" (p. 68). A second concern is intersectionality's blind spots, where—similar to most epistemologies and methodologies—it can conceal just as much as it reveals (Crenshaw, 1991; Yuval-Davis, 2011).

To expand the scope of analysis, progressive feminist scholars utilize intersectionality throughout a multitude of disciplines, thus filling in gaps within their respective fields where intersectionality has value to employ, given the inquiry focus. This approach is considered duly malleable and amenable to the contingencies of rigorous empirical research (Ali, 2010; Davis, 1992). As intersectionality is a relatively recent development, Bryant and Hoon (2006) reinforce the significance of building a theoretical and empirical foundation by studying how other social theorists—who are not necessarily intersectionality scholars—engage with research, and how they investigate the embeddedness of gender, class, and ethnicity for the distinct purpose of making more nuanced and compelling claims.

Critics of intersectionality arguably express more disadvantages than advantages when operationalizing the interpretative framework, and largely attribute these disadvantages to the historically divergent logics associated with gender, class, race/ethnicity, disability, and sexuality.

Furthermore, the academic market of sociological and educational research, comprised of peer-reviewed high-impact journals (McCall, 2005), has continued to maintain a narrow silo focus, thereby hindering ongoing engagement with intersectionality. For example, to date, there is no scholarly handbook of intersectionality, and few peer-reviewed journals dedicated to intersectionality. Senior scholars, while economizing use of the term, do make full use of the constructs associated with the theoretical lens (compare Archer & Yamashita, 2003; Lareau, 2008; Lyng, 2009; Nayak, 2003). Our contention is that intersectionality still harbors the potential to foreground a "richer and more complex ontology, than approaches that attempt to reduce people to one category at a time" (Phoenix, 2004, p. 232).

Exploring Intersectional Identity Processes

Social theorists posit that identity is infused with history and shaped discursively (Hall, 1996; McLeod, 2000), and hence the concept of identity opens out onto a set of complex and deeply reflexive processes. Social divisions and positions have different organizing discourses or logics, whereby the ontological dimensions of race, class, and ethnicity, should not be treated similarly or equally (Skeggs, 2002, 2004). Stuart Hall (1996) writes:

> I use "identity" to refer to the meeting point, and the point of suture between, on the one hand, the discourses and practices which attempt to "interpellate"—to speak to us or hail us into place as the social subjects of particular discourse—and, on the other hand, the processes which produce subjectivities, which construct us as subjects which can be "spoken." Identities are thus points of temporary attachment to the subject positions, which discursive practices construct for us. They are the result of a successful articulation or "chaining" of the subject into the flow of the discourse. (pp. 5–6)

What we call identities and positionalities refer to "processes of becoming rather than being: "not 'who we are' or 'where we came from,' so much as what we might become, how we have been represented, and how that bears on how we might represent ourselves, therefore it is about 'routes' as opposed to 'roots'" (Hall, 1996, p. 4). Thus, more specifically, while engaging with intersectionality, the fluidity of identity processes must be thoroughly considered. For example, gender, considered from within a post-structuralist framework, is not a singular or self-same entity, but processed as such, and thus infused throughout social contexts (Yuval-Davis, 2006). Context (i.e., time and place) becomes essential for interpreting and theorizing how participants narrate their positionalities and subjectivities. Each division presents "ideological and organizational principles within which the others operate ... in different historical contexts and different social arenas, their roles will differ" (Anthias & Yuval-Davis, 1983, p. 68). Michelle Fine (1997) broadly insists on social analysis not pursued as if "races and ethnicities [and class groups] were distinct, separable, and independent; [but] rather [as] produced, coupled, and ranked" (p. 64).

Intersectional analysis is pertinent to identity research, but as such it needs to remain a site of contestation (Phoenix, 2010). When intersectionality is deployed as an analytic tool, Lykke (2011) maintains it can make significant scholarly contributions by historically unearthing the specific array of power differentials, or constraining social norms, emanating from how "discursive, institutionally or structurally constructed socio-cultural categories of gender, ethnicity, race, class, age/generation, dis/ability, nationality, mother tongue, and so on, interact, and in so doing produce different kinds of societal inequalities and unjust social relations" (p. 50). Within these sociocultural categories, intersectional analysis will, to varying extents, show how subjectivities cohere around binaries of "dominance/subordination, possession/dispossession, privilege/lack of privilege, majoritizing/minoritizing and so on" (p. 50), and define the myriad ways "people subjectively experience their daily lives in terms of inclusion and exclusion, discrimination and disadvantage, specific aspirations and specific identities" (Yuval-Davis, 2006, p. 198).

Categories tend to be problematic, and they must be shown to be. Their purpose typically is to establish inclusionary and exclusionary boundaries, differentiate between the self and other, determine what is *normal* and what is not, and who is entitled to certain resources (e.g., programs, interventions, etc.), and who is not. The interlinking grids of differential positions related to class, race/ethnicity, gender and sexuality, ability, stage of life cycle, and other social divisions, regularly create, in specific historical situations, hierarchies of differential access to a variety of economic, political, and cultural resources (Yuval-Davis, 2006).

In a seminal study of intersectionality, McCall (2005) distinguished three approaches to intersectional inquiry which illustrate how different methodologies produce different types of knowledge, and that a wider range of methodologies is required to fully engage with issues and topics under the heading of intersectionality: (a) *anticategorical*—which considers social life to be irreducibly complex, multiple, and fluid, and that any effort toward "fixing" categories is ultimately counterproductive; (b) *intercategorical*—which requires research to provisionally adopt existing categories to document "relationships of inequality among social groups and changing configurations of inequality among multiple and conflicting dimensions" (p. 1773); and (c) *intracategorical*—where the focus is on particular social groups at neglected points of intersection, "in order to reveal the complexity of lived experience within such groups" (p. 1774). These approaches sit on a continuum, allowing overlaps, which subsequently fosters complex thinking with regard to the interpellation of identities.

In current social research, should intersectionality be limited to understanding individual experience, to collective experience, or to theorizing identity (Wetherell, 2010)? Or should intersectionality be considered merely the outgrowth of larger shifts in societal structures, and the acceptance of post-structuralism? In the next section, we attempt to have the core facets of intersectionality speak to pivotal scholarship on masculinity and schooling. Connections are made using two case studies of scholarship (Connell, 1995; Mac an Ghaill, 1994), whereby attention is drawn to how intersectionality, or its understanding, arguably does not comprise an "approach" per se, but rather the questioning of a too-narrow approach.

The Cases: Masculinity and Schooling

We argued above that a rich conceptual knowledge of intersectionality needs to be applied to research centered on boys' schooling and identity, and this educational research is essential for the future of the field. Below, we assert that a key component of this argument is a return to seminal texts. The scholarship of Raewyn Connell and Mairtin Mac an Ghaill has contributed significantly to the foundations of gender theory, boys' schooling, and the study of identities. In their early research, which is widely referenced, both theorists incorporate class, ethnicity and sexuality/heteronormativity in their analysis of masculinity. Through our focus on two prominent theorists we consider how certain theoretical constructions and approaches have been counterproductively degraded. The result is similar to a photocopy of a copy, where with each copy, the actual picture—or in this case—the theoretical construct—becomes unrecognizable from the original.

Appreciating Seminal Works

Both Connell and Mac an Ghaill clearly grapple with intersectionality and its problematics—though not explicitly—and this effort adds a new degree of complexity. In *Masculinities*, Connell (1995) offers a theory of masculinity largely focused on the social construction of gender, and, to date, this theoretical construct remains the most influential conceptualization in the field of men and masculinities, and other empirical studies of gender, boyhood, and men (Wedgewood, 2009). Different from sex-role theory, masculinity is here being deemed a discursive construct and, as such, accessible to poststructuralist, postmodernist, discursive psychological and Foucauldian (Foucault, 1966) approaches. Masculinity, for Connell (1995), is a "process toward understanding" (pp. 10–17) that involves raising concern with a pluralistic model of power relations, whereby gender, while it intersects with other forms of power, is constituted out of interaction between social structure and social actors. "Structures," within this modernist paradigm, fail to simply determine subjects; instead "structure" involves a range of power dynamics (Beasley, 2012). Gendered power is a form of power rooted in patriarchal oppression, where it is constantly producing gendered beings, and in turn shapes wider societal structures. Intersections of power structure the analysis of Connell's research. Class and ethnicity, and to a lesser extent sexuality, and how these operate in relation to the social construction of gender, are fully engaged.

This approach to analysis enabled Connell to open-up new "spaces" for understanding masculinity, though in recent years, Connell has been primarily considered a gender theorist. Our concern is with how this limited perception of the scholar has led to reductive interpretations throughout subsequent scholarship, which ultimately defuses Connell's original intersectional analysis. Concerned with the role intersectionality has played and should play in the boys' schooling discourses, is Connell's (1995) construct of hegemonic masculinity, mostly used to explore *dominant* and *subordinate* or *marginalized* masculinities. Hegemonic masculinity maintains the focus on gender relations among men, which is "necessary to keep the analysis dynamic, to prevent the acknowledgement of multiple masculinities collapsing into a character typology" (p. 76). Taking a clear intersectional approach, Connell provided multiple examples of White masculinity constructed in relation to White women, and Black men in relation to Asian women, and how significant "othering" (p. 116) is in relation to subordinated identities. Connell's focus on power is in the tradition of intersectionality, whereby power interfaces with hegemonic masculinity in myriad ways. The intersections of race, class, and ethnicity allow Connell to analyze masculinities as socially constructed in relation to ethnicity and gender, which becomes a far more elaborate and theoretically challenging task than a straight-forward analysis of problematizing the masculinities of working-class males.

Despite hegemonic masculinity's "over-utilization, or rather, overemphasis" (Wedgewood, 2009, p. 335), it remains a powerful, illustrative construct within the masculinities literature. The concept, however, has endured criticism (Connell & Messerschmidt, 2005; Hall, 2002; Wetherall & Edley, 1999). Ensuing debates, we argue, are important in that they exemplify the manner in which boys' education literature—like most scholarly literatures—is subject to trends, which can lead to theoretical gaps, and a lack of reflexivity with regard to original scholars' intent. Prominent contestations concerning hegemonic masculinity have centered on how it can appear sociologically deterministic, or become a free-floating, ambiguous concept. Another concern lies with hegemonic masculinity's lack of attention to class and ethnicity. It is often assumed that hegemonic masculinity operates similarly for all men. As a construct, hegemonic masculinity's purpose, or validity, is not questioned, but made to function within a configuration of practices steeped in ethnic identity and class background. Exploring the dynamics of hegemonic masculinity and subordinated masculinity in a single context provides minimal insight into how identity-based fluidity or mobility functions, and how the dominant-subordinate dichotomy might play out differently in other contexts. As shown in intersectional approaches, power differentials emanate from "discursive, institutionally or structurally constructed socio-cultural categories," which interact to produce societal inequalities and unjust social relations (Lykke, 2011, p. 50). We contend scholars should actively investigate how men can adopt hegemonic masculinity when it is socially desirable, but at other times, strategically distance themselves from dominant masculinity when it is advantageous. Intersectionality, when operationalized thoroughly, allows for "distancing" from certain masculinities, where class, race, and gender are better integrated.

Critiquing hegemonic masculinity, Hall (2002) states, "Hegemonic cultural production, in conjunction with the recurring enacted practices that it encourages (Butler, 1993), reproduces the belief that it is legitimate and natural for men to use violence as a means of oppressing women and less belligerent males" (p. 37). It is indeed essential to consider the cultural production of hegemony. Scholarship that deploys hegemonic masculinity in isolation veers far from its intent. Intersectional analysis requires engagement of how such cultural production is formed through intersections of class, ethnicity, and gender, and across contexts. Undoubtedly, it is reductive to focus exclusively on gender and its relationship to power structures. Exploring deficiencies of hegemonic masculinity through intersectional lenses involves raising questions related to the capacity to challenge and subvert hegemonic discourses; how ethnicity and class function to foster fixity or fluidity of person-hood or the self; how hybridized identities operate; the dynamics of intergroup and intragroup differences; and how the organizing logics of race, class, and gender constitute subjects.

In *The Making of Men: Masculinities, Sexualities, and Schooling* (Mac an Ghaill, 1994), which was published almost concurrently with *Masculinities* (Connell, 1995), Mac an Ghaill provides a conceptualization of masculinity grounded in Foucauldian theory. This seminal ethnography of boys' education and identity primarily explores the "processes involved in the *interplay* between schooling, masculinities, and sexualities," where "microcultures of management, teachers, and students are key infrastructural mechanisms through which masculinities and femininities are mediated and lived out" (pp. 3–4). Within the school, boys' subjectivities were greatly influenced by the "administration's regulation and reification of sex and gender boundaries, and its institutionalization of interrelated social and discursive practices of staffroom, classroom, and playground" (p. 45). Hegemonic masculinity was not at the forefront but otherwise hegemonic discourses in the school were apparent; for instance "the constitutive cultural elements of dominant modes of heterosexual subjectivity informed male students' learning to act like men" (p. 9). Mac an Ghaill established four typologies of the boys in which they perform their gendered and sexual identities amid changing family networks, labor markets, sexual patterns of consumption, leisure practices, and media representations—the *macho lads*, the *academic achievers*, the *new entrepreneurs*, and the middle-class *real Englishmen*. Relations among these researcher-constructed groupings of boys were additionally explored, as well as the range of subject positions the boys occupied.

From an intersectional perspective, Mac an Ghaill's (1994) scholarship primarily considers class, particularly with the *new entrepreneurs* and *real Englishmen*. However, there is a clear effort to engage with the intersections and overlapping of masculine identities and classed identities. Building on earlier work by Connell, hegemonic masculinity was employed to examine the *academic achievers*. The *ideal pupil* literature (Mac an Ghaill, 1996) was also consulted, and applying the concept revealed how teachers regularly identify with middle-class students, and therefore contributed to the constitution of certain boys in ideal terms. The differentiation of masculinities proved a critical learning opportunity, especially given how the four typologies of young men existed within distinct school domains, and where the elements of gendered and classed identities are validated, reinforced, and kept under surveillance by the institution. To more fully engage intersectionality, *The Making of Men* might have interrogated what occurs when there are disjunctions, whereby class subjectivities are sanctioned, but gendered subjectivities are not, and what these disjunctions mean for boys' engagement with school. Few allowances are granted for how boys may shift between certain typologies, given the eponymous hint that their masculine identities were still "in the making". As Connell's and Mac an Ghaill's scholarship ultimately provides a compelling portrait of complex male identities in social and educational arenas as they are shaped and reshaped through intersectional identity processes.

Making Intersectionality Explicit

While the scholarship of both Connell and Mac an Ghaill clearly grapples with intersectionality and its problematics, our focus now turns to two theorists who more explicitly utilize intersectionality to investigate boys' schooling experiences. Both Anne-Marie Nuñez and Louise Archer analyzed boys' masculinities at school, and their approaches revealed how identity was informed by multiple overlapping logics of practice. Núñez (2014) consulted Anthias and Davis-Yuval (1983) to develop new conceptual models for educational research involving intersectional analysis. While examining Latino immigrant and migrant students' access to college, a three-pronged procedure was designed to explore how separate or integrated social categories affected educational opportunities. The first prong entailed conceptualizing the social categories and mapping their relations and interrelatedness. In using intersectionality to trace how social dynamics create inequitable outcomes and constitute multiple axes of disadvantage, lies the danger of a singular focus on individual identities, such that it "becomes all too easy to ascribe educational inequities to perceived characteristics and (in)abilities of marginalized individuals or groups, rather than the economic, social, and political practices that perpetuate these inequities" (Núñez, 2014, p. 88). A second prong explicates the multiple arenas of influence: "(a) organizational (e.g., structural positions of society such as work, family, and education); (b) representational (e.g., discursive processes); (c) intersubjective (e.g., relationships among individuals and other group members); (d) experiential (e.g., narrative sense-making)" (p. 88). A third prong is concerned with historicity, in which the broader interlocking systems of inequality and classification are thoroughly considered as they "evolve over time in specific places, as well as [instigate] social movements to challenge these systems" (p. 89). Collectively, the prongs of Núñez's (2014) approach are to illuminate *intersectionality in action*.

Also examining boys' masculinities at school, Archer (2001a, 2001b; see also Archer & Hutchings, 2010; Archer et al., 2010; Archer & Yamashita, 2003) makes a significant contribution to the field of intersectionality studies. In *Race, Masculinity, and Schooling: Muslim Boys and Education* (Archer, 2001a), the nature of aspiration and working-class identity is longitudinally explored in the United Kingdom, and from varied sociological angles, integrated with consideration of ethnic identity constructions. Of particular interest were Muslim boys' identities, which were shown to be embedded within the context of schooling, and related identity processes of class, race, and gender. Each dimension of intersectionality was engaged, although the use of the term itself was limited. The theoretical construct of *habitus*, for instance, was utilized to:

> help explain how young people are simultaneously unique individuals with agency and subjects who are produced by their structural locations in the sense that their ways of thinking about and engaging with the world are strongly inflected by identities and inequalities or "race," social class, and gender. (Archer & Hutchings, 2010, p. 31)

Archer's theoretical inquiries of gender and aspiration (Archer & Hutchings, 2010; Archer & Yamashita, 2003), alongside class and ethnicity, pull from a robust inter-sectional lens that gives careful attention to youth cultural elements, and the cross-pollination of social identities and learner identities. Archer's concern is with how masculinities constructed *through* discourse were explicated, but more importantly how these masculinities are enacted *in* discourse.

Conclusion: Intersectionality Inquiry and Its Implications for Boys' Education

In this article we have set out to encounter intersectionality theory's tenuous relationship with boys' education literature. In the spirit of a strong intersectionalist focus, we encourage social theorists of education to investigate the overlapping and mutually informing identities among diverse groups of boys. Our critical review has spotlighted the use of conceptual lenses that are too gender-specific, but which may not reflect their originators' intent. In order for future research on boys' schooling and identities to remain theoretically robust, we compel scholars, from the outset, to not be selective with concepts appropriated from theorists who have pioneered the field of masculinity studies. Additionally, we urge researchers to: (a) examine the use intersectionality to develop other innovative frameworks of inquiry for both masculinity studies and educational research; (b) delineate pre-defined and emerging conceptualizations of intersectional identity processes; (c) detail operationalizations of intersectionality throughout methodological approaches, and (d) spell out practical implications for masculinity-based and educational analysis, practice, and policy.

Thus oriented, empirical explorations of boys' identities and schooling should enable researchers to begin to unearth how intersectionality facilitates in-depth understandings of key issues associated with boys' education broadly, and particularly of alarmist references to "boy crisis." Boys' conceptions of *who they are*, or *who they wish to become*, and the quality of and propensity for positive school engagement, greatly influence boys' social and learner identities. The critical edge necessary throughout educational research on, and with, boys diminishes in the absence of an investigation and an accounting for boys' intersectional identities. Researchers themselves need to consider their own reflexivity (Luttrell, 2010), such that their own intersected and intersecting identities are systematically reflected upon.

We contend intersectional analysis of boys' experiences at school allows for disrupting essentialist, archetypal constructs of boys situated within learning environments. Ramifications of race, ethnicity, and class are critical to understand boys and girls in any context (Sewell, 1997; Harper, 2004; Noguera, 2003a). Intersectionality, according to Martino et al. (2009), Kimmel (2010), Noguera (2003a; 2003b), and Way and Chu (2004), permits sociological and educational research on boys' schooling to ask at every turn, *which boys?* Intersectional approaches moreover bolster interpretations of the depth and breadth of boys' subjectivities as these relate to achievement, school engagement, and identities, and help gaining more complex insights into boys' schooling experiences overall; make explicit the nuanced interplay of boys' social and learner identities, whereby boys draw upon separate, although interrelated, discourse communities to construct their identities, which in turn influences boys' engagement with schooling; and amplify the multidimensionality of boys' *voice* and perspectives characterizing their educational experiences and academic performance.

Utilizing intersectionality to explore dynamics among school opportunity structures tied to power relations and boys' identity work, would complicate and enrich scholarship exploring boys' aspirations and social mobility. Lastly, intersectional analysis is methodologically crucial (notably in ethnography, phenomenology, and case studies). The goal should be to enhance design and efficacy of school interventions, instructional strategies, and social programming for all boys, and to promote more expansive educational aspirations for boys, along with facilitating boys' positive identity construction.

Notes

1   Attention deficit disorder, and medication use to moderate school behavior, disproportionality impacts boys (Gurian, 2001).
2   U.S. Department of Education reported women outnumber men in college enrollment at 2–4 year institutions (NCES, 2007). The gap is expected to steadily increase through 2017. Up 2% since 2000, women constitute 60% of registered students in graduate programs. Although down 2% since 2000, men still account for 51% of students enrolled in professional programs, but their overall enrollment has declined 8.5% since 1976. (Martino et al., 2009).

References

Ali, S. (2010). *Intersectionality: Who needs it?* London, England: Institute of Education.

Anthias, F., & Yuval-Davis, N. (1983). Introduction. In N. Yuval-Davis & F. Anthias (Eds.), *Woman, nation, state* (pp. 1–16). New York, NY: Macmillan.

Archer, L. (2001a). *Race, masculinity, and schooling: Muslim boys and education.* Philadelphia, PA: Open University Press.

Archer, L. (2001b). 'Muslim brothers, Black lads, traditional Asians:' British Muslim young men's constructions of race, religion, and masculinity. *Feminism Psychology, 11*(1), 79–105.

Archer, L., Hollingworth, S., & Mendick, H. (2010). *Urban youth and schooling: The experiences and identities of educationally 'at risk' young people.* Philadelphia, PA: Open University Press.

Archer, L., & Hutchings, M. (2010). 'Bettering yourself'? Discourse of risk, cost and benefit in ethnically diverse, young, working-class, non-participants' constructions of higher education. *British Journal of Sociology of Education, 21*(4), 555–574.

Archer, L., & Yamashita, H. (2003). Theorising inner-city masculinities. *Gender and Education, 15*(2), 115–132.

Bae, Y., Choy, S., Geddes, C., Sable, J., & Snyder, T. (2000). Trends in educational equity of girls and women (NCES 2000–2030). Washington, DC: U.S. Department of Education, National Center for Education Statistics.

Beasley, M. (2012). *Opting out: Losing the potential of America's young Black elite.* Chicago, IL: University of Chicago Press.

Bowles, S., & Gintis, H. (1976). *Schooling in capitalist America.* New York, NY: Basic Books.

Bryant, L., & Hoon, E. (2006). How can the intersections between gender, class, and sexuality be translated to an empirical agenda. *International Journal of Qualitative Methods, 5*(1), 2–12.

Butler, J. (1993). *Bodies that matter: On the discursive limits of "sex."* New York, NY: Rout-ledge.

Carnoy, M., & Lavin, H. (1985). *School and work in a democratic state.* Palo Alto, CA: Stanford University Press.

Cho, S., Crenshaw, K., & McCall, L. (2013). Toward a field of intersectionality studies. *Signs: Journal of Women in Culture and Society, 38*(4), 785–810.

Connell, R.W. (1995). *Masculinities*. Cambridge, MA: Blackwell.

Connell, R.W., & Messerschmidt, J.W. (2005). Hegemonic masculinity: Rethinking the concept. *Gender and Society, 19*(6), 829–859.

Crenshaw, K. (1991). Mapping the margins: Intersectionality, identity politics, and violence against women of color. *Stanford Law Review, 43*(6), 1241–1299.

Davis, K. (1992). Toward a feminist rhetoric: The Gilligan-debate revisited. *Women's Studies International Forum, 15*(2), 219–213.

Eckholm, E. (2006, March 20). Plight deepens for Black men. *New York Times*, p. 2.

Epstein, D., Elwood, J., Hey, V., & Maw, J. (1998). *Failing boys? Issues in gender and achievement*. Philadelphia, PA: Open University Press.

Fine, M. (1997). Witnessing whiteness. In M. Fine, L. Weis, L.C. Powell & L.M. Wong (Eds.), *Off white: Readings on race, power, and society* (pp. 57–66). New York, NY: Rout-ledge.

Fordham, S., & Ogbu, J.U. (1986). Black students' school success: Coping with the "burden of acting White." *The Urban Review, 18*(3), 176–206.

Foster, V., Kimmel, M., & Skelton, C. (2001). What about the boys? An overview of the debates. In W. Martino & B. Meyenn (Eds.), *What about the boys? Issues of masculinity in schools* (pp. 1–23). Philadelphia, PA: Open University Press.

Foucault, M. (1970). *The order of things: An archeology of the human species*. New York, NY: Vintage. (Original work published in 1966)

Francis, B. (1999). Lads, lasses and (new) labour: 14–16 year old student responses to the laddish behaviour and boys. *British Journal of Sociology of Education, 20*, 355–373.

Glazer, N., & Moynihan, D. (1963). *Beyond the melting pot*. Cambridge, MA: MIT Press.

Griffin, C. (2000). Discourses of crisis and loss: Analysing the 'boys' underachievment' debate. *Journal of Youth Studies, 3*(2), 167–188.

Gurian, M. (2001). *Boys and girls learn differently!* San Francisco, CA: Jossey-Bass.

Hall, S. (1995). Who needs 'identity'? In S. Hall & P. Du Gay (Eds.), *Questions of cultural identity* (pp. 1–18). London, UK: Sage Publications.

Hall, S. (2002). Daubing the drudges of fury: Men, violence and the piety of the "hegemonic masculinity" thesis. *Theoretical Criminology, 6*(1), 35–61.

Harper, S. (2004). The measure of a man: Conceptualizations of masculinity among high-achieving African American male college students. *Berkeley Journal of Sociology, 48*(1), 89–107.

Hill-Collins, P. (2000). Black sexual politics: African Americans, gender, and the new racism. New York, NY: Routledge.

Hill-Collins, P. (2015). Intersectionality's definitional dilemmas. *Annual Review of Sociology, 41*, 1–12.

Kenway, J., & Willis, S. (1998). *Answering back: Girls, boys and feminism in schools*. New York, NY: Routledge.

Kimmel, M. (2010). Boys and school: A background paper on the 'boy crisis'. Swedish Government Official Reports. Retrieved from http://www.government.se/boys-and-school-a-background-paper-on-the-boy-crisis-sou-201053.

Lewis, O. (1966). *La vida: A Puerto Rican family in the culture of poverty—San Juan and New York*. New York, NY: Random House.

Luttrell, W. (2010). *Qualitative educational research: Readings in reflexive methodology and transformative practice*. New York, NY: Routledge.

Lykke, N. (2011). Intersectionality revisited: Problems and potentials. *Kvinnovetenskaplig Tidskrift, 2*(3), 7–17.

Mac an Ghaill, M. (1994). *The making of men: Masculinities, sexualities and schooling*. Buckingham, UK: Open University Press.

Mac an Ghaill, M. (1996). *Understanding masculinities: Social Relations and Cultural Arenas*. Buckingham, UK: Open University Press.

MacLeod, J. (1987). *Ain't no makin it: Aspirations and attainment in a low-income neighborhood*. New York, NY: Westview.

Martino, W., Kehler, M., & Weaver-Hightower, M. (Eds.). (2009). *The problem with boys' education: Beyond the backlash*. New York, NY: Routledge.

Martino, W., & Meyenn, B. (Eds.). (1999). *What about the boys? Issues of masculinity in schools*. London, UK: Open University Press.

McCall, L. (2005). The complexity of intersectionality. *Signs: Journal of Women in Culture and Society, 30*(3), 1771–1800.

McLeod, J. (2000). Subjectivity and schooling in a longitudinal study of secondary students. *British Journal of Sociology of Education, 21*(4), 501–521.

National Center for Educational Statistics (NCES). (2007). The nation's report card: Reading and writing. Washington, DC: U.S. Department of Education.

Nayak, A. (2003). "Boyz to men": Masculinities, schooling and labour transitions in deindustrial times. *Educational Review, 55*(2), 147–159.

Noguera, P.A. (2003a). *City schools and the American dream: Reclaiming the promise of public education*. New York, NY: Teachers College Press.

Noguera, P. (2003b). The trouble with Black boys: The role and influence of environmental and cultural factors on the academic performance of African-American males. *Urban Education, 38*(4), 431–459.

Noguera, P. (2008). *The trouble with Black boys and other reflections on race, equity, and the future of public education*. San Francisco, CA: Jossey-Bass.

Núñez, A.M. (2014). Employing multilevel intersectionality in educational research: Latino identities, contexts, and college access. *Educational Researcher, 43*(2), 85–92.

Office of Special Education and Rehabilitation Services. (2005). *25th Annual report to Congress on the implementation of the Individuals with Disabilities Education Act, Vol. 1*. Washington, DC: U.S. Department of Education.

Omi, M., & Winant, H. (1994). *Racial Formation in the United States*. New York: Routledge.

Phoenix, A. (2004). Neoliberalism and masculinity: Racialization and the contradictions of schooling for 11-to-14-year-olds. *Youth Society, 36*(2), 227–246.

Phoenix, A. (2009). De-colonising practices: Negotiating narratives from racialised and gendered experiences in education. *Race, Ethnicity, and Education, 12*(1), 101–114.

Phoenix, A. (2010). Ethnicities. In M. Wetherell & C.T. Mohanty (Eds.), *Sage handbook of identities* (pp. 297–320). Los Angeles, CA: Sage Publications.

Prins, B. (2006). 'Narrative accounts of origins:' A blind spot in the intersectional approach. *European Journal of Women's Studies, 13*(3), 277–290.

Rollock, N., Gillborn, D., Ball, S. & Vincent, C. (2012). "You got a pass, so what more do you want?" Race, class and gender intersections in the educational experiences of the Black middle class. *Race, Ethnicity, and Education, 15*(1), 121–139.

Sadker, D., Sadker, M., & Zittleman, K. (2009). *Still failing at fairness: How gender bias cheats girls and boys in school and what we can do about it*. New York, NY: Simon and Schuster.

Sewell, T. (1997). *Black masculinities and schooling: How Black boys survive modern schooling*. London, UK: Trentham.

Sewell, T., & Majors, R. (2001). Black boys and schooling: An intervention framework for understanding the dilemmas of masculinity, identity and underachievement. In R. Majors (Ed.), *Educating our Black children: New directions and radical approaches* (pp. 183–202). New York, NY: Routledge.

Skeggs, B. (2002). *Formations of class and gender*. Nottingham, UK: Sage Publications.

Skeggs, B. (2004). *Class, self, culture*. London, UK: Routledge.

Skiba, R.J., Simmons, A.D., Ritter, S., Gibb, A., Rausch, M.K., Cuadrado, J., & Chung, C.G. (2008). Achieving equity in special education: History, status, and current challenges. *Exceptional Children, 74*, 264–288.

Smalls, C., White, R., Chavous, T., & Sellers, R. (2007). Racial ideological beliefs and racial discrimination experiences as predictors of academic engagement among African-American adolescents. *Journal of Black Psychology, 33*(3), 299–330.

Smith, E. (2003). Failing boys and moral panics: Perspectives on the underachievement debate. *British Journal of Educational Studies, 51*(3), 282–295.

Swain, J. (2005). Masculinities in education. In M. Kimmel, J. Hearn, & R. Connell (Eds.), *Handbook of men and masculinities* (pp. 13–24). Thousand Oaks, CA: Sage Publications.

Way, N., & Chu, J.Y. (Eds.). (2004). *Adolescent boys: Exploring diverse cultures of boyhood*. New York, NY: NYU Press.

Weaver-Hightower, M. (2009). Issues of boys' education in the United States: Diffuse contexts and futures. In W. Martino, M. Kehler, & M. Weaver-Hightower (Eds.), *The problem with boys' education: Beyond the backlash* (pp. 1–35). New York, NY: Routledge.

Wetherall, M., & Edley, N. (1999). Negotiating hegemonic masculinity: Imaginary positions and psycho-discursive practices. *Feminism and Psychology, 9*(3), 335–356.

Wetherall, M., & Mohanty, C. (2010). *The Sage handbook of identities*. Thousand Oaks, CA: Sage Publications.

Willis, P. (1977). *Learning to labor: How working class kids get working class jobs*. London, UK: Saxon House.

Younger, M., & Warrington, M. (1996). Differential achievement of girls and boys at GCSE. *British Journal of Sociology of Education, 17*, 299–314.

Yuval-Davis, N. (2011). *The politics of belonging: Intersectional contestations*. Thousand Oaks, CA: Sage Publications.

Overview of Chapters 1 Through 6

Chapter 1: Race and Ethnicity

This chapter covers the topic of race and ethnicity as it relates to individuals and families. Structural diversity is one of the main premises of this chapter, along with hegemony. Also, a discussion about microaggressions toward people of color, particularly Black people in the United States, and how they are perpetrated is included. We also dissect in-group microaggressions and discrimination between native-born and foreign-born Black people. Intersectionality, specifically regarding religion and racial identity, are also covered in this chapter. The need for representation in the context of studying race and ethnicity is also addressed. The assignments and reflections related to the chapter articles is included. Finally, the impact of race and ethnicity on family life education is addressed.

Chapter 2: Social Class

Class status plays a major role in the lives of families. It can determine access to opportunities and resources for success. The class types and definitions are discussed in this chapter. The difference between social class and social status is clarified. Microaggressions, particularly microassaults, that occur are considered for each of the class types. Privilege based on class as well as the discrimination and oppression that can accompany class status is reviewed through a breakdown by race, gender, and sexuality. There are assignments associated with the articles provided in this chapter. Recommended videos based on the chapter topic are included for in-class assignments. Additionally, impact and implications for family life education are provided.

Chapter 3: Gender and Sexual Orientation

For this chapter, the rationale for combining these two topics is provided. Additionally, historical perspectives on gender and sexual orientation are reviewed. Intersectionality theory and the intersection of gender and sexual orientation and race and class are significant and are part of this chapter's discourse as well. Next, based on literature, the definitions of the gender types are provided. Sexual orientation types are also covered in this chapter. Historical perspectives of race, gender, and sexual orientation in the United States are explored. Terms are defined, discussion questions are included, and implications for family life education are discussed.

Chapter 4: Religion

This chapter's discourse is specific to religion and the role it plays in cultural diversity. Specific to this topic is a discussion of the role of religion in diversity and families. The intersectionality of religion, class, race, and gender are significant and explained in this chapter. We are aware that there is privilege regarding religious practices, and this is discussed as well. Discrimination and oppression based on religion are very prevalent and are addressed in this chapter. For perspective and comparison, the historical view of religion is also explained. Regarding the assignments, there are some blogs provided and reading questions associated with them. Also, there is a reaction paper assignment associated with these blog posts. The implications for family life education are also included.

Chapter 5: Ageism

Issues related to ageism are prevalent across class, race, gender, sexual orientation, and religious spectrums. This chapter provides explanations of the intersections of those issues. U.S. historical perspectives are included, and microaggressions and their detrimental impact on aging are detailed as well. Recommendations for in-class processing of ageism as well as activities are listed. The implications for family life education are provided.

Chapter 6: Fathers, Fathering, and Fatherhood

The role of fathers and expectations in society vary and are sometimes ambiguous. This chapter covers different forms of fathering as well as historical perspectives from the United States regarding the transition to fatherhood. The intersections of class, race, gender, and sexual orientation play a major role in determining the role of a father and are examined. Recommended assignments/educational experiences include interviews with fathers and observations of father-child interactions. Movie suggestions also are provided, and family life education implications are offered.

Goals of the Textbook

There are many goals for this textbook. We aim to provide family science instructors and professors with a tool that encompasses many of the unique types of cultural diversity that families experience all in one textbook. The family itself and the definition of family are not simplistic concepts. They involve so many aspects that can be overlooked if one does not purposely seek to know those things that affect families directly. Our text describes the difficulties that families face regarding aging, fatherhood, race, ethnicity, class, gender, sexual orientation, and religion. The readings that are included in each chapter encourage students and educators to go deeper to increase their understanding of the subject matter.

The exercises and assignments are also designed to help students engage with the material. Additionally, suggested implications for family life education when working with families are included. Intersections of each of these areas are very significant. Each area in every family will intersect, and we want students to be prepared to examine the ways the families they work with are interacting based on their social location. Our hope is that the material and information contained in this text will be utilized to advance the work that is done with families. We aim to help students transition from the classroom to the field, armed with information that assists in shaping their work with diverse people and families.

References

Beitin, B., Duckett, R., & Fackina, P. (2008). Discussions of diversity in the classroom: A phenomenological study of students in an MFT training program. *Contemporary Family Therapy, 30*(4), 251–268.

Carbado, D. W., Crenshaw, K. W., Mays, V. M., & Tomlinson, B. (2013). Intersectionality: Mapping the movements of a theory. *Du Bois Review, 10*(2), 303–312.

Clark, C. (2004). Diversity initiatives in higher education: Multicultural education as a tool for reclaiming schools organized as breeding grounds for prisons. *Multicultural Education, 11*(3), 50–53.

Ferree, M. M. (2010). Filling the glass: Gender perspectives on families. *Journal of Marriage and Family, 72*(3), 420–439.

Gurin, P., Dey, E. L., Hurtado, S., & Gurin, G. (2002). Diversity and higher education: Theory and impact on educational outcomes. *Harvard Educational Review, 72*, 330–366. http://doi.org/10.1353/rhe.0.0172

Hancock, A. (2007). When multiplication doesn't equal quick addition: Examining intersectionality as a research paradigm. *Perspectives on Politics, 5*(1), 63–79.

Hanson, M. J., & Lynch, E. W. (1992). Family diversity: Implications for policy and practice. *Topics in Early Childhood Special Education, 12*(3), 283–306.

Harrison, L. (2017). Redefining intersectionality theory through the lens of African American young adolescent girls' racialized experiences. *Youth & Society, 49*(8), 1023–1039. http://doi.org/10.1177/0044118X15569216

Hu, S., & Kuh, G. D. (2003). Diversity experiences and college student learning and personal development. *Journal of College Student Development 44*(3), 320–334.

Levon, E. (2015). Integrating intersectionality in language, gender and sexuality research. *Language and Linguistics Compass, 9*(7), 295–308.

McBride Murry, V., Phillips Smith, E., & Hill, N. E. (2001). Race, ethnicity, and culture in the studies of families in context. *Journal of Marriage and Family, 63*(4), 911–914.

McTighe Musil, C., Garcia, M., Hudgins, C. A., Nettles, M. T., Sedlacek, W. E., & Smith D. G. (1999). *To form a more perfect union: Campus diversity initiatives.* Association of American Colleges & Universities.

Misra, S., & McMahon, G. (2006). Diversity in higher education: The three Rs. *Journal of Education for Business, 82*(1), 40–43. http://doi.org/10.3200/JOEB.82.1.40–43

National Association of Social Workers (NASW). (2015). Diversity and cultural competence. *Standards and Indicators for Cultural Competence in Social Work Practice,* 13–15.

National Council on Family Relations (NCFR). (2018). Inclusion and diversity. https://www.ncfr.org/about/inclusion-and-diversity

NCFR Task Force on the Development of a Family Discipline. (1987). Family science. *Family Science Review, 1,* 49.

Pitre, N. Y., & Kushner, K. E. (2015). Theoretical triangulation as an extension of feminist intersectionality in qualitative family research. *Journal of Family Theory and Review, 7*(3), 284–298.

Schueths, A. M., Gladney, T., Crawford, D. M., Bass, K. L., & Moore, H. A. (2013). Passionate pedagogy and emotional labor: Students' responses to learning diversity from diverse instructors. *International Journal of Qualitative Studies in Education, 26*(10), 1259–1276. http://dx.doi.org/10.1080/09518398.2012.731532

Tanner, T., Hermond, D., Vairez, M., & Leslie, L. (2017). Does diversity really matter? The interplay between students' race and their teachers' level of cultural responsiveness. *International Journal of Diversity in Organizations, Communities, and Nations: Annual Review, 17*(1), 1–11.

Wiley, A. R., & Ebata, A. (2004). Reaching American families: Making diversity real in family life education. *Family Relations, 53*(3), 273–281.

CHAPTER 1

Race and Ethnicity

Lorenza Lockett and Lover Chancler

R ACE AND ETHNICITY cover a broad spectrum of people, cultures, subcultures, and diverse population groups from all walks of life across the globe. Although they are often addressed at the same time, they are two different phenomena. For this learning experience, we utilize the native-born African American (i.e., Black people[1]) as a model to convey the learning objectives of this pedagogy as we cover the topic of race and ethnicity in relation to the family.

As noted in the introduction, an increase in "diversity" has become a goal for many institutions of higher learning across the country. McClain and Perry (2017) brought to our attention the importance of an inclusive approach, referred to as structural diversity, which exposes students across colleges and universities to the diverse experiences, insights, and language available through curriculum derived from inclusive sources. One of the tenets of a structural diversity challenge is for learning institutions to incorporate inclusive curriculum materials from a minority platform rather than from dominant culture sources only. As future family scientists, it is of the utmost importance to serve individuals and families by meeting their needs in their current environment—which includes people from a multitude of origins. For example, people seem to be more eager to learn and accept assistance in parenting techniques when they can see themselves reflected in the teaching materials. Therefore, to effectively address the nuances of presenting materials that underscore cultural competency means that social scientists and helping professionals must include etic and emic perspectives[2] and experiences associated with cultures across the spectrum; their language, social, and economic realities; as well as day-to-day experiences that validate them as inclusive members of the global family.

---

1   Throughout the text Black people and African Americans are used interchangeably.

2   Etic: Of, relating to, or involving analysis of cultural phenomena from the perspective of one who does not participate in the culture being studied; emic: of, relating to, or involving analysis of cultural phenomena from the perspective of one who participates in the culture being studied.

The central premise for Chapter 2 is for the learning experience to be drawn from an inclusive lens. Despite the influences that White racial framing might present, this investigation explores this phenomenon from within—from an Afrocentric perspective. Asante (2009) defines afrocentricity as a paradigm based on the idea that people of African descent should reassert a sense of agency in order to formulate novel ways of analyzing information about their perceptions that are based on their own ideals. This approach looks at information from "a Black perspective" as opposed to what had been considered the "White or Eurocentric perspective" of most information in the American academy. Asante (2009) emphasized that since immigrant Black people came to America from different ancestral origins, geographical areas, and historical contexts, it should not be assumed that their perceptions of native-born Black members are congruent or that they readily identify with or have strong affiliations with non-native-born Black people. Asante further stipulated that since assimilation experiences were not the same, these variant experiences might influence perceptions and attitudes across a plethora of life events, affecting, for instance, the level of closeness Black group members feel toward each other.

This chapter draws on insights from the native-born African American (i.e., Black) community within the U.S. family continuum. Not only is race and ethnicity explored, but the information that you are reading includes an inside view (emic), as the authors of this text are of African American descent. Additionally, intersectionality, specifically regarding religion, racial identity, gender, social class, and sexual orientation, are highlighted in this chapter.

Hegemony, Racial Identity, and Racism

"We cannot talk about racial identity without talking about racism" (Tatum, 1999). Racial framing is not the central focus of this text. However, it provides a conceptual framework that explains how such framing in contemporary America disrupts associations between African Americans and Black immigrant group members. This subsequently interrupts progression in the identity process of Black group memberships in America. This view or experience is not limited to within the Black community but extends well beyond to other minority group members and the dominant White community. The construct of *hegemony* describes a system of universally accepted domination through the use of powerful and imposed cultural norms. Hegemony is not easily seen as a factor or goes unnoticed in the works of cultural attitude formulation, specifically as it is related to racial identity formation and attaining the American way of life (Burrell, 2009). A hegemonic situation occurs when people of color consent in various ways to this ideology. Williams (2011) noted that such disruptions are reported as a lack of shared identity, and thus "division" pervades the literature in describing the nature of the relationship between different Black groups in America. This is evidenced by the dominant group members' view of what it means to be American (Burrell, 2009). Burrell further noted that the formation of the American identity is woven into the social fabric. This is illustrated by the *American Citizens Handbook*, proclaiming that it is important that people who live and work together have a common mind—a heritage of purpose, shared religious ideals, love of country, beauty, and wisdom to guide and inspire them.

The racialized structures of this society imposed on Black group members by the history of slavery in America, and the intersections of contemporary race and identity issues among Black people, may be powerful enough to breed tensions between these ancestral siblings. These groups include native–born African Americans, Black Caribbean immigrants, and Other Black immigrants (e.g., Black people from Somalia, the Philippines, Nigeria, or other nations) (Feagin, 2013; Williams, 2011). These same issues can be observed in other minority groups, as this behavior is often explained through the lens of colorism.[3]

There is a common ideology that collectively all Black people living in America are among the dominant population. The idea that Black people are a monolithic community in America, that all Black people are alike, and that there is little variation on perceptions of what it means to be Black in the 21st-century America is seen as truth (Burrell et al., 2014; Feagin, 2013; McAdoo, 2002). However, this stereotypical assumption by the dominant group in America rarely applies this monolithic view regarding other groups, such as Asians or Hispanics, but it is clear that these groups, because of their diverse ancestral heritages and backgrounds, are considered different. Such distinctions are not readily made for Black people, and yet it is apparent to members of the Black community that Black membership consists of Black people from a variety of ethnicities, origins, and backgrounds. All Black people are not the same (Burrell, 2009; Burrell et al., 2014; Newby & Dowling, 2007; Springer, 2010).

Lockett (2015) addressed the importance of image ideations and the sense of closeness or social distance between variant Black group members residing in 21st-century America. He coined the term "Black propinquity," which is defined as self-identified closeness in ideas and feelings with native-born Black people, and image ideations toward native-born Black people by immigrant Black people also living in contemporary America. His study identified that although there is considerable research on concepts of Blackness in America, much of this research was conducted with a Eurocentric (etic) perspective as opposed to an Afrocentric (emic) perspective. Social research has established that ideals, social norms, and values about Black minority groups may be shaped by dominant culture premises and that the dominant culture of any society can influence the attitudes, perceptions, and behaviors of minority group members coexisting in that culture.

Afrocentrism, Intersectionality, and the Learning Experience

The intent is not to be anti-White or anti-other, but to highlight information and views from perspectives other than the dominant culture, which shapes much of thinking in Western

---

3   Colorism: Prejudice or discrimination against individuals with a dark skin tone, typically among people of the same ethnic or racial group.

society. The central concept of the White racial frame (Feagin, 2013) is one that helps in understanding the operation of racial oppression as it is engaged by different elements of society. For some populations, groups, and cultures, racial oppression has little to no effect on their daily lives. For others, there is a profound effect on life and reactions to life events. Several contemporary sciences, especially the cognitive, neurological, and social sciences, have made use of the idea of a perspectival frame that gets embedded in the individual mind, as well as in collective memories and histories, and helps people make sense out of everyday situations. Since people are "multi-framers," they have numerous frames for understanding and interpreting in their minds, and their frames vary in complexity from specific micro-level framing on situations to a broad framing by society (Lockett, 2015). Racial socialization is one frame that is used by other cultures, and specifically Black families.

Identity and Socialization

Socialization of children is the process of teaching children to function in society (Hill, 1999; Thomas & Speight, Witherspoon, 2010). In essence, it is a map or guide designed to help navigate through the outside world. Thus, racial socialization is the transmission of information, norms, and values about race and ethnicity to children (Hughes et al., 2006; Martin & McAdoo, 2007; Thomas et al., 2010). The key role of racial socialization is to provide children with a shield from the shattering effects of racism. This is done by the immediate family as well as the extended family (Chancler, 2014; Martin & McAdoo, 2007; Snyder, 2012). In the literature, the systems approach to racial socialization is the most common. Children and families do not exist in a bubble; their extended families, community, society, and societal beliefs all play a role in their racial socialization (Chancler, Webb, & Miller, 2017).

Racial socialization from a Black person's perspective includes exposure and development of knowledge in regard to cultural practices to help negotiate between broader society and their own community, promotion of racial pride, and preparation for bias and discrimination (Delgado & Stefancic, 2001; Peters, 2002). In essence, parents are teaching their children how to be a Black person in a White society (Martin & McAdoo, 2007; Thomas et. al, 2010). Keep in mind, as found by Lockett (2015), the perspectives and the message are not monolithic, only based on the ethnicity and nationality of the Black family.

Intersectionality of Race and Ethnicity

Intersectionality as a theoretical framework requires us to examine the different processes that individuals use to "negotiate competing and harmonious social identities" (Few-Demo et al., 2016, p. 76). The intersectionality of race, ethnicity, gender, and even social class must be examined as they impact individual and family development. Wilkins's (2014) article compares the experiences of first-generation White males to Black males as they transition from high school to college. Although both groups struggle, the difficulties experienced by Black males are race related while the White males are class related. The identity struggles for Black males involved stepping away from how they are viewed by society (e.g., athletic, or overly masculine), whereas the White males did not express a need to change their disposition. Additionally, Black males who were not athletes experienced social invisibility, not only by White students but by Black students as well.

Conclusions

Race and ethnicity are not the same. Race is a social construct and created as a system of social stratification based on domination. Ethnicity is based on the origin of one's ancestry. It refers to biological attributes and cultural practices. Therefore, it is a more accurate description of a person than race. However, many use these terms interchangeably, thus causing confusion, which allows many to view those of a certain racial group as if they are monolithic. This results in certain history to be ignored and/or not given the significance and consideration it deserves. For example, an African student may be praised for being able to trust things being said to them are not racially based; an African American student may view content through the lens of how they have been perceived in their country for centuries. Sue et al. (2007) described this as a microaggression, and in this case the Black student would be in a "catch-22" situation. Although both share a racial connection, they do not share the same ethnicity and thus have different views of the same situation.

Implications for Family Life Educators

As we continue to find ways to educate others about race and ethnicity and its impacts on the lives of those who are a part of the minority cultures, it is important that we reach as wide an audience as possible. As conversations continue about the multifaceted phenomena of race and ethnicity, we must encourage those in the field to stay current on the latest offerings on these topics. As family dynamics change and our definitions of racial categories evolve, it becomes our responsibility to provide family life educators with the tools to serve these families and communities. It is imperative that we know and share the benefits of preparing families to live in a world where race, although a sociological concept, is a functional tool used in society while supporting and validating students, individuals, or families when they share their experiences about microaggressions and perceived bias.

Additionally, it is important for family life educators to consider what this knowledge means regarding their personal biases. Each person has a frame of reference they adhere to based on the life script they have received through socialization. It is important that one's own preconceived notions about groups of people who are different from us are examined. It is the professionals' ethical duty to maintain open lines of communication with one another and educate ourselves about the differences between racial and ethnic group experiences. When we commit to knowledge, we can assist our communities and the family that reside within them.

Additional Readings

The readings that have been included in this chapter assist the learner in understanding the intersectionality of race, ethnicity, privilege, and gender. These intersections show how certain behaviors are viewed differently based on age and the race of male students. Entering college is new and exciting, but it can be challenging. This is often the first time young people of color may be away from daily affirmation (racial socialization) from their family and community. As helping professionals, it is our responsibility to recognize and provide guidance to individuals who find themselves being judged, whether it be outwardly or through microaggressions as a result of bias.

Activities for Further Exploration and Discussion

Article Analysis

1. Read the following articles:
    - Sue, D. W., Capodilupo, C. M., Torino, G. C., Bucceri, J. M., Holder, A. M. B., Nadal, K. L., & Esquilin, M. (2007). Racial microaggressions in everyday life: Implications for clinical practice. *American Psychologist, 62*(4), 271–286
    - *New York Times* (2017, July 17). Was that racist? https://nyti.ms/2uzqpw8. The first incident is provided.

    Not So Black and White

    A barista had just finished preparing an order and then called out "tall, black Marques; tall, black Marques." Marques, a 6-foot-2 African American man who works for a demolition company based in Colorado, stood bewildered by what seemed to be a racially charged incident inside a Starbucks.

    After realizing the misunderstanding—"tall, black" was referring to the coffee, not the person ordering it—he laughed and defused the situation with a joke: "That's me, tall black Marques!"

    Everyday life brings awkward moments for everyone, but some of our daily stories are infused with added tension, especially if one or more of those involved perceive that race is a determining factor.

We collected three more experiences from colleagues—on the sidewalks of New York, at a restaurant in Kansas City, MO, and in the business world. Each case carries a different degree of clarity, and what took place can be a matter of perception.

—Adeel Hassan

2. Using the concepts of catch-22 found in the Sue et al. (2007) article, analyze the *NY Times* article and answer the following questions. Be prepared to share your responses.
    - Did what I think happened really happen?
    - Was this a deliberate act or an unintentional slight?
    - How should I respond?
    - Sit and stew on it or confront the person?
    - If I bring the topic up, how do I prove it?
    - Is it really worth the effort?
    - Should I just drop the matter? If so, what aspects caused you to come to that conclusion? If not, why not?
    - Have you ever been left wondering whether an experience was racism? What is the right way to respond if something like that happens?
    - Have you ever been in a situation where you worried about being perceived as racist?

Video Analysis

Watch the following video and read the article:

Video: Race and Ethnicity

https://tinyurl.com/h4wnala

Article: Is Being Hispanic a Matter of Race, Ethnicity, or Both?

https://tinyurl.com/yb95tcxr

Be prepared to answer these questions in class:

1. What are sociologists interested in as it relates to race according to the video?
2. Is Black, Black; Is White, White? Explain.
3. How are stereotypes defined in the video?
4. Give an example used in the video of pre-judgment.
5. Give one of the sociological theories used and how it is used as it relates to race.
6. Personal reflection: What prior knowledge do you have about race and racial categories? Where did you learn this information?
7. How do we end racism according to the video?
8. What race is included under the umbrella of "Hispanic"?
9. Reflect on the idea of changing the federal racial categories.
10. Would it be better to provide more education on what is ethnicity versus what is race? Explain your answer.
11. What are other gray areas related to this that you can think of?

Video: Let's Talk About Race

https://tinyurl.com/ybfq9caa

1. What is the number one surgical procedure completed?
2. Based on the example given by the presenter, where you live affects what areas of your life?
3. Where is the TED Talk taking place?
4. What groups was the researcher studying?
5. What was the makeup of those who did not fit the description?
6. Give two examples of racial discourse that were presented.
7. What is the word for race in Norwegian? Why is this potentially problematic?
8. What are the potential implications of not discussing race and the implications it can have on society?

References

Asante, M. K. (2009). *Afrocentricity*. South African City Press.

Burrell, J., Webb, F., Russell, C., Schumm, W., & Stoney, B. (2009). *The influences of gender, generation, and racial /ethnic groups on adaptations to hegemony in contemporary America* (ProQuest Dissertations Publishing). Retrieved from http://search.proquest.com/docview/304914605/

Chancler, L.L.M. (2014). *Role of Black grandmothers in the racial socialization of their biracial grandchildren* (ProQuest Dissertations Publishing). Retrieved from http://search.proquest.com/docview/1559110956/

Delgado, R., & Stefancic, J. (2001). *Critical race theory: An introduction.* New York University Press.

Hughes, D., Smith, E., Stevenson, H., Rodriguez, J., Johnson, D. & Spicer, P. (2006). Parents' ethnic-racial socialization practices: A review of research and directions for future study. *Developmental Psychology, 42*(5), 747–770.

Feagin, J. R. (2013). *The White racial frame: Centuries of racial framing and counter-framing* (2nd ed.). New Routledge.

Few-Demo, A. L., Humble, A. M., Curran, M. A., & Lloyd, S. A. (2016). Queer theory, intersectionality, and LGBT-parent families: Transformative critical pedagogy in family theory. *Journal of Family Theory & Review, 8*(1), 74–94.

Lockett, L. (2015). *Black propinquity in 21st century America* (ProQuest Dissertations Publishing). Retrieved from http://search.proquest.com/docview/1727125956/

Martin, P. P. & McAdoo, H. P. (2007). Sources of Racial Socialization: Theological Orientation of African American Churches and Parents. In McAdoo, H. P. (Ed.), *Black Families*, pp. 125–142. Sage Publications.

McClain, K. S., & Perry, A. (2017). Where did they go: Retention rates for students of color at predominately white institutions? *College Student Affairs Leadership, 4*(1). https://scholarworks.gvsu.edu/csal/vol4/iss1/3/

Newby, C. A., & Dowling, J. A. (2007). Black and Hispanic: The racial identification of Afro–Cuban immigrants in the southwest. *Sociological Perspectives, 50*(3), 343–366.

Peters, M. F. (2002). Racial socialization of young black children. In H. P. McAdoo (Ed.), *Black children: Social, educational, and parental environments* (2nd ed.) (pp. 57–72). SAGE.

Snyder, C. (2012). Racial socialization in cross-racial families. *Journal of Black Psychology. 38*(2), 228–253.

Springer, J. T. (2010). Fractured diaspora: Mending the strained relationships between African American and African Caribbeans. *Wadabagei: A Journal of the Caribbean and its Diaspora. 13*(2), 2–34.

Sue, D. W., Capodilupo, C. M., Torino, G. C., Bucceri, J. M., Holder, A. M. B., Nadal, K. L., & Esquilin, M. (2007). Racial microaggressions in everyday life: Implications for clinical practice. *American Psychologist, 62*(4), 271–286

Tatum, B. D. (1999). *Why are all the Black kids sitting together in the cafeteria? And other conversations about race.* Basic Books.

Thomas, A., Speight, S., & Witherspoon, K. (2010). Racial socialization, racial identity, and race-related stress of African American parents. *Family Journal, 18*(4), 407–412.

Williams, V.V. (2011). *Brothers of the trade: Intersections of racial framing and identity processes upon African Americans and African immigrants in America—ancestral kinsmen of the American slave trade* (ProQuest Dissertations Publishing). Retrieved from http://search.proquest.com/docview/885230751/

Wilkins, A. C. (2014). Race, age, and identity transformations in the transition from high school to college for Black and first-generation White. *Sociology of Education, 87*(3), 171–187.

CHAPTER 2

Social Class

T HE ORIGIN OF social class and social status has been covered by many researchers. Parkin (1962) reported the term emerged due to the conversion from barbarism to civilization and later work edited by Rhonda Levine (2006), which is a collection of works that examined the role class plays in current in stratification. Therefore, it is not the intention of this chapter to discuss the origin of social class and status, but to define and clarify these terms and their differences and to examine the intersectional aspects of social class and social status. Additionally, ancillary readings are provided to deepen the understanding of race and social class, along with suggested activities to apply the concepts from the chapter.

Social Class

Social class as proposed by Marx was the division of individuals into categories in proximity to their level of access to power, now commonly known as *upper, middle,* and *lower* class (Grabb, 1980; Schooler, 1994). Since these categories are broad, there are further classifications within each of the classes. The middle class is the most common category that is subdivided (i.e., lower-middle or upper-middle class).

Social class plays a major role in the lives of families and can determine access to opportunities and resources for success. There are many things that influence one's social class, including family size and geographic location. For example, income data from 2012–2013 collected by the Pew Research Center (2016) determined the social class of a three-person household living in a metropolitan area. The study determined the following: **Upper class** consists of households earning $124,925 per year or more. Midland, Texas, had the highest share of adults (37%) in this tier (Pew Research, 2016). The **middle class** comprises household earnings between $41,641 and $124,924 per year. At 67%, Wausau, Wisconsin, had the highest number of families in this group. The **lower class** includes those who earn $41,640 per year or less. Forty-seven percent of adult households in Brownsville-Harlingen, Texas, and Laredo, Texas, fit this criterion.

Understanding the Differences Between Class and Social Status

It is important for family scientists to understand the difference between social status and social class. Although the two are often used interchangeably, they have distinct differences. Social class is defined as groups of individuals bound by their possessions and their level of control (Schooler, 1994). In contrast, social status is determined by how one is seen by society. Social status, in essence, is the measurement of one's value to society. For example, if we examine the social status and class of a college student who recently became a professional athlete, one may conclude that the athlete's contract with a professional team puts them in the upper social class category. However, their social status may not immediately change. Although predicated on how one is perceived by society and the decisions they make with their new wealth, they may gain social status; thus, they will not or at the very least have difficulty getting on the private country club invite lists or being welcomed in neighborhoods their new wealth affords them. Comparatively, professions like ministers or pastors have high social status in most communities even though most of them, at best, would classify as middle class. Another distinct difference is that social status is not linear, meaning it is measured using many variables, unlike income, which is linear and used to define social class. For example, Flitter (2019) wrote an article addressing racism in the banking industry for the *New York Times*. The article was about former NFL player Jimmy Kennedy who had earned over $13 million during his career. Although he had the income (over $250,000) to become part of the elite clientele with JPMorgan Chase, he was not allowed to reap these benefits. The financial advisor who informed him of these perks was later fired for his advocacy for Mr. Kennedy and replaced by an individual who was a Black man. According to the article, this advisor was appointed because he was a Black male. The new advisor advised Mr. Kennedy that his social status (i.e., "big Black man") prevented him from joining this higher social status and perks afforded to wealthy individuals due to the perception of his physical stature. Additionally, Mr. Kennedy earned his money through athletics, thus his wealth did not have historical value and was deemed less "worthy," resulting in his admittance to that social status to be denied. The microaggressions, specifically microinvalidations, were used to justify him being excluded from membership.

Intersectionality of Social Class

As defined in this text, *intersectionality,* as a theoretical framework, requires us to examine the different processes that individuals use to "negotiate competing and harmonious social identities" (Few-Demo et al., 2016, p. 76). There are several factors that influence one's social class and their ability to navigate changing social classes. For example, in working families, their ability to care for their loved ones is highly dependent on the amount of money one makes. What we find is the amount one makes is not solely based on the job/career they have. These other influences include, but are not limited to, gender, race, and sexuality. Once you have read the role each intersection of an individual as presented in this chapter, critically examine the multiple intersections and the effects they have on individuals and their ability to provide for their families (i.e., limited earning potential or changing a social status).

The Difference in Wages Earned by Gender

It is widely reported that women earn less than men (Patten, 2016). There are several factors in the past that have been used to justify this. First, men have been expected to be the head of the family and thus need to earn more because they are responsible for taking care of their families. This may have had some credence in the 1950s or even the 1960s. However, with more homes being headed by single women, the wage gap automatically creates problems for these households. Second, women often take more service-oriented jobs with more flexibility to be able to attend events and activities that their children or partners are involved in. These jobs tend to pay lower wages because service industry jobs are not valued as much as the private sector and business jobs.

This excuse is becoming obsolete as the workplace expands beyond the brick and mortar it was once confined to. Additionally, task completion is no longer tied to a strict 9-to-5 schedule. Other tried and true explanations have been that women are not as educated and they work less than men, mostly due to their responsibilities at home, which explains part of the gap, although not as much as commonly believed (Gould et al., 2016). Additionally, it is important to point out that career choices play a role in the wage differential, taking into consideration the role of gender-based career bias (i.e., steering women away from the science and technology field) (Gould et al., 2016), thus, leaving one to draw the conclusion that gender discrimination may be the root cause for the approximate 85 cents to the dollar general wage gap difference between men and women.

The Difference in Wages Earned by Race

When examining the difference in earnings and adding race as an additional layer, the numbers are far more staggering. In a 2015 study conducted by Pew Research Center, White men out-earn Black and Hispanic/Latinx men and women of all races. However, they did not hold the title of highest earner (Patten, 2016). This title is held by Asian men who earned an average hourly wage of $24 to White men's $21 (Patten, 2016). Asian women and White women are $18 and $17 dollars, respectively, behind White men, whereas Black women and Hispanic/Latinx women earned $13 and $12, respectively. The earnings of Asian women and White women also surpassed that of Black men and Hispanic/Latinx men, who earned an average of $15 and $14 hourly. This demonstrates that race has a larger influence than gender in explaining the wage gap.

The Difference in Wages Earned Based on Sexuality

Many states and principalities, including Washington DC, prohibit discrimination in hiring based on sexual orientation. However, since there are no federal laws that prohibit sexual orientation from being a factor in the decisions on promotion or compensation, that leaves the population of people who do not ascribe to heteronormativity especially vulnerable (Baumle, 2013). Mize (2016) found that since many sexual minorities are believed to be "less competent," they are less likely to be recommended or considered for promotion. According to Mize (2016), lesbian women and gay men experience this differently. Lesbian women fare better than gay men regarding the pay gap, and lesbian women earn more than their heterosexual counterparts. This did not hold true for bisexual women, as they earn about 7% less when all factors were considered. The likely reason they earned less is due to the perception of being sexually promiscuous and being perceived as being disingenuous about their sexual orientation (Mize, 2016).

As discussed previously, when considering gender, women earned less due to beliefs that men had children to support. The same reasoning is used to explain why gay men, who are less likely to have children, earn less than their heterosexual counterparts. However, the data shows that gay men and heterosexual men have similar earnings when controlling for these factors, but the difference, when disaggregating the data and looking at bisexual men, in these findings cannot be as easily accounted for. The study found that bisexual men earn 16% less than their heterosexual counterparts (Mize, 2016). The difference in earning potential when using the lens of sexual orientation demonstrates the power prejudicial treatment can play in determining earning potential.

Conclusions

In the 1983 movie *Trading Places,* actors Dan Aykroyd and Eddie Murphy are placed in a life situation by two wealthy businessmen, played by actors Don Ameche and Ralph Bellamy. The businessmen make a bet for a dollar on the power of opportunity (i.e., nurture versus nature). The results of the wager showed that if one is given the opportunity for success, the potential for success is unlimited. The opposite is the case when those opportunities are taken away. The underlying intersectionality is that one of the men was Black, whereas the other was White. Just like in this movie, race and social class are connected in American society; those who are not members of the dominant racial group face similar struggles, not only financially but in academic achievement as well. It could be a result of discrimination or lack of academic exposure due to limited educational and financial resources (Harackiewicz et al., 2015).

Often, the difference in how we act, how we feel about ourselves, and how we see others is tied to social class and social status. Children perform better when they do not know their social class. Anxiety and other mental health disorders are higher in societies with greater wealth disparities, thus showing inequality is contentious and corrosive (Wilkinson & Pickett, 2014).

Implications for Family Life Educators

As we continue to find ways to educate others about social class and the role it plays in the lives of families, we must keep in mind how the other roles they occupy also contribute to the outcome of the individual, family and/or their role in society. It is important, when working with families of different income levels, to have an understanding of their social class as well as their social status, as both can influence their willingness to and the way they interact with you. Additionally, as a professional, it is important to look beyond the surface when examining a family's status. As discussed previously, there are several factors besides income that need to be considered.

Additionally, we must remember individuals often equate wealth with a sense of superiority, or lack thereof with inferiority. Wilkinson and Pickett (2014) found Indian children performed almost equally when they did not know what social class they occupied. However, once those who are seen as stereotypically inferior were made aware of this fact, even subtlety, their performance changed. This demonstrated the social effects that social class plays in how children see themselves and their abilities. Your ability to help them separate social class and status from self-worth is extremely important.

Additional Readings

The readings included in this chapter show the intersectionality of social class and the other identities one may hold. These intersections show how certain class levels influence how one sees themselves and their abilities as well as what they believe others can accomplish. They also explain the difference between social class and social status.

Mindful of Inequality?

By Richard Wilkinson and Kate Pickett

The naïve view of inequality is that it only matters if it makes the poor poorer, or if it is unfair. But the truth is that we have deep-seated psychological responses to the levels of inequality in society. Our tendency to equate outward wealth with inner worth means that inequality colors our social perception. It invokes deep psychological responses—feelings of dominance and subordination, superiority and inferiority—and affects the way we see and treat each other.

Our extraordinary sensitivity to being regarded as inferior is only too easily demonstrated. Indian children from different castes may do almost equally well in pen-and-paper tests when they don't know each other's caste. (Hoff & Pandey 2006) But the lower-caste children do much less well as soon as their status is known. Even the most subtle reminder that someone belongs to a social class, ethnic group or gender which is stereotypically regarded as inferior is enough to reduce performance. (Steele & Aronson 1995)

A few years ago, we published evidence that major and minor mental illnesses are three times as common in more equal developed countries as in the more equal ones. (Pickett, James & Wilkinson 2006) An American is likely to know three times as many people with depression or anxiety problems as someone in Japan or Germany. The differences are not a matter of awareness, definitions or access to treatment. To compare mental illness rates internationally, World Health Organization surveys asked people in each country about their mood, tiredness, agitation, concentration, sleeping patterns, self-confidence and so on, which have been found to be good indicators of mental illness.

Inequality affects the way we see and treat each other.

More recent studies have found the same pattern. One, looking at the 50 U.S. states, found that after taking account of age, income and educational differences, depression is more common in states with more income inequality. Another study, which combined data from over 100 surveys in 26 countries, found that schizophrenia is around three times as common in more unequal than in less unequal societies.

Mental Disorders

So what is happening? In an important research paper, Sheri Johnson, a psychologist at Berkeley, and her colleagues have reviewed a vast body of evidence from biological, behavioral and self-reported accounts, suggesting that a wide range of mental disorders may originate in a "dominance behavioral system." (Johnson, Leedom & Muhtadie 2012) Part of our evolved psychological make-up and almost universal in mammals, it is a system for recognizing and responding to social ranking systems—to hierarchy, power and subordination. Brain imaging studies suggest that there are particular areas of the brain and neural mechanisms dedicated to processing social rank. (Zink et al. 2008)

Johnson suggests that conditions such as mania and narcissism are related to inflated perceptions of, or striving for, status and dominance. In contrast, anxiety and depression seem to involve responses to, or attempts to avoid, subordination. Conditions like antisocial personality disorder and psychopathy, which involve egocentrism and lack of empathy, are probably also features of a strong social dominance drive. Bipolar disorder may involve oscillations between striving for status and dominance and feelings of defeat and inferiority.

If these conditions are related to dominance and subordination, you might think it suggests only that things like narcissism would be more common at the top of the social hierarchy, and others, like depression, at the bottom. But while depression is much more common lower down the social ladder, it exists at all levels in society: Few are immune to feelings of defeat or failure. Similarly, people can be narcissistic or strive for dominance at any level in the hierarchy, even though psychologist Paul Piff has shown that higher status is associated with more unethical and narcissistic behavior. (Piff et al. 2012) He found that drivers of more expensive cars were less likely to give way to pedestrians or to other cars; higher-status people were also more likely to help themselves to candies they had been told were intended for children. They also had a greater sense of entitlement and were less generous.

Dominance and Subordination

One of the important effects of bigger income differences between rich and poor is to intensify issues of dominance and subordination, superiority and inferiority. Although there is always some connection between people's income and the social class they feel they belong to, the match between the two is closer in societies with bigger income differences between rich and poor. (Andersen & Curtis 2012)

A recent study of 34,000 people in 31 countries found that, in countries with bigger income differences, status anxiety was more common at all levels in the social hierarchy. (Layte & Whelan 2013) Another international study found that self-enhancement or self-aggrandise-ment—presenting an inflated view of yourself—was more common in more unequal societies. (Loughnan et al. 2011) That may be why 93% of American students thought they were more skilful drivers than average, while only 69% of Swedes did. (Svenson 1981) We had predicted several years earlier that, because greater inequality increases status insecurity and competition, people in more unequal societies would feel they couldn't afford to be modest about their achievements and abilities. (Wilkinson & Pickett 2010)

The recorded increases in narcissism rates in the USA (as measured by the Narcissistic Personality Inventory) coincide with widening income differences. (Twenge et al. 2008) Bigger material differences create bigger social distances. Feelings of superiority and inferiority increase, status becomes an essential part of how we judge each other, and we all become more neurotic about impression management and how we are seen.

The Imprint of Status and Class

With rising inequality strengthening all the ways in which status and class imprint themselves on us from early childhood onwards, we should not be surprised by the evidence that social mobility has slowed and equality of opportunity for children has become a more distant dream. (Wilkinson & Pickett 2010; Krueger 2012) Nor should we be surprised that all the problems more common lower down the social ladder—including violence, poor health, bullying, incarceration, low math and literacy scores, teenage births and lower levels of child well-being—all become anything from twice to ten times as common in more unequal countries. (Wilkinson & Pickett 2010) The USA pays a high price for being one of the most unequal of the rich developed societies.

Humans have lived in every kind of society, from the most egalitarian hunter-gatherer bands of our pre-history (described by Christopher Boehm in his recent book *Moral Origins*), to the most brutal tyrannies. We instinctively know how to be caring and sharing, creating social bonds of friendship, mutuality and cooperation. We also know how to do status competition, how to be snobs, looking up to superiors and down on inferiors, and how to talk ourselves up. We use these alternative social strategies almost every day of our lives, but inequality shifts the balance between them. A study covering 26 European countries found that people in more unequal countries were less willing to take action to help others—whether the sick, elderly, disabled or others in the community. (Paskov & Dewilde 2012)

It is hard to avoid the conclusion that we become less nice people in more unequal societies. One of the better-known costs of inequality is that people withdraw from community life and are less likely to feel that they can trust others. This is partly a reflection of the way status anxiety makes us all more worried about how we are valued by others. But good social relationships are key to human well-being. Study after study shows that they are highly protective of health (Holt-Lunstad, Smith & Layton 2010) and essential to happiness. (Layard 2005; Dunn, Aknin & Norton 2008) And now that we can compare robust data for different countries, we are reminded of what we once knew intuitively—that inequality is divisive and socially corrosive.

References

Andersen R. & Curtis J. "The polarizing effect of economic inequality on class identification: Evidence from 44 countries" *Research in Social Stratification and Mobility* 2012; 30(l):129–41

Dunn E.W., Aknin L.B. & Norton M.I. "Spending money on others promotes happiness" *Science* 2008; 319(5870):1687–88

Hoff K. & Pandey P. "Discrimination, social identity, and durable inequalities" *The American Economic Review* 2006; 96(2):206–11

Holt-Lunstad J., Smith T.B. & Layton J.B. "Social relationships and mortality risk: A meta-analytic review" *PLoS Medicine* 2010; 7(7):e1000316

Johnson S.L., Leedom L.J. & Muhtadie L. "The dominance behavioral system and psychopathology: Evidence from self-report, observational, and biological studies" *Psychological Bulletin* 2012; 138(4):692–743

Krueger A.B. "The rise and consequences of inequality in the United States" Center for American Progress, Washington, D.C., 2012

Layard R. *Happiness: Lessons from a New Science* (London: Allen Lane, 2005)

Layte R & Whelan C.T. "Who feels inferior? A test of the status anxiety hypothesis of social inequalities in health" GNI Discussion Papers 78, AIAS, Amsterdam Inst. For Advanced Labour Studies, 2013

Loughnan S., Kuppens P., Allik J., Balazs K., de Lemus S., Dumont K. et al. "Economic inequality is linked to biased self-perception" *Psychological Science* 2011; 22(10):1254–8

Paskov M. & Dewilde C. "Income inequality and solidarity in Europe" *Research in Social Stratification and Mobility* 2012

Pickett K.E., James O.W. & Wilkinson R.G. "Income inequality and the prevalence of mental illness: A preliminary international analysis" *J. Epidemiol and Community Health* 2006; 60(7):646–7

Piff P.K, Stancato D.M., Cote S., Mendoza-Denton R. & Keltner D. "Higher social class predicts increased unethical behavior" *Proceedings of the National Academy of Sciences Acad Sci USA* 2012; 109(11):4086–91

Steele C.M. & Aronson J. "Stereotype threat and the intellectual test performance of African Americans" *Journal of Personality and Social Psychology* 1995; 69(5):797

Svenson O. "Are we all less risky and more skillful than our fellow drivers?" *Acta Psychologica* 1981; 47(2):143–48

Twenge J.M., Konrath S., Foster J.D., Campbell W.K. & Bushman B. J. "Egos inflating over time: A cross-temporal meta-analysis of the Narcissistic Personality Inventory" *Journal of Personality* 2008; 76(4):875–902; discussion 03–28

Wilkinson R. & Pickett K. *The Spirit Level: Why Greater Equality Makes Societies Stronger* (Bloomsbury Publishing USA, 2010)

Zink C.F., Tong Y., Chen Q., Bassett D.S., Stein J.L. & Meyer-Lindenberg A. "Know your place: Neural processing of social hierarchy in humans" *Neuron* 2008; 58(2):273–83

Complexities of Race, Class and Gender in Reconstructing Identities

AFRO-CUBAN AND AFRO-AMERICAN IMMIGRANT OPPOSITIONAL STRATEGIES TO RACISM IN THE TWENTIETH CENTURY

By Rosalyn Terborg-Penn

Introduction

Confronting institutional racism, Cubans, and other Caribbean immigrants of African descent, have long challenged the perpetuation of power through domination. Their challenges took various forms, yet they were often made invisible by the powers in mainstream societies. Strategies varied also, including constructing identity with hopes of mitigating adversity. The ability to deconstruct an identity was often determined by the individual's social class and gender, because both categories limited one's ability to make choices. Comparing and contrasting the ways that racism and colonialism have thwarted successful efforts to deconstruct alterity reveal how we can make the invisible visible as scholars examine systems of domination cross-culturally.

The focus here is on the voices of the once invisible—Maria de los Reyes Castillo Bueno (aka) Reyita (1902–1997), a Black Cuban female, contrasted with Richard B. Moore (1893–1978), an educated, Coloured (Mulatto) male, who migrated to the United States from Barbados. These two individuals serve as models for revealing differences in antidomination strategy

Rosalyn Terborg-Penn, "Complexities of Race, Class and Gender in Reconstructing Identities: Afro-Cuban and Afro-American Immigrant Oppositional Strategies to Racism in the Twentieth Century," *Journal of Caribbean History*, vol. 43, no. 2, pp. 228-245. Copyright © 2009 by The University of the West Indies Press. Reprinted with permission. Provided by ProQuest LLC. All rights reserved.

construction based on class, colour and gender.[1] Nonetheless, similarities emerge in the ways that each person faced domination by the powerful in racialized societies.

In addition to the words of these two Caribbean-born individuals who came of age in the early twentieth century, references to domination and race can be seen through the lens of two academicians, Lisa Brock, co-editor of *Between Race and Empire: African-Americans and Cubans before the Cuban Revolution*, and Kevin K. Gaines, author of *Uplifting the Race: Black Leadership, Politics and Culture in the Twentieth Century* [*USA*]. Each provides contemporary themes for scholarly analysis of race and culture in global contexts about identity formation of individuals living under the forces of racial segregation and domination.

In recent years, historians of the African diaspora have been using testimony found in individual narratives to interrogate alterity among colonized or proscribed groups. Analysis of such works does not always seek to learn about truth, but rather how testimony reveals the subject's representation of self.

Personal Cuban narratives appear cyclically, as do life stories of African Americans, both native-born and immigrant. For example, in Cuba, the autobiography of Juan Francisco Manzano, a formerly enslaved poet, was first published in English in 1840, rather than in Spanish, revealing a strategy to connect to a broader abolitionist base developing outside of Cuba.[2] The work was the first of many narratives about formerly enslaved men, some of whom, like Esteban Montejo, fought in nineteenth-century Cuban wars of liberation. The narratives appeared in the late nineteenth and early twentieth centuries.[3] By the late twentieth century the narratives or diaries of Caribbean and South American women began to appear in print. One such was a collection of diaries written in the 1950s by Brasilian Carolina Maria de Jesus, but it was not edited, translated and published by a major press until the 1990s.[4]

In the United States various slave narratives and autobiographies by free people of colour emerged throughout the nineteenth century, when narratives were aimed to raise the consciousness of the general public about the evils of slavery. In addition, men, and especially women, published autobiographies as fundraisers. For instance, Sojourner Truth, an illiterate formerly enslaved woman, engaged an amanuensis to record and edit her life story. Then she sold the narrative to support herself.[5] Even North American Free Blacks who were literate engaged editors and publishers to assist them with developing autobiographies. An example is Solomon Northrup. A free-born musician, Northrup was kidnapped and sold into slavery. With the assistance of several individuals, he was able to escape from the Louisiana plantation where he toiled and return to his home in New York. Shortly thereafter, he wrote his narrative with the help of a newspaper publisher, who marketed the book as well.[6]

By the late nineteenth century, published writings by educated North Americans of colour emerged among politicians and the clergy, in particular, some of whom were Caribbean immigrants to the United States, such as David Augustus Straker. Like Richard B. Moore, Straker was a native Barbadian. He earned his law degree from Howard University in Washington, D.C., and became a Detroit, Michigan, lawyer and civil rights activist, who wrote from the post–Civil War era in the United States until his death in 1909. However, unlike Moore's written works a generation later, Straker's speeches and newspaper articles were never collected and published in an anthology.[7] Nonetheless, his militancy as a West Indian and naturalized US citizen was a prelude to future immigrants like Richard Moore.

As for the two works focused upon in this study, there are similarities and differences regarding their origins. Both books were published in the United States by university presses during the late twentieth century. In each case educated daughters became the amanuensis who provided expertise so that the parent's life story could be told. However, in the case of "Reyita" (Maria de los Reyes Castillo Bueno), her book was published with several photographs before her death. On the other hand, in the case of Richard B. Moore, his daughter wrote her father's biography and included his writings with the biography and several photographs collected in one volume, which she edited with W. Burghardt Turner, her husband. The book was published after Moore's death.[8]

The role of amanuensis as the editor and perhaps interpreter of another person's life story may prevent the true meaning of the subject that is being conveyed. Questions may be raised about whether the meaning of each historical analysis had been compromised. However, in the two cases under discussion, the parent trusted the daughter to be the keeper of the record as well as the facilitator to bring to light how the elder was to be remembered. Consequently, I argue that we must trust the work performed by these amanuenses: historian Joyce Moore Turner, and Santiago de Cuba Fernando Ortiz African Cultural Centre's founder Daisy Rubiera Castillo.

Contextualizing Cross-Cultural Alterity and Responses to Domination

Interrogating the complexities of race, class and gender reveals similarities often overlooked in the way nonelites have challenged domination. In the minds of imperialists and colonizers, "the other"—nonelites in the state of alterity—remained people of colour who had been subjugated through cultural as well as economic and political manipulation. Despite "the other" being different and marginalized from the elites in society, scholars have found overlapping diasporas where, despite alterity, marginalized people identify with those in similar circumstances within a global context.

Subverting a "Co-Habitable Universe"

When Lisa Brock, an African-American historian at the Art Institute of Chicago, teamed up with Digna Castaneda Fuertes, a Black Cuban historian at the University of Havana, they prevailed over the ideological and political barriers erected by their respective governments and successfully edited a study of African-American and Cuban relations before the Cuban Revolution. Brock noted how she, Castaneda Fuertes and the other contributors realized, in researching their essays, that there is centrality of struggle among people of colour. Over time, from various jurisdictions in the Western Hemisphere—representing both genders, diverse colours, phenotypes, economic classes, means of work, languages and politics—nonelite people have centred themselves in their efforts to "subvert" their nation's elite. In so doing, the nonelite created what Brock called "a co-habitable universe" with the elite. The scholars found overlapping struggles against racism and imperialism, where "a body of non-elite pan-African *and* pan-American political, social, and cultural relations evolved".[9] However, in reviewing this analytical framework, two categories, class and gender, seemed missing and needed to be added to the list of overlapping struggles. Consequently, I have included class differences and "sexism", along with racism and imperialism, as analytical themes in this study.

In making her case for a historical continuum of African-American identification with Blacks in Cuba, Brock looked at nineteenth-century Black abolitionists in the United States, who, in 1872, organized the Cuban Anti-Slavery Society, in solidarity with Black Cuban freedom fighters such as Antonio Maceo.[10] He had come to New York City to garner support for the Cuban anti-slavery struggle, the goal of which was to end both slavery and Spanish colonial domination. Solidarity continued in social and political ways into the twentieth century, as did domination of people of colour who migrated from Cuba and other Caribbean jurisdictions to the United States, where manifestations of racism, sexism and classism existed in a very profound manner.

African-American and Caribbean Immigrant Negus: Nationalist Yearnings

Historian Kevin Gaines explored the nexus between native-born African Americans and Caribbean immigrants to the United States by interrogating their early twentieth-century political and intellectual exchanges about colonialism and imperialism during the period after the First World War. Many educated Caribbean immigrants to the United States settled in the Harlem neighbourhood of New York City where there was a critical mass of like-thinking men and women. Many of them became socialists, then black nationalists, as they looked globally at the plight of nonelite people of African descent. Gaines argued that black nationalists varied in ideology, but basically fell into two categories: those who based their sense of cultural authority on what Gaines described as "ethnocentric conceptions of an African continent in need of redemption", or those who based their "cultural authority on biological fictions of race purity". Marcus Garvey's approach would fall into the latter, because he promoted the belief in racial purity. On the other hand, Gaines concluded that there were nationalists who were anti-imperialist and pan-Africanist, a consciousness, which "opposed affinities with racialized thought", yet challenged "oppressive white civilization".[11]

Gaines noted how black nationalism in the United States at the turn of the twentieth century was different from late twentieth-century ideology. However, in placing black nationalism in historical meaning, Gaines saw no change in how African Americans related to people of African descent in the diaspora, past and present. He found that diaspora visions of the past expressed "contemporary yearnings". On one hand, Gaines observed, nationalists called for what they believed to be normative in traditional Africa—patriarchal gender relations—a belief Gaines felt came at the expense of Black women, especially the intellectuals who were often marginalized by Black men in their organizations. At the same time, Gaines showed how nationalist yearnings called for freeing people of African descent from deplorable poverty and exploitation experienced at the hands of imperialists and colonizers.[12]

Harlem Radicalism from 1900 to the 1920s

Militant African-Americans of the 1920s embraced anticolonialism and antiracism movements that drew Caribbean-born men and women to Harlem in particular. Among these were Arturo Schomburg of Puerto Rico and Hubert H. Harrison of St Croix (a neighbouring Danish Virgin Island before it became a US territory). By the 1920s Harrison, himself a bibliophile, was involved in helping to create the Schomburg collection of books and writings about Black life, a part of the New York City Public Library's Harlem branch. This branch later became the Schomburg Research Center. In writing about Harrison, who emigrated to the United States in 1900, Gaines foretold the experiences of other Afro-Caribbean immigrants in search of opportunities who found, instead, racism and marginalization even in Harlem.[13]

Harrison, who was probably self-educated before coming to the United States, may have found a position teaching elementary school in St Croix, but preferred to be a journalist in the United States. He became a contributing editor to the *Negro World*, the Universal Negro Improvement Association's (UNIA's) newspaper, a position he held for many years, although he engaged in oratory, adopting both pro- and anti-UNIA positions on different issues. Gaines viewed Harrison as a prototype of Harlem's street-corner orators, and argued that Garvey owed many of his political ideas to Harrison.[14] Jeffrey B. Perry, his biographer, supported Gaines's argument.[15]

In spite of Harrison's influence on Garvey, Harrison became a mentor to the younger members of the African Blood Brotherhood, a secret society of primarily West Indian men and women, founded by Cyril Briggs, a Nevisian immigrant living in Harlem. Harrison joined the Socialist Party, as did others like Richard Moore. Many of the members of the brotherhood, including Briggs, were also anti-Garveyites. In addition, most were identified as what in the late twentieth century were called "black nationalists"; they regarded Garvey as not being radical enough.[16]

Moore and Complexities of Identity Formation: Anti-Racism Strategies

Both Richard B. Moore, a teenaged Barbadian immigrant to New York City's Harlem, and Reyita Castillo Bueno, who was nine years his junior and lived most of her life in the Oriente Province of Cuba, negotiated the difficult terrain forged by imperialism and colonialism. Moore's family decided to migrate from Barbados to seek a better life in the United States, while Castillo Bueno's choices were class and gender limited, first by poverty and then by marriage. Migration was not an option. Nonetheless, she faced the prejudices and racism Cubans inherited in the post-colonial twentieth century that were bolstered by US occupation, just as Moore faced US-style racism while living in New York City.

Among the younger members of the developing Caribbean cadre of Harlem radicals, Richard B. Moore appeared in New York City at age fifteen in 1909, after arriving from Barbados with his stepmother. Richard Henry Moore (Richard B. Moore's father), having passed away when Richard was eight, had arranged for his son's schooling in Barbados. However, when Richard B. Moore's family could no longer afford his school fees, his formal education ceased. His education to that point had been quite good, so he began working as a clerk at age eleven to help his family meet expenses. The Moores considered themselves to be among the Barbadian middle class. The senior Moore had been an entrepreneur and a lay preacher in the evangelical tradition. However, hard times after his death made the family's middle-class lifestyle impossible, so Richard B. Moore and his stepmother followed two older sisters who had migrated to the United States in 1908 to find work. They joined the thousands of Barbadians who could afford to leave the island as hardship found its way to many in Barbados who remained.[17]

Joyce Moore Turner noted that her father attempted to further his education by applying to take classes at the Young Men's Christian Association (YMCA) in Manhattan, but that he was barred because of his colour. In addition to the YMCA not providing services to African Americans, some New York City churches segregated parishioners by race. When Moore visited the Christian Missionary Alliance, he was instructed to sit in the gallery. Finding employment was also difficult. Through connections that fellow Barbadians had made, he was able to obtain a job as a clerk. Not understanding US racial mores, Moore began to woo a white woman who worked in the office, which resulted in his losing his job. According to Moore Turner, by the First World War her father had experienced several racial episodes with which he struggled to cope. His middle-class Barbadian upbringing had simply proved inadequate for the changed circumstances of his life in early twentieth-century New York City society. This reality revealed the difference between the way racial classification differed in the British colonies and in the United States.[18]

In Barbados, Moore's family were middle-class gentry, whereas in New York he was relegated to working-class "Negro" with visions of upward mobility. During those years, he worked in positions of service, either as an elevator operator or as a hotel bellhop. Many of the African-American and Afro-Caribbean men in these positions were over-educated for the menial jobs they held. Their escape from poverty had resulted in what Lisa Brock described earlier as living "a co-habitable universe" with the elite, who in this case were wealthy white businessmen. These individuals discriminated against men of colour by hiring them to do menial, low-paying jobs. With the help of a neighbour, Moore obtained a job with a silk manufacturer and moved from being an elevator operator to a clerk and then to head of the stock department. He worked for the company from 1913 to 1923. Thereafter, as Moore Turner explained, her father's paid work became erratic.[19] Apparently, he could not bring himself to continue the survival strategy of "a co-habitable universe" with the white power elite.

In the meantime, Moore was pulled to the street philosophy that he was hearing and the books that he was reading. He articulated how he saw religion and empire as forces designed to exploit Africa and its peoples. He also discovered the book, *The Life and Times of Frederick*

Douglass, a man who had been enslaved in the United States, but had escaped and later had written his narrative to tell about his upward climb, commencing with freedom. Douglass's story revealed to Moore how in alterity an individual may still be able to free himself from exploitation. This revelation connected him to African Americans, and he became a Frederick Douglass specialist.[20]

As Harlem developed culturally during the First World War, Moore enjoyed what Gaines called the West Indian/Black American nexus, and it lured him to make Harlem home. He and his cohorts opposed the war, because they saw the conflict as one among major imperialist powers who subjugated people of colour in their African and Caribbean colonies. At Madison Square Park he heard Hubert Harrison, the street corner orator, expressing his socialist ideology. He sought out Harrison and ways to combat racism and colonialism.[21]

At the same time, Moore was attracted to the socio-economic analyses of A. Philip Randolph and Chandler Owens, two native-born Black American socialists who published the journal, the *Messenger*. Consequently, he joined the Socialist Party in 1918, at the age of twenty-five, the year before he married Kathleen Ursula James, a Jamaican immigrant of very light complexion. Their daughter, Joyce, was born in 1920 and, in the gender conventions of the times, Moore Turner noted, Richard left the childrearing to Kathleen, although she worked in a garment district factory to help support her family. Shortly after their marriage, both Kathleen and Richard applied for US citizenship, which they obtained in 1924. By the 1930s, Kathleen, dissatisfied with her husband's irregular employment and frequent absence from home, reacted against the lifestyle of radical agitation. Moore Turner wrote that her mother obtained a legal separation and put Richard out. For a while, her father left his job in New York City to travel to Chicago with the Communist Party, where he felt white members accepted him for his views, not his colour.[22]

Throughout those years, Moore's strategy for surviving racism and domination was personal as well as group defined. Back in New York City, he believed in education as a vehicle toward upward mobility. However, he knew from experience how discrimination prevented many people of colour in the United States from entering most educational institutions. However, he continued to educate himself. At this point in his life, Perry confirms, Moore saw education of the masses via the community action of socialists through the People's Educational Forum, a venue to bring the sociopolitical changes needed to save African Americans and their Afro-Caribbean cohorts.[23]

Castillo Bueno and Complexities of Identity Formation: Subverting Poverty and Sexism

Around the same time, in Cuba, Castillo Bueno continued to experience an impoverished and racially proscribed life as a teenager who had been pushed from one family member to the next throughout her childhood. In recalling her mother's life story, Daisy Rubiera Castillo, the youngest child, started with her African-born maternal great grandmother who had been enslaved and transported to Cuba from West Africa. Once in Cuba, her owner sexually abused her.

Consequently, Castillo Bueno's mother was a Mulatto who also struggled to survive through using sexual liaisons and becoming a "kept woman". She bore at least ten children (several of whom died at an early age), ranging in skin colour from "black" to "white". In writing the introduction to the narrative, historian Elizabeth Dore noted that Castillo Bueno was the child of a black soldier whom her mother joined during the second Cuban War for Independence from Spain. Castillo Bueno noted that he was the only black man who fathered any of her mother's children. Consequently, Castillo Bueno and her brother by the same father were the only ones of African phenotype, a reality that their mother seemed to abhor, driving her to denigrate her physically black offspring.[24] Not surprising, identity based on race denigration moves poor and/or colonized people of lighter-skin phenotype to a position above that of the others of darker phenotype, despite the subjugation of both groups. Once again, we can see how Castillo Bueno's mother used the survival strategy of literally living "a co-habitable universe" with white elite men.

As Castillo Bueno developed as a teenager, like Moore, she sought to be educated, although her mother felt that her dark-skinned children should pursue menial employment and forgo formal education. Nonetheless, she secretly learned to read and write. Rubiera Castillo noted that her mother's experience in the communities of Oriente Province where she lived as a child convinced her that being black was a liability. She had witnessed the results of the 1912 massacre of black political leaders and members of *El Partido Independiente de Color* (PIC). The political party had been founded during the US occupation of Cuba, because many Blacks realized that the white Cuban leaders of the independence movement had betrayed them. Afro-Cubans had played a leading role in the anticolonial struggle, but had been denied acceptance and political recognition. According to Dore, this was true for Castillo Bueno's mother and grandmother, both of whom participated in the anti-colonial struggle, but continued to live impoverished lives thereafter.[25]

Significantly, Casillo Bueno did not mention the US occupation of and/or interventions in Cuba from 1899 to 1917. However, Richard Moore, as a 1926 delegate to the American Negro Labor Congress, joined others in signing a declaration to sanction US imperialism. Among the tenets of the declaration was the "abrogation of the unequal treaties making virtual protectorates of Panama, Cuba, and other countries in the Caribbean area".[26]

Castillo Bueno's recollections about gender conventions throughout the political struggles in Cuba were even more vivid than those of the US occupation. Her accounts to her daughter Daisy Rubiero Castillo revealed a gendered view of Cuban struggle, where women of colour, both Cuban-born and West Indian, took active leadership roles on the island, yet remained invisible beyond the locale where they provided leadership. This was true for women of colour in the anticolonial movement at the turn of the century, the 1920s Garvey movement, and the 1940s Socialist movement. These two movements engaged Castillo Bueno personally. In addition, she recalled the colour discrimination among Cubans of even the more educated classes, who joined different political associations for Whites, for Blacks and for Mulattos. Castillo Bueno viewed the problem as the result of racial discrimination. However, the reality of race identification and identity formation led her to develop a personal strategy to help her future children escape the discrimination that she faced. Castillo Bueno consciously sought to marry a white man, a strategy she discusses at the beginning of chapter 2 of her narrative, subtitled "Why I Married a White Man". In recalling her goal, Castillo Bueno told her daughter Daisy, "I know you understand why I wanted to marry a white man. It goes without saying now that I love my race, that I am proud to be black, but in those days, marrying white was vital."[27]

The man whom she married in 1920 was Antonio Amador Rubiera, ten years her senior. Castillo Bueno was eighteen and working in a restaurant, located in her town of Cuerto, Oriente Province, where Rubiera frequented. Apparently, his attraction to her was sexual. His family refused to accept his decision to marry her and, according to Castillo Bueno, he broke with them. She played the role that he wanted of her, providing him with the services of a submissive wife who catered to his every whim. Like her mother before her, she lived in "a co-habitable universe". She did this for the first twenty years of their marriage. Together, they produced eight sons and daughters, the photos of whom reflect various hues of brown.[28]

Nonetheless, through her narrative, Castillo Bueno talked about love of her race and her African heritage, which she distinguished from her strategy to bring children of a lighter complexion than her own into the world so that they would not have to face the discrimination that she faced. What appears to be dichotomous thinking fades as Castillo Bueno recalled the communities where she lived in the eastern end of the island and interacted apart from her husband as a community activist.[29]

Dore concluded that Castillo Bueno's life reflected the "multiple contradiction of living in a society with a myth of racial democracy".[30] This reality played out in the way that Rubiera discouraged his black children from seeking education and self-improvement, as he encouraged the males, in particular, to find manual jobs. Castillo Bueno resented this characteristic in her husband, yet he mirrored the society dominated by the white colonial elite, where even Blacks themselves practised self-denigration. In Cuerto, a black woman named Marcelina explained to Castillo Bueno why the married white women were called Dona, and why she was not. Marcelina stated, "Why are they going to call you Dona? These people are called Dona because they're white and rich; but you, *negra prieta*—married to a white man, yes, but poor—mistress of what? Simply Reyita [Castillo Bueno]!"[31]

Confounding Domination: Complexities of Race, Class and Gender

Truly the complexities of race, class and gender often impacted differently the lives and strategies for resisting domination among males and females of colour. Yet sometimes the impact was similar. Although Castillo Bueno and members of the poor black communities where she lived sought to confound domination, at times their strategies and goals differed from those of middle-class Caribbean men like Moore living in the United States. However, the politics of skin colour appeared to remain the same for European-colonized people cross-culturally. We know that Richard Moore was attracted to a white American woman in the United States, whom he wooed unsuccessfully in New York City. Perhaps, he would have done similarly, living as an adult in Barbados, where he may not have lost his job as he did in the United States. Nonetheless, in the nineteenth and twentieth centuries, skin colour was critical in determining class hierarchy in both the United States and the Caribbean. Castillo Bueno acknowledged this problem as a young woman, after experiencing the negative way that her Mulatto mother treated her darker-skinned children and the limitations to upward mobility that Blacks encountered in Cuba. When she deliberately sought to marry a white man to produce lighter-skinned children, Castillo Bueno adopted the only viable strategy available to a poor woman of African phenotype. Nonetheless, comparing the strategies of Moore and Castillo Bueno to seek a white partner reveals the prevailing taboo against men who did so. However, for women of African descent, cohabitation with mates of European descent was acceptable in Cuba. In addition to issues arising about skin colour in selecting a mate, both Moore and Castillo Bueno adopted other similar strategies to confound domination by elites. Caribbean immigrants of colour in the United States interacted in the same organizations as their Cuban cohorts—the UNIA and the Socialist Party.

However, in Harlem there were several choices for West Indian and other Caribbean immigrants with regard to affiliation. Moore Turner noted that Grace Campbell, a prominent member of the 21st AD Socialist Club, was the only female member of this organization in which Richard Moore was also affiliated. Campbell, her father, a Jamaican immigrant, later joined the African Blood Brotherhood, as did Moore in 1919. However, all the organizations found a home in close proximity on 135th Street, in Harlem. Grace Campbell apart, the lack of women's voices in the various militant associations reveals the differences in class mobilization for change between the working-class militancy remembered by Castillo Bueno in Cuba from the late 1910s to the 1940s, and the middle-class militancy remembered by Richard Moore.[32]

Castillo Bueno recalled in detail her membership in the Cuerto chapter of the UNIA, whose leader was Malvaina Grand, a Jamaican immigrant woman. As an adolescent, on Sundays Castillo Bueno would sneak to the house that Grand shared with Charles Clark, her Jamaican husband, to attend UNIA meetings. Grand was a laundress who specialized in stiff-collared white shirts. She also made and sold candies. A very resourceful woman, Castillo Bueno emulated her and took on the assignment to recruit others to the Garvey movement. She noted that the Jamaicans in Cuba wanted to go to Africa, a desire that she also shared. She learned from those whom she recruited why they were interested in going to the continenst. They believed "Africa" would give them greater opportunities for employment, but, most importantly, they would not be restricted to serving white people. Castillo Bueno estimated that fifty Cubans in Cuerto were members of the UNIA.[33]

In 1921 Marcus Garvey was drawn to Cuba by a large following of Jamaica-born Cubans. He held a meeting in Santiago de Cuba, but Castillo Bueno had to work and could not attend. Following his visit, she testified, the Blacks who led UNIA chapters in Cuba were persecuted and some were deported to their Caribbean countries of origin. As a result, the movement's strategy was to go underground. Castillo Bueno was sad because she concluded, "I had to stay in Cuba, keep suffering because I was black. After that I was sure of one thing: I had to prevail over discrimination."[34]

In Harlem, the UNIA attracted a large following in Harlem, where Garvey maintained his headquarters in the early 1920s. His vision for black empowerment was only one of competing dreams among Harlemites. However, it attracted the working class, primarily Blacks as opposed to educated Mulattos. Garvey's special antagonism toward Mulattos who had migrated to the United States from British colonies was clearly articulated and caused resentment. Nonetheless, many socalled Mulattos disliked him because he was dark-skinned. Apparently, after ten years of experiencing racial discrimination living in New York, Moore seemed not to be prejudiced against people with dark skin. For that matter, Hubert Harrison, his mentor, was dark-skinned. As for the UNIA, Moore never became a member, but avoided making negative public statements against the organization. Moore Turner stated that her father's accounts of the Garvey movement were sketchy, but that he made it clear that radical Blacks in New York City used to debate the causes and effects of oppression against people of colour, and had already developed strategies to confound it by the time Garvey first arrived in Harlem. Moore and his cohorts were Socialists at this point in their development. They did not consider Garvey to be radical enough, and many members of the African Blood Brotherhood—Cyril Briggs and Wilfred A. Domingo, in particular—were involved in a "Garvey Must Go" campaign. According to Moore Turner, her father objected to, and refused to be part of, the efforts of some black intellectuals to pressure the US government to deport Garvey.[35]

Clearly, Moore had more choices than Castillo Bueno for a variety of reasons, including colour, class and gender. Nonetheless, at various points in their lives both Moore and Castillo Bueno became Socialists. As noted above, Moore was converted to Socialism by Hubert Harrison, who became disillusioned by the Socialist leadership's lack of interest in race issues. Harrison left the party shortly after Moore and his younger cohorts joined him. Moore and his group also became disillusioned with Socialism for the same reasons. Consequently, the Harlembased 21st AD Socialist Club had little connection with headquarters. Its members developed their own agendas and study groups. Campbell, Moore and others organized the People's Educational Forum in order to educate the public. Soon the US government began to investigate the various radical groups in Harlem, and arrests followed surveillance. As it was, the Socialist Party offered no protection for African Americans. However, fear of persecution was not what caused Moore and his Socialist cohorts to leave the party. They concluded, as had Hubert Harrison before them, that the party leadership was not ready for black Socialists or to tackle racial issues. Most of them left the Socialist camp in 1921 and headed for the Communist Party.[36]

In Cuba, Castillo Bueno became a Socialist twenty years later, in a different country with a different set of historical circumstances. In the 1940s she was actively involved with the Socialists. Party members were persecuted, as had been the UNIA members. Nonetheless, Castillo Bueno allowed the members in her community to hold meetings at her house because Pura, her daughter, was a seamstress and clients were coming and going from her house regularly.

Castillo Bueno sold the party newspaper, *Hoy*, and became very active, despite her husband's disapproval. She ignored him and told Rubiero Castillo, "I was waking up—you know?" During this period in her life, Castillo Bueno began to steer a course independent of her husband, who seemed ashamed of his family. Her role as the submissive wife ended. Several years later, when she joined the Popular Socialist Party, Castillo Bueno explained that she liked the organization because it called for race and gender equality.[37] Clearly, her feminist consciousness was developing as she entered middle age and struggled to help her children move up in the world, even as her husband attempted to keep them down. In so doing, she abandoned the "co-habitable universe" strategy.

Gender complexities appear to have been more significant in affecting the later lives of both Richard Moore and Castillo Bueno as they entered middle age. Both continued to struggle against the domination of the elites who controlled their communities. Like Castillo Bueno, Moore's personal strategies also changed.

Moore and others were ousted from the Communist Party because of their demand for pro-black strategies. Among these strategies was fighting for jobs in Harlem for coloured workers. The white leadership, on the other hand, lacked black nationalist commitments. They disagreed because jobs for Whites would be lost in so doing.[38] Moore continued to agitate, but he apparently needed another woman in his life, after his wife separated from him. In 1942, Lodie Biggs provided him with the funds needed to launch the Frederick Douglass Book Center on 125th Street in Harlem. According to Moore Turner, Biggs was quite a militant, one who had joined other female members of the Communist Party in Harlem to agitate against the chauvinism among the male members. Lodie Biggs, a Seattle, Washington, native of dark-brown hue, was a bacteriologist who worked for the City of New York. She provided the business and Richard with steady income, companionship and philosophical compatibility at a time when, according to Moore Turner, her father really needed it. Richard and Lodie married in 1950 and lived in Brooklyn, New York—truly a nexus between a native-born African American and a Caribbean immigrant.[39] Moore's militancy was redirected from joining radical political organizations back in the direction of where he had started—a desire to educate the common people. At this point in his life, his goal was supporting the pan-Caribbean movement, although he never put aside his black nationalism and kept his membership in scholarly groups, such as the Association for the Study of Negro Life and Culture, based in the District of Columbia.

As for Castillo Bueno, she raised her children, especially her sons, to confound the domination of the elites, and at the same time she confounded her husband's attempts to be seen as a white "gentleman". Two of her sons joined the "Twenty-sixth of July Movement", which was instrumental in producing the Cuban Revolution. Rubiero was furious, but also worried about the fate of his sons, one of whom ultimately gave his life for the Revolution. When the family fled their community because of government intimidation of the movement's supporters, they moved to Chicharrones, an impoverished but pro-revolutionary town outside of Santiago de Cuba. Castillo Bueno continued her community activism while Rubiera retreated into solitude. She did not know until soon both her son's and her father's deaths that she was not legally married to Rubiera. Although they had had a wedding ceremony, the notary had colluded with Rubiera not to have the marriage papers registered with the court. Castillo Bueno learned of her fraudulent marriage when she sought to receive her father's pension as the daughter of a war veteran. Another notary from whom she inquired informed her that only single daughters could collect the pensions of deceased veterans; but he checked the marriage records anyway, and found that she had been a single woman all along. "Reyita", the "black" woman, had been deceived by her so-called white husband. She did not tell him immediately that she knew about the deception, but when Castillo Bueno received the papers approving the pension, she showed them to Rubiera and he tried to explain what had happened. However, Castillo Bueno declared that she "wouldn't give him the chance to be free of his deceit".[40]

Confounding institutional racism, a Cuban and an African American of Barbadian descent challenged the perpetuation of power through domination. Their strategies took various forms, including living within "a co-habitable universe" with the elite, and constructing new identities in hope of mitigating adversity. Significantly, two educated daughters, Joyce Moore Turner in the United States and Daisy Rubiera Castillo in Cuba, made possible the lifting of the shrouds of invisibility concerning these individuals. By comparing and contrasting the ways that racism and colonialism affected efforts to deconstruct alterity, we have tried to give greater visibility to two persons—a lower-class Black woman and a middle-class Mulatto man—and show through their life stories how they challenged systems of domination cross-culturally to emerge finally from alterity.

Acknowledgements

My thanks go to historians Glenn O. Phillips and Derick A. Hendricks of Morgan State University, and to historian Joyce Moore Turner for reading this essay and making constructive suggestions.

The origin of this essay was my presentation under a similar title to the delegates at the 2005 Association of Caribbean Historians Conference in Cartagena, Colombia. During the discussion period following my presentation, historian Jean Stubbs, whose specialty is Afro-Cuban History, commented about Daisy Rubiero Castillo, Maria de los Reyes Castillo Bueno's daughter, who had prodded her mother to tell her story and have it published in book form. Rubiero Castillo is the founder of the Fernando Ortiz African Cultural Centre in Santiago de Cuba.

Notes

1 Joyce Moore Turner, in discussion with Rosalyn Terborg-Penn, 15 June 2009, revealed that her father rejected words such as "Mulatto", "West Indian", and "Negro", because they were "white terms" of definition. He preferred "Afro-Caribbean" and "Afro-American" (see Richard B. Moore, *The Name "Negro", Its Origin and Evil Use*, edited by Joyce Moore Turner and W. Burghardt Turner [orig. pub. 1960. Baltimore, MD: Black Classic Press, 1992]).

2 Juan Francisco Manzano, *Autobiografia de un Esclavo*, edited by Evelyn Picon Garfield and Ivan A. Schulman (Detroit: Wayne State University Press, 1996); Carmen Gomez Garcia, "Cuban Social

Poetry and the Struggle against Two Racism", in *Between Race and Empire: African-Americans and Cubans before the Cuban Revolution,* edited by Lisa Brock and Digna Castaneda Fuertes. (Philadelphia: Temple University Press, 1998), 210–11.

3   See Serafin Portuondo Linares, *Los Independientes de Color,* cited by Gisla Arandia Covarrubia, "A Panorama of Afrocuban Culture and History: One Way to Strengthen Nationality", *AfroCubaWeb,* www.afrocubaweb.com (accessed 8 September 2003).

4   *The Unedited Diaries of Carolina Maria de Jesus,* ed. Robert M. Levine and Jose Carlos Sebe Bom Meihy; trans. Nancy P.S. Naro and Cristina Mehrtens (New Brunswick, NJ: Rutgers University Press, 1999).

5   *Narrative of Sojourner Truth, A Bondwoman of Olden Times and Book of Life,* edited by Frances W. Titus (orig. pub. 1875; Chicago: Johnson Publishing, 1970).

6   Solomon Northrup, *Twelve Years A Slave,* edited by Sue Akin and Joseph Logsdon (orig. pub. 1853. Baton Rouge: Louisiana State University Press, 1968).

7   See, for example, D. Augustus Straker, *Citizenship, Its Rights and Duties, Woman Suffrage* (Washington, DC: New National Era Printers, 1974); Glenn O. Phillips, "The Responses of a West Indian Activist: D.A. Straker, 1842–1908", *Journal of Negro History* 66, no. 2 (1981): 130.

8   Maria de los Reyes Castillo Bueno, *Reyita: the Life of a Black Cuban Woman in the Twentieth Century, as Told to her Daughter Daisy Rubiera Castillo* (Durham, NC: Duke University Press, 2000); W. Burghardt Turner and Joyce Moore Turner, eds., with biography by Joyce Moore Turner, *Richard B. Moore, A Caribbean Militant in Harlem: Collected Works, 1920–1972* (Bloomington: Indiana University Press, 1988).

9   Lisa Brock, "Introduction: Between Race and Empire", in *Between Race and Empire*, 2.

10 Ibid., 8–12.

11 Kevin K. Gaines, *Uplifting the Race: Black Leadership, Politics and Culture in the Twentieth Century* (Chapel Hill: University of North Carolina Press, 1996), 7–8.

12 Ibid., 2–3.

13 Ibid., 234–36.

14 Ibid., 239–40; Jeffrey B. Perry, *Hubert Harrison: The Voice of Harlem Radicals, 1883–1918* (New York: Columbia University Press, 2009), 47.

15 Ibid., 5; Gaines, 236–37.

16 Joyce Moore Turner, "Biography of Richard B. Moore", in *Richard B. Moore*, 19–21; Franklin W. Knight, "Introduction", in *Richard B. Moore*, 4–5.

17 Moore Turner, *Richard B. Moore*, 20–24.

18 Ibid.; Joyce Moore Turner, *Caribbean Crusaders and the Harlem Renaissance* (Urbana, IL: University of Illinois Press, 2005), 34.

19 Moore Turner, *Richard B. Moore*, 25.

20 Perry, 273; Moore Turner, *Caribbean Crusaders*, 58.

21 Moore Turner, *Richard B. Moore*, 27, 46–48, 58, 107fn42.

22 Perry, 12.

23 Richard B. Moore, "Afro-Americans and Radical Politics", in Turner and Moore Turner, *Richard B. Moore*, 216.

24 Elizabeth Dore, "Introduction: Afro-Cuban History from Below", in Castillo Bueno, 7; see also 21–26, 78.

25 Dore, 1–3; Castillo Bueno, 48–50.

26 Moore Turner, *Richard B. Moore*, 53–54.

27 Castillo Bueno, 30–31, 48–50, 59.

28 Ibid., 95–104.

29 Ibid., 27, 83.

30 Dore, 5.

31 Castillo Bueno, 62–63.

32 Moore Turner, *Richard B. Moore*, 30–32.

33 Castillo Bueno, 26–27.

34 Ibid., 28–29

35 Moore Turner, *Richard B. Moore*, 38–39.

36 Ibid., 28–42, 46.

37 Castillo Bueno, 83.

38 Moore Turner, *Caribbean Crusaders*, 238.

39 Moore Turner, *Richard B. Moore*, 70.

40 Castillo Bueno, 122–23, 168–69.

Activities for Further Exploration and Discussion

Video Analysis 1

In class, view the following videos and then discuss the following questions as a class.

Video: 1957 1 of 2 Social Class in America

https://tinyurl.com/ycw9ryzq

Video: 1957 2 of 2 Social Class in America

https://tinyurl.com/yabpepua

Questions for Class Discussion

1. What are the statuses that were ascribed?
2. What are the statuses that were achieved?
3. Did these statuses change or stay the same? Provide a rationale for your answer.
4. What role did geographic location play in their ascribed and achieved statuses?
5. What were the influences on each of their choices?
   - Education: Why did they go to the same high school?
   - What were their future goals?
   - What role did their families play in their decisions about the future?
   - What role did class play in their decisions?

Video Analysis 2

In class, view the following video and then discuss the following questions as a class.

Video: Introduction to Social Stratification

https://tinyurl.com/ycdtyn4b

Questions for Class Discussion

1. Summarize the video in your own words.
2. What is social stratification?
3. What is the purpose of categories?

- When can categorization be helpful?
- When can categorization be detrimental?
4. List the economic classes that were highlighted in the video.
5. Provide an overall analysis of the video.

Video Analysis 3

In class, view the following video and then discuss the following questions as a class.

Video: Social Class & Poverty in the US: Crash Course Sociology #24

https://tinyurl.com/ya5r3y5s

Questions for Class Discussion

1. How did Marx define social class?
2. How did Weber define social class?
3. How many social classes are there?
   - Which of the classes are divided? List the divisions.
4. What is the federal poverty level and how many Americans are in it?
5. What is the difference between relative poverty and absolute poverty?
6. Explain the effects of the intersection gender and race on your social class.

Article Analysis

Read the following article:

Kraus, M. W., & Tan, J. J. X. (2015). Americans overestimate social class mobility. *Journal of Experimental Social Psychology, 58*, 101–111. https://doi.org/10.1016/j.jesp.2015.01.005

Reflection Paper Instructions

Write a reflection paper describing your reactions to the discussions, videos, and article.

References

Baumle, A. K. (2013). The demography of sexuality and the labor market. In A. Baumle (Ed.), *International handbook on the demography of sexuality* (pp.243–256). Springer.

Few-Demo, A. L., Humble, A. M., Curran, M. A., & Lloyd, S. A. (2016). Queer theory, intersectionality, and LGBT-parent families: Transformative critical pedagogy in family theory. *Journal of Family Theory & Review, 8*(1), 74–94.

Flitter, E. (2019, December 14). This is what racism sounds like in the banking industry. *New York Times.* https://www.nytimes.com/2019/12/11/business/jpmorgan-banking-racism.html

Gould, E., Schieder, J., & Geier, K. (2016, October 20). *What is the gender pay gap and is it real? The complete guide to how women are paid less than men and why it can't be explained away.* Economic Policy Institute. https://www.epi.org/publication/what-is-the-gender-pay-gap-and-is-it-real/

Grabb, E. (1980). Marxist categories and theories of class: The case of working-class authoritarianism. *Pacific Sociological Review, 23*(4), 359–376. https://doi.org/10.2307/1388730

Harackiewicz, J. M., Canning, E. A., Tibbetts, Y., Priniski, S. J., & Hyde, J. S. (2015, November 2). Closing achievement gaps with a utility-Value intervention: Disentangling race and social class. *Journal of Personality and Social Psychology, 111*(5), 745–765. https://doi.org/10.1037/pspp0000075

Levine, R. F. (Ed.). (2006). *Social class and stratification: Classic statements and theoretical debates.* Rowman & Littlefield.

Marx, K. (1972). *The Marx–Engels reader* (Vol. 4). Norton.

Mize, T. (2016). Sexual orientation in the labor market. *American Sociological Review, 81*(6), 1132–1132.

Parkin, A (1962). Social class: Historical origins and psychological influences. *Canadian Psychiatric Association Journal, 7*(4), 178–185.

Patten, E. (2016). *Racial, gender wage gaps persist in U.S. despite some progress.* Pew Research Center. https://www.pewresearch.org/fact-tank/2016/07/01/racial-gender-wage-gaps-persist-in-u-s-despite-some-progress/

Pew Research Center. (2016, May 11). *The American middle class: Who is in it, and who is not, in U.S. metropolitan areas.* https://www.pewsocialtrends.org/interactives/middle-class-metro-map/

Schooler, C. (1994). A working conceptualization of social structure: Mertonian roots and psychological and sociocultural relationships. *Social Psychology Quarterly,* Special Issue: *Conceptualizing Structure in Social Psychology. 57*(3), 262–273. https://doi.org/10.2307/2786880

Wilkinson, R., & Pickett, K. (2014). Mindful of Inequality? *Poverty & Race, 23*(2), 3–5.

CHAPTER 3

Gender and Sexual Orientation

I N THIS CHAPTER, we have chosen to put gender and sexual orientation together as they are phenomena that intersect. Therefore, it is our belief that they are better together than they are separate. Further, gender is a factor in family functioning and is a crucial part of sexual orientation. It is important to understand each one as they exist on their own; they both affect the individual and the family separately in addition to where they intersect.

In recent years, issues with gender equality and acceptance have become more prevalent. Although there have been large gains in terms of gender inequality, there are more issues that need to be addressed (Morgenroth & Ryan, 2018). The definitions of gender have changed, and there is no longer a primarily binary approach (i.e., male/female). People are able to better identify their *gender identity* because there is language to support them. Traditionally, the language used to refer to those who are *transgender* (man or woman), *genderqueer, gender-fluid, gender-neutral, bigender, agender,* and many others were not available.

Sociolinguistic research for the past 20 years has been largely associated with social theory. Thus, "the development of a more nuanced understanding of the relationship between individuals, society, and observed patterns of language variation" has yielded positive results (Levon, 2015, p. 295). Through the development of language to describe one's gender identity, those who have been marginalized because of their perceived gender expression have been given a voice and a way to define who they are.

McDowell and Fang (2007) pointed out that there has been a large increase in attention to family diversity and relations of gender with other inequalities that families may face. In social practice, one must consider how multiple systems of social categorizations intersect with one another in dynamic and constructive ways (Levon, 2015). The ways these categories intersect will be discussed later in this chapter. Before we get to that, let's talk about gender identity and the different definitions.

Gender Identity and Definitions

Ferree (2010) suggested that "thinking of gender in a more multilevel and dynamic way would also demand thinking of families differently" (p. 420). The way that family interactions can change around gender identity is important to consider when working with individuals who have a member with a gender identity that is not the male-female binary. When discussing gender identity with families and individuals, it is important to distinguish between gender and sex.

Gender is a socially constructed way of defining female and male, femininity and masculinity. *Sex* is biological and refers to anatomy (genitalia), which is the basis of the gender that a person is assigned at birth. Many people use gender and sex interchangeably, so much so that Pryzgoda and Chrisler (2000) stated that "the words 'sex' and 'gender' are deceptive" (p. 553). People tend to use the words without much effort or thought of what they mean to others.

In their study, Pryzgoda and Chrisler (2000) found that there are a variety of ways people understand gender and sex. Common responses include that gender and sex are the same; others equate gender with females or discrimination. "Gender is generally used to refer to the cultural or attitudinal qualities that are characteristic of a particular sex" (Greenberg, 1999, p. 274), and therefore it is socially constructed. Additionally, the law has typically utilized the assumption that "male" and "female" are fixed and unambiguous (Greenberg, 1999). As more consideration has been given to the language used to delineate the dynamics of gender, there has been an expansion of awareness of how people would like to be identified regarding their gender. "*Gender identity* is defined as a personal conception of oneself as male or female" (Ghosh, 2015, p. 1).

The definitions and scope of what gender means have changed as society has progressed. More recently, gender has been defined in many different ways to reflect those who need ways to identify themselves outside of the male-female binary. Some of the types and definitions of gender that have come to light in recent years are included.

Cisgender

The first type of gender identity that we will discuss is *cisgender*. A *cis*gender or *cis*person is someone whose gender identity is congruent with the anatomical sex and gender assignment they were given at birth. Those who identify as cisgender are sometimes seen as having *heteronormative* privilege. Heteronormative refers to conformity to prescribed gender roles and sexual orientation that is linked to biological sex (Nagoshi et al., 2017). This person chooses to adhere to the male-female gender binary because of their identification with their sex and gender assignment at birth. Those who identify as cisgender are seen as privileged because their gender and sex align with what is socially and culturally acceptable.

Transgender

Outside of the gender binary of male-female, *transgender* is the most known gender identity that is outside of the binary gender. According to *Merriam-Webster Dictionary* (n.d.), a transgender or transperson is someone

> whose gender identity differs from the sex the person had or was identified as having at birth, *especially* of, relating to, or being a person, whose gender identity is opposite the sex the person had or was identified as having at birth.

A person who is anatomically male (sex), identifies as a woman (gender), and expresses their gender as feminine is considered a *transgendered woman.* Further, a person who is anatomically female, identifies as a man, and expresses their gender as masculine is considered a *transgendered man.* Although those who have had sex reassignment surgery are included as transgendered, not all transpeople have a sex change (Nagoshi et al., 2017). However, just as the definition says, they do not identify with the anatomical sex assignment they received at birth.

Genderqueer, Bi-gender, Gender-Fluid, and Agender

Gender-queer or "*GQ* or *nonbinary* person is someone who feels that their felt gender does not fit with socially constructed norms for their biological sex. This may be in terms of their thoughts, feelings, behaviors, and most importantly, their gender identity" (Savin-Williams, 2018, p. 1). *Bi-gender* refers to a person who has two gender identities that exist either simultaneously or they switch between the two. *Gender-fluid* persons may identify as male, female, or nonbinary depending on the circumstances. *Agender* people lack gender, are considered genderless, or seem not to care about gender identity (Savin-Williams, 2018).

Gender is a more complex and nuanced phenomenon than what it was believed to be by previous generations. For centuries it has been relegated to the binary, male/female, concept. Now, as knowledge of the gender spectrum has become more prominent, the simple binary no longer dominates the discussion. Gender non-conforming people who do not conform to any particular gender role are also included in this discussion. There are some who still believe that male and female are the only gender categories. The trends in the lived experience of those who ascribe to the gender spectrum are very significant. This is especially true when it comes to sexual orientation.

Sexual Orientation

Sexual orientation and gender are commonly used interchangeably. The preferred term of *sexual orientation* is used to define who a person is attracted to sexually. Gender, as previously explained, is about the expression of a particular identity. They are similar but definitely not the same concept. Researchers have a difficult time defining and identifying sexual orientation.

Sexual orientation comprises psychological and behavioral components. However, not all definitions include both (Sell, 1997).

Some definitions of sexual orientations include both the psychological and the behavioral components; "The determining factor [in homosexuality] is the demonstration of perverse feelings for the same sex; not the proof of sexual acts with the same sex. These two phenomena must not be confounded with each other" (Krafft-Ebing, 1886, as cited in Sell, 1997, p. 647). LeVay (1993) said that sexual orientation was the direction of feelings or behavior regarding sexual attraction toward people of the opposite sex, same-sex, or some combination of the two. These descriptions were used to define those who were heterosexual, homosexual, and bisexual.

Heterosexual and Homosexual

Heterosexual refers to someone who is sexually attracted only to the opposite sex and/or gender than they identify. The most common pairing in a heterosexual couple is female- and male-identifying people. *Heteronormativity* is the belief that to be heterosexual is the only "normal" sexual orientation. All other expressions of sexuality are seen as abnormal. Those who have a heteronormative mentality value "conformity to prescribed gender roles, gender identity, and sexual orientation…linked to one's assigned biological sex" (Nagoshi et al., 2017, p. 19). Those who ascribe to the heteronormative mentality often enforce these beliefs through societal prejudice and discrimination. It "promotes gender conventionality, heterosexuality, and family traditionalism as the correct way to be" (Oswald et al., 2005, p. 143).

Homosexual refers to someone who is sexually attracted to those who are of the same sex and/or gender with which they personally identify. There is a history of demonizing homosexuality in the social and family science realms. With this history has come debates about whether homosexuality is a mental disorder, nature, nurture, or both. Although there is not a clear origin of homosexuality, the reality is that being homosexual does not negate a person's value and importance to society. It is important to know that people are not the sum total of their sexual orientation; it is just a small part of the larger scope of who they are.

Bisexual and Lesbian

People who identify their sexual orientation as *bisexual* are most commonly sexually attracted to people who are a part of the gender binary male/female. Their sexual attraction is to both males and females instead of one or the other. Keep in mind that some bisexual people find that they are attracted to a number of different people who are on the gender and sexual orientation spectrum. Someone who identifies as a *lesbian* has sexual attraction to women. That is not to say that women who are lesbians cannot be attracted to those who identify as male or transsexual male. The attraction is not to the sexual organs but to the gender expression of the partner or potential mate.

Transsexual and Transgender

Transsexual and *transgender* are oftentimes used interchangeably. In fact, most of the definitions of each are very similar. As mentioned earlier in the chapter, a person who identifies as transgender is someone whose gender identity and gender expression are different from what was assigned at birth. Similarly, a person who identifies as transsexual is a transgender person who wants to take the next step and have their sex medically reassigned (sex reassignment surgery).

Sexual orientation and gender are very significant parts of families and individuals' livelihood. There are varied definitions of gender, and what they mean is very important to those who have different expressions outside of the gender binary male/female.

Sexual orientation is the level of sexual attraction that a person has to another person. Sexual orientation and gender cannot be used interchangeably and have separate meanings for each person. Someone who is transsexual has decided that they want to have the sex reassignment surgery and has started to take steps toward that end.

There are some clear distinctions between the different gender expressions. Remember that genderqueer, gender-fluid, transgender, bi-gender, and agender are just a few distinctions and gender types. However, they are not the complete and total list of gender descriptions. These are just a few that are highlighted in this text. Further reading is encouraged to learn more about the gender spectrum. (For more information, see itspronouncedmetrosexual.com.)

Intersectionality of Gender and Sexual Orientation

Intersectionality, as a theoretical framework, requires us to examine the different processes that individuals use to "negotiate competing and harmonious social identities" (Few-Demo et al., 2016, p. 76). Intersectionality of gender, race, class, and sexual orientation must be considered as we talk about the effects these phenomena have on family development. It is necessary to view them all in the context of the various ways they intersect to gain a greater understanding of each one.

Sometimes the places where gender, sexual orientation, race, and class intersect can cause a great deal of distress to the person(s) experiencing the intersection. For example, Janice identifies as a single Black woman, her sexual orientation is lesbian, and her class is middle class. Janice decides that she wants to adopt a child. During the orientation process, the interviewer commented on Janice's sexual orientation and her marital status. As the process ensues, Janice is informed that she does not qualify to be an adoptive parent based on exigent circumstances. Despite having the financial assets and being willing to care for a child, she still was denied the opportunity. Based on the interaction with the interviewer, one would gather that this decision was based on her marital status and sexual orientation.

When discussing intersectionality and how gender, sexual orientation, class, race, and religion intersect, we must acknowledge that these phenomena do not intersect in the same way for everyone. Some experience the intersections in positive ways, depending on their social location. For others, their experiences of these intersections, no matter the combination of the phenomena, are negative in nature. For example, in the narrative, it is probable that because Janice identified as a lesbian (sexual orientation) and a Black woman (race), her experience with these intersections was not positive. As a result of these intersections, Janice was prevented from being able to expand her family.

Conclusions

Gender and sex are not the same. Some people use them interchangeably, and that causes confusion for those who are truly seeking correct definitions of each. Gender comprises the felt sense of who a person is; that is, gender is based on a set of behaviors that one ascribes to or does not ascribe to. For example, as noted previously, there are people who identify as agender, which means that they do not care about gender identity and believe they are genderless. Sex is determined by the biological sex organs one is born with. Gender is the outward expression; sex is based on sex organs (genitalia).

Sexual orientation is just that: how one is sexually oriented. This describes who one is sexually attracted to and it may be based on the gender expression and characteristics the mate has. There are people who do not have a particular sexual attraction to anyone. Asexual is the term that describes someone who does not have a sexual attraction to another person, regardless of their gender expression or lack thereof.

Implications for Family Life Educators

As family life educators continue to find ways to educate others about gender and sexual orientation, it is important to reach as many people as possible. The topic of gender identity has moved to the forefront of conversations about sexualities and expressions. Many people are just beginning to pay attention to the important place these conversations have in our social world. As family life educators, it is imperative to understand the need for and create safe spaces for families and individuals to continue the conversations. For families who have a member who is questioning their gender identity and/or sexual orientation, it is our responsibility to provide education about how to deal with these potentially unexpected occurrences.

For information about educating yourselves and others, it may be helpful to seek to understand as much as you can about the different types of gender identities and sexual orientations. Being informed as a provider is your responsibility. There is literature about these topics, as well as websites, individuals, and families who have a wealth of information about how to help. As a starting point, additional readings are provided to add to your knowledge gained in this chapter.

Additional Readings

The readings that have been included in this chapter bring to light the difficult intersect of race, gender, and sexual orientation. These intersections are significant to acknowledge, particularly when it relates to adolescents and their sexual exploration. Children and adolescents may have a difficult time understanding what their felt gender and gender expression should be. As helping professionals, it is our responsibility to provide guidance and assist with what may amount to mental health and relational difficulties.

An Overview of the Resolution on Gender and Sexual Orientation Diversity in Children and Adolescents in Schools

By Karla Anhalt, Cristina L. Magalhães, and Mary Beth Klotz

This article provides an overview of the joint *Resolution on Gender and Sexual Orientation Diversity in Children and Adolescents in Schools* that was adopted by the American Psychological Association's (APA) Council of Representatives (CoR) and the National Association of School Psychologists' (NASP) Leadership Assembly during the summer of 2014 (APA & NASP, 2014). We begin by describing the original resolution adopted by APA and NASP in 1993, highlighting aspects that were incorporated in the 2014 version, and noting the various groups that participated in writing the updated document. A summary of the 2014 resolution follows, along with a review of supplemental resources, and a discussion of potential school psychologist roles in implementing the resolution.

A resolution focusing on sexual minority youth in schools was first adopted by APA in 1993 (DeLeon, 1993). At the time, the limited psychological research focused on the needs of lesbian, gay, and bisexual (LGB) adolescents. The 1993 document addressed health and mental health risks that had been reported at the time (e.g., increased risk of self-injurious behavior and HIV infection) and the experience of harassment and physical violence in school settings. The *Lesbian, Gay, and Bisexual Youths in the Schools* 1993 resolution called for APA and NASP to take leadership roles in promoting safe and secure educational environments for LGB youth, to develop and evaluate interventions addressing the needs of these students, and to advocate for funding targeting prevention and risk reduction for this population (DeLeon, 1993).

Approximately 20 years after the 1993 resolution on LGB Youths in the Schools was adopted by NASP and APA, a workgroup was formed to develop an updated resolution. The workgroup was composed of representatives from NASP and APA. It included representation from APA's Division 44 Children, Youth, and Families Committee; Division 44's Committee for Transgender People and Gender Diversity; and Division 16. Individuals from the APA's Committee on Children,

Youth, and Families and APA's Committee on Sexual Orientation and Gender Diversity also participated in the workgroup. Additionally, staff from the APA's Lesbian, Gay, Bisexual, and Transgender Concerns Office served as the liaison to APA governance. Workgroup members representing NASP included the LGBTQI2-S committee chairperson and the staff liaison to this committee.

Although there is still a great deal of work to be done in research and policy arenas, the scientific literature focusing on sexual minority and gender diverse children and adolescents has been flourishing in the last two decades. While writing the 2014 resolution, the workgroup identified many new areas to address. First, this document is applicable to students of all ages in K–12 school settings and the language incorporates issues of children and adolescents throughout the document. Second, the 2014 resolution integrates the needs of students who are transgender, intersex, and/or gender diverse. It acknowledges that gender identity develops in early childhood and that some young children do not identify with the sex assigned to them at birth. The 2014 resolution calls for affirmation of diverse gender expressions, regardless of gender identity, and an understanding of gender beyond a binary classification. It calls for school staff to support the decisions of children, adolescents, and families regarding a student's gender identity or expression, and endorses access to sex-segregated facilities consistent with an individual's gender identity. The 2014 resolution stresses how the right to privacy with regard to sexual orientation, gender identity, intersex/disorders of sex development (DSD) condition, or transgender status is critical to a student's well-being and safety. Third, the 2014 resolution emphasizes issues of intersectionality and includes unique needs of students with disabilities, and students from diverse racial/ethnic groups, religious identities, and geographic locations, among others (APA & NASP, 2014). A summary of the resolution components follows.

> Awareness of one's sexual attractions toward people of the same gender can occur by the onset of adolescence; questioning of, confusion about, and fluidity in one's sexual and gender identity is common among children and adolescents.

Summary of the 2014 Resolution

The 2014 resolution consists of 30 statements summarizing empirical and practice-based knowledge about gender and sexual diversity in children and adolescents, followed by 18 resolves (APA & NASP, 2014). The first part of the document (hereafter referred to as the WHEREAS statements) starts with acknowledging the existence of gender and sexual orientation diversity in the general population, the rapid cultural and political changes that are occurring in our communities regarding the treatment of sexual minorities and gender diverse people, and the rights of all people to equal opportunity and safe environments within all public educational institutions (WHEREAS statements 1 through 3). These opening statements provide a rationale for the 2014 resolution and remind mental health professionals of the importance of their advocacy role in supporting gender diverse and sexual minority children and adolescents in schools.

The remaining 27 WHEREAS statements are organized under five sections: Sexual Orientation and Gender Identity, Gender Diversity, Consequences of Stigma and Minority Stress, Concerns and Issues in the Context of Schools, and The Role of Mental Health Care Professionals in Schools. Supported by a large body of literature, statements in these sections represent the consensus of experts in the field regarding gender and sexual orientation identity development; common experiences of gender and sexual orientation diverse (GSOD) children and adolescents in the United States; unique challenges GSOD children and adolescents experience in schools; and what mental health care professionals can do to reduce risks, foster resilience, and promote healthy development of GSOD children and adolescents.

In the Sexual Orientation and Gender Identity section, WHEREAS statements 4 through 7 assert that awareness of one's sexual attractions toward people of the same gender can occur by the onset of adolescence; that gender and sexuality are different aspects of one's experience; that questioning of, confusion about, and fluidity in one's sexual and gender identity is common among children and adolescents; and that there are few resources and supports available for them, especially in rural areas. WHEREAS statements 8 and 9 in the Gender Diversity section assert that gender identity develops in early childhood, that some young children do not identify with the sex assigned to them at birth, that it may be medically and therapeutically indicated for children and adolescents to transition from one gender to another, and that this transition can take different forms (e.g., name change, hormonal treatment, surgical procedures).

The Consequences of Stigma and Minority Stress section includes WHEREAS statements 10 through 22. This section asserts that stigma and minority stress affect the health and well-being of GSOD children and adolescents and reports on increased rates of emotional and behavioral problems, substance use, homelessness, pregnancy, and other adverse outcomes among this population. It also reports that, compared to cisgender (nontransgender) peers, transgender and gender diverse children and adolescents can experience even higher rates of depression, anxiety, self-harm, and other health risk behaviors, and that other subgroups within the population of GSOD children and adolescents are at heightened risk for HIV and other sexually transmitted infections (i.e., young men who have sex with men, homeless adolescents, racial/ethnic minority adolescents, transgender women of color, and adolescents enrolled in alternative schools). Additionally, this section recognizes that many GSOD children and adolescents have multiple minority identities or statuses (e.g., racial/ethnic minorities, children and adolescents from impoverished or low-income families) or live in rural areas or small towns with limited access to affirming community-based supports, which can result in additional challenges and risks. Lastly, this section also describes research findings on the experience of children, adolescents, and adults with intersex/DSD conditions. Many children and adolescents report a history of silence, stigma, and shame regarding their bodies and the medical procedures imposed on them; some report a history of self-harm and suicidality at rates comparable to those reported by children and adolescents who have experienced physical or sexual abuse; and there is evidence to suggest that these negative effects often persist into adulthood. Despite this, unnecessary invasive medical procedures continue to be recommended to parents of children and adolescents with intersex/DSD conditions with the intent of "normalizing" them.

WHEREAS statements 23 through 28 refer to Concerns and Issues in the Context of Schools. This section reports on high rates of harassment, bullying, and physical violence toward GSOD students; increased risks and potential negative outcomes associated with hostile or unsupportive school climates; and interventions by school personnel that are known to help reduce risks and improve well-being. Research findings indicate that children and adolescents who are transgender or gender diverse are especially vulnerable. School personnel are less likely to intervene to stop harassment targeting these students, and may even participate in the harassment. School victimization can lead to a range of negative outcomes for GSOD children and adolescents, including increased risk for mental health problems, suicidal ideation and attempts, substance use, high-risk sexual activity, high level of absenteeism, low grade point averages, and low interest in pursuing postsecondary education. According to some studies, transgender and gender diverse students show even lower achievement levels, lower educational aspirations, and higher incidences of truancy and weapons possession compared to sexual minority students; and they are also more likely to be "pushed out" of high school prior to graduation. While unsupportive schools can have a significant and long-lasting negative impact on GSOD children and adolescents, they can also be places of respite when appropriate policies, programs, and practices are put in place. GSOD students report increased school connectedness and school safety when school personnel actively respond to these challenges by demonstrating commitment to improving school climate. Interventions shown to be most effective include addressing and stopping bullying and harassment when they occur; developing administrative policies that prohibit discrimination based on sexual orientation, gender identity, and gender expression; supporting the use of affirming classroom activities and the establishment of gender and sexual orientation diverse-affirming student groups; and valuing education and training for students and staff on the needs of GSOD students.

The last two WHEREAS statements (29 and 30) are included in The Role of Mental Health Care Professionals in Schools section. These statements urge mental health care professionals to advocate for inclusive policies, programs, and practices within schools systems, and to work toward promoting the healthy development of all students, regardless of sexual orientation, gender identity, or gender expression.

The second part of the document (hereafter referred to as the BE IT RESOLVED statements) starts with APA and NASP's affirmation that "same-sex sexual and romantic attractions, feelings, and behaviors are normal and positive variations of human sexuality regardless of sexual orientation identity," and that "diverse gender expressions, regardless of gender identity, and diverse gender identities, beyond a binary classification, are normal and positive variations of the human experience" (APA & NASP, 2014, The Role of Mental Health Care Professionals in Schools section, para. 3 and 4).

The remaining 16 BE IT RESOLVED statements are organized under four headings: Policies, Programs and Interventions, Training and Education, and Practices. Under Policies, statements

3 through 7 include the following resolutions: APA and NASP will advocate for local, state, and federal policies and legislation that promote safe and positive school environments for GSOD students; recommend that schools develop policies protecting the right to privacy for students, parents, and school employees with regard to sexual orientation, gender identity, or transgender status; recommend that school administrations and mental health providers develop networks, collaborate, and create policies that will positively affect GSOD students; and encourage the collection of data on sexual orientation and gender identity by state educational agencies to monitor and study risk behaviors and to help inform effective interventions to support GSOD children and adolescents in schools.

BE IT RESOLVED statements 8 through 12 refer to Programs and Interventions. APA and NASP will support efforts to secure funding for research that will help address the needs of GSOD students; recommend the continued development and evaluation of school-level interventions aimed at reducing risks and improving well-being for GSOD students; recommend that attention be given to the diversity that exists within the population of GSOD students and that interventions incorporate the concerns and needs of those who have other minority identities or are underserved; support affirmative interventions with transgender and gender-diverse children and adolescents; and encourage mental health care providers who work in school settings to participate in the education and training of other school professionals about the full range of sex development, gender expression, gender identity, and sexual orientation.

Two BE IT RESOLVED statements address Training and Education (statements 13 and 14). APA and NASP encourage education and training about the needs and available supports of GSOD students for all school personnel, and also recommend that such training and education be made available to students, parents, and community members. Beliefs and attitudes based on strictly binary notions of sex, sex development, and gender can negatively impact all students. Thus, APA and NASP encourage mental health care professionals who work in school settings to learn more about the full range of human experiences in regards to sexuality and gender.

The last four BE IT RESOLVED statements (15 through 18) address practices. APA and NASP encourage mental health care professionals who work in school settings to serve as allies and advocates for GSOD children and adolescents in schools, particularly in effecting the creation of new antibullying and antidiscrimination policies, or modifying existing ones to include gender identity, gender expression, and sexual orientation. School staff members are encouraged to support the decisions of students and families regarding gender identity and expression, and discouraged from requiring proof of medical treatments as condition for having access to such support. Additionally, APA and NASP recommend that school administrators create a safer environment for transgender, gender-diverse, and intersex/DSD students and school personnel. Access to facilities, activities, and programs that are consistent with gender identity, and provision of gender-neutral bathrooms for individuals who prefer to use them, are two ways in which improved safety can be achieved.

Supplemental Resources

Although not formally part of the 2014 resolution, the workgroup developed various supplemental materials to assist in the implementation and dissemination process. These materials include an Introduction to the Resolution, Context for the Resolution, Definitions, and Limitations of Language, and References for Definitions. Further, a series of five informational pamphlets related to the 2014 resolution were produced through funding received from an interdivisional grant between APA's Divisions 44 and 16. The series, "Promoting Resiliency for Gender Diverse and Sexual Minority Students in Schools" is structured in short pamphlet format and outlines best practices for school personnel based on the latest related research. Topics covered in the pamphlets include key terms and concepts, school-based risk and protective factors, recommendations for supporting transgender and gender diverse students in schools, and suggestions for how educators can support families with gender diverse and sexual minority youth. Additionally, LGBTQ youth resources from APA and NASP have been organized around nine of the recommendations from the 2014 resolution to aid school personnel and others in implementing these recommendations. Users will find position statements, fact sheets, research summaries, model school district policies, and links to websites of allied organizations. These supplemental materials as well as a link to the resolution can be found on APA's website at: http://www.apa.org/pi/lgbt/programs/safe-supportive/lgbt/default.aspx.

Role of the School Psychologist

School psychologists promote fairness and justice and use their expertise to cultivate school climates that are safe and welcoming to all persons (NASP, 2010). In keeping with NASP's ethical principles and professional policies, and with the recommendations in the 2014 resolution, school psychologists can engage in various educational and advocacy activities.

Offer education, training, and ongoing professional development about the needs for gender and sexual orientation diverse students. For example, school psychologists can disseminate the 2014 resolution to teachers and administrators and hold discussions at staff meetings using conversation starters such as, "Do we offer safe and inclusive school spaces and activities for transgender, intersex, and gender diverse students?" Or, utilize the supplementary pamphlet, "School-Based Risk and Protective Factors for Gender Diverse and Sexual Minority Children and Youth: Improving School Climate" (http://www.apa.org/pi/lgbt/programs/safe-supportive/lgbt/risk-factors.pdf) to discuss the suggested steps educators can take to help create a safe school climate for gender diverse and sexual minority children and adolescents.

Advocate for local, state, and federal policies and legislation that promote safe and positive school environments free of bullying and harassment for all children and adolescents. At the district level, school psychologists can disseminate the 2014 resolution to their school board members when advocating for antibullying and anti-discrimination school policies that enumerate gender and sexual orientation diverse children and adolescents. At the building level, school psychologists can set up appointments with their principal to discuss students' rights to privacy and confidentiality regarding their sexual orientation, gender identity, and transgender status. See supplementary resources for policy implementation at http://www.apa.org/pi/lgbt/programs/safe-supportive/lgbt/default.aspx.

Summary

Perhaps the most compelling BE IT RESOLVED statement in the 2014 resolution is the recommendation that school-based mental health professionals serve as allies and advocates for gender and sexual orientation diverse children and adolescents—which is at the heart of any effort to enhance school climate and safety. To accomplish the recommendations and goals outlined in the 2014 resolution, APA and NASP pledged to work together and with other organizations so that gender and sexual orientation diverse children and adolescents will have the same opportunities as any other student to be affirmed for who they are and to feel connected, accepted, and respected in their schools.

Related Resources

Klotz, M. B. (2014). Welcoming and safe schools. *Communiqué, 43*(1), 13. Retrieved from http://www.nasponline.org/publications/cq/43/1/welcoming.aspx

National Association of School Psychologists. (2011). *Lesbian, gay, bisexual, transgender, and questioning (LGBTQ) youth* [Position Statement]. Bethesda, MD: Author.

National Association of School Psychologists. (2014). *Safe schools for transgender and gender diverse students* [Position statement]. Bethesda, MD: Author.

References

American Psychological Association & National Association of School Psychologists. (2014). Resolution on gender and sexual orientation diversity in children and adolescents in schools. Retrieved from http://www.nasponline.org/about_nasp/resolution/gender_sexual_orientation_diversity.pdf.

DeLeon, P. H. (1993). Proceedings of the American Psychological Association, Incorporated for the year 1992; Minutes of the annual meeting of the Council of Representatives. *American Psychologist, 48*, 745–788. doi:10.1037/0003-066X.48.7.745

National Association of School Psychologists. (2010). *Principles for professional ethics.* Bethesda, MD: Author. Retrieved from http://www.nasponline.org/standards/2010standards/1_%20Ethical%20Principles.pdf

The Impact of Sexual Orientation and Gender Expression Bias on African American Students

By Kamilah F. Majied

Overview

This article discusses sexual orientation and gender expression bias as they impact African American students. Although there is ample literature on anti-gay prejudice and gender bias as they impact educational settings in general (Espelage et al., 2008; O'Conor, 1993; Russell et al., 2009; Walter & Hayes, 1998), less attention has been given to these matters as they affect Black students. For that reason this article focuses on the experiences of African American students with regard to homophobia, heterosexism, and gender expression bias.

Issues related to sexuality have an impact on the educational experience of Black students regardless of sexual orientation. Adolescence is a burgeoning period of libidinal development; therefore, the educational milieu cannot help but be impacted. According to the Centers for Disease Control Youth Risk Behavior Surveillance System (YRBSS, Mohsen & West, 2006), 46.7% of high school students have sexual intercourse during their high school years and Black and Latino students engage in sexual activity at significantly higher rates than their white counterparts (Mohsen & West, 2006). Analyzing longitudinal data from the YRBSS, Cavazos-Rehg and colleagues (2009) found that African American males experienced their sexual debut earlier than all other groups. In fact, 74% of African American females and 82% of African American males experienced their sexual commencement by age 17.

Concomitantly, Black people accounted for 49% of the new HIV/AIDS diagnoses in the United States in 2005. The data show that of the 18,849 people under the age of 25 who were diagnosed between 2001 and 2004, 61% are Black (CDC, 2006). These data articulate that unprotected sex (heterosexual and non-heterosexual) is the principal means of transmission of the virus and thereby is a prominent cause for the disproportionate representation of Black youth among those infected. African Americans also have the highest teen pregnancy rates in the United States which significantly increases the likelihood that they will not complete high school (Mohsen & West, 2006).

The neoteric uproar over "sexting" (Manzo, 2009; "Teen 'sexting' attracts attention," 2009), whereby students send each other sexually explicit texts or photographs using mobile telephone devices and over the Internet during school, is yet another tocsin indicating students' heightened sexuality in their learning environment. While students' preoccupation with sexuality and engagement in sexually risky behavior may create a distraction from the learning process, these also portend serious legal, psychosocial, and health consequences for Black youth.

Distorted gender norms and gender bias also have influence on the education of Black students with varied manifestations. The emasculation of academic achievement among some Black males, especially in disciplines such as art, literature, and the social sciences, is one indicator (Bailey, 2002). Black female students' preoccupation with their appearance and sexual attractiveness more than their academic achievement also highlights the agency of sexism in perceived gender appropriate roles and behavior.

The abstruse and divaricated consequences of all sexual behavior and gender identity issues among adolescents, although beyond the purview of this article, must be assessed for their impact on Black students of all sexual orientations and genders. The purpose of this article is to contribute to that broader topic by addressing homophobia, heterosexism, and internalized negative stereotypes about Black sexuality and their impact on heterosexual and non-heterosexual Black students.

Homophobia and heterosexism are often identified as paradigms of oppression faced primarily by lesbian, gay, bisexual, transgendered, and questioning (LGBTQ) people. However, they are also social processes that negatively impact all facets of society, including the educational experience of heterosexuals and non-transgendered persons. Homophobia and heterosexism are often used to reinforce gender bias and force individuals to adhere to strict gender prescriptions for fear that they will be labeled "gay" if they do not. This is particularly true in secondary and higher educational contexts where sexuality and gender issues are being negotiated as students try to develop and maintain social cohorts and construct their individual and social identities. Socio-politically construed norms and archetypes also proliferate in the educational context so that often students aspire to define themselves accordingly. In an effort to create environments where intellectual freedom and academic achievement are not harnessed by these oppressive paradigms, educators and school administrators must address dehumanizing notions of sexuality, as well as sexual orientation and gender expression bias as factors in students' educational experience and overall success.

In examining the impact of these phenomena on African American educational purlieu, the framework of intersectionality suits best. Through the lens of their behavior in school one often finds students expressing their conceptualizations of their gender identity, and their sexuality as it has developed thus far, as well as their racial and ethnic identity.

Internalized Racism

Part of the legacy of slavery and racism in America is the distorted conceptualization of Black sexuality which has been promoted and internalized by Black people (Hill Collins, 2004). Therefore, sexual orientation and gender expression bias have a unique presentation in Black educational settings. In fact, such settings are often confounded by the combination of stereotypic views of what it means to be Black and to be gay. For these reasons, it is worthwhile to consider how Black youth are impacted by sexual orientation issues and conceptualizations of Black sexuality.

In her exegesis on Black sexuality and gender, Hill Collins (2004) identified the personal and social implications of distorted historical images of Black men and women. She discussed the early American prevailing conviction that all Black men were potential rapists deserving of lynching and all Black women were so immoral that they invited rape. She described the internalization of these ideas among contemporary Black youth. Hill Collins also highlighted the influence of prison culture on urban youth which often glorifies connections between sex and violence. Notions of sexuality that are informed by internalized racism and aggression along with anti-gay prejudice and gender expression bias can produce negative social and behavioral outcomes, particularly in a hypersexual climate. "Corrective rape" ("Murdered soccer star," 2009), wherein females presumed to be lesbian are sexually assaulted with the purported intent to make them heterosexual, is a prime example of the combined effect of violence, anti-gay prejudice and insalubrious notions of the meaning and purpose of sex.

For more clarity on internalized racist notions of Black sexuality, one can further descry America's history of gross misrepresentation of Black sexuality and the remnants of that ideology which endure. During the colonial era, Black men who were accused of raping or sexually molesting White women were subject to the death penalty or castration. The same punishment did not hold true for White men accused of the same crime. As far as Black females were concerned, early American laws did not protect Black women from rape and sexual assault by either White or Black men. In the antebellum South, the rape of enslaved Black women was common and not considered criminal. The law provided human property no protection from sexual assault. Even free Black women had little legal recourse because the laws preventing Black people from testifying in court or serving on juries would have made successful prosecutions of their assailants impossible.

The conveniently dehumanizing pretext used to justify slavery—that Black people required the civilizing influence of subjugation to tame their sexual appetites—was pressed into the service of rationalizing rape and sexual exploitation. Since colonial rape laws denied protection to all unchaste women, Black women and girls who were considered inherently unchaste would never fall within the law's ambit. The rape of enslaved women also had a powerful economic justification because a child inherited the legal status of its mother, not its father. Rape was therefore a mechanism for increasing the labor force. Even after the Civil War when rape laws became race neutral, law enforcement entities were indolent toward punishing the assailants of Black women. The rape of African American women also became a tool for inspiring terror and ensuring continued subordination in the Reconstruction South. Even when prosecutions for the rape of African American women did occur, inequality in sentencing of White offenders and recourse for Black victims persisted (The Feminist Sexual Ethics Project, 2009).

After the law forbade the execution of Black men for alleged sexual offenses against White women, historical records indicate that lynching of Black men who had been accused of raping White women became increasingly common, especially in the mid- to late 19th century (Hodes, 1997). During the Civil War and the Reconstruction Period, public outrage about sexual relations between Black men and White women increased, as evidenced by government hearings and media coverage on the subject (Hodes, 1997), as well as American literature and folklore describing Blacks as promiscuous (Staples, 2006). Fear of newly freed slaves lusting after White women was systematically spread as an attempt to maintain the antebellum racial hierarchy. As a result, White preoccupation with Black sexuality intensified significantly after emancipation (Hodes, 1997). In a speech before the Senate in March of 1900, Senator Benjamin R. Tillman (South Carolina) described Blacks as hot-headed and lustful toward White women, which, according to him, justified the common practice of lynching Blacks in the South ("Speech of Senator," 1900). It is this ideology that led to the emergence of the Ku Klux Klan (D'Ooge, 1994). Until the Supreme Court struck down the use of the death penalty as punishment for rape, Black men convicted of raping a White woman received that punition far more often than those convicted of raping an African American woman (Staples, 2006).

From the earliest times in American history, Black men were seen as "hungry" for sex and dangerous to White women. Black women were typecast as sexually aggressive, promiscuous, and lacking in moral virtues (Greene, 2000). These enduring perceptions predispose Black males to be defined by an ever present sexual need and Black females to be considered perpetually sexually available (Greene, 2000).

The legacy of these racialized notions of sexuality is that popular culture presents African American women as this same sexual stereotype, linking sexual promiscuity to the nature and identity of African American women (Bounds Littlefield, 2008). African American women are continually portrayed as concupiscent sexual objects. Contemporary media propagates and profits from this image, popularizing it, and presenting it as the defining characteristic of African American women. In this conceptualization, the goal for some Black girls and women is to become the penultimate video vixen, incessantly lustful, insatiable, and procurable. Concurrently, Black males are praised in popular culture for their capacity to accrue sexual conquests. It is also regarded highly if one is able to do so without emotional attachment. This is most evident in the music and videos popular on rap segments of music and entertainment networks and on Black hip hop radio stations. In 1992 Dr. Dre released *The Chronic,* which received rave reviews from music critics and sold over three million copies. One of the most popular singles on this album was titled "Bitches Ain't Sh**" in which Dr. Dre declared what became a hip hop anthem promoting sex without sentiment, "we don't love them hoes" (Dr. Dre, 1992). Presently, there are 1,210 popular singles containing the word "hoes" in the title (Billboard, 2009). The influence of this music on the sexual self-concept of African American males and females cannot continue to be underestimated.

Sexual Orientation and Anti-Gay Prejudice

The following section will differentiate the authentic LGBTQ experience from what is often abstractly referred to as "gay" with definitions of the relevant terms. LGBTQ is an acronym that refers to individuals who are lesbian, gay, bisexual, transgendered, or questioning. Lesbians are females who are oriented toward other females emotionally, socially, politically, and sexually.

Similarly, males who are gay are oriented toward other males emotionally, socially, politically, and sexually. Bisexual individuals can be oriented toward both males and females in these same ways. Transgendered individuals have a gender identity that is different from the physical characteristics with which they were born. An example of this is an individual who is born in a female body but psychologically, emotionally, and socially identifies as a male or vice versa. Transgendered persons may sexually identify themselves as heterosexual, homosexual, or bisexual and may sometimes undergo surgery or other sexual reassignment procedures. The term "questioning" refers to individuals who are in an evaluative or re-evaluative stage regarding their sexuality (Majied, 2008).

Heterosexism

Heterosexism refers to the predominant worldview that heterosexuality is the norm and that all other intimate relationships and expressions of sexuality are considered to be outside of and in contrast to the norm (Brown, 1989). American society and culture are built on heterosexist ideals, as is evidenced in the American legal system, the educational system, and the national media which generally disregard and diminish the existence of LGBTQ persons. Many states, for example, deny same-sex couples the right to marry and some states deny same-sex couples the right to adopt children. Same-sex couples therefore often cannot access the rights and benefits that marriage affords, which poses risk factors for the psychosocial well-being and stability of LGBTQ individuals and families.

Heterosexist sentiments are epitomized in policies such as "Don't ask, don't tell" which "protects" homosexuals serving in the military from being dismissed only if they agree to hide their sexual identity. Non-heterosexual experiences and relationships are generally left out of the discussions of family and human sexuality that occur in the educational system. In the media, LGBTQ individuals and families are often mocked and stereotypically portrayed (Herek, 2000). Heterosexism is often evident in the context of the typical rearing of children. Many parents do not discuss homosexuality with their children as a natural form of intimate human relationships. In fact, some parents often teach their children that homosexuality is errant and wrong. This paradigm has been referred to as compulsory heterosexuality and speaks to the lack of options and limited range of knowledge about human sexuality of which most people are exposed (Kauer, 2009; Rich, 1993; Trotter, 2009). Furthermore by taking traditional gender roles for granted as the correct and natural order of things, the heterosexist paradigm also reinforces sexism (Pharr, 2006).

Heterosexism is a pervasive social problem that contributes to the invisibility of LGBTQ persons and the conceptualization of them as the odd and insignificant "other." Philosopher and educator Daisaku Ikeda pointed out that when human beings are viewed as abstractions in this way, the humanity of those perceived as "other" is obscured and the potential for delusion and violence manifests (Ikeda, 2009). Furthermore, the breadth of knowledge and insight regarding the world and its people is curtailed for those who hold such views, since their capacity to engage with human diversity, a skill needed for personal and professional growth in contemporary society, is diminished.

Homophobia

The term homophobia was popularized by psychologist George Weinberg (1972) who used it to refer to heterosexuals' irrational fear of homosexuals. Unlike heterosexism, which ignores homosexuality and takes heterosexuality for granted, homophobia refers to the visceral negative emotional and cognitive reaction to perceived homosexuality. Homophobia is the fear, hatred, and disgust felt by homophobic individuals when they are confronted with anything considered non-heterosexual. Homophobic sentiment which is often fueled by anti-gay religious fervor contributed to such historical abuses as torture, imprisonment and killing of homosexuals and is the principal cause of contemporary anti-gay violence (Herek, 2000).

Homophobia in Schools

Research on homophobia in educational settings reveals that homosexuals as well as those believed to be homosexual are often victims of prejudice which manifests in various ways ranging from marginalization to outright assault (Burdge, 2009; Greene, 2000; Poteat, Espelege, & Koenig, 2009; Trotter, 2009). LGBTQ teachers often opt not to disclose their sexual orientation or gender identity for this reason and research indicates that if they do disclose their sexual orientation, they risk being subject to discrimination or loss of employment (DeJean, 2007; Duke, 2007; Ferfolja, 2008, 2009).

Homophobia is a social pathology that has significant socio-cultural sequela. The most obvious consequence is the suppression and marginalization of homosexuals. However, the less recognized social repercussion is enforcement and reinforcement of antiquated gender role prescriptions. In discussing the role homophobia plays in school violence, Kimmel and Mahler (2003) purported that the high incidence of physical assault in American schools can be imputed not only to the media (video games, rap and goth music, film, etc.), dysfunctional family history (i.e., child abuse), or individual psychological pathology, but also to an ungovernable operose effort to conform to social constructions of masculinity that endorse the use of violence as a reply to shame. Using recent school shootings as an example, the authors posited that the majority of the shooters were "gay-baited" or at the very least were accused of not adhering to the normative codes of masculinity (Kimmel & Mahler, 2003). The horrific violence that ensued was the response to homophobic bullying—not that any of the young men identified as gay in the first place. They were however, "different"—"non-athletic, bookish, weird" and the like—and for that reason they were accused of being gay.

The salient point is that it is homophobia, not being gay, that makes one a target. School violence is often the result of bullying and threats toward individuals who are perceived to be gay, as well those trying to let others know they are "real men". Carl Joseph Walker-Hoover, a Black youth, was 11 years old when he hung himself in his bedroom with an extension cord in

April 2009 (James, 2009). He never identified as either gay or straight although his mother remonstrated with the school he attended about the homophobic bullying he was experiencing. The relative silence about this incident from African American social justice advocates has been documented (Farrow, 2010).

History of Homophobia in Schools

The history of homophobia in school settings is long. In an article titled "Masculinity as homophobia," Kimmel (2007) quoted a 19th century educator describing school house institutionalization of anti-gay bias:

> Boys among boys are ashamed to be unmanly. I have a standing bet with a friend that I can walk into any playground in America where 6 year olds are happily playing and by asking one question I can provoke a fight. That question is 'who's a sissy around here?' Once posed the challenge is made. One of two things is likely to happen. One boy will accuse another of being a sissy to which that boy will respond that he's not a sissy and that the first boy is. They may have to fight it out to see who's lying. Or the whole group of boys will surround one boy and shout "he is, he is". That boy will either burst into tears and run home crying disgraced or he will have to take on several boys at once to prove that he's not a sissy (and what will his father or older brothers tell him if he chooses to run home crying?) It will be some time before he regains any sense of self-respect. (Kimmel, 2007, p. 328)

As much as homophobia is used to codify masculinity, it is also used to enforce sexism and to qualify what is and is not appropriately feminine. In her seminal work on this topic Pharr (2006) pointed out that:

> It is not by chance that when children approach puberty and increased sexual awareness, they begin to taunt each other with names such as "queer," "faggot," or "pervert." It is at puberty that the full force of society's pressure to conform to heterosexuality and prepare for marriage is brought to bear. Children have been given clear messages that those who deviate from standard expectations are to be made to get back in line. The best controlling tactic at puberty is to be treated as an outsider, to be ostracized at a time when it feels most vital to be accepted. Those who are different must be made to suffer loss. It is also at puberty that misogyny begins to be more apparent and girls are pressured to conform to societal norms that do not permit them to realize their full potential. (p. 172)

Conformity to biased social norms can impact educational achievement in various ways such as girls "dumbing themselves down" to not appear smarter than the boys whose attention they seek. Girls with this mindset tend to focus more on being provocative and alluring in appearance and behavior in school than they do on academic achievement.

This mentality is particularly evident in high school and college because in those settings, adolescents are working through the identity versus role confusion stage (Erikson, 1959) and are negotiating burgeoning sexual feelings. There is a tremendous need to fit in and give shape to one's identity through a connection to others and to align one with social and cultural norms, which must be done at the same time that one endeavors to establish a unique personality and manage a unique experience of sexual feelings and orientation. It is amidst all these developmental challenges that students endeavor to learn. Hence the educational process is clearly confounded when the environment is rife with homophobia and distorted notions of sexuality.

Having considered the interplay of these oppressive phenomena on the school community and students in general, it is appropriate to consider what the impact is on students who are lesbian, gay, bisexual, transgendered, and questioning.

Homophobia and the African American LGBTQ Student

A study using data from the 2007 National School Climate Survey revealed that 80% of students of color reported hearing homophobic remarks in school and 60% reported being verbally harassed because of their gender expression (Diaz & Kosciw, 2009). Thirty-three percent of African American students in this study reported having been subject to physical violence in school due to their sexual orientation. Only 38% of African American students who experienced homophobia and harassment reported the incidents and of those students, the majority felt that the issues were not addressed effectively by the authorities.

Black students who identify as LGBTQ in the research indicated that they often avoid coming out as gay, may feel alienated from the LGBTQ community at large, and find it difficult to integrate their sexual orientation and their Black identity (McCready, 2004a, 2004b; Parks, 2001; Vaught, 2004). In addition, Black youth who are attracted to the same sex appear to be at risk for emotional disturbances due to their experience of homophobia or heterosexism (Parks, 2001).

It is not only social scientists who recognize the prevalence of anti-gay sentiment among Black youth. Homophobic words are often used to describe "weaker" or "lesser" men in hip hop music, even though some rappers have openly condemned these sentiments (R. Johnson, 2007). In his documentary "Hip Hop: Beyond beats and rhymes," filmmaker Byron Hurt explored homophobia and exaggerated notions of masculinity as an unfortunate constituent of hip hop culture (Hurt, 2006). Rapper Ice-T stated

> there isn't anybody in the ghetto teaching that some peoples' sexual preferences are predisposed. You're just ignorant, you got to get educated, you got to get out of that jail cell called the ghetto to really begin to understand. All you see is a sissy, a soft dude, a punk. (Hill Collins, 2004, p. 124)

Adolescents must accomplish crucial developmental tasks that include "adjusting to the physical and emotional changes of puberty, establishing effective social and working relationships with peers, achieving independence from primary caretakers, preparing for a vocation, and moving toward a sense of values and definable identity" (Radkowsky & Siegel, 1997, p. 191). Because of homophobia and the stigmatization of homosexuality, reaching these developmental milestones can be harder for LGBTQ adolescents. Murdock and Bolch (2005) reported that victimization by peers is one of the strongest predictors of school disengagement for gay, lesbian, bisexual, or questioning youth. Mufioz-Plaza, Quinn, and Rounds (2002) described the classroom as "the most homophobic of all social institutions" (p. 53).

In an article discussing homophobic bullying, Dominique Johnson (2007a) posited that the formation and behavior of the African American lesbian high school gang, "DTO (Dykes Taking Over)," reflected these students attempt to take a proactive stance against homophobia and "re-establish a power differential after they experienced bullying based on their sexuality and gender expression" (p. 87).

In a speech before the Gay Lesbian Straight Education Network (GLSEN), a nationally recognized training and advocacy organization that focuses on ending homophobia in schools, the 28-year-educator and wife of the Vice President of the United States, Dr. Jill Biden stated that all "students deserve to be safe in school, regardless of sexual orientation or gender identity/ expression" (GLSEN, 2009) She referenced the recent suicides of two young boys, who had suffered constant anti-gay bullying as examples of the national "failure to confront a hostile school climate where bullying and harassment can be daily occurrences" (GLSEN, 2009).

Homophobia in schools also has been linked to negative mental health outcomes. LGBTQ students with the highest frequency of homophobic teasing and who perceived the least positive school climate reported the highest rate of depression and suicidal feelings as well as the highest alcohol and marijuana use. LGBTQ students who reported moderate to high levels of school support conversely reported significantly less depression and suicidal feelings (Kosciw, Diaz, & Greytak, 2008). What this research clearly discerns is that the determining factor is not the students' sexual orientation but the hostility and homophobia of the educational environment.

In "Sticks and Stones can Break my Bones and Words Can really Hurt Me" (Conoley, 2008), the author stated that young people who are either LGBTQ or (according to preconceived stereotypes) look like they could be LGBTQ are at risk for being bullied which in turn can lead to reduced physical, academic, and psychological well-being. There is ample research that confirms this risk (e.g., Mudrey & Medina-Adams, 2006; Poteat, 2008; Swearer et al., 2008; Whitman, Horn, & Boyd, 2007).

Regarding how academic institutions respond to the bullying of LGBTQ students, Conoley (2008) stated:

> Some educators may not know how to intervene effectively. … They may normalize physical bullying as gender specific to males and relational bullying as specific to females, and therefore part of their normal development. Further, adults may believe that children learn to be tough and resilient by dealing with same-age bullies and thus resist intervening as a way to promote self-confidence in victimized children. Finally, and of most concern, some may allow bullying, especially of children

from certain minority groups, as a way to satisfy their own aggressive impulses toward those children or groups. ... (p. 218)

Recommendations

Having deconstructed the core components of the problem of sexual orientation and gender bias for African American students, how does one divest the schools of these complex problems that limit both students and faculty and confound the whole process of developing emotionally healthy, progressive scholars who can thrive in the increasingly diverse contemporary world? The process can begin by highlighting existing efforts to address the problem. Most of the efforts to address sexuality in predominantly Black schools have focused on bridling the rampant spread of HIV/AIDS. As such, the research and practice interventions developed, thus far, focus largely on family makeup, religious background, and other risk and protective factors. Some social scientists have proffered that the use of education and human service paradigms informed by an Afrocentric perspective are the most effective contradiction to internalized racism and its cognitive and behavioral manifestations (Schiele, 2000). Further query into the age-specific manifestations of internalized racism and internalized homophobia in educational contexts is needed, but there is evidence that both can predict negative self-esteem in African American LGBTQ persons (Szymanski & Gupta, 2009). Interventions that draw from the more positive and holistic presentations of African Americans can help challenge the hypersexual and homophobic notions that inform the psychosocial malfunctioning of some Black students.

Policy

As policy informs practice, it is logical that some policy interventions can help address these issues. Legislative interventions in this regard are already underway. There are currently 24 states with general school anti-bullying and harassment laws. Nine states and the District of Columbia prohibit bullying and harassment based on both, sexual orientation and gender identity (Family Equality Council, 2008). On the federal level, Representative Linda Sanchez introduced a bill "To amend the Safe and Drug-Free Schools and Communities Act (2009)" to include bullying and harassment prevention programs. The amendment was introduced in May 2009 and then referred to a subcommittee for review in June of that year. No further action has been taken on this proposed legislation.

Programming and Infrastructure

Policy needs to translate into practice in order to affect real change. This process is underway in some schools through the development of programmatic interventions. School curricula, for example are beginning to include and reflect LGBTQ people from diverse backgrounds and some educators are beginning to help students understand and embrace the different ways in which gender identity and sexual orientation are expressed (Diaz & Kosciw, 2009; D. Johnson,

2007a; McCready, 2004b; Parks, 2001). There are also several school-based violence preven-tion programs throughout the country. Development of school infrastructure that supports on-going dialogue about respect for diversity is a proven resource for increasing school safety and ensuring a supportive environment for all students. One example of such infrastructure is the emergence of gay-straight alliance groups in secondary and higher educational institutions.

School-Based Tolerance and Respect Advocacy Groups

Gay-straight alliances (GSAs) are student-led, school-based clubs open to all members of the student body regardless of sexual orientation. The emergence of GSAs is generally believed to have begun in California and Massachusetts in the late 1980s (Fetner & Kush, 2008). What is not so well-known is that a group of students of color started an earlier group in the Bronx in 1972 (D. Johnson, 2007b). GSAs often advocate for improved school climate, educate the larger school community about LGBTQ issues, and support LGBTQ students and their allies (Griffin et al., 2004). Some qualitative studies indicate that participation in GSAs can lead to an increased sense of empowerment (Russell et al., 2009), as well as positive identity development (May-berry, 2006) for LGBT youth. Even though some local school boards and school administrators often resist the formation of GSAs because of their own homophobia or heterosexism, the legal system has often ruled in favor of these programs as a means of protecting the rights of LGBTQ students (Mercier, 2009). There is empirical evidence that shows that GSAs are more likely to form in larger schools, in urban and suburban settings, and in more liberal and progressive regions of the United States (Fetner & Kush, 2008).

The 2007 National School Climate Survey (NSCS) highlighted major findings regarding school safety, access to education, academic achievement for LGBTQ students, and access to GSAs in school (Kosciw, Diaz, & Greytak, 2008). The NSCS studied 6,209 middle and high school students. LGBTQ students in schools with GSAs were found to be less likely to hear homophobic remarks than students in other schools (57% versus 75%). They were also found to experience less harassment and assaults based on their sexual orientation and gender expres-sion and were more likely to report such incidents when they did happen. In general, LGBTQ students in schools with GSAs were less likely to feel unsafe based on sexual orientation or gender expression and they were less likely to miss school out of fear for their safety. LGBTQ students in schools with GSAs were also found to feel a greater sense of belonging to their school communities.

Active organized school groups that support respect for human diversity may also play an important role in helping students identify staff who are supportive and to whom they can report any struggles with their sexual identity as well as any incidents of victimization. The presence of such groups may offer evidence of a school's commitment to LGBTQ students and their allies, creating a source of perceived support for students even if they are not actively engaged with the school-based group themselves. Although the number of such programs is increasing, less than one quarter of high school students nationally have a GSA in their school.

Students in small towns, rural areas, and in the South are least likely to have access to this type of support in school. LGBTQ students of color also have less access to the resources of GSAs and comparable visible sources of support than their White peers (Diaz & Kosciw, 2009; Kosciw, Diaz, & Greytak, 2008). It is also important to note that such organizations are only a part of what helps to make schools safer for LGBTQ students and their allies. GSAs should be combined with a larger comprehensive safe schools initiative that includes school policies specifically addressing sexual orientation and gender identity/expression bias, as well as training for school administrators, faculty, and other staff. As part of a comprehensive safe schools initiative, such alliances can create positive changes in school climate that endure beyond transitions in the student body, faculty, or administration.

Training

Schools conduct training for faculty and staff to promote tolerance and respect around ethnic diversity. "Respecting persons of varied sexual orientations and gender identities" included as a topic at such training will enhance the understanding of human diversity for both students and teachers and help ensure that teachers and administrators are better equipped to support a multifaceted student population.

In predominantly African American schools training would provide an excellent opportunity to affirm the benefits of Black culture as well as the diversity of the experience of people of African heritage, including diversity in sexual orientation and gender expression. Increased culturally responsive teaching is often a natural outcome of such training (Gay, 2002). Finally, training around issues of sexual diversity can increase the number of teachers and other school staff who recognize verbal and physical harassment based on sexual orientation and gender identity who could then skillfully intervene when these incidents occur (Diaz & Kosciw, 2009; D. Johnson, 2007a).

Bibliotherapy

Bibliotherapy uses literature, such as books, articles, or poems, as a strategy to work with individuals or groups to increase motivation, self-confidence, and address misconceptions. As an intervention to increase understanding of and respect for diversity around sexual orientation and gender expression, bibliotherapy can be used in training specifically to the topic of diversity, or as a means of integrating knowledge about human diversity into core content courses. For example, Elie Wiesel's "Night" (1982) and Anne Frank's "The Diary of a Young Girl" (1993) are often used in English or history classes to give students the opportunity to simultaneously improve reading skills to understand anti-Semitism and its historical consequences. Bibliotherapy identifies appropriate literature and then reads these texts with individuals who can benefit from them. The goal is for readers to naturally identify with characters or themes, have an emotional reaction to them, gain some self-awareness in the process, and realize their connection to people or circumstances that are described (McCoy & McKay, 2006). Boykin's "One More River to Cross" (1997) and Hull and colleagues "But Some of Us Are Brave" (1993) are examples of stories about Black LGBTQ people that can serve to sensitize and educate Black students about the diversity of the Black experience. Readings on diversity and healthy sexuality can contribute to consciousness-raising, which helps to ameliorate muddled and often pathological notions about sex.

School faculty can familiarize themselves with the literature on diversity and human sexuality, particularly as it relates to their subject areas and incorporate such readings, where appropriate, for the students' educational and social development. Increased awareness about the multifarious nature of human sexuality and gender expression can help heterosexual and non-heterosexual Black students negotiate the realities of modern society. Whether or not they are comfortable with homosexuality or diversity around gender expression, today's youth will invariably encounter non-heterosexuals and transgendered persons, sometimes as employers, college professors, colleagues, or potential friends. Such knowledge of and appreciation for human diversity, can enrich African American students' capacity to advance personally and professionally.

Peer Mediation

Peer mediation refers to a process whereby individuals are empowered to resolve conflicts within their cohorts in order to reach a given goal. Peer mediators in school safety initiatives are trained to manage conflict among their peers. The goal of peer-mediated conflict resolution is to get all parties to listen to each other and resolve the conflict in a non-violent way (Skiba & Peterson, 2000). Peer mediation may be a helpful strategy for addressing conflicts between LGBTQ students and students who exhibit homophobic attitudes and behaviors. One caveat is that the school climate must support tolerance and respect for all types of diversity in order for peer mediators to successfully advocate for inclusiveness.

Social Support for LGBTQ Youth

Another way to improve academic and mental health outcomes for LGBTQ youth is through creating social support groups. Research indicated that such support groups provide a space for students to share problems with one another, meet other LGBTQ students thereby decreasing isolation, exchange ideas, advocate for their needs, and engage in social activities (Alvarez & Schneider, 2008).

McCready (2004b) cautioned; however, that in order for such support groups to become meaningful for Black students, they need to operate under a multidimensional framework that takes other oppressive paradigms impacting Black students (e.g., racism and classism) into consideration. A focus on issues of gender and sexuality does not suffice because the social and cultural realities of the student body and the community need to be taken into consideration in order for social support groups to become successful (McCready, 2004a).

School Media

As youth are often targeted and heavily influenced by media, the use of varied platforms to highlight the history and contributions of Black LGBTQ people is necessary to counter the notion that such groups do not exist or have not made seminal contributions to the legacy of Black people. Media that focus on LGBTQ African Americans (e.g., activists, authors, educators and artists) can improve faculty and student understanding of the real diversity of the African American experience and the long history of contributions made by Black LGBTQ persons. Often educators and students are unaware that noted activists, famed artists and dancers, athletes, playwrights, and politicians are LGBTQ persons. Famous individuals can serve as role models on many levels because, in addition to their extraordinary achievements, they overcame not only racism but homophobic and heterosexist social prejudice and as such they can provide breadth and depth to students' understanding of Black heroes and heroism.

Advocacy

Advocacy efforts will make a difference in securing safe, healthy learning environments free of the toxins of anti-gay bias and gender stereotyping. Educators have a key role in such advocacy efforts. Recognizing the limitations placed on the Black community by homophobia and heterosexism, African American leaders are beginning to speak out. In the opening speech for the 20th LGBT activists' convention, Julian Bond, chairman emeritus of the NAACP and civil rights leader, discussed his support for gay marriages, drawing a comparison to interracial marriages that were also publicly criticized as morally wrong in the not too distant past (Resnick, 2008). He clarified that gay rights are basic civil rights and that all members of society deserve to be treated equally. Bond acknowledged that some African Americans may feel resentful when comparisons between the struggle for gay rights and the civil rights movement are drawn, but he pointed out that this resentment can be transformed into pride based on the realization that the civil rights movement has served as an inspiration for other oppressed groups in their fight for equality (Resnick, 2008). It should also be noted that from its inception, the movement for gay rights has been supported and often led by LGBTQ people of African heritage.

Conclusion

As educational institutions are a principal site of social learning and behavioral instruction for African American students, it is critical that dehumanizing, prejudicial notions of Black sexuality not be allowed to proliferate. Additionally, the heterosexist and homophobic attitudes and behaviors that prescribe gender roles and lead to aggression against those who fall outside the perceived norm must be eliminated. In order to create safety and support for the academic achievement and overall development of all students, educators, and school administrators must be actively involved in addressing these issues. Anti-gay bullying policy that prohibits all sexuality and gender based harassment is the foundation on which increased safety and respect for diversity can be cultivated in schools. *School programs* and training based on the wealth of literature and media available about human diversity are also vital for students, parents, staff, and faculty. Distorted notions of Black sexuality must be contradicted in both the implicit and the explicit curricula. Students must be empowered to lead in fostering a safe progressive educational context for themselves and for their peers. These interventions combined with advocacy in support of human diversity will contribute to the psychological, intellectual, and social evolution of Black youth as well as that of the institutions charged with educating them.

References

Alvarez, S. D., & Schneider, J. (2008). One college campus' need for a safe zone: A case study. *Journal of Gender Studies, 17,* 71–74.

Bailey, B. (2002). Gendered realities: Fact or fiction? The realities in a secondary level coeducational classroom. In P. Mohammed (Ed.), *Gendered realities: Essays in Caribbean feminist thought* (pp. 164–182). Kingston, JM: University of West Indies Press.

Billboard. (2009). *Find artists and music.* Retrieved from http://www.billboard.com

Bounds Littlefield, M. (2008). The media as a system of racialization: Exploring images of African American women and the new racism. *American Behavioral Scientist, 51,* 675–685.

Boykin, K. (1997). *One more river to cross: Black and gay in America.* Harpswell, ME: Anchor.

Brown, L. S. (1989). New voices, new visions: Toward a lesbian/gay paradigm for psychology. *Psychology of Women Quarterly, 13,* 445–458.

Burdge, B. J. (2009). Legal discrimination against lesbian, gay, and bisexual employees: A multi-theoretical model to explain an elusive civil rights law. *Journal of Policy Practice, 8,* 4–20.

Cavazos-Rehg, P. A., Krauss M.J., Spitznagel E.L., Schootman M., Bucholz K.K., Peipert J.F. et al. (2009). Age of sexual debut among U. S. adolescents. *Contraception, 80,* 158–162.

Centers for Disease Control and Prevention-CDC. (2006). Racial/ethnic disparities in diagnoses of HIV/AIDS—33 states, 2001–2004. *MMWR, 55,* 121–125.

Conoley, J. C. (2008). Sticks and stones can break my bones and words can really hurt me. *School Psychology Review, 37,* 217–220.

DeJean, W. (2007). Out gay and lesbian K-12 educators: A study in radical honesty. *Journal of Gay & Lesbian Issues in Education, 4,* 59–72.

Diaz, E. M., & Kosciw, J. G. (2009). *Shared differences: The experiences of lesbian, gay, bisexual, and transgender students of color in our nation's schools.* New York: Gay, Lesbian and Straight Education Network.

D'Ooge, C. (1994). 'The birth of a nation.' Symposium on classic film discusses inaccuracies and virtues. *The Library of Congress Information Bulletin, 53,* 263.

Dre, Dr. (1992). Bitches ain't sh**. [Recorded by Dr. Dre and Da Nigga Daz]. On *The Chronic* [CD]. Los Angeles: Priority Records.

Duke, T. S. (2007). Hidden, invisible, marginalized, ignored: A critical review of the professional and empirical literature (or lack thereof) on gay and lesbian teachers in the United States. *Journal of Gay & Lesbian Issues In Education, 4,* 19–38.

Erikson, E. H. (1959). *Identity and the life cycle.* New York: International University Press.

Espelage, D. L., Aragon, S. R., Birkett, M., & Koenig, B. W. (2008). Homophobic teasing, psychological outcomes, and sexual orientation among high school students: What influence do parents and schools have? *School Psychology Review, 37,* 202–216.

Family Equality Council. (2008). *State-by-state: Anti-bullying laws in the U. S.* Boston, MA: Author.

Farrow, K. (2010). *Anti-gay bullying is a deadly threat to children of color.* Retrieved from http://www.thegrio.com/opinion/teasing-is-more-than-childs-play.php

The Feminist Sexual Ethics Project. (2009). *Slavery, sexuality and religion.* Retrieved from http://www.brandeis.edu/projects/fse/slavery/slav-index.html

Ferfolja, T. (2008). Discourses that silence: Teachers and anti-lesbian harassment. *Discourse: Studies in the Cultural Politics of Education, 29,* 107–119.

Ferfolja, T. (2009). Stories so far: An overview of the research on lesbian teachers. *Sexualities, 12,* 378–396.

Fetner, T., & Kush, K. (2008). Gay-straight alliances in high schools: Social predictors of early adoption. *Youth & Society, 40,* 114–130.

Frank, A. (1993). *The diary of a young girl.* New York: Bantam Books. (Original work published 1947)

Gay, G. (2002). Preparing for culturally responsive teaching. *Journal of Teacher Education, 53,* 106–116.

Gay Lesbian Straight Education Network (GLSEN). (2009). Dr. Jill Biden speaks at GLSEN Respect Awards. Retrieved from http://blog.glsen.org/2009/06/dr-jill-biden-speaks-at-glsen-respect.html

Greene, B. (2000). African American lesbian and bisexual women. *Journal of Social Issues, 56,* 239–250.

Griffin, P., Lee, C., Waugh, J., & Beyer, C. (2004). Describing roles that gay-straight alliances play in schools: From individual support to social change. *Journal of Gay & Lesbian Issues in Education, 1,* 7–22.

Herek, G. M. (2000) The psychology of sexual prejudice. *Current Directions in Psychological Science, 9,* 19–22.

Hill Collins, P. (2004). *Black sexual politics: African Americans, gender, and the new racism.* New York: Routledge.

Hodes, M. (1997). *White women, Black men: Illicit sex in the nineteenth century South.* New Haven, CT: Yale University Press.

Hull, G. T., Bell Scott, P., & Smith, B. (Eds.). (1993). *All the women are White, all the Blacks are men, but some of us are brave: Black women's studies.* New York: The Feminist Press at CUNY.

Hurt, B. (Director). (2006). *Hip hop: Beyond beats and rhymes* [Television broadcast]. U. S.: PBS.

Ikeda, D. (2009). *Toward humanitarian competition: A new current in history.* Tokyo, JP: Soka Gakkai International.

James, S. D. (2009, April 14). *When words can kill: 'That's so gay.'* Retrieved from http://abcnews.go.com/Health/MindMoodNews/story?id=7328091&page=l

Johnson, D. (2007a). Taking over the school: Student gangs as a safety strategy for dealing with homophobic bullying in an urban public school district. *Journal of Gay & Lesbian Social Services, 19,* 87–104.

Johnson, D. (2007b). 'This is political!' Negotiating the legacies of the first school-based gay youth group. *Children, Youth and Environments, 17,* 380–387.

Johnson, R. (2007). *Cornel West, hip hop and homophobia. Ramon's gay life blog.* Retrieved from http://gaylife.about.com/b/2007/09/07/cornel-west-hip-hop-and-homophobia.htm

Kauer, K. (2009). Queering lesbian sexualities in collegiate sporting spaces. *Journal of Lesbian Studies, 13,* 306–318.

Kimmel, M. S. (2007). Masculinity as homophobia: Fear, shame, and silence in the construction of gender identity. In P. S. Rothenberg (Ed.), *Race, class, and gender in the United States* (pp. 80–92). New York: Macmillan.

Kimmel, M., & Mahler, M. (2003) Adolescent masculinity, homophobia, and violence: Random school shootings, 1982–2001. *American Behavioral Scientist, 46,* 1439–1458.

Kosciw, J. G., Diaz, E. M., & Greytak, E. A. (2008). *The 2007 National School Climate Survey: The experiences of lesbian, gay, bisexual and transgender youth in our nation's schools.* New York: Gay Lesbian Straight Education Network.

Manzo, K. (2009, June 17). Administrators confront student "sexting": Schools urged to develop policies and programs to curb the practice. *Education Week, 28,* 8.

Majied, K. (2008). A conceptual analysis of homophobia and heterosexism: Experiences of lesbian, gay, bisexual, transgendered, and questioning people (LGBTQ) in Trinidad. *The Caribbean Journal of Social Work, 6/7,* 144–166.

Mayberry, M. (2006). The story of a Salt Lake City Gay-Straight Alliance: Identity work and LGBT youth. *Journal of Gay & Lesbian Issues in Education, 4,* 13–31.

McCoy, H., & McKay, C. (2006). Preparing social workers to identify and integrate culturally affirming bibliotherapy into treatment. *Social Work Education, 25,* 680–693.

McCready, L. T. (2004a). Some challenges facing queer youth programs in urban high schools: Racial segregation and de-normalizing Whiteness. *Journal of Gay & Lesbian Issues in Education, 1,* 37–51.

McCready, L. T. (2004b). Understanding the marginalization of gay and gender non-conforming Black male students. *Theory into Practice, 43,* 136–143.

Mercier, M. T. (2009). Fighting to fit in: Gay-straight alliances in schools under United States jurisprudence. *International Journal of Human Rights, 13,* 177–191.

Mohsen, B., & West, K. (2006). Correlates of the intention to remain sexually inactive among underserved Hispanic and African American high school students. *Journal of School Health, 76,* 25–32.

Mudrey, R., & Medina-Adams, A. (2006). Attitudes, perceptions, and knowledge of pre-service teachers regarding the educational isolation of sexual minority youth. *Journal of Homosexuality, 51,* 63–90.

Mufioz-Plaza, C., Quinn, S. C., & Rounds, K. A. (2002). Lesbian, gay, bisexual and transgender students: Perceived social support in the high school environment. *The High School Journal, 85,* 52–63.

Murdered soccer star—A victim of 'corrective rape'? (2009). *Contemporary Sexuality, 43,* 9–10.

Murdock, T. B., & Bolch, M. B. (2005). Risk and protective factors for poor school adjustment in lesbian, gay, and bisexual (LGB) high school youth: Variable and person-centered analyses. *Psychology in the Schools, 42,* 159–172.

O'Conor, A. (1993). Who gets called queer in school? Lesbian, gay, and bisexual teenagers, homophobia and high school. *The High School Journal, 77,* 7–12.

Parks, C. W. (2001). African-American same-gender-loving youths and families in urban schools. *Journal of Gay & Lesbian Social Services, 13,* 41–56.

Pharr, S. (2006). Homophobia as a weapon of sexism. In P. S. Rothenberg (Ed.), *Race, class, and gender in the United States* (pp. 168–177). New York: Macmillan.

Poteat, V. P. (2008). Contextual and moderating effects of the peer group climate on the use of homophobic epithets. *School of Psychology Review, 37,* 188–201.

Poteat, V. P., Espelage, D. L., & Koenig, B. W. (2009). Willingness to remain friends and attend school with lesbian and gay peers: Relational expressions of prejudice among heterosexual youth. *Journal of Youth & Adolescence, 38,* 952–962.

Radowsky, M., & Siegel, L. J. (1997). The gay adolescent: Stressors, adaptations, and psychosocial interventions. *Clinical Psychology Review, 17,* 191–216.

Resnick, E. (2008). *Julian Bond: Gay rights are civil rights.* Gay People's Chronicle. Retrieved from http://www.thetaskforce.org/TF_in_news/08_0227/stories/2_julian_bond.pdf

Rich, A. (1993). Compulsory heterosexuality and lesbian existence. In H. Abelove, M. A. Barale, & D. Halperin (Eds.), *The Lesbian and Gay Studies Reader* (pp. 227–254). New York: Routledge.

Russell, S. T., Muraco, A., Subramaniam, A., & Laub, C. (2009). Youth empowerment and high school gay-straight alliances. *Journal of Youth & Adolescence, 38,* 891–903.

Schiele, J. H. (2000). *Human services and the Afrocentric paradigm.* New York: Routledge.

Skiba, R., & Peterson, R. (2000). *Creating a positive climate: Peer mediation. What works in preventing school violence.* Bloomington, IN: Safe and Responsive Schools Project.

Speech of Senator Benjamin R. Tillman. 56th Cong. (1900). Cong. Rec. §§ 3223–3224.

Staples, R. (2006). *Exploring Black sexuality.* Lanham, MD: Rowman & Littlefield.

Swearer, S., Turner, R. K., Givens, J. E., & Pollack, W. S. (2008). 'You're so gay!" Do different forms of bullying matter for adolescent males? *School Psychology Review, 37,* 160–173.

Szymanski, D. M., & Gupta, A. (2009). Examining the relationship between multiple internalized oppressions and African American lesbian, gay, bisexual, and questioning persons' self-esteem and psychological distress. *Journal of Counseling Psychology, 56,* 110–118.

Teen "Sexting" attracts attention of prosecutors. (2009). *Contemporary Sexuality, 43.*

To amend the Safe and Drug-Free Schools and Communities Act to include bullying and harassment prevention programs, H.R. 2262, 111th Cong. (2009).

Trotter, J. (2009). Ambiguities around sexuality: An approach to understanding harassment and bullying of young people in British schools. *Journal of LGBT Youth, 6,* 7–23.

Vaught, S. (2004). The talented tenth; Gay Black boys and the racial politics of southern schooling. *Journal of Gay & Lesbian Issues in Education, 2,* 5–26.

Walter, A., & Hayes, D. (1998). Homophobia within schools: Challenging the culturally sanctioned dismissal of gay students and colleagues. *Journal of Homosexuality, 35,* 1–20.

Weinberg, G. (1972). *Society and the healthy homosexual.* New York: St. Martin's.

Whitman, J. S., Horn, S. S., & Boyd, C. J. (2007). Activism in the schools: Providing LGBTQ affirmative training to school counselors. *Journal of Gay & Lesbian Psychotherapy, 11,* 143–154.

Wiesel, E. (1982). *Night.* New York: Bantam.

Activities for Further Exploration and Discussion

1. When it comes to gender identity, there are many debates about the "rightness" or "wrongness" of the spectrum. Some would say it is a moral issue and that the gender binary is the only way. What are some questions that you have about the gender identity spectrum? What methods of research will you use to find answers to your questions?

2. As we learned in this chapter, sexual orientation is specifically about the sexual attraction one has to another. Gender is the expression of the felt gender someone has. Sometimes gender identity, sexual orientation, and race intersect in people's lives and cause issues and distress. What are some examples of where the intersection of these three phenomena can be problematic? Why?

3. Family life educators have the responsibility of educating individuals and families regarding ways that they can be healthy. Some families do not have the resources available to understand the intersections of their different stations in life. Develop a five-step plan to help families with issues related to race, class, gender, and sexual orientation. Be sure to include the part you will play in the plan. How do you envision this plan will assist families with the different intersections they face?

Terms

Agender: Lacking gender, genderless, or not caring about gender identity

Bigender: Having two gender identities either simultaneously or switching between the two

Bisexual: Sexual attraction that most commonly consists of attraction to both of those members of the gender and sex binary, male/female

Gender-fluid: Someone who identifies as male, female, and/or nonbinary at different times and/or circumstances

Genderqueer: Someone who feels that their felt gender does not fit with socially constructed norms for their biological sex; encompasses thoughts, feelings, behaviors, and gender identity

Heteronormativity: Belief that heterosexism is normal and should be adhered to regarding gender roles, identity, and sexual orientation based on assigned biological sex

Heterosexual: Sexual attraction to the opposite sex and/or gender with which an individual identifies

Homosexual: Sexual attraction to the same sex and/gender with which an individual identifies

Intersectionality: The places in a person's or family's life where all their identities and social locations connect and intersect to define who they are and potentially how they behave in the context of life situations

Lesbian: Sexual attraction and orientation is commonly toward others who identify as female, transgender, and/or transsexual

Sexual orientation: Defines who a person is sexually attracted to

Transgender (man or woman): Someone whose gender identity differs from the sex they were assigned at birth

References

Ferree, M. M. (2010). Filling the glass: Gender perspectives on families. *Journal of Marriage and Family, 72*(3), 420–439.

Few-Demo, A. L., Humble, A. M., Curran, M. A., & Lloyd, S. A. (2016). Queer theory, intersectionality, and LGBT-parent families: Transformative critical pedagogy in family theory. *Journal of Family Theory & Review, 8*(1), 74–94.

Ghosh, S. (2015). *Gender identity*. Medscape. https://emedicine.medscape.com/article/917990-overview

Greenberg, J. (1999). Defining male and female: Intersexuality and the collision between law and biology. *Arizona Law Review, 41*(2), 265–328.

LeVay, S. (1993). *The sexual brain*. MIT Press.

Levon, E. (2015). Integrating intersectionality in language, gender and sexuality research. *Language and Linguistics Compass, 9*(7), 295–308.

McDowell, T., & Fang, S. R. S. (2007). Feminist-informed critical multiculturalism: Considerations for family research. *Journal of Family Issues, 28*(4), 549–566.

Merriam-Webster. (n.d.). *Transgender*. https://www.merriamwebster.com/dictionary/transgender

Morgenroth, T., & Ryan, M. K. (2018). Addressing gender inequality: Stumbling blocks and the roads ahead. *Group Processes & Intergroup Relations, 21*(5), 671–677.

Nagoshi, J. L., Hohn, K. L., Nagoshi, C. T. (2017). Questioning the heteronormative matrix: Transphobia, intersectionality, and gender outlaws within the gay and lesbian community. *Social Development Issues, 39*(3), 19–31.

Oswald, R., Blume, L., & Marks, S. (2005). Decentering heteronormativity: A model for family studies. In V. L. Bengtson, A. C. Acock, K. R. Allen, P. Dilworth-Anderson, & D. M. Klein (Eds.), *Sourcebook of family theory and research* (pp. 143–165). SAGE.

Pryzgoda, J. & Chrisler, J. C. (2000). Definitions of gender and sex: The subtleties of meaning. *Sex Roles, 43*(7–8), 553–569.

Savin-Williams, R. C. (2018, July 29). A guide to genderqueer, non-binary, and gender fluid identity: A new gender identity is confusing to many over 30, yet critical to some youths. [Weblog comment]. https://www.psychologytoday.com/us/blog/sex-sexuality-and-romance/201807/guide-genderqueer-non-binary-and-genderfluid-identity

Sell, R. L. (1997). Defining and measuring sexual orientation: A review. *Archives of Sexual Behavior, 26*(6), 643–658.

CHAPTER 4

Religion

T HIS CHAPTER'S DISCOURSE is specific to religion and the role it plays in cultural and family diversity. The history of religion in the world, as well as its presence around the world, is important to explore. The intersectionality of religion, class, race, and gender are significant and extrapolated further in this chapter. We are aware that there is privilege regarding religious practices, and this is discussed as well. Discrimination and oppression based on religion are very prevalent and are included in this chapter. For perspective and comparison, the historical view of religion is also explained. Regarding the assignments, there are suggestions to incorporate media and reaction papers into the learning experience. The implications for family life education are also included.

History of Religion

Ristuccia (2013) posited that

> in the standard history of the term, *religion* as a comparative category first appeared in the West during the sixteenth century. On this view, religion is not a native category but rather an implicitly anthropological one: the imposition of colonial minds contrasting themselves with the conquered or perhaps the creation of tolerant intellectuals seeking peace amid religious wars. (p. 170)

There were historians during medieval times who rejected the narrative of religion being socially constructed during this time period. Colonization of formerly Islamic and pagan lands are examples of conditions that caused the concept of religion to be in place by the 12th century (Ristuccia, 2013). During the unification of Spain under the reign of the Roman Catholic monarchs Isabella and Ferdinand in 1492, there were a significant number of non-Christian people in the kingdom (Casares & Delaigue, 2013). These ethnic groups included enslaved people brought from sub-Saharan West Africa, Moriscos, and Arab-Berber people from North Africa, also referred to as *berberiscos,* who were taken captive by corsairs, a group who practiced a legalized form of piracy in the Mediterranean.

The enslaved people from West Africa who were brought to Spain were *animists,* those whose doctrine emphasizes the vital principle of organic development as immaterial spirit. They attribute conscious life to objects and phenomena in nature and believed in the existence of spirits that were separable from bodies (Merriam-Webster, n.d.). Some of the enslaved Africans belonged to ethnic groups that had converted to Islam. Moriscos were descended from Spanish-born Muslims. They were initially allowed to keep their religion and traditions but were eventually forced to convert to Christianity through baptism. This happened as early as 1502 (Casares & Delaigue, 2013).

Historically, religion and culture are very closely related. In some societies, they are one in the same. For Judaism, people identify racially with their religion (Beyers, 2017). When someone is referred to as Jewish, often they are being identified based on their race and religion. Sometimes people who practice Islam, commonly called Muslims, are referred to as an ethnic group with a unique culture of their own. During Bible times, Christians were seen as a sect of people who did not practice Judaism. However, some who were Jewish converts to Christianity were referred to as Jewish-Christians. When used in this way, their former religion was used as a descriptor.

In ancient times, religion was often viewed to measure morality and the general "goodness" of a person. It was believed that if one was religious, they were held in high esteem. Clergy, such as priests in the Catholic church, rabbis in Judaism, and pastors and ministers in the Christian and Protestant religions, can be viewed with the respectability and reverence of a deity. The expectation was that the clergy of the religious tradition would represent the best interests of the people who ascribed to the religious principles. The culture of a people, their race and/or ethnic group, in part, was determined by their religion.

Saroglou (2011) identified some universal dimensions and functions of religion that include believing, bonding, behaving, and belonging. Most world religions include the belief in a personal god. *Believing* was described as being characterized by having "a set of some or many beliefs relative to what many people would consider as being an (external) transcendence—and its "connection" with humans and the world— [and] is a basic universal component of religion" (p. 1323). This does not only include one god but can be many gods and divine beings. Some are nonpersonal divinities or impersonal forces or principles.

Bonding is an emotional dimension. Religion is comprised of beliefs, but there must also be "self-transcendent experiences" that bind the person or persons with each other and their deities (Saroglou, 2011). This bonding can take place through acts of worship, which may include, but are not limited to, prayer, public meetings, and/or pilgrimages. *Behaving* is the dimension of religiosity where the idea of morality is examined. "Religion not only is particularly concerned with morality as an external correlate but includes morality as one of its basic dimensions" (Saroglou, 2011, p. 1326). The fourth dimension is *belonging.* This speaks more specifically to the idea of culture and identity with religion. Those who ascribe to certain religious beliefs automatically seem to become a part of a community of people who are presupposed to support and guide them through their lives and help to meet their needs.

Depending on the region of the world and prior to colonization, there were many religions operating with these dimensions in various ways that are necessary for the progression of culture and community. About 72% of the world's population likely belong to four major religions: Christianity, Islam, Hinduism, and Buddhism, respectively (Barrett, 2001). Each of the religion's historical and contemporary impact on culture and family will be discussed, including the intersections of class, race, gender, and sexual orientation.

Christianity and the Family

According to Hackett and McClendon (2017), in a study conducted by Pew Research, Christians remain the largest religious group in the world; it makes up nearly a third of the Earth's 7.3 billion people (~31%), and "Christians had the most births and deaths of any religious group in recent years" (p. 1). In fact, it is estimated that 223 million babies were born to Christian mothers between 2010 and 2015.

Psalm 127:3–5 says, "Sons are indeed a heritage from the Lord, children, a reward. Like arrows in the hand of a warrior are the sons born in one's youth. Happy is the man who has filled his quiver with them. Such men will never be put to shame when they speak with their enemies at the city gate (HCSB). There are many passages in the Bible that encourage Christians to have children and assert that children are a blessing from the Lord. Having children and a family is a part of the "heritage" that Christians receive as a result of their faith. The culture of Christianity has largely centered around family, rearing children who remain faithful to their spiritual heritage as they go on to live their own lives and create their own families.

The Couple That Prays Together
RACE AND ETHNICITY, RELIGION, AND RELATIONSHIP QUALITY AMONG WORKING-AGE ADULTS

By Christopher G. Ellison, Amy M. Burdette*, and W. Bradford Wilcox**

A substantial body of research has shown that relationship quality tends to be (a) lower among racial and ethnic minorities and (b) higher among more religious persons and among couples in which partners share common religious affiliations, practices, and beliefs. However, few studies have examined the interplay of race or ethnicity and religion in shaping relationship quality. Our study addresses this gap in the literature using data from the National Survey of Religion and Family Life

Christopher G. Ellison, Amy M. Burdette, and W. Bradford Wilcox, "The Couple That Prays Together: Race and Ethnicity, Religion, and Relationship Quality Among Working-Age Adults," *Journal of Marriage and Family*, vol. 72, no. 4, pp. 963-975. Copyright © 2010 by Blackwell Publishing. Reprinted with permission. Provided by ProQuest LLC. All rights reserved.

(NSRFL), a 2006 telephone survey of 2,400 working-age adults (ages 18–59), which contains oversamples of African Americans and Latinos. Results underscore the complex nature of the effects of race and ethnicity, as well as religious variables. In particular, we found that couples' in-home family devotional activities and shared religious beliefs are positively linked with reports of relationship quality.

During the past half century, the United States has witnessed dramatic changes in the nature, quality, and stability of intimate relationships—from increases in divorce, nonmarital childbearing, and cohabitation to delays in the age of first marriage. Most notably, marriage has become increasingly fragile over the same period (Cherlin, 2004). Although these changes have influenced all sectors of U.S. society, they have been particularly consequential for racial and ethnic minorities, especially African Americans (Landale & Oropesa, 2007; Lichter, McLaughlin, Kephart, & Landry, 1992; Tucker & Mitchell-Kernan, 1995). For instance, according to recent Census estimates, fewer than half of Blacks (34% of men, 28% of women) and Hispanics (43% of men, 46% of women) are now married and living with their spouse; by contrast, more than half of all non-Hispanic White adults (58% of men, 54% of women) are married and living with their spouse (Kreider & Simmons, 2003). Studies have also shown that African Americans who do marry experience lower relationship quality and greater risk of marital disruption (i.e., divorce or separation) than do non-Hispanic Whites (Broman, 2005; Phillips & Sweeney, 2006). Finally, African Americans and especially Hispanics are more likely to have children born into cohabiting unions than are non-Hispanic Whites, and such cohabiting relationships are more likely to be characterized by instability and lower relationship quality than are marital relationships (Kennedy & Bumpass, 2008; Landale & Oropesa, 2007).

Although scholarly attention has increasingly been directed toward the causes and correlates of relationship quality among Blacks and Hispanics (Broman, 2005; McLoyd, Cauce, Takeuchi,& Wilson, 2000), as well as differences in relationship quality by race and ethnicity (Blackman, Clayton, Glenn, Malone-Colon, & Roberts 2005), there has been surprisingly little attention to the role that religion may play in influencing the quality of marriages and intimate relationships for Blacks and Hispanics, or in accounting for racial and ethnic differences in relationship quality. This is surprising given that, in recent years, family researchers have refocused attention on the role of religious factors in shaping relationship quality among married and cohabiting couples. Although some studies have reported little or no association between religion and relationship quality (Booth, Johnson, Branaman, & Sica, 1995), most studies have shown salutary or protective effects of religious involvement on relationship quality (Call & Heaton, 1997; Myers, 2006; Wolfinger & Wilcox, 2008). This oversight is also surprising because a wealth of evidence reveals that African Americans tend to be more religious, by virtually any conventional indicator, than are non-Hispanic Whites from otherwise similar backgrounds (Taylor, Chatters, & Levin, 2004). Although one recent study focused on religion and relationship quality among African Americans and non-Hispanic Whites (Furdyna, Tucker, & James, 2008), we are aware of no published work that explores this topic among Mexican Americans or other Latino groups, a striking gap in the literature in light of the rapid growth of the Hispanic population in the United States (Suro, 2005), as well as the distinctive religious cultures of Latinos (Espinosa, Elizondo, & Miranda, 2003). Moreover, no study has sought to explore how religion may augment or reduce racial and ethnic differences in relationship quality.

Our study augments the literature in several notable ways. We concentrate on the potentially salutary effects for Black, Hispanic, and non-Hispanic White couples of several specific aspects of religion: (a) denominational homogamy, (b) joint regular religious attendance, (c) shared beliefs and values, and (d) shared home worship activities. Specifically, we explore the links between religion and relationship quality by analyzing data from a new, nationally representative sample of working-age (18–59 years) adults with oversamples of African Americans and Latinos: the National Survey of Religion and Family Life (NSRFL). We discuss results in terms of (a) our understanding of the mechanisms through which religion may contribute to relationship quality among married and unmarried couples, (b) the distinctive role of religious beliefs and values among racial and ethnic minority communities, and (c) the role that religion plays in reducing racial and ethnic differences in relationship quality.

Religion and Relationship Quality

How and why might religious involvement be linked to relationship quality? Previous research on religion and relationship quality has suggested that family-centered norms and social networks associated with religious congregations, along with the subjective well-being fostered by religious belief, help account for the association between religion and higher quality relationships (for a review, see Mahoney, Pargament, Tarakeshwar, & Swank, 2001). First, religious communities typically promote generic norms (e.g., the Golden Rule) and relationship-specific norms (e.g., forgiveness) that help define appropriate marital and relationship conduct, encourage partners to fulfill their familial roles and responsibilities, and handle conflict in a constructive manner (Fincham, Hall, & Beach, 2006; Lambert & Dollahite, 2006; Wilcox, 2004). Second, family-centered social networks found in religious communities offer formal and informal support to couples and families—from financial help to models of healthy relationships—that can help couples navigate the challenges of married or romantic life (Edgell, 2006; Stolzenberg, Blair-Loy, & Waite, 1995). Such networks also tend to lend explicit or implicit support to conventional and religiously grounded norms about appropriate relationship conduct—such as sexual fidelity (Atkins & Kessel, 2008; Burdette, Ellison, Sherkat, & Gore, 2007). Third, subjective religious belief seems to provide people with a sense of purpose and meaning about life in general and their relationship in particular. This general sense of purpose and meaning is valuable as a buffer against the stresses that can harm relationships (Ellison, 1994). For all these reasons, religious persons may enjoy higher quality relationships.

The literature on religion and relationship quality suggests that religious homogamy is a particularly powerful influence on the quality of married and unmarried intimate relationships. Indeed, recent research exploring the family-religion nexus suggests that religious homogamy generally facilitates better relationships within the family, whereas religious heterogamy can be linked to negative outcomes within the family—from domestic violence to poor-quality parent-child relationships (Ellison, Bartkowski, & Anderson, 1999; Pearce & Axinn, 1998; Regnerus & Burdette, 2006). In particular, homogamy in religious affiliation, attendance, and belief appears to foster higher quality relationships among contemporary couples.

According to several studies, marital happiness and satisfaction are somewhat higher in same-faith unions (Heaton & Pratt, 1990; Vaaler, Ellison, & Powers, 2009; Wilcox & Wolfinger, 2008). Why is denominational homogamy associated with higher levels of relationship quality? Religious affiliation is linked with beliefs about marriage, sexuality, gender roles and household organization, child rearing, and a host of additional issues that confront domestic partners. Couples from similar denominational backgrounds may find relatively few points of disagreement when negotiating these choices, whereas partners from disparate religious backgrounds may harbor discordant assumptions about appropriate lifestyles and conduct that become evident when reaching concrete decisions (Curtis & Ellison, 2002). Studies also indicate that when mixed-faith marriages involve one conservative (i.e., fundamentalist or Evangelical) Protestant or one sectarian (e.g., Mormon) partner, they are especially prone to disharmony and dissolution, in part because partners in such relationships are probably more likely to have serious disagreements about important family or relationship choices facing them (Lehrer & Chiswick, 1993; Vaaler, Ellison, & Powers, 2009).

Research also has indicated that joint religious participation or similarities in participation patterns are positively linked with relationship quality among married and unmarried couples, for several possible reasons (Call & Heaton, 1997; Heaton & Pratt, 1990; Wilcox & Wolfinger, 2008). For example, couples who attend services together on a regular basis may be expressing their common commitment to faith and their relationship. It is also reasonable to expect that each partner may gain insight and inspiration, and may receive consistent, compatible feedback from coreligionists about relationship and family issues. Further, couples who attend services together are more likely than others to be subject to the social controls of coreligionist networks. Finally, religious attendance may simply be part of a longer list of religious practices by which partners strengthen their bonds through shared meaning systems and activities. Thus, couples who engage in regular devotional practices, such as family prayer or scriptural study within the home, may enjoy richer unions than others.

There are also sound reasons to consider the possible role of theological similarities or dissimilarities. The significance of denominational labels as markers of differences in values and lifestyles appears to be on the wane in recent decades (Wuthnow, 1988). Rates of interfaith marriage have been increasing for most non-conservative religious groups (Sherkat, 2004), and many denominations have become quite internally diverse, both theologically and attitudinally (Alwin, 1986; Gay, Ellison, & Powers, 1996). Consistent with this argument, one recent study suggested that the link between denominational homogamy and marital satisfaction has waned across generations (Myers, 2006). In contrast, empirical studies continue to reveal strong associations between theological beliefs (e.g., beliefs about scriptural interpretation) and a wide range of family-related attitudes and practices (Curtis & Ellison, 2002; Ellison, Bartkowski, &

Anderson, 1999). Indeed, core tenets may be more closely connected to lifestyles and behavioral choices than either denominational identities or self-reported religious attendance patterns. In data from the National Survey of Families and Households, the degree of spouses' theological dissimilarity is significantly associated with the risk of domestic violence (Ellison, Bartkowski, & Anderson, 1999), the frequency and type of arguments among partners (Curtis & Ellison, 2002), and the degree of satisfaction with the marriage (Heaton & Pratt, 1990). By contrast, couples who share core religious beliefs are probably more likely to hold similar family and gender attitudes and to agree more about the choices they confront in their relationship and family life.

Race and Ethnicity, Religion, and Relationships

To date, researchers have largely ignored possible racial and ethnic differences in the links between religious homogamy and dissimilarity or similarity and relationship quality. This is an oversight, not only because of racial and ethnic variations in marital and relationship quality and duration but also because patterns of religious affiliation, practice, and belief differ across racial and ethnic lines. This oversight is particularly noteworthy because of what might be called the African American religion—marriage paradox, where Blacks combine comparatively high levels of religiosity with comparatively low levels of marriage, marital quality, and relationship stability (Wilcox & Wolfinger, 2007).

The literature on African American religion indicates that Blacks exhibit significantly higher levels of religious attendance and congregational involvement, as well as nonorganizational religious practices and doctrinal conservatism (e.g., beliefs in the inerrancy and centrality of the Bible), than do non-Hispanic Whites from similar backgrounds (Taylor, Chatters, & Levin, 2004). African American religiosity may be linked to higher quality relationships. African American congregations and clergy exhibit broad concern and involvement with the lives of church members and their families, and they often play leading roles in identifying and responding to community needs (Billingsley, 1999). In many urban communities, religious congregations are crucial in sustaining traditional norms of nuclear family life and personal deportment in the face of alternative cultures and norms of "the street"; indeed, religion seems to be particularly important in protecting Black men from the lure of the street (Anderson, 1999; Wilcox & Wolfinger, 2008). Numerous studies underscore the importance of organizational and nonorganizational religious resources for African Americans coping with major crises and chronic stressors, including family and relationship problems (Taylor et al., 2004). These studies would suggest that religiosity, and religious homogamy in particular, fosters higher-quality relationships among Blacks; indeed, religion may be particularly valuable for African Americans insofar as it helps buffer against the stresses of poverty, neighborhood disorder, under- or unemployment, and discrimination that they face at markedly higher levels than do non-Hispanic Whites (Wilson, 1996). If religion fosters higher quality relationships, this suggest two possibilities: (a) suppressor patterns, in which statistical controls for variations in religiousness will increase the estimated net deficit in relationship quality for African Americans relative to non-Hispanic Whites, and (b) statistical interactions of religiousness and race and ethnicity (i.e., differences in slope coefficients), in which each unit of religiousness will yield greater dividends in relationship quality for African Americans than for non-Hispanic Whites.

The body of empirical work on religion and African American relationships is surprisingly modest. In a study of working White and Black married women, Furdyna, Tucker, and James (2008) found that Black women who rated themselves as more religious reported higher levels of marital happiness. A study of Michigan couples found that wives' attendance of religious services was linked to lower divorce rates for both non-Hispanic Whites and Blacks, but the effect was stronger for non-Hispanic Whites (Brown, Orbuch, & Bauermeister, 2008). In contrast, another study found that the protective effects of religious attendance on domestic violence were stronger for African Americans than for others (Ellison, Trinitapoli, Anderson, & Johnson, 2007). Although there is some evidence that religious involvement is positively associated with overall family satisfaction and closeness among African Americans (Ellison, 1997), no research has investigated the links between multiple aspects of religiousness and of a range of religious indicators on Blacks' relationship quality or specifically examined the effect of religious homogamy on relationship quality among African Americans. This is the case despite (a) the combination of high religiousness and relatively low rates of relationship quality among African Americans and (b) the fact that stable African American couples who are interviewed about such issues spontaneously mention religious faith (Carolan & Allen, 1999; Marks et al., 2008).

Even less is known about the links between religion and family life in general, or intimate relationships in particular, among Hispanics. With regard to religious tradition, a recent study found that 70% of Hispanics are Catholic and 23% are Protestant (Espinosa, Elizondo, & Miranda, 2003). Both traditions lend normative and social support to a long-standing tradition of familism found in many Hispanic cultures (Wilcox & Wolfinger, 2007). Familism is essentially the idea that one's family should be accorded a high priority, both subjectively and practically, and it is common among Hispanics, especially foreign-born Hispanics (Oropesa & Landale, 2004). Both traditions also combat the excesses of a machismo ethic among some Hispanic men that has been linked to higher levels of domestic violence, infidelity, and alcohol abuse (Frias & Angel, 2005; McLoyd et al., 2000). Similarly, religion can be helpful in protecting Hispanics, especially Hispanic men, from assimilating downward to a code of "the street"—marked by work in the underground economy, drug use, infidelity, and a violent way of life—which is found in many low-income communities and is not conducive to high-quality relationships (Anderson, 1999; Portes & Rumbaut, 1990; Wilcox & Wolfinger, 2008). Finally, we also expect that the social support and subjective meaning provided by religious attendance and beliefs may be more valuable for Hispanic relationships than for White relationships because—somewhat as with Blacks—Hispanics are more likely than non-Hispanic Whites to be buffeted by the stresses of poverty, discrimination, acculturation, and neighborhood disorder (Portes & Rumbaut, 1990; Telles & Ortiz, 2008). But no research has specifically examined the links between religion and relationship quality among Hispanics. We hypothesize that religion will be particularly valuable to Hispanics, given the range of structural and cultural challenges facing Latinos in the United States. This may be particularly true for Hispanic couples who enjoy religious homogamy, in part because less religious Latino men may be more likely to embrace a macho identity that is not conducive to a high-quality relationship.

Method
Data

Our data come from the National Survey of Religion and Family Life (NSRFL), a 2006 telephone survey of working-age adults (ages 18–59) in the continental United States, conducted by SRBI, a New York–based survey firm. The NSRFL contains extensive data on the religious affiliation, beliefs, and practices of individual respondents and (where applicable) their partners, as well as detailed information on relationship characteristics and quality. On average, the survey took 30 min to complete. If respondents desired, the survey was conducted in Spanish.

Sampling Procedures and Characteristics

Households were selected to participate in the survey using random-digit dialing (RDD) techniques, and one respondent was chosen at random from each household. African Americans and Hispanics were oversampled by dialing into area codes containing at least 10% concentrations of those racial and ethnic subgroups. Notification letters, refusal conversion letters, and noncontact letters were mailed to all sampled households for which addresses were available.

The overall cooperation rate (the proportion of all cases interviewed of all eligible units ever contacted) was 54%, with greater cooperation rates in the racial and ethnic oversamples. The response rate (the number of complete interviews with reporting units divided by the number of eligible reporting units in the sample) for the NSRFL was 36% (33% in the cross-sectional sample, and 41% and 34% in the African American and Hispanic oversamples, respectively). Although the response rate is low by traditional standards, it compares favorably with most recent national RDD-based studies (Council on Market and Opinion Research [CMOR] 2003). Moreover, studies show few differences between government surveys with high response rates (e.g., the Current Population Survey) and RDD-based surveys with lower response rates (Keeter, Miller, Kohut, Groves, & Presser, 2000; Pew Research Center for People and the Press, 2004).

The full sample contains roughly equal numbers of African Americans, Hispanics, and non-Hispanic Whites. Because our analytic sample is limited to those who are currently in a relationship, it contains a smaller percentage of African Americans (25%). Table 4.1 indicates that the overwhelming majority of respondents were married (89%); however, this number is lower among those respondents who are members of racial and ethnic minorities. Conversely, African Americans, Mexican Americans, and other Hispanics were all more likely to be in cohabiting relationships than their non-Hispanic White counterparts. Most respondents were women (63%), employed full-time (63%), and had children (an average of 1.35 children). The average number of children was greater for African Americans and Mexican Americans than for non-Hispanic Whites. The average respondent was

TABLE 4.1 Unadjusted means by race and ethnicity on key variables

	TOTAL SAMPLE (N = 1,387)	SD	NON-HISPANIC WHITE (N = 539)	AFRICAN AMERICAN (N = 352)	MEXICAN/MEXICAN AMERICAN (N = 348)	OTHER HISPANIC (N = 148)
Dependent variable						
Relationship satisfaction	4.80	0.98	4.88[b]	4.70[a]	4.80	4.75
Religion variables						
Respondent and partner attend regularly	0.32	—	0.29[b]	0.40[acd]	0.31[b]	0.23[b]
Respondent attends regularly; partner does not	0.10	—	0.07[b]	0.17[acd]	0.08[b]	0.11[b]
Partner attends regularly; respondent does not	0.06	—	0.04[b]	0.09[a]	0.07	0.07
Partners share affiliation	0.78	—	0.76[c]	0.73[c]	0.86[ab]	0.79
Partners share similar beliefs	3.45	0.88	3.45	3.42	3.49	3.43
Family religious activities	3.34	2.04	3.05[b]	4.10[acd]	3.16[b]	3.03[b]
Sociodemographics/controls						
Cohabitating	0.11	—	0.07[bcd]	0.12[ad]	0.13[ad]	0.20[abc]
Married	0.89	—	0.93[bcd]	0.88[ad]	0.87[ad]	0.80[abc]
Male	0.37	—	0.43[cd]	0.37	0.30[a]	0.32[a]
Employed full-time	0.63	—	0.69[c]	0.66[c]	0.52[ab]	0.60
Age	41.47	10.27	43.85[bcd]	42.28[ac]	37.22[abd]	40.84[ac]
Education	4.47	1.75	5.10[bcd]	4.64[acd]	3.43[abd]	4.25[abc]
Educational similarity	0.46	—	0.48[b]	0.39[ac]	0.51[b]	0.42
Income	4.84	2.15	5.81[bcd]	4.65[ac]	3.69[abd]	4.47[ac]
Partner employed full-time	0.73	—	0.72	0.77	0.71	0.74
Number of children	1.35	1.35	1.07[bc]	1.31[ac]	1.88[abd]	1.21[c]

[a]Indicates significant differences from non-Hispanic Whites ($a = p < .05$). [b]Indicates significant differences from African Americans ($b = p < .05$).
[c]Indicates significant differences from Mexican Americans ($c = p < .05$). [d]Indicates significant differences from other Hispanics ($d = p < .05$).

approximately 41 years of age, with at least some education beyond college. Finally, racial and ethnic minorities tended to report lower levels of education and income than their non-Hispanic White counterparts.

Dependent Variable: Relationship Satisfaction

We measured relationship satisfaction by mean responses to two questions: "Taking all things considered, how would you describe your relationship?" and "How happy are you with the love and affection you receive from your partner?" Responses for both items range from *very unhappy* (1) to *extremely happy* (6) ($r = 0.77$).

Key Independent Variables: Religious Involvement

We measure several distinct aspects of religious involvement. First, we include a measure of organizational religious involvement: frequency of church attendance. The frequency of attendance at religious services is gauged via the following item: "How often do you attend religious services?" In addition, the respondent was asked how often his or her partner attended religious services. Responses for both of these items range from *never* (1) to *more than once a week* (6). The two items were used to construct three dummy variables capturing whether the respondent and partner attended regularly (i.e. once a week or more), the respondent attends regularly but the partner does not, or the partner attends regularly but the respondent does not. Those couples not regularly attending services served as the reference category for our analysis.

Respondents were also asked their own religious affiliation as well as the religious affiliation of their partner. These items were used to construct a dummy variable for whether partners share the same religious affiliation. Those partners not sharing a religious affiliation served as the reference category for our analysis.

Similarly, respondents were asked about the degree of dissimilarity or similarity between their own religious beliefs and those of those of their partner. Shared religious values were gauged via responses to the question, "Please tell me if you agree or disagree with the following statement: You feel that your partner shares your core religious or spiritual values." Responses to this item capturing whether partners share similar beliefs ranged from *strongly agree* (1) to *strongly disagree* (5).

Finally, respondents were asked how often they prayed or participated in other religious activities with their partner or children at home, excluding grace at meals. Responses for this item measuring family religious activities ranged from *never* (1) to *more than once a week* (6).

Background Factors

Previous research establishes a number of individual-level sociodemographic characteristics as correlates or predictors of relationship satisfaction (Amato, Johnson, Booth, & Rogers,

2003). We can be confident of our conclusions regarding possible religious variations in relationship satisfaction only if we include statistical adjustments for the potentially confounding factors. Therefore, our models include controls for the following variables: race and/or ethnicity (dummy variables for African American, Mexican American, and other Hispanic, with non-Hispanic White as the reference category); relationship status (a dichotomous variable coded 1 = *married*, with *cohabitating* as the reference category); gender (a dichotomous variable coded 1= *male*); employment status (a dichotomous variable coded 1 = *employed full-time*, with other work status as the reference category); age (dummy variables for *age 26–33, age 34–41, age 42–49,* and *50 and older,* with 25 and younger as the reference category); education (dummy variables for *less than high school, some college, bachelor's degree,* and *graduate degree,* with high school as the reference category); educational similarly (a dichotomous variable coded 1 = *respondent and partner have the same level of education,* with otherwise educationally matched as the reference category); income (eight categories ranging from less than $15,000 to more than $100,000); partner's employment status (a dichotomous variable coded 1 = *partner employed full-time,* with other employment status as the reference category); number of children (actual number); ages of children in the household (dummy variables for children *under 6 years in the household* and children *between 6 and 11 in the household,* with children *over 11 in the household* as the reference category).

Statistical Procedures

Table 4.1 presents descriptive statistics for all variables used in these analyses for the total sample as well as comparisons by race or ethnicity (N = 1,387). Table 4.2 presents a series of ordinary least squares (OLS) regression models estimating the net effects of religious variables and covariates on relationship satisfaction (N = 1,381). Models are organized as follows: Model 1 (the baseline model) includes nonreligious predictors, such as sociodemographic factors and other key variables. Model 2 adds a series of dummy variables to capture frequency of church attendance. Model 3 replaces church attendance with a measure of whether the respondent and his or her partner share a religious affiliation. Model 4 includes a measure of whether the respondent and his or her partner share similar core religious or spiritual beliefs. Model 5 includes a measure of whether the respondent participates in home religious activities with his or her family. The final model, Model 6, includes all of our religion measures simultaneously.

Results
Unadjusted Means by Race or Ethnicity

On average, NSRFL respondents reported high levels of relationship satisfaction (4.80 on a 6-point scale); however, African American respondents reported being significantly less happy in their partnerships than non-Hispanic Whites. In contrast, African American respondents reported significantly higher levels of church attendance, both with and without their partners, in comparison to non-Hispanic White respondents. Whereas approximately 29% of

TABLE 4.2 Ordinary least squares regression of relationship satisfaction on religious involvement and background factors ($N = 1,381$)

	MODEL 1		MODEL 2		MODEL 3		MODEL 4		MODEL 5		MODEL 6	
	B	SE	B	SE	B	SE	B	SE	B	SE	B	SE
Respondent and partner attend regularly			0.30	0.06***							-0.00	0.06
Respondent attends regularly; partner does not			-0.16	0.09							-0.18	0.09*
Partner attends regularly; respondent does not			0.07	0.10							-0.09	0.10
Partners share affiliation					0.24	0.06***					-0.05	0.06
Partners share similar beliefs							0.30	0.03***			0.26	0.03***
Family religious activities									0.11	0.01***	0.09	0.01***
African American	-0.11	0.07	-0.13	0.07	-0.11	0.07	-0.12	0.06	-0.21	0.07**	-0.18	0.07**
Mexican American	-0.08	0.07	-0.11	0.07	-0.10	0.07	-0.11	0.07	-0.09	0.07	-0.10	0.07
Other Hispanic	-0.12	0.09	-0.11	0.09	-0.13	0.09	-0.12	0.09	-0.13	0.09	-0.12	0.08
Married	0.29	0.08***	0.24	0.08**	0.26	0.08***	0.25	0.07***	0.21	0.07**	0.20	0.07**
Male	0.11	0.06	0.09	0.06	0.11	0.06	0.07	0.06	0.12	0.06*	0.07	0.06
Employed full-time	0.10	0.06	0.11	0.06	0.09	0.06	0.11	0.06	0.11	0.06	0.12	0.06*
Age 26–33	-0.03	0.11	-0.07	0.10	-0.04	0.11	-0.04	0.10	-0.01	0.10	-0.03	0.10
Age 34–41	-0.23	0.11*	-0.27	0.11*	-0.24	0.11*	-0.19	0.10	-0.22	0.11*	-0.18	0.10
Age 42–49	-0.11	0.11	-0.15	0.11	-0.12	0.11	-0.09	0.10	-0.13	0.10	-0.10	0.10
Age 50 and older	-0.26	0.11*	-0.31	0.11**	-0.26	0.11*	-0.24	0.11*	-0.27	0.11*	-0.23	0.11*
Less than high school	0.20	0.08*	0.19	0.08*	0.18	0.08*	0.20	0.08*	0.17	0.08*	0.18	0.08*
Some college	-0.11	0.07	-0.12	0.07	-0.09	0.07	-0.12	0.07	-0.14	0.07*	-0.15	0.07*
Bachelor's degree	-0.00	0.08	-0.04	0.08	-0.00	0.08	-0.05	0.08	-0.04	0.08	-0.07	0.08
Graduate degree	0.02	0.10	-0.02	0.10	0.03	0.10	-0.00	0.10	-0.03	0.10	-0.04	0.10
Educational similarity	0.02	0.05	0.01	0.05	0.02	0.05	-0.00	0.05	0.01	0.05	-0.01	0.05
Income	0.04	0.02*	0.04	0.02*	0.04	0.02*	0.04	0.02**	0.04	0.02**	0.04	0.02**
Partner employed full-time	0.04	0.06	0.04	0.06	0.03	0.06	0.00	0.06	0.02	0.06	-0.00	0.06
Number of children	0.04	0.02	0.04	0.02	0.04	0.02	0.05	0.02*	0.01	0.02	0.03	0.02
Children under six in the household	0.13	0.08	0.13	0.07	0.12	0.08	0.15	0.07*	0.10	0.07	0.12	0.07
Children between 6 and 11 in the household	0.03	0.09	0.04	0.09	0.03	0.09	0.02	0.08	-0.00	0.09	0.01	0.08
Constant	4.31		4.34		4.18		3.37		4.11		3.38	
Model F	3.38***		4.47***		3.97***		9.09***		7.15***		9.64***	
R^2	0.04		0.07		0.06		0.12		0.10		0.16	

*$p < .05$. **$p < .01$. ***$p < .001$.

non-Hispanic White respondents attended religious services regularly and are partnered with someone who attended services on a regular basis, almost 40% of African American respondents fit this description. African American respondents were also significantly more likely than non-Hispanic Whites to have partners who regularly attended religious services, even when they themselves did not attend services. Of the total sample, approximately 78% of couples shared a religious affiliation; however, roughly 86% of Mexican American couples shared an affiliation, a significantly greater percentage than among non-Hispanic White couples. Finally, African Americans were significantly more likely than non-Hispanic Whites to participate in family religious activities.

Main Effects

Table 4.2 displays the results of OLS regression models. To conserve space, we confine our discussion to findings involving religious and racial and ethnic variables, which are central to our study. Several important patterns involving couples' religious involvement and relationship quality emerged from the analyses. First, according to Model 2, satisfaction with the relationship tended to be higher among couples who attend services regularly ($b = .30, p < .001$). However, when other religious dimensions were controlled in Model 6, this pattern disappeared. Second, although religious homogamy (i.e., shared religious affiliation) was positively associated with relationship quality in Model 3 ($b = .24, p < .001$), the association was also eliminated by controls for the other religious variables. Third, the degree to which core religious and spiritual values are shared among partners was positively linked with relationship satisfaction in Model 4 ($b = .30, p < .001$); in contrast to the estimated effects of shared affiliation and attendance, this association persisted even in the full model ($b = .26, p < .001$). Finally, the frequency with which couples practice in-home devotional activities, such as prayer or scriptural study, was also linked with relationship quality ($b = .11, p < .001$). Despite the inclusion of controls for other aspects of couples' religiousness, such in-home worship activities remained positively associated with satisfaction in Model 6 ($b = .09, p < .001$).

Table 4.2 also sheds new light on the complex interplay of race, ethnicity, and couples' religiousness in shaping relationship quality. Although the baseline model (Model 1) revealed no significant net racial or ethnic differences in relationship satisfaction, subsequent models showed that the true magnitude of racial and ethnic gaps in this outcome is masked, or suppressed, by the comparatively high levels of religiousness among African American and, to a lesser extent, Latino couples. A sizable gap in relationship satisfaction between African Americans and non-Hispanic Whites existed in the full model ($b = -.18, p < .01$). Taken together, the findings indicate that racial and ethnic differences in relationship quality would be even greater than they are if not for the higher average levels of religiousness among African American and Hispanic couples.

In addition to the analyses presented in Table 4.2, we also estimated several sets of ancillary models (not shown but available on request). First, we explored the possibility that the links between couples' religiousness varies by race and ethnicity by adding cross-product interaction terms (Race and ethnicity × Religious variables) to Model 6 in Table 4.2. However, no clear or consistent pattern of such interactions surfaced in these models. We interpret the null effects as evidence that the subgroups examined here differ in levels, but not effects, of couples' religiousness. Second, we also examined several potential explanations for the religious patterns observed in Table 4.2. Specifically, we added controls for the following variables to Model 6: (a) the self-rated spirituality and religiousness of the respondent, (b) the degree of guidance the respondent received from his or her religious faith, and (c) the extent to which the respondent perceived the religious congregation (if any) to be a potential source of social support when needed. Ultimately, however, the variables did not account for the estimated net effects reported herein, and they did not significantly improve the predictive power of the model. Third, given that our data were collected from only one of the relationship partners, we added Gender × Religion interactions to gauge whether the role of religiousness was more pronounced for women than for men. The null findings indicate otherwise.

Discussion

Some academics and policymakers have expressed concern about the shifting fortunes of marriage in the contemporary United States. This has led to a growing body of research on patterns and determinants of relationship quality. In addition, investigators have shown a long-standing interest in the role of religion as a source of validation and support for marriage, and for traditional nuclear family arrangements more generally, although some recent findings suggest that the link between religion and marriage may be waning or at least changing. Scholars have also pointed to an intriguing paradox: Religious belief and practice tend to be higher among members of racial and ethnic minority populations, for whom relationship quality is also more elusive. This raises an important set of questions regarding the interplay of race and ethnicity and multiple dimensions of couples' religiousness in shaping variations in relationship quality. We have explored these issues using data from a nationwide sample of working-age adults (ages 18–59) that includes oversamples of African Americans and Hispanic (Latino) Americans.

Several patterns involving couples' religious affiliation and practices are especially noteworthy. Consistent with a number of previous studies, persons in homogamous (i.e., same-faith) relationships and those in which both partners attend religious services regularly tended to report greater relationship satisfaction than do others. In addition, the frequency with which couples engage in regular in-home worship activities (e.g., prayer, scriptural study) was also positive linked with relationship quality. Although controls for other dimensions of religiousness attenuated or mediated the net effects of couples' institutional religious engagement, the net effect of in-home devotional activities persisted even in the full model. On the one hand, the findings are broadly consistent with the popular aphorism that "couples who pray together stay together." On the other hand, they also raise interesting questions about (a) how religious communities and the social relationships within them may nurture and sustain the quality of intimate bonds, and (b) whether more religiously devoted couples may differ from their counterparts on other, unmeasured variables that may also be linked with relationship quality (Wilcox & Wolfinger, 2008). Our results also dovetail with recent studies that conclude that religious homogamy is a weaker predictor of relationship quality than it once was (Myers, 2006), perhaps because denominational labels have become less meaningful as markers of theological, attitudinal, or lifestyle differences over the past several decades, as more individualistic expressions of faith and spiritual seeking have gained popularity.

Another major finding is that couples in which partners share core religious beliefs and values tended to report greater satisfaction than others. Indeed, such subjective and nonorganizational indicators of couples' religiousness appear to be even more predictive of relationship quality than shared affiliation or attendance. This pattern is broadly consistent with the findings of other religion–family studies, which tend to show that core religious beliefs, especially indicators of Evangelicalism, such as beliefs about the inerrancy and authority of the Bible, are more predictive of family-related attitudes and practices (e.g., childrearing and child discipline, division of household labor) than is affiliation or practice (Ellison & Bartkowski, 2002; Wilcox, 1998). Further, the degree of partners' dissimilarity in such beliefs also predicts frequency and types of conflict and exacerbates the risk of marital dissolution (Curtis & Ellison, 2002; Ellison, Bartkowski, & Anderson, 1999; Vaaler, Ellison, & Powers, 2009).

Our study also reveals the interplay of race and ethnicity and religion in shaping relationship quality. In particular, our results demonstrate a substantial racial and ethnic gap in relationship quality, the full magnitude of which is suppressed by the comparatively high levels of multiple dimensions of religiousness among African American and Latino respondents. We found no evidence of statistical interactions between religiousness and race and ethnicity (i.e., differences in religion slope coefficients across racial and ethnic groups). Taken together, the findings provide an important window to the crucial role of religious faith for minority couples. We speculate that this pattern may partly reflect the chasm between "decent" and "street" cultures that are thought to characterize some African American and Latino communities (Anderson, 1999). This possibility is particularly plausible in light of other recent research showing that couples who attend church together in urban America are significantly less likely than others to use drugs, to have conflicts over sexual infidelity, or to experience domestic violence (Wilcox & Wolfinger, 2008). By contrast, rates of domestic violence are markedly elevated among African American men who rarely or never attend religious services (Ellison et al., 2007).

Future research could clarify and extend these findings. It would be useful to identify and distinguish among the various explanations for observed religious variations in relationship quality. On the one hand, partners who share common values may engage in more positive emotion work (e.g., supportive exchanges, companionship, compliments, routine acts of kindness) and less negative emotion work (e.g., criticism, demands). They may also employ more constructive strategies for communicating, compromising, and resolving disagreements. Religious differentials in other relationship-related behaviors (e.g., infidelity, domestic violence, drug or alcohol use, gambling and other risky or impulsive behaviors) may also help to explain these patterns. In addition, personal or subjective religiousness has been linked with commitment to family roles and willingness to sacrifice one's self-interest in favor of the needs or desires of one's partner (Mahoney et al., 2001). Clearly future research should specify the mechanisms that connect couples' religiousness with relationship quality.

Several limitations of this study should also be acknowledged. First, the data are cross-sectional, which precludes the establishment of causal order among variables. For example, it is not possible to establish whether high-quality relationships promote religiousness, or vice versa, or to rule out the possibility that pro-religious and pro-relationship values are rooted in dispositional factors (e.g., impulse control, conscientiousness) or other variables that cannot be measured here. Second, our survey relies on the survey responses of one partner to report on couples' religiousness and relationship quality. It would be helpful to have independent responses from both individuals and their spouses or partners, as well as observational data on interaction and conflict resolution styles. This would enhance confidence that sources of bias related to the method of data collection did not influence our findings. Third, although the large minority oversamples are a major strength of this survey, our data are also characterized by rather low response rates, and for that reason, too, it would be useful for future investigators to replicate the findings using data gathered via other methods. Fourth, our analysis focuses on heterosexual couples. Although there is emerging evidence that religiousness may also foster relationship commitment among same-sex couples (Oswald, Goldberg, Kuvalanka, & Clausell, 2008), research on the links with relationship quality in that population remains in its early stages, and more investigation is needed concerning possible racial and ethnic variations in such associations.

Despite these limitations, our study has made an original contribution to the research literature by examining the interplay of race and ethnicity, multiple aspects of couples' religiousness, and relationship quality. Results indicate that the linkages are more complex than previous studies have recognized. Although religious factors bear a nontrivial association with the relationship quality of non-Hispanic White couples, our findings confirm and augment a broader literature showing that religion can be especially important within racial and ethnic minority populations, for whom religious resources and worldviews can counter the effects of structural barriers and other obstacles to relationship quality. Further investigation along the lines sketched here is needed to clarify the mechanisms via which religious factors contribute to relationship quality in the increasingly diverse American society of the 21st century.

Note

This work was supported by a grant from the Lilly Endowment (2002 2301–000). An earlier version of this article was presented at the 2009 meetings of the American Sociological Association, San Francisco (August 8–11). We thank Stacy Haynes for helpful comments and suggestions.

References

Alwin, D. F. (1986). Religion and parental child rearing orientations: Evidence of a Protestant-Catholic convergence. *American Journal of Sociology, 92,* 412–440.

Amato, P. R., Johnson, D. R., Booth, A., & Rogers, S. J. (2003). Continuity and change in marital quality between 1980 and 2000. *Journal of Marriage and Family, 65,* 1–22.

Anderson, E. (1999). *Code of the street.* New York: Norton.

Atkins, D. C., & Kessel, D. E. (2008). Religiousness and infidelity: Attendance, but not faith and prayer, predict marital fidelity. *Journal of Marriage and Family, 70,* 407–418.

Billingsley, A. (1999). *Mighty like a river: The Black church and social reform.* New York: Oxford University Press.

Blackman, L., Clayton, O., Glenn, N., Malone-Colon, L., & Roberts, A. (2005). *The consequences of marriage for African Americans: A comprehensive literature review.* New York: Institute for American Values.

Booth, A., Johnson, D. R., Branaman, A., & Sica, A. (1995). Belief and behavior: Does religion matter in today's marriage? *Journal of Marriage and the Family, 57,* 661–671.

Broman, C. L. (2005). Marital quality in Black and White marriages. *Journal of Family Issues, 26,* 431–441.

Brown, E., Orbuch, T. L., & Bauermeister, J. A. (2008). Religiosity and marital stability among Black American and White American couples. *Family Relations, 57,* 186–197.

Burdette, A. M., Ellison, C. G., Sherkat, D. E., & Gore, K. (2007). Are there religious variations in marital infidelity? *Journal of Family Issues, 28,* 1553–1581.

Call, V. R., & Heaton, T. B. (1997). Religious influence on marital stability. *Journal for the Scientific Study of Religion, 36,* 382–392.

Carolan, M. T., & Allen, K. R. (1999). Commitments and constraints to intimacy for African American couples at midlife. *Journal of Family Issues, 20,* 3–24.

Cherlin, A. (2004). The deinstitutionalization of American marriage. *Journal of Marriage and Family, 66,* 848–861.

Council on Market and Opinion Research. (2003). *Tracking response, cooperation, and refusal rates for the industry: 2003 results.* Wethersfield, CT: Council on Market and Opinion Research.

Curtis, K. T., & Ellison, C. G. (2002). Religious heterogamy and marital conflict: Findings from the National Survey of Families and Households. *Journal of Family Issues, 23,* 551–576.

Edgell, P. A. (2006). *Religion and family in a changing society.* Princeton, NJ: Princeton University Press.

Ellison, C. G. (1994). Religion, the life stress paradigm, and the study of depression. In J. S. Levin (Ed.), *Religion in aging and health: Theoretical foundations and methodological frontiers* (pp. 78–121). Thousand Oaks, CA: Sage.

Ellison, C. G. (1997). Religious involvement and the subjective quality of family life among African Americans. In R. J. Taylor, L. M. Chatters, & J. S. Jackson (Eds.), *Family life in Black America* (pp. 117–131). Thousand Oaks, CA: Sage.

Ellison, C. G., & Bartkowski, J. P. (2002). Conservative Protestantism and the division of household labor among married couples. *Journal of Family Issues, 23,* 950–985.

Ellison, C. G., Bartkowski, J. P., & Anderson, K. L. (1999). Are there religious variations in domestic violence? *Journal of Family Issues, 20,* 87–113.

Ellison, C. G., Trinitapoli, J., Anderson, K. L., & Johnson, B. R. (2007). Race/ethnicity, religious involvement and domestic violence. *Violence Against Women, 13,* 1094–1112.

Espinosa, G., Elizondo V., & Miranda, J. 2003, *Hispanic churches in American public life: Summary of findings.* South Bend, IN: University of Notre Dame Institute for Latino Studies.

Fincham, F. D., Hall, J., & Beach, S. R. (2006). Forgiveness in marriage: Current status and future directions. *Family Relations, 55,* 415–427.

Frias, S. M., & Angel, R. J, (2005). The risk of partner violence among low-income Hispanic subgroups. *Journal of Marriage and Family, 67,* 552–564.

Furdyna, H. E., Tucker, M. B., & James, A. J. (2008). Relative spousal earnings and marital happiness among African American and White women. *Journal of Marriage and Family, 70,* 332–344.

Gay, D. A., Ellison, C. G., & Powers, D. A. (1996). In search of denominational subcultures: Religious affiliation and "pro-family" attitudes revisited. *Review of Religious Research, 38,* 3–17.

Heaton, T. B., & Pratt, E. L. (1990). The effects of religious homogamy on marital satisfaction and marital stability. *Journal of Family Issues,11,* 191–207.

Lambert, N. M., & Dollahite, D. C. (2006). How religiosity helps couples prevent, resolve, and overcome marital conflict. *Family Relations, 55,* 439–449.

Landale, N., & Oropesa, R. S. (2007). Hispanic families: Stability and change. *Annual Review of Sociology, 33,* 381–405.

Lehrer, E. L., & Chiswick, C. U. (1993). Religion as a determinant of marital stability. *Demography, 30,* 385–404.

Lichter, D. T., McLaughlin, D. K., Kephart, G., & Landry, D. J. (1992). Race and the retreat from marriage: A shortage of marriageable men? *American Sociological Review, 57,* 781–799.

Keeter, S., Miller, C., Kohut, A., Groves, R. M., & Presser, S. (2000). Consequences of nonresponse in a national telephone survey. *Public Opinion Quarterly, 64,* 125–148.

Kennedy, S., & L. Bumpass. (2008). Cohabitation and children's living arrangements: New estimates from the United States. *Demographic Research, 19,* 1663–1692.

Kreider, R. M., & Simmons, T. (2003). *Marital status: 2000.* Washington, DC: U.S. Census Bureau.

Mahoney, A., Pargament, K. I., Tarakeshwar, N., & Swank, A. B. (2001). Religion in the home in the 1980s and 1990s: A meta-analytic review and conceptual analysis of links between religion, marriage, and parenting. *Journal of Family Psychology, 15,* 559–596.

Marks, L. D., Hopkins, K., Chaney, C., Monroe, P. A., Nesteruk, O., & Sasser, D. D. (2008). "Together, we are strong": A qualitative study of happy, enduring African American marriages. *Family Relations, 57,* 172–185.

McLoyd, V. C., Cauce, A. M., Takeuchi, D., & Wilson, L. (2000). Marital processes and parental socialization in families of color: A decade review of research. *Journal of Marriage and the Family, 62,* 1070–1093.

Myers, S. M. (2006). Religious homogamy and marital quality: Historical and generational patterns, 1980–1997. *Journal of Marriage and Family, 68,* 292–304.

Oropesa, R. S., & Landale, N. (2004). The future of marriage and Hispanics. *Journal of Marriage and Family, 66,* 901–920.

Oswald, R. F., Goldberg, A., Kuvalanka, K., & Clausell, E. (2008). Structural and moral commitment among same-sex couples: Relationship duration, religiosity, and parental status. *Journal of Family Psychology, 22,* 411–419.

Pearce, L. D., & Axinn, W. D. (1998). The impact of family religious life on the quality of mother-child relations. *American Sociological Review, 63,* 810–828.

Pew Research Center for People and the Press. (2004). *Polls face growing resistance, but still representative.* Washington, DC: Author. Retrieved from http://people-press.org/reports/pdf/211.pdf

Phillips, J. A., & Sweeney, M. M. (2006). Can differential exposure to risk factors explain recent racial and ethnic variation in marital disruption? *Social Science Research, 35,* 409–434.

Portes, A., & Rumbaut, R. (1990). *Immigrant America: A portrait.* Los Angeles: University of California Press.

Regnerus, M., & Burdette, A. (2006). Religious change and adolescent family dynamics. *Sociological Quarterly, 47,* 175–194.

Sherkat, D. E. (2004). Religious intermarriage in the United States: Trends, patterns, and predictors. *Social Science Research, 33,* 606–625.

Stolzenberg, R. M., Blair-Loy, M., & Waite, L. (1995). Religious participation over the early life course: Age and family life cycle effects on church membership. *American Sociological Review, 60,* 84–103.

Suro, R. (2005). *Hispanics: A people in motion.* Washington, DC: Pew Hispanic Center.

Taylor, R. J., Chatters, L. M., & Levin, J. S. (2004). *Religion in the lives of African Americans.* Thousand Oaks, CA: Sage.

Telles, E. E., & Ortiz, V. (2008). *Generations of exclusion: Mexican Americans, assimilation, and race.* New York: Russell Sage Foundation.

Tucker, M. B., & Mitchell-Kernan, C. (1995). *The decline in marriage among African Americans.* New York: Russell Sage Foundation.

Vaaler, M. L., Ellison, C. G., & Powers, D. A. (2009). Religious influences on the risk of marital dissolution. *Journal of Marriage and Family, 71,* 917–934.

Wilcox, W. B. (1998). Conservative Protestant childrearing: Authoritarian or authoritative? *American Sociological Review, 63,* 796–809.

Wilcox, W. B. (2004). *Soft patriarchs, new men: How Christianity shapes fathers and husbands.* Chicago: University of Chicago Press.

Wilcox, W.B., & Wolfinger, N. H. (2007). Then comes marriage? Religion, race, and marriage in urban America. *Social Science Research, 36,* 569–589.

Wilcox, W. B., & Wolfinger, N. H. (2008). Living and loving "decent": Religion and relationship quality among urban parents. *Social Science Research, 37,* 828–843.

Wilson, W. J. (1996). *When work disappears.* New York: Vintage.

Wolfinger, N. H., & Wilcox, W. B. (2008). Happily ever after? Religion, marital status, gender, and relationship quality in urban families. *Social Forces, 86,* 1311–1337.

Wuthnow, R. (1988). *The restructuring of American religion.* Princeton, NJ: Princeton University Press.

APPENDIX A   Bivariate correlations among relationship satisfaction and religion variables

	1	2	3	4	5	6	7
1. Relationship satisfaction	—						
2. Respondent and partner attend regularly	.14***	—					
3. Respondent attends regularly; partner does not	−.15***	−.23***	—				
4. Partner attends regularly; respondent does not	.01	−.17***	−.09**	—			
5. Partners share affiliation	.37***	.28***	−.21***	−0.03	—		

6. Partners share similar beliefs	.28***	.26***	−.15***	0.01	.37***	—
7. Family religious activities	.20***	.41***	.04	0.04	.17***	.20***	—

** *p* < .01. *** *p* < .001.

Christianity and Race

The intersections of race and religion, in this case, Christianity and race, have had significant impacts on the ways race has been viewed, specifically in the United States. Even with its popularity, Christianity as a practiced religion has been under scrutiny. As noted earlier, it is considered the most practiced religion throughout the world. When colonization took place around the world, Christianity was used as the means for colonizers, especially Europeans, Spanish, and the British, to control those who were considered savage and uncivilized. Christianity has also been seen and used as a way to justify the mistreatment of others. The control exercised by the church over the spirituality of Black Africans and those who were of Muslim descent has caused division in this country and around the world (Casares & Delaigue, 2013). African civilizations were not the same as European ones. However, there were comparable cultural, economic, and even political developments. The arrival of the Christians and the enslavement of Africans by Europeans were the catalysts for the decline of the history of Africans across the continent (Casares & Delaigue, 2013).

Black Africans were kidnapped and sold into slavery all over the world by those who were from various countries in Europe and other regions of the world through the Middle Passage. The most widespread approach used to exert control over them was religion, particularly Catholicism and Christianity. When brought to America, Black Africans were stripped of their culture, including their names and religious practices, and made to believe in and profess their allegiance to their masters, who kept them bound in servitude of which they owed no debt, through the very religion that taught freedom in Christ was the answer to their troubles. Fear was used as a means to teach and instill Christian doctrine, comparing God to the master and threatening people with punishment for sins. Passages in the Bible were used to instill submission and resignation of the enslaved Africans to their masters.

Nat Turner, a Black man born enslaved, who learned to read with the Bible, became "the preacher" of the "gospel" to the other enslaved Black people on the plantation. Turner was leased out by his master to other plantations where he preached the importance of slaves obeying their masters. When Turner saw how the other slave owners were treating their enslaved people and that he was emphasizing the importance of obeying their masters through the Bible, he became convicted and knew that he could no longer participate in such activity. In 1831, Turner led an insurrection with a handful of other enslaved Black people to escape enslavement that led to the deaths of 57 White people. He believed that if freedom in Christ was the way to heaven, he was going to fight to ensure that he and other enslaved people would experience at least a measure of that freedom. He was captured, tried in court in Southampton, Virginia, and found guilty and put to death by lynching (Fabricant, 1993; Kunka, 2011).

Islam

Second to Christianity, Islam is the second most common religion practiced across the world (Hackett & McClendon, 2017). Those who practice Islam are called Muslims, similar to the identification of those who practice Christianity being called Christians. Over time, Islam as a religious practice has been riddled with controversy and sometimes downright disdain. Since September 11, 2001, when the Islamic extremist committed acts of terror on U.S. soil, Muslims have been under siege in the United States. Contrary to popular belief, Islam is a faith that is about peace and service to others.

Islam is a faith that is misunderstood. Many who profess the faith are granted freedoms that those outside of the faith are not aware of. Seeing women wear hijabs and some who cover themselves from head to toe may cause some people to view the religion as restrictive and oppressive toward women. The reality is that there are women who choose to wear the hijab and cover their body as a statement of their devotion to their faith. Similarly, some men who wear turbans have been largely seen as suspicious because they are automatically associated with terrorist organizations such as ISIS and Al Qaeda. For fear of more terrorist activity, the United States issued a travel ban for people traveling to and from countries that were known to have Islam as their major religion. Those countries include Iran, Libya, Somalia, Syria, and Yemen (Travel.state.gov, 2018). The idea was to prevent extremists from entering the country. What actually happened was that some families were not allowed to reunite, and individuals were not allowed to visit their loved ones. If people had already traveled to or from those regions of the world, they were sometimes kept from returning to their homes for weeks at a time. This caused many individuals to be separated from their families.

There are pillars of Islam that all Muslims ascribe to. The first pillar is the profession of faith. This requires the believer to profess the unity of God and the mission of Muhammad. Also, it involves the repetition of the formula "There is no God but Allah and Muhammad is the messenger of Allah." It forms every part of the prayers, which leads to the second pillar, prayer. Prayer is required four times per day: at dawn, mid-afternoon, sunset, and dusk. It must be performed in a state of ritual purity, and worshippers can pray privately in the open air, in a house, with a group outdoors, or in a mosque.

Almsgiving embodies the principle of social responsibility. This pillar teaches that what belongs to the believer also belongs to the community as well. Only by donating a portion of their wealth for public use does a person legitimize what they retain. Fasting means observing Ramadan, the month during which it is written that God sent the Qur'an to the lowest heaven where Gabriel received it and revealed it to Muhammad. Fasting demands complete abstinence from food and drinks from dawn to sunset every day during Ramadan. The Pilgrimage to Mecca is the final pillar. Mecca is the place where Allah's (God's) revelation was first revealed to Muhammad. Believers worship publicly at the Holy Mosque, expressing full equality among

Muslims with a common objective: seeking the favor of God. Every Muslim is expected to make the pilgrimage at least once during their lifetime.

Buddhism

"Scholars of religion have long thought about how written religious history in metaphorical terms [] reify religions as entities of certain particular kinds—as liquids or conquering armies that spread themselves over geographical landscapes" (Company, 2012, p. 100). Buddhism has its roots in China and Chinese tradition. Regarding family, the Chinese tradition is the practice of filial piety. This is where older generations are regarded as deserving of a higher status than younger generations. The lines of authority in the family are very clear. The extended family is central to the organization of the Chinese family. These same views on family hold true for Buddhists.

Chinese Buddhism allows for the international range and fruitful comparison with developments in other cultures, such as India and Japan, countries that also have Buddhist traditions (McRae, 1995). The contemporary identity of Buddhism is a missionary, adoptable, religion, "providing a continuing audience and community of scholars" (p. 354). The maturity of the religion has allowed for an emphasis on the study of Buddhism and led to new and exciting directions. Even with the renewed interest in Buddhist traditions and practice in recent centuries, a full understanding of Buddhist religious practice is still disjointed.

The Westerners who first came into contact with Buddhism identified the Buddha and the buddhas as god(s). This mind-set was guided by their Christian background. "Although the Buddha and the buddhas are not regarded as gods by Buddhists, they clearly fulfill the criteria of 'counter-intuitive agents,'" meaning buddhas are not gods but they are not human beings either (Pyysiäinen, 2003, p. 147). Buddhists believe that religion can be understood as human thought, action, and experience. The Buddha is a perfectly enlightened one and is also enlightened by himself and wants to lead others to enlightenment (Pyysiäinen, 2003).

Hinduism

Fundamental to the practice of Hinduism as a religion is the idea of "coming to know and develop one's fullest potentialities" (Mehta, 2004, p. 108). Hinduism is a millennia-old practice that is indigenous to India (Hacker, 2006). The word "Hindu" comes from the same root as the name of the modern-day country of India. It is not a term that is self-identifying but one that has been "used by visitors from the west who originally meant it as shorthand for 'those who live east or south of the Indus River'" (Mehta, 2004, p. 109). The word "Hinduism" came into use only in the 19th century (Hacker, 2006).

Central to Hinduism "is a belief in reincarnation, in which the status, condition and cost of each life is determined by the behaviour in the last life" (Anonymous, 2005, pp. 8–9).

This means that each person is responsible for who they are and what they do. Hindus believe that there is only one god and god can only be understood or worshipped in many different forms (Anonymous, 2005). A large part of the life lived before reincarnation is family. For those of the Hindu faith, marriage is an important social institution. Marriage in India takes place between two families, not just two individuals (Sharma et al., 2013).

The marriage is the basis of the family. Arranged marriages and dowry are customary. There have been attempts by the Indian legislation, as well as Indian society, to protect marriage. Because society is predominantly patriarchal, there are gender roles from which individuals rarely deviate. For example, women have a passive role and the husband has an active, dominating role. The primary statuses from women are marriage and motherhood (Sharma et. al., 2013). The value of family is paramount. The function of marriage is sexual regulation, reproduction, protection of children, and nurturance.

> For a Hindu, marriage is essential, not only for begetting a son in order to discharge his debt to the ancestors but also for the performance of other religious and spiritual duties. The institution of marriage is considered sacred even by those who view it as a civil contract. (Sharma et al., 2013, p. S244)

Intersectionality of Religion

So far in this text we have defined intersectionality as a theoretical framework that requires us to examine the different ways that individuals and families navigate their lives to "negotiate competing and harmonious social identities" (Few-Demo et al., 2016, p. 76). In a secular and academic approach, religion has "been defined in terms of beliefs, internal conditions, and systems of symbols" (Olsson & Stenberg, 2015, p. 204). Thus, the intersections of religion and sexual orientation, religion and class, religion and gender, and religion and race have significance as we discuss families in the context of culture and diversity.

Religion and Sexual Orientation

Some who are Christians have professed judgment and have been adversarial against those who are members of the LGBTQIA+ community. There are passages in the Bible that speak to homosexuality, and based on their interpretation of the scripture, the view of some Christians is that homosexuality is a sin. Additionally, Muslims have a view of sexual orientation that is similar to that of Christians. Both groups believe that heteronormative sexual orientation and traditional gender roles are what is natural and as God intended. The gender binary, male/female, is how the scriptures of the Bible and Qu'ran are interpreted.

Religion and Class

In some cultures, class structures determine status. Class and religion have been associated with each other since ancient times. Many of the religious leaders in the Protestant cultural histories had more wealth than those who were considered common people of the faith. For example, in Judaism, the Pharisees and Sadducees, who were considered the religious leaders of the law of

Moses, were very wealthy. Hayward and Kemmelmeier (2011) conducted research on Weber's Protestant ethic hypothesis.

This "hypothesis holds that elements of theology gave Protestants a cultural affinity with economic demands of early market capitalism" (Hayward & Kemmelmeier, 2011, p. 1406). Early Protestant theology shifted the relationship that each person had with God. This was so that the individual, not the community, was seen as a self-contained spiritual unit. This is not to say that those who are members of the Protestant tradition are selfish and only seek wealth. Many who are members of the Protestant/Christian faith serve on mission trips and give to the poor and those in need. In fact, there are numerous passages in the Bible that talk about how the one who gives is blessed. The belief is that to whom much is given, much is expected. In the Old Testament, tithing 10% of what a family earned to the church was expected as a believer in God. However, prosperity and success in earthly endeavors were emphasized as a sign of divine grace (Hayward & Kemmelmeier, 2011).

Islam, Buddhism, and Hinduism are faith traditions that honor those who give of their time and material wealth. Almsgiving, which is one of the tenets of Islam, is an example of the giving that is required of those who have received much financially and materially. The study by Hayward and Kemmelmeier (2011) found the presence of an Islamic work ethic that promotes hard work for communal purposes. Muslims and Protestants were similar because they endorsed hard work. Muslims were less supportive of competition and the value of the individual than government responsibility (Hayward & Kemmelmeier, 2011). Buddhist monks take a vow of poverty and live with the most modest conditions. They abstain from sexual activity and focus on their inner sanctuary through meditation, interaction with nature, and maintaining inner peace.

Hindus focus their time and energy trying to live the best life possible. As discussed earlier in this chapter, because they believe in reincarnation, living their lives as good and honorable people is an important goal. Accumulation of wealth and capitalists' viewpoints are not significant and are not seen as "living one's best life." The way that this is lived out is through service to others to reach their fullest potential. That way, when they return in their next life, they reap the benefits of how they lived in their previous life.

Religion and Gender

In many religions, the male (i.e., husband, father, son) is seen as the leader of the home. Second to the male or husband, the female (i.e., wife, mother, sister, daughter) is to be submissive to the male influence in the household. In some religions, if the father dies or leaves the family for some reason, the son is to be the head of the household and provider. In other more indigenous religious traditions, the female is the dominant one in the home.

Christianity and Islam have a long history of the family being male dominated. There are passages in the Qu'ran and the Bible that speak of wives being submissive to their husbands. There are some who take those admonishments to the extreme, which can lead to abusive family relationships. As one of the four dimensions of religion, behaving is particularly concerned with morality, practicing and defining what is "right" and "wrong" (Saroglou, 2011). This is where the intersection of religion and gender comes in. There is a significant overlap between what it means to be a follower of Christ or Allah if you are a woman than there is if you are a man. In ancient times, it was customary for men of Islam, Judaism, and Christianity to have more than one wife. However, this was not permitted for women. The double standard exists because of the ways women are viewed in most religions as inferior beings: too weak, irrational, and/or too emotional to make sound judgments. Thus, women are not ideal people to lead families.

Religion and Race

Race and religion have a long history in most major religions. During the Holocaust, Adolf Hitler convinced the majority of the German population that Jewish people were inferior. This is a case where the religion and race of people were considered the same. Because of this government-sanctioned hatred, millions of people were murdered, and thousands of others were permanently injured, emotionally as well as physically. The Jewish people who were relegated to concentration camps were stripped of their dignity, safety, sense of self, and, ultimately, their lives.

As mentioned earlier, Christianity was weaponized against Black Africans and Black people during the beginning of and throughout slavery and into the Jim Crow South in the United States. There was government-sanctioned hatred, discrimination, and racism that occurred during this time, and still, some Christians have the same racist and discriminatory view of Black people in the United States. During biblical times, those who were Jewish and those who were Greek were pitted against each other based on religious practices and beliefs.

Conclusions

Religion and spiritual practices affect how people live their lives. They provide guiding principles for how and why people do what they do, how and why families function the way they function, and the decisions that people make daily. While we appreciate freedom of religion in the United States, there are some barriers for certain members of the religious groups discussed in this chapter. For example, Christianity has a history of using its doctrine to justify the mistreatment of enslaved people. Islam has a history of marginalizing those whose sexual orientation deviates from the heteronormative ideals that were discussed in Chapter 4. As we continue to develop and understand the intersections that are in each area of a person's life, we must be aware of how our interactions with them at those intersections can affect the way people experience the world.

Implications for Family Life Educators

As family life educators, our focus is to teach and equip families with the tools necessary to continue to function well in the various ways they interact with the world. For example, we must examine their different social locations and consider all the ways their lives intersect, including religion intersections. While it is true that some families do not practice any formal religion, more often than not families have some roles they play that are the direct result of their religious beliefs. Our work, then, is to gather information about those intersections, inform the families of their effect, and teach them to navigate their lives with this knowledge. We must not assume that families are unaware of how their race, class, gender, sexual orientation and religion intersect. Even still, we must be prepared to help them understand those roles inside as well as outside of their family.

Additional Readings

The readings that have been included in this chapter emphasize how race, class, and gender intersect with religion. These intersections are significant to acknowledge, particularly when it relates to families functioning and how it may differ based on religious practice. As helping professionals, it is our responsibility to provide guidance and assist with what may amount to role strain and relational difficulties.

Religiosity, Citizenship and Attitudes to Social Policy Issues

By Peter Saunders

Introduction

There has always been a close affinity between religious belief and social goals. Whether it is the emphasis given to the importance of compassion for the poor in traditional Western Christian teaching or the role of Confucian philosophical values in shaping the role of the family under the different forms of welfare orientalism, these influences have been profound. The impact of religion has been reinforced in a country like Australia, where religious organisations have long played a major role in the provision and delivery of welfare services across the life cycle, from schooling and health care to aged care. This role has been increasing under a contracting-out agenda that has extended the long-established service delivery role of religious organisations into new areas, including employment and disability services. This trend, in part, reflects the view that these organisations are run economically and have an institutional ethos of care and

Peter Saunders, "Religiosity, Citizenship and Attitudes to Social Policy Issues," *Australian Journal of Social Issues*, vol. 47, no. 3, pp. 336-352. Copyright © 2012 by Australian Social Policy Association. Reprinted with permission. Provided by ProQuest LLC. All rights reserved.

compassion that makes them better providers of social services in an era characterised by the twin imperatives of economic efficiency and personal responsibility.

Despite the strong links between religious beliefs and social policy goals, the relationship between them remains relatively under-researched. A recent review of the role of religion in the development of social policy concluded that its role 'has not always been understood properly or appreciated particularly well' (van Kersbergen & Manow 2010: 265). Much of the existing work on the topic has been narrowly focused on the experience of Western countries, yet the changing relationship between religion and social policy in all countries makes the topic of growing global significance. Van Kersbergen and Manow argue that religion can impact on social policy through three main channels; first, religious values (such as the Protestant work ethic or the 19th century papal encyclicals) provide a framework that can have a profound impact on the assumptions and objectives that shape social policy; second, religious movements can exert pressure by advocating in support of specific issues and/or groups through the political process; third, religious organisations can influence (and be influenced by) policy outcomes in their role as service delivery agents. The balance between these three roles will influence how religious organisations are structured, shape their relationships with the state, and affect how religious individuals engage with social policy issues and debates.

The traditional alignment of religious values with the underlying goals of the welfare state has been matched by a closer relationship between church and state in the ways in which welfare benefits (broadly defined) are delivered. The positive impacts of this relationship are assumed to work both ways: the state is freed from responsibility for the minutiae of service provision as a result of contracting out, while religious organisations become more economically powerful and socially and politically influential. There are many facets of these changes that warrant detailed examination from the perspective of their impact on social policy, but this paper focuses on the degree to which the attitudes held by those who describe themselves as religious are consistent with welfare state goals, programmes and policies.[1] It examines the extent to which some of the conclusions drawn recently by Putnam and Campbell (2010) for the United States apply to Australia, focusing specifically on whether it is the case that when religiosity is identified and defined *on the basis of practice as opposed to belief*, those who are identified as being religious are 'better citizens' in relation to the kinds of attitudes and behaviours that suggest an affinity with the principles of the welfare state.

There is, of course, no reason why having a more compassionate attitude towards those who are less economically fortunate should be associated with a higher level of support for *state* interventions designed to improve their circumstances. It may instead lead to a conviction that 'charity should begin (and end) at home' and that state programmes undermine the individualist values on which such charity relies. However, when it comes to attitudes or beliefs about the causes of poverty and inequality (as opposed to what actions should be taken to address them) there is a presumption that those who are religious should lie at the compassionate end of the spectrum, expressing values that are more consistent with the underlying social objectives of fairness, need satisfaction and poverty relief.

Background to the Approach

There is a vast literature—much of it comparative—that examines how public attitudes in general affect support for, and the design of, different forms of social policy intervention (for example, Taylor-Gooby 1985; van Oorschot et al. 2008; Svallfors 1997, 2010). Many of these studies highlight the fact that people's attitudes are not only hard to shift ('coins that do not readily melt' as Schumpeter (1942: 12) noted), but can also reveal information about how social problems are perceived and guide the kinds of ameliorative actions that will attract widespread political support.[2] Such studies also highlight the difficulty involved in explaining the considerable attitudinal diversity that exists by a small set of observable variables.

In relation to attitudes to inequality for example, studies have shown (for Australia and other countries) that a large proportion of the population regard the existing level of inequality—as reflected in the gap between rich and poor—as too large.[3] However, the same survey data often also indicates that this belief does not translate into support for income redistribution designed to reduce the income gap (Saunders & Wong 2013).[4] Attitudes matter, but it is also clear that there is currently an incomplete understanding of the nature of those attitudes and the underlying values that they represent. In this context, it is important to get a better understanding of the nature of the attitudes expressed by different groups in the population in order to explain the lack of consistency between the attitudes held and the strength of support for action.[5]

Addressing such issues requires a more thorough examination of the data and a reduced willingness to accept at face value what the expressed attitudes appear to represent. A better understanding of attitudes to such issues as inequality and state social provision can also assist the policy process because existing attitudes can be an obstacle to the introduction of new policies—particularly when those attitudes are mobilised politically. It is also possible to use attitudinal surveys to 'road test' new policies against public opinion and modify the policies to better fit the existing patterns of belief.[6] Attitudes can be changed, but only if they are known and understood.

Many studies have shown that different dimensions of religious belief and behaviour are correlated with attitudes to social objectives (such as equality), social policies (such as welfare provision), and social activities (such as volunteering). The key findings to emerge from these studies include that religious belief and participation in religious activities is associated with conservative attitudes to social issues such as abortion (Huber 2005), and that there is an inverse relationship between religious participation and support for welfare spending after controlling for the other effects of modernization (Gill & Lundsgaarde 2004).[7] Chang (2010) used data from the *Taiwan Social Change Survey* to examine a range of factors affecting social policy preferences and concluded that 'Religion plays a significant role in shaping people's beliefs about fairness, causes and consequences, the reward for hard work, individual responsibility, altruism, and the relationship between personal interests versus the collective well-being of society' (2010: 83). Despite these seemingly powerful conclusions, there is no agreement from empirical studies about precisely how religiosity and social attitudes are related. Differences exist in how to measure the strength (or even the existence) of religious belief, and studies differ in the policy goals of interest and the sophistication of the statistical methods used to identify the underlying relationships.

One important recent study examines data from the United States *Faith Matters* survey that was conducted specifically to examine the role of religion on a range of social attitudes and practices (Putnam & Campbell 2010). The study provides a detailed examination of the relationships between religiosity and different aspects of social behaviour in the United States, focusing on what the authors refer to as 'the three B's of religiosity'—believing (adherence to religious principles and values), belonging (to a religious community) and behaving (through attendance at religious services and events).[8] The authors draw on a broad body of evidence to show that it is behaving and belonging (which are closely linked) rather than believing that matter when it comes to understanding the *impact* of religion. This is an important finding, because it suggests that those earlier studies that have focused on the role of religious beliefs may have missed the more important mechanisms through which the *practice* of involvement in religion and engagement with like-minded others influences support for specific goals or policies.

The key variable used in the Putnam and Campbell study is a composite religiosity index (RI) which captures the frequency of attending religious services, the frequency of praying outside of religious services, the importance of religion in daily life, the importance of religion in one's sense of who one is, the strength of religious belief and the strength of belief in God (see Putnam & Campbell 2010: 18–23 and Appendix 1). The RI was derived for each individual and the sample was split into quintiles, which were then compared in order to identify the underlying attitudinal gradients.

The resulting evidence reveals a number of important findings, including that for the most part religiously observant Americans are more civic and in some respects simply 'nicer' (Putnam & Campbell 2010: 44). The results also indicate that religiously observant men and women are more philanthropic—especially towards organisations that serve the needy. In relation to volunteering, the authors found that '[the] primary predictor of generosity is the strength of one's religious commitment, regardless of one's religious tradition' (2010: 453), and that: 'religious people are more satisfied with their lives mostly because they build religious social networks, thus reinforcing a strong sense or religious identity' (2010: 491). Combining these findings, the study concludes that: 'For happiness as for neighbourliness, praying together seems to be better than either bowling together or praying alone' (2010: 492). The remainder of this paper examines whether similar conclusions can be drawn (at least tentatively, given the available data) in the Australian context.

Data and Methods

The data used in the analysis is drawn from two surveys, the *Community Understanding of Poverty and Social Exclusion* (CUPSE) survey, conducted in 2006, and the *Poverty and Exclusion in Modern Australia* (PEMA) survey, conducted in 2010. Both surveys were distributed by mail to a random sample of 6,000 adults drawn from the Australian electoral roll and achieved response rates of around 46 per cent.[9] The PEMA survey was accompanied by a follow-up survey of 1,000 of the CUPSE respondents as a way of providing an insight into the dynamics of social disadvantage, and the resulting two-period panel is also used in the analysis that follows.

Comparisons with official Australian Bureau of Statistics data reveal that the CUPSE and PEMA samples are broadly representative of the general population, although the following groups are under-represented: males; those who have never been married; those who live alone; Indigenous Australians; those with lower levels of education; those in private rental accommodation; and those with incomes over $1,000 a week (in 2006) and over $2,000 a week (in 2010). The main area where the samples in both years differ from the population is in relation to age structure: as with many social surveys of this type, older people (aged 50 and over) are disproportionately represented among the respondents compared to younger people (aged under 30). A weighting system has been derived to adjust for any resulting bias, although the results presented below are based on the raw (un-weighted) data because the focus here is on comparing groups within the total sample and weighting by age should not affect these comparisons. A third data source used later is the 2009 *Australian Survey of Social Attitudes* (AuSSA), which attracted 3,243 respondents equivalent to a response rate of around 35 per cent.[10]

The PEMA, CUPSE and PEMA follow-up surveys included a set of core questions which included the following: *Would you describe yourself as a religious person?*[11] Participants were given the three response options shown below and these were used to segment the sample into those who were religious in practice (RP); those who were religious in belief only (or nominally religious) (RB); and those and those who said they were not religious (NR).

> Yes—but I do not regularly attend church or other places of religion (RB)
> Yes—I regularly attend church or other places of religion (RP)
> No—I do not follow any religion (NR)

The question asked in AuSSA 2009 asked about the frequency of attendance at religious services (*How often do you attend religious services?*). This presents problems in deciding how frequently one must attend services before being regarded as a religious in practice, although the following classification has been used:[12]

> Attend more than once a month (RP)
> Attend up to once a month (RB)
> Never attend (NR)

The use of the reported incidence or frequency of service attendance to identify those who are religious in practice can be criticised as being somewhat crude; however, it is all that is possible given the available data. It is relevant to note here that Putnam and Campbell conclude from their study (2010: 19) that: 'Church attendance is ... an excellent measure of religious commitment in most cases'—an assessment which suggests that the religiosity measures used here capture a central aspect of the concept.

The initial approach used to examine the impact of religion involves comparing the mean values of a range of wellbeing, behavioural and attitudinal variables that are relevant to social status and social policy concerns across the RP, RB and NR sub-samples. These variables include several indicators of subjective well-being (SWB), of the incidence of community and social participation (CSP) and of attitudinal support for a range of social policy issues (ASSP). The mean values of these variables are compared across the three religious categories (RP, RB & NR) and the following null hypotheses are tested:[13]

H_1: SWB (or CSP or ASSP)/RP > SWB (or CSP or ASSP)/RB
H_2: SWB (or CSP or ASSP)/RB = SWB (or CSP or ASSP)/NR

The vexed issue of causality is examined using the linked panel of respondents to the CUPSE and PEMA follow-up surveys. Finally, a multivariate (regression) approach is used to assess the extent to which the relationships between religiosity and attitudes to social policy issues are robust after controlling for other factors that exert an influence on social behaviour and attitudes.

Results

Because much of the initial analysis is based on the 2010 PEMA survey, Table 4.3 provides a breakdown of the demographic composition of the three sub-samples of the PEMA sample

TABLE 4.3 Demographic composition of the three religiosity sub-samples (unweighted percentages)

CHARACTERISTIC	RELIGIOUS IN PRACTICE (16.2%)	RELIGIOUS IN BELIEF (42.5%)	NOT RELIGIOUS (41.3%)	SHARE OF TOTAL SAMPLE
Gender				
Female	62.5	60.1	50.3	56.4
Age				
Under 30	9.6	11.7	13.7	12.2
Aged 65+	37.1	23.6	17.0	23.1
Country of birth				
Australian-born	64.9	75.2	78.9	75.1
Born in a NES country (a)	20.9	11.5	6.7	11.1
Marital status				
Never married	11.2	14.4	17.1	15.0
Married	74.1	67.8	67.4	68.7
Educational attainment				
Did not complete high school	30.6	33.9	28.3	31.1
Bachelor degree or higher	36.6	24.6	30.5	29.0
Labour force status				
Employed	43.5	54.1	59.5	54.6
Income				
Family income (equiv.) < $600	66.4	61.2	54.0	59.0
Political affiliation (b)				
ALP voter	23.5	33.8	36.5	32.5
Liberal/National voter	47.7	37.5	25.5	35.8

that are classified according to the reported religiosity of the respondent. Comparisons between the compositions of the religious in practice sub-sample and the sample as a whole indicate that the following groups are over-represented in the actively religious sample: females, those aged 65 and over, those born in an overseas non English-speaking country, those who are married, those with a tertiary qualification, those who are not employed, those who have a low income, and those who (in 2006) described themselves as a Liberal/National party voter. In contrast, the religious in practice group contains an under-representation of people who are aged under 30, Australian-born, never married, employed and ALP voters.

The upper panel of Table 4.4 suggests that those who practise religion as defined here are more satisfied with their standard of living, are somewhat happier, lead more active social lives, and report a higher level of participation in community activities than the other two groups. Against this, they also say that they have less control over their own lives and the things that happen to them. In terms of the null hypotheses specified earlier, the values of two of the five

TABLE 4.4 Subjective wellbeing, autonomy and participation by religiosity (unweighted percentages)

VARIABLE	DEFINITION	RELIGIOUS IN PRACTICE	RELIGIOUS IN BELIEF	NOT RELIGIOUS
Satisfaction with Standard of Living	% 'very satisfied' or 'satisfied'	71.2*	65.9	69.5*
Happiness	% 'very happy'	89.2	88.2	88.2
Autonomy	% scoring of 8–10 on a 10-point scale	39.7	45.2	48.0
Social life	% with 'fairly' or 'very' active' social life	61.1	55.5	51.4
Overall level of Community Participation	% scoring 9-10 on a 10-point scale	17.6*	13.8	13.7
Participation in[a]				
Education/school activities	% that participated	28.4	22.3	22.8
Volunteer in health or community services	% that participated	26.0	17.8	15.4
Church groups/activities	% that participated	59.5	6.6	1.7
Cultural activities	% that participated	25.3	17.4	21.2
Neighbourhood activities	% that participated	18.8	17.2	17.4
No Participation	% that did not participate in any of 8 identified activities	21.2***	33.7	31.5

Notes: (a) Data refer to the percentage that participated in each activity over the last 12 months; (b) The asterisks (*/**/***) indicate that the differences between those shown and those in the middle column are statistically significant (ρ =0.10/0.05/0.01).
Source: PEMA survey.

wellbeing variables shown in the upper panel of Table 4.4 are significantly higher for the religious in practice group than for the religious in belief group, while all but one of the differences for the last two groups are not significantly different. This initial evidence thus provides some support for the two hypotheses (particularly for the latter) although there are a number of cases that do not conform to the expected pattern.

The lower panel of Table 4.4 compares rates of participation in specific community activities between the three religious sub-groups.[14] The results indicate that those who practise religion are more likely to participate in education-based, voluntary and cultural activities, are (not surprisingly) much more likely to take part in church activities, and have the highest participation rates for all of the other activities. In contrast, only a small proportion (6.6 per cent) of those who say they are religious but do not attend a place of religion regularly participate in church groups or activities. The one area where there are very small between-group differences is in relation to participation in neighbourhood activities. With this exception, all of the specific participation rates are significantly higher in the RP than in the RB group, and while there are also some significant differences between the RB and NR groups (contrary to the second hypothesis specified above), overall the results in Table 4.4 are consistent with the findings reported by Putman and Campbell for the United States in showing that those who actively practise their religious beliefs seem more content with their lives and more engaged as citizens.

One possible criticism of the results presented so far is that the correlation between religiosity and wellbeing or community participation does not imply causality. Are religious people more content and more actively engaged socially because of their religious practices, or is it that more content social beings are drawn to religion? This issue was addressed by Putnam and Campbell in two ways. First, they examined whether the simple relationships between religiosity and indicators of good neighbourliness still existed after controlling for other factors such as gender, education, race, location, home ownership, length of residence, marital and parental status, and ideology. They found that the correlation was robust. Second, they examined longitudinal data extracted from the two waves of the *Faith Matters* survey and found that changes in religiosity (though infrequent and small) gave rise to changes in philanthropic generosity and community involvement that were consistent with causation running from religiosity to these other civic variables.[15]

The role of confounding factors is examined later using a regression framework, but before that the causality issue is examined using data from the linked panel data. Panel members have been separated into three groups: those who were actively religious in both years using the definition applied above; those who were not actively religious in either year; and those who were actively religious in 2006 but not in 2010.[16] If it is the case that being actively involved in religion (i.e. by frequently attending religious services) is a causal factor explaining the other variables, then one should find that those who stopped being religious between 2006 and 2010 should look much like others who were religious in 2006, but by 2010 should look more like those who were not actively religious in 2010.

The results in the upper panel of Table 4.5 provide little evidence to support the causality hypothesis: in fact, contrary to expectations, those who stopped being actively religious between 2006 and 2010 report an *increased* level of satisfaction with their standard of living, no change in their happiness, and a sharp rise in control over their lives. They also experienced a substantial *fall* in the level of their social life activity—although so too did the other two groups. However, none of the changes for the group that stopped being actively religious are statistically significant. The changes in community participation in the lower panel of Table 4.5 are (at least in some regards) more consistent with the causality hypothesis, although even here the results are not compelling. While those who ceased being actively religious experienced sharp declines in their participation in education-based, voluntary, church-related and cultural activities, their participation in neighbourhood activities increased sharply. Again, however, the reported changes in participation are not statistically significant, aside from the reduced participation in church activities.

Table 4.5 provides some support for the hypothesis that those who stopped being actively religious between 2006 and 2010 shifted from being like those who were actively religious in 2006 to being like those who were not actively religious in 2010. However, the hypothesis that the mean values for *all three groups* are the same cannot be rejected, reinforcing the view that

TABLE 4.5 Changes in religiosity, wellbeing and community/social participation, 2006 to 2010 (linked panel, unweighted percentages)

ACTIVITY	ACTIVELY RELIGIOUS IN BOTH YEARS (N = 94)		STOPPED BEING ACTIVE-LY RELIGIOUS (N = 33)		NOT ACTIVELY RELIGIOUS IN BOTH YEARS (N = 372)	
	2006	2010	2006	2010	2006	2010
Satisfaction with standard of living	73.4	73.4	75.8	78.1	70.8	73.8
Happiness	94.6	93.6	90.9	90.6	92.4	89.9
Autonomy	45.7	43.6	43.8	53.1	46.6	49.9
Social life	70.1	67.4	61.3	54.6	61.5**	53.4
Participation rate (previous 12 months):						
Education/school activities	25.0	22.6	32.3	24.2	28.7**	21.8
Volunteer in health or community services	23.9	28.0	16.1	6.1	20.0	19.1
Church groups/activities	68.2	65.6	32.3*	12.1	2.5	3.3
Cultural activities	25.0	23.7	25.8	15.2	20.0	18.5
Neighbourhood activities	18.2	15.1	9.7	24.2	23.1	21.0
No participation	12.5	15.1	19.4	27.3	21.7	26.4

Note: (a) The activity variables are defined in Table 4.4; (b). The asterisks (*/**/***) indicate that the differences between the two years are statistically significant (p = 0.10/0.05/0.01).
Sources: CUPSE and PEMA follow-up surveys.

these results cannot be claimed to support the hypothesis under review. The only exception to this pattern occurs for participation in church activities, where the differences between the first and third column values and between the fourth and sixth column values are both statistically significant (although these test outcomes are not shown in Table 4.5). Thus, participation in church activities in 2006 among those who stopped being actively religious after 2006 was significantly below that of those who remained active after 2006, but in 2010 was significantly above that for the group that was not religious in that year. This suggests that the middle group of 'shifters' differs from the other two groups in terms of their church attendance, rather than revealing anything about causality as such.

Table 4.6 draws on the cross-sectional CUPSE and PEMA data to examine differences in attitudes to a number of aspects of inequality and redistribution among the three religious sub-groups identified in Table 4.3. The survey questions relate to different aspects of inequality,

TABLE 4.6 Religiosity and attitudes to inequality and redistribution (unweighted percentages that strongly agree/agree with each proposition)

	RELIGIOUS IN PRACTICE	RELIGIOUS IN BELIEF	NOT RELIGIOUS
Poverty in Australia today is a big problem	26.5	32.5	31.3
The rich are getting richer and the poor are getting poorer	77.0	74.8	71.2
Large differences in income are necessary to maintain Australia's economic prosperity	15.7	16.3	14.9
The gap between rich and poor is too great and should be reduced	76.0	69.3	70.0
Incomes at the top are too high and should be reduced	74.3	70.7	69.6
Incomes at the bottom are too low and should be increased	81.8	83.8	82.6
It is fair that taxes paid by the majority help to support those in need[b]	79.8***	72.0	75.9*
It is not fair that some people pay a lot of tax and hardly use the services that taxes pay for[b]	41.0	43.4	35.2***
It is not fair that people benefit from services that they haven't helped to pay for[b]	35.6	39.6	33.4***
It is fair that people with higher incomes can buy better health care than those with lower incomes[b]	40.5	38.6	34.9*
It is fair that people with higher incomes can buy better education for their children than those with lower incomes[b]	40.2	37.6	34.5

Notes: (a) The asterisks (*/**/***) indicate that the differences between those shown and those in the middle column are statistically significant (p = 0.10/0.05/0.01); (b) These estimates refer to 2006.
Sources: PEMA and CUPSE surveys.

focusing on outcomes (in the income space) and fairness (in relation to taxes, government welfare spending and the relationship between taxes paid and benefits received). The response categories provided were 'strongly agree', 'agree', 'neither agree nor disagree', 'disagree', and 'strongly disagree', although only the percentages in the first two categories are shown in Table 4.6. The results indicate that, relative to the other two groups, the religious in practice group are less convinced that poverty is a big problem, are more likely to agree that the income gap is too high and should be reduced, regard it as fair that taxes should be used to support those in need, but also believe that those on higher incomes should be free to purchase better health care and education for their children.

Only one of the attitudinal differences between the religious in practice and religious in belief groups is statistically significant, while two of the differences between the last two groups (which were hypothesised to be the same) are significantly different. There is also no clear attitudinal gradient across the three religious sub-groups, with the highest values appearing for the middle group in several instances. The evidence in Table 4.6 does not therefore suggest any clear patterns between religiosity and attitudes to inequality, fairness and redistribution.

Table 4.7 complements the results in Table 4.6 by comparing attitudes to a broader range of social policy issues across religious sub-groups using data from the 2009 *Australian Survey of Social Attitudes* where religiosity is defined, as noted earlier, by the frequency of attendance at religious services. These results indicate that, compared to the other two groups, those who attend a religious service at least once a month (identified here as the religious in practice group) are more supportive of government efforts to reduce the income gap, and are more concerned about the negative impact of cutting welfare benefits for the unemployed. They also express more confidence in both charities and the welfare system (which suggests an affinity with a 'mixed economy of welfare' approach), and for providing support that allows sole parents to stay at home to raise their children. All three groups express similar levels of support for sole parents as for all families with children, with such support well below that for providing a decent minimum for the unemployed. Again, however, most of the group differences in Table 4.7 are not statistically significant, a finding which provides little evidence to support the null hypotheses under examination.

The analysis conducted so far has focused on bivariate relationships between religiosity and a number of attitudinal variables that capture support for the goals of social policy, or with the mechanisms used to achieve those goals. The focus now shifts to examining whether the findings are robust when a multivariate approach is taken that controls for the effects of other variables that are likely to influence the relationship between religiosity and social attitudes. A number of alternative dependent variables that capture different aspects of attitudes to social goals and policies have been specified for this purpose. The first two relate to attitudes to overall income inequality and fairness and are based on responses to the following survey questions:[17]

TABLE 4.7 Religiosity and attitudes to selected social policy interventions (unweighted percentages)

SOCIAL POLICY OBJECTIVE	FREQUENCY OF ATTENDING RELIGIOUS SERVICES:		
	MORE THAN ONCE A MONTH (N=485; 15.7%)	UP TO ONCE A MONTH (N=1,318; 42.5%)	NEVER (N=1,295; 41.8%)
Complete/a great deal of confidence in charities	44.3	39.3	30.7***
Complete/a great deal of confidence in Australia's social welfare system	30.6	25.4	18.5***
Strongly agree/agree that government privatisation has more benefits than costs	23.2	20.9	17.9*
The gap between high incomes and low incomes is much too large/too large	74.5	74.2	74.3
Strongly agree/agree that it is the government's responsibility to reduce income differences	57.8**	49.3	51.3
The government should provide a decent standard of living for the unemployed	56.8	50.5	51.9
The government should spend less on benefits for the poor	9.0	10.1	9.6
Cutting welfare benefits would damage too many people's lives	76.8**	71.7	74.1
Families deserve payments to help with the costs of raising children	44.8	45.8	38.5***
Single parents deserve government payments so that they can be at home to raise their children	44.1	40.1	38.9

Note: (b) The asterisks (*/**/***) indicate that the differences between those shown and those in the middle column are statistically significant (ρ = 0.10/0.05/0.01).
Source: Author's calculations based on AuSSA 2009.

1. The gap between rich and poor is too great and incomes should be reduced
2. Incomes are too high at the top and should be reduced
3. Incomes are too low at the bottom and should be increased
4. It is fair that taxes paid by the majority help to support those in need
5. It is not fair that some people pay a lot of tax and hardly use the services their taxes pay for
6. It is not fair that people benefit from services that they haven't helped to pay for
7. It is fair that people with higher incomes can buy better health care than those with lower incomes
8. It is fair that people with higher incomes can buy better education for their children than those with lower incomes

In each case, the response categories provided (strongly agree, agree, neither agree nor disagree, disagree and strongly disagree) were assigned a score of 1 through to 5, where the higher score indicated greater support for either income redistribution or for the fairness criterion implied in the question. These scores were then summed for questions 1–3 and for questions 4–8 and these aggregate scores represent the first two dependent variables.[18] The third (zero-one) dependent variable reflects one of the assumed characteristics of good civic citizens highlighted in the earlier discussion, and refers to whether or not the respondent acted as a volunteer in health and community services over the last 12 months. The final variable is designed to capture compassion in attitudes to the plight of the poor, and is based on responses to the following 2 questions:

1. People are poor because they have been unlucky in life
2. People are poor because they have not had the opportunities that other people have

In this case, a scale was constructed by assigning a strongly agree response to each question a score of 5, down to a score of 1 for strongly disagree responses; these scores were then summed across the two questions (so that a higher score indicates greater agreement with the propositions in each question and thus a greater willingness to see the poor as the victims of external circumstances).

The same set of explanatory variables was included in each regression model and these are defined in the Appendix—the results themselves are presented in Table 4.8. When reviewing these results, it is important to note that the dependent variables have been defined so that a positive coefficient implies that the relevant explanatory variable is associated with a more egalitarian attitude, greater civic engagement, or a more compassionate attitude towards the causes of poverty and the poor. The first point to note about the results is that the explanatory power of all four models is very low and relatively few of the explanatory variables are statistically significant. This reflects the difficulty in explaining the variability in attitudes to complex social issues using a small set of observable socio-demographic variables.

With these caveats in mind, the results in Table 4.8 indicate that younger people, those born in a non English-speaking country and those on higher incomes tend to be less egalitarian (in the income space). On the question of fairness more generally (specifically in relation to access to basic services), wage and salary earners are less egalitarian, as are those born in a non English-speaking overseas country, while females and graduates are more egalitarian. Broadly similar patterns relate to those engaged in volunteering. The final column of estimates show that graduates, those who regard themselves as poor, and those on lower incomes, hold more compassionate views towards the poor.

When it comes to the role of the religiosity variables, the parameter estimates in Table 4.8 indicate that those who are actively religious hold more egalitarian views when it comes to access to basic services and are more likely to have volunteered over the last year. In contrast, those who are not religious hold even more egalitarian views on service fairness and are more compassionate when it comes to views about how responsible the poor are for their plight.

TABLE 4.8 Regression results

	DEPENDENT VARIABLE:			
INDEPENDENT VARIABLE	INCOME GAPS (PEMA)	SERVICE FAIR-NESS (CUPSE)	VOLUNTEER (CUPSE)	CAUSES OF POVERTY (CUPSE)
Intercept	11.19***	16.05***	−1.10***	5.62***
Gender: female	0.15	0.38*	0.34**	0.13
Age: <30	−1.04***	−0.36	0.01	−0.28*
Age: 65+	−0.16	−0.52	−0.13	0.15
Income: W or S	0.61*	−0.84*	−0.92***	−0.03
Income: SSP	0.13	−0.70	−0.66**	−0.15
Income: other	−0.12	−1.77**	−0.76*	−0.99***
Subjectively poor	0.95***	0.22	−0.23	0.52***
COB: English-speaking	−0.18	−0.35	−0.03	−0.16
COB: Non English-speaking	−0.53**	−0.82*	−0.60*	−0.23
Indigenous	−0.10	−2.09*	0.52	0.17
Disability	0.38*	−0.13	−0.32	0.26*
Housing: renter	−0.08	0.30	−0.19	0.06
Housing: other	0.27	−0.28	−0.30	0.17
Education: primary	0.09	−0.35	−0.43*	0.02
Education: trade certificate	0.22	0.43	−0.03	0.02
Education: degree	−0.16	1.74***	0.41*	0.50***
Income: < $600	0.61**	0.13	0.27	0.44**
Income: $600–$1,000	0.44**	0.11	0.21	0.32**
Income: $2,000+	−0.78***	−0.05	0.48*	0.01
LFS: unemployed	−0.07	0.17	0.40	0.26
LFS: other	0.24	−0.03	0.25	0.12
Religious in practice (RP)	0.24	0.47*	0.42*	0.12
Not religious (NR)	0.15	0.68***	−0.13	0.22*
Sample size	2,066	2,090	2,052	2,062
R-squared	0.083	0.055	0.045	0.045

Notes: (a) The asterisks (*/**/***) indicate that the differences between those shown and those in the middle column are statistically significant (ρ = 0.10/0.05/0.01).
Sources: CUPSE and PEMA surveys.

The patterns of size and significance of the religiosity variables do not conform to the hypotheses set out earlier, but the important point is that religiosity is shown to have an impact on social attitudes even after the influence of other factors is taken into account. In fact, religiosity shows up as statistically significant in at least as many cases as any of the other broad classes of variables included in the modelling. The results are thus not definitive, but they do suggest that religiosity exerts an influence on social attitudes and has the potential to influence support for different social goals and policies.

Conclusions

Religious beliefs reflect and reinforce people's wider value system and one might expect that those values influence how people feel about the goals of social policy and the methods used to achieve them. However, there is no simple relationship between personal values and attitudes towards state action in the social policy field—in part because of the lack of agreement about what those goals are, and because of the uncertainty and confusion that surrounds debates about the impact and effectiveness of different policy choices. This paper has presented a range of data on Australian attitudes to social policy issues and explored whether they differ systematically with religiosity, measured in terms of the frequency of attending religious services.

The focus here has been on examining the impact of religious practice rather than of religious belief itself, because other studies have shown that the former variable is a better predictor of social attitudes than the latter. It is, however, important to acknowledge that the variable used to capture the strength of religious practice is rather crude and can only be expected to map the actual differences that exist in general terms. Further research is needed (along the lines of that conducted for the United Sates by Putnam and Campbell (2010)) that allows a more sophisticated specification of the religiosity variable and importantly, is also able to breakdown the responses by type of religion.

Despite these limitations, the results suggest that some of the attitudes expressed about the role, design and delivery of social policy programs vary systematically across religious groups defined on the basis of both religious service attendance and reported non-belief. Future research in this field will clearly benefit from better data on which to identify a person's religiosity and from samples that are large enough to allow its overall (and diverse) effects to be better isolated and quantified. Although there is some evidence that those who are actively religious have more egalitarian, pro-welfare attitudes, there is no consistent pattern linking pro-welfare attitudes (such as aversion to inequality, support for redistribution, compassion for the poor) or more civically-minded behavior (such as in relation to the incidence of volunteering) systematically to religious activity or non-belief. Those involved in religious activity appear to hold a diversity of views about the importance of the ends and the effectiveness of the means of social policy.

Acknowledgements

The author acknowledges the helpful comments provided on the original version of this paper by John Nevile and two anonymous referees. Statistical support was provided by Melissa Wong. Financial assistance from the Australian Research Council under Linkage project grants LP0560797 and LP100100562 is also acknowledged.

References

Chang, W.C. (2010) 'Religion and preferences for redistributive policies in an East Asian country', *Poverty & Public Policy*, 2 (4), 81–109.

Chesters, J. & Western, J. (2010) 'Evidence and perceptions of inequality in Australia', *CEPR Discussion Paper No. 635*, Centre for Economic Policy Research, Research School of Economics, Australian National University.

Gill, A. & Lundsgaarde, E. (2004) 'State welfare spending and religiosity: a cross-national analysis', *Rationality and Society*, 16 (4), 339–436.

Huber, J.D. (2005) 'Religious belief, religious participation, and social policy attitudes across countries', mimeo, Department of Political Science, Columbia University.

Kelley, J., Evans, M. & Sikora, J. (2004) 'Is there too much inequality in Australia?', *Australian Social Monitor*, 7 (3/4), 92–100.

Meagher, G. & Wilson, S. (2008) 'Richer, but more unequal: perceptions of inequality in Australia 1987–2005', *The Journal of Australian Political Economy*, 61 (June), 220–243.

Oorschot, W.V., Opielka, M. & Pfau-Effinger, B. (eds.) (2008) *Culture and the Welfare State. Values and Social Policy in Comparative Perspective*, Cheltenham, Edward Elgar.

Osberg, L. & Smeeding, T.M. (2006) '"Fair" inequality? Attitudes toward pay differentials: the United States in comparative perspective', *American Sociological Review*, 71 (30), 450–73.

Pusey, M. & Turnbull, N. (2005) 'Have Australians embraced economic reform?'. In S. Wilson, G. Meagher, R. Gibson, D. Denemark & M. Western (eds), *Australian Social Attitudes. The First Report,* Sydney, UNSW Press, 161–81.

Putnam, R.D. & Campbell, D.E. (2010) *American Grace. How Religion Divides and Unites Us,* New York, Simon & Schuster.

Saunders, P., Eardley T. & Evans, C. (2000) 'Community attitudes towards unemployment, activity testing and mutual obligation', *Australian Bulletin of Labour*, 26 (3), 211–35.

Saunders, P., Naidoo, Y. & Griffiths, M. (2008) 'Towards new indicators of disadvantage: deprivation and social exclusion in Australia', *Australian Journal of Social Issues*, 43 (2), 175–94.

Saunders, P. & Wong, M. (2012) *Promoting Inclusion and Combating Deprivation: Recent Changes in Social Disadvantage in Australia*, Social Policy Research Centre, University of New South Wales.

Saunders, P. & Wong, M. (2013) 'Examining Australian attitudes to inequality and redistribution', *Journal of Australian Political Economy*, forthcoming.

Schumpeter, J. (1942) *Capitalism, Socialism and Democracy*, New York, Harper.

Sikora (2003), 'Tastes for privatisation and tastes for subsidisation: have Australians been getting cold feet?, *Australian Social Monitor*, 6(2), 34–40.

Stilwell, F. & Jordan, K. (2007) *Who Gets What? Analysing Economic Inequality in Australia*, Cambridge, Cambridge University Press.

Svallfors, S. (1997) 'Worlds of welfare and attitudes to redistribution: A comparison of eight Western nations, *European Sociological Review*, 13(3), 331–52.

Svallfors, S. (2010) 'Public attitudes'. In F. G. Castles, S. Leibfried, J. Lewis, H. Obinger & C. Pierson (eds), *The Oxford Handbook of the Welfare State*, Oxford, Oxford University Press, 241–51.

Taylor-Gooby, P. (1985) *Public Opinion, Ideology, and State Welfare*, London, Routledge & Kegan Paul.

van Kersbergen, K. & Manow, P. (2010) 'Religion'. In F.G. Castles, S. Leibfried, J. Lewis, H. Obinger & C. Pierson (eds), *The Oxford Handbook of the Welfare State*, Oxford, Oxford University Press, 265–77.

Notes

1   It is acknowledged that this is only one aspect of what is a much broader set of issues relating to the actual interaction between religion and the welfare state that includes, for example, working conditions, the notion of a 'just wage', the ownership of private property and relations between the church and the state more generally.

2   The source of the quote from Schumpeter is Svallfors (2010: 241).

3   Among the many recent contributions to the Australian literature are Sikora (2003); Kelley and colleagues (2004); Pusey and Turnbull (2005); Stilwell and Jordan (2007); Meagher and Wilson (2008); Chesters and Western (2010); and Saunders and Wong (2013, forthcoming).

4   Data from the 2005 *Australian Survey of Social Attitudes* (*AuSSA*) indicates that although over 86 per cent agreed that the income gap was too high, support for income redistribution from better-off to less well-off was less than half of this, at below 42 per cent (Saunders & Wong 2013: Table 4.3). In other words, a majority of the 86 per cent who thought that the income gap is too large were either opposed to redistribution or were ambiguous about it, with almost one-third of them opposed to redistribution from high to low income. Part of the contradiction apparent in these findings may reflect the use of undefined terms like 'rich' and 'poor' to gauge people's attitudes, as Osberg and Smeeding (2006) have observed, or the (unknown) impact of the context in which a particular question is embedded.

5   This apparent lack of consistency may also reflect a lack of faith in the effectiveness of the redistributive policies proposed to deal with the problem, or a concern that they may give rise to unacceptable side effects (e.g. on incentives).

6   An example of this occurred in the late 1990s when surveys of public attitudes to the introduction of mutual obligation requirements (MOR) on social security recipients were used to better tailor MOR to those groups where support for them was strongest (see Saunders et al. 2000).

7   Huber argues that the relationship between religious belief and religious participation (e.g. in services) varies cross-nationally, and is strongest in those countries that are most economically and politically developed.

8   The need to distinguish between religious belief and church attendance has been emphasised by Huber (2005: Figures 4 and 5), who notes that a 'disconnect' exists between religious belief and church attendance in a cross-country sample derived from the *World Values Survey*, which reveals

that many who attend church weekly do not adhere to standard religious beliefs (for example, about the existence of heaven, or being very spiritual), while many believers do not attend church regularly. Gill and Lundsgaarde (2004: Tables 4.4, 4.6 and 4.7) find that there is a statistically significant cross-national relationship between welfare spending and church attendance, the percentage of the population who describe themselves as non-religious, and the percentage who express comfort in religion.

9   Further details of the CUPSE and PEMA surveys can be found in Saunders and colleagues (2008) and Saunders and Wong (2012), respectively.

10 Further details of AuSSA (including the 2009 questionnaire) can be found at www.aussa.anu.edu. au. The AuSSA response rate varied slightly between the two versions of the questionnaire that were applied in 2009 and the figure of 35 per cent is the average.

11 Information on the form of religion practised by respondents was not requested, making it impossible to examine the impact of type of religion on the issues examined.

12 Despite the differences in formulation of the religiosity variable, the sample sizes shown in Tables 4.3 and 4.7 below indicate that the boundary used to distinguish between the first two groups in the AuSSA sample produces a breakdown of the sample that is very close to that produced by the three-way classification derived from the PEMA survey.

13 Note that a one-tailed test is appropriate when testing the first hypothesis.

14 The survey asked about more activities than those shown in Table 4.4 and the 'no participation' variable refers to all of the specified activities, not just those identified in Table 4.4.

15 Putnam and Campbell acknowledged that these latter tests do not 'prove' that religious change 'caused' civic change, although they argue that the panel results 'make it less plausible to suppose that some enduring personal trait, such as generic niceness or generic activism, explains the correlation' (2010: 462).

16 A fourth group consisting of those who were not actively religious in 2006 but were in 2010 contains only seven individuals and is not large enough to conduct statistical analysis.

17 Questions 1–3 were included in both the CUPSE and PEMA surveys, while questions 4–8 were included in CUPSE only. The following results are based on the PEMA survey for questions 1–3 and on CUPSE for questions 4–8.

18 Reliability tests indicate that the resulting two scales are robust, with Cronbach alpha values of 0.726 and 0.678, respectively.

APPENDIX   Specification of the independent variables used in the regression analysis (reference categories shown in italics)

Variable name	Specification
Gender	1 if female, 0 if male
Age	Under 30 years; *30–64 years*; 65 and over
Main source of income last week	Wages or salaries (W or S); *interest, dividends, superannuation, etc.*; social security payment (SSP); other

Subjectively poor	Would you describe yourself as poor? 1 if response is yes, 0 otherwise
Country of birth	*Australia*; another English-speaking country; another non English-speaking country
Indigenous status	1 if yes, 0 otherwise
Disability status	1 if yes, 0 otherwise
Housing status	*Home owner/purchaser*; public or private renter; other
Educational attainment	Primary/some secondary; *completed secondary school*; trade certificate or similar; degree/postgraduate degree
Gross weekly income	Under $600; $600–$999; *$1,000–$1,999*; $2,000 and over
Labour force status	*Employed*; unemployed; other
Religiosity	Religious in practice, *religious in belief only/nominally religious*; not religious

On Ecumenism and The Peace of Religions

By Madeea Axinciuc

Introduction

The aim of the present study is to address a complex and, at the same time, delicate subject, whose ramifications will be analysed and reexamined by following several lines of research.[1]

Put succinctly, the general subject matter is the prerequisites and preconditions required in order to make interreligious communication possible. The issue will be addressed within the broader framework of the debate surrounding ecumenism and "the peace of religions"[2], making explicit reference to the particular case of Central and Eastern Europe. Particular attention will be given to describing and interpreting the current stage of religious cohabitation, touching on the situation of post-communist countries, on the one hand, and, on the other hand, to predicting, in a rather pragmatic manner, the possible directions in which this will evolve, as well as the potential mechanisms and triggers that might reconfigure the framework for discussion in the medium and long term.

The approach to the topic under examination is from a perspective pertaining mainly to the fields of the philosophy of religion and the history of religious ideas.

The chosen viewpoint brings together and integrates debates and issues relevant, on the one hand, to the historical developments of the various embodied "faces" of the religious, grasped in their political and communal aspects, and, on the other hand, to the reappraisal of

Madeea Axinciuc, "On Ecumenism and Peace of Religions," *Journal for the Study of Religions and Ideologies*, vol. 10, no. 30, pp. 160-182. Copyright © 2011 by SACRI The Academic Society for the Research of Religions and Ideologies. Reprinted with permission. Provided by ProQuest LLC. All rights reserved.

meanings and interpretations, divested of diachrony and revealed in religious and/or theological discourse, with regard to "the peace of religions"[3].

These two coexisting "viewpoints" naturally interweave the communal, institutionalised dimension of the understanding of religion, and the personal (and personalised) dimension of religious experience.

The political extent of interreligious dialogue, in its secular and institutionalised dimension, is emblematically reflected in the different usages of the term "ecumenism", which posit communication at the level of individuals following different religious traditions, as well as at the level of the institutions meant to represent, traditionally or officially, coexisting religions, in a more or less politicised manner.

The non-secularised dimension of interreligious communication, envisaged as a non-politicised dialogue stemming from spiritual premises alone, will be further addressed drawing upon the suggestive formulation used by Nicolaus Cusanus: "the peace of religions".

Thus, the present study intends to analyse the two aspects as they reflect each other, explicitly emphasising that their differentiation is purely methodological, and their edges of interference will be brought into close discussion.

Theology, Ideology and Interreligious Communication

There are several terminological delimitations pertaining to the religious-political realm, denoting, by virtue of their common occurrences and implicit meanings, a belonging to structures, systems, and configurations of an institutional nature, and indicating, by their very definition, a specific type of relation established within the framework of different forms of communal organisation. Thus, terms or expressions such as "religious minority", "denomination", "canon", "Church", "sect", "religious toleration", "religious conflict", "official/unofficial religion", "ecumenism" etc., make sense only within the bounds of systems which, by their nature, presuppose a certain order or ordering in accordance with one or more reference points or guide marks, grounded in the "social contract" and regulated politically.

We may, for example, talk about religious minorities in a systemically ordered context, wherein any "minority" would emerge and define itself as being different from the "majority". The ratio of forces between "minority" and majority" is regulated in the same manner that is employed in order to decide the authority of "voices" and their hierarchy, if it is possible to talk about hierarchy in this case.

The theological, perceived as an institutionalised "measure" of the religious phenomenon, becomes the "exorcised" expression of the individual (or collective) experience, adjusted within a framework, and adopted as a model or formative matrix at the communal level. The discourse of theology, by openly imparting knowledge to the masses, is inevitably contaminated by the imprint of ideology, since it is uncritically adopted and appropriated as such.

Propaganda and ideology are here to be understood, based on their ultimate meaning (divested of their usual negative outlook), as a "(pre)fabricated" message, coming "from the outside", and efficiently dominating the mechanisms of insinuation: "as if" it came "from the inside", "as if" it were naturally "yours", and for that reason, it ought to be embraced without any reservations and redemptively conveyed to others. They are always ready to provide and propose concrete, tangible solutions. Seemingly insoluble situations and problems are instantly solved. The guilty persons, as well as the saviours, are immediately nominated and we are offered the key destined to possibly unlock every door.[4]

Ideology and propaganda pretend to meet the fundamentally human aspiration to "(re-)solve all the problems in the world". This aspiration, usually laden with spiritual connotations, fails whenever it persists in affixing itself to palpable, "politically" wrought solutions, made in the image and likeness of man.

Thus, the solutions brought by social-political systems that programmatically deny any religious influence (explicitly excluding this dimension from the sphere of their own message or setting it apart, as a tolerant move) succeed in configuring a redemptive ideology, similar to the way in which religious doctrines operate in their own field. This fact has led an Eric Voegelin to put forward the suggestive formula of "political religions"[5].

The vision according to which the theological and the political are organically co-generated categories was exemplarily expounded by Spinoza, in his *Theological-Political Treatise*[6], for example. Theology implies a systematic vision (or, at least, clearly defined landmarks), expressed by means and devices intended to facilitate its transmission and reception. The text usually provides the supporting structure or the medium instrumentalised by theology in order for it to take shape, to be preserved and transmitted. Theological discourse is circumscribed and confined to the specific vision whence it stems and which it further represents. The power and durability of the text to withstand and constitute the "depositary" of the message in time, as well as its "vehicle" in space (since the text seems to be the easiest way to "convey" a message), form the nucleus and the core of any doctrine or ideology. The permanence of the message, accompanied by its political influence and authority, gives rise to ideology, understood as sterile repeatability, assumed from outside, by virtue of compatibilities, constraints or interests.

The nature of permanence also rests under the sign of uniqueness, in a creative gesture, this time implying a new mode of transmission and/or reception of the message.

It is the means of conceiving and approaching a message that is particular to the oral and, later, to the scriptural traditions, prior to the articulation of any theology.

Interreligious communication considered as ecumenical dialogue is endowed with an implicit political dimension, and creates the possibility of building a bridge between ideologies through the very acceptance of their (peaceful) cohabitation. This dialogue is a dialogue of "texts" and doctrines, without actually succeeding in bringing together, face to face, the real message of the theologies involved—the endeavour is rather to defend, protect or mindfully delineate a particular vision. Ecumenism, as political standpoint, puts forward and constructs a "honeycomb" wherein "theologies" may rest untroubled, without interfering with each other.

The effective dialogue of religions should therefore also take place within frameworks other than the merely exterior ones provided by official meetings, political agreements or shared events and ceremonies.

Genuine dialogue and, consequently, living ecumenism would first and foremost involve the co-operation of theologians (rather than theologies!), by connecting and joining the text to the spiritual message from which the theological vision has originated. The emphasis would be laid on the practical dimension of religion and the sharing of the religious experience. Religions as such do not exist: their *embodied* message is more than theology. The main reason for the practice of religion can (and should) not remain the producing and perpetuating of theology, but the transformation of man. This understanding of ecumenism could, in my opinion, permit the next step in the development of interreligious communication.

How could this new stage of ecumenism be envisaged or depicted?

Passing from the level of interreligious conflict and the imposition of one religion as supreme, the first step in the hierarchy of interreligious communication is religious tolerance, which requires and takes for granted the *de jure* cancellation of the doctrinal supremacy of any one religion over others. Numerical superiority might thus become, through a lack of political prerogatives, the criterion and instrument for further discrimination—necessary from the viewpoint of the "defeated" religion rejecting, as a first reaction, the "equality" of religions.

After the level of religious tolerance, envisaged as weak ecumenism, the next step brings into attention *de facto* communication among religions, at the level of theological doctrines, by removing the veil and partaking in the "core" of the corresponding visions. More precisely, respect and mere cohabitation without interference are step by step transformed into lively communication. To the 'negative' understanding of interreligious communication as non-violence and avoidance of conflict, the positive dimension of sharing religious experience and indulging in common spiritual endeavour would thus be added. As a result, theologies will no longer speak in their own language, for their own sake, while indifferently tolerating the "neighbouring" discourse; on the contrary, they will finally speak to each other, freed from the belligerent intentions usually come moulded in apologetics and proselytism. It is only at this point that the passage from ecumenism to what Nicolaus Cusanus called "the peace of religions" will become possible.

At this new level, a certain receptivity, readiness, and generosity of understanding are required—accompanied, as a mirror image, by a genuine search for self-apprehension, in order to find the adequate methods and tools to open up and make a particular theology and knowledge available not only to those who serve and practise it, by tradition or out of habit, but above all to those who want to approach it from outside. Dialogue does not imply renunciation of one's own tradition or condemnation of others'.

The risks assumed by this kind of openness are huge from the perspective of the political stability of the doctrine: in fact, this kind of communication would lead, in a creative manner, to inevitable renewal and thus to a rebirth of the religious and spiritual message, which might take unexpected, unpredictable turns, one easily embraced by those who are always ready to renounce, without any precaution, a dusty doctrine in exchange for a living message.

This kind of communication among religions would no longer develop within pre-established frameworks, confined to the boundaries of a particular theological vision, indefinitely using the same language (transformed in jargon or, even worse, *langue de bois*), but would favour new frameworks and contexts, shifting the emphasis from doctrine and its substantiation towards religious experience. The approach is not meant to find a solution in order to impose a new doctrine, and what is at stake is not to provide evidence for a system or to refute it, but rather to raise honest questions and give answers relevant not to the logic of the various systems, but to our knowledge as humans.

The emphasis is no longer laid on highlighting and exacerbating specific differences, by continuously setting boundaries for one's own territory, but rather on what "unites us". The doctrines, theologies or systems are no longer at the forefront; the leading position is taken over by the search for the first and ultimate principle. The unity of religions and their authentic communication is not to be found in the common lines or issues of their theologies. Sealing the dialogue of the doctrines by listing and totalising the common landmarks and lines of thought, at the textual and ideological level, is neither eloquent, nor convincing to us nowadays. The transition from political tolerance to doctrinal tolerance is but a small step, which preserves ideological contamination, as well as the immobility of the systems still regarded as being the ultimate reference point.

Even so, the ultimate principle cannot be "captured" and reduced to a system, nor can it express itself fully through a systematic theory. The risk of replacing the ultimate principle with a doctrine or a system bearing human face, due to its multiple secularised ramifications, is evident. Whenever the religious followers listen to the "voice" of the system rather than paying attention to the "voice" made present and manifest *by means of* the system, the situation may be easily compared to the parable of someone who, instead of looking at the moon, is staring at the finger pointing to the moon. It is only a short step from this to believing that the finger itself is the moon, or, in the best case, that this particular finger alone can point to the moon.

In conclusion, the endeavour to confront different theologies and religious doctrines might offer a framework for ideological substantiations, as well as for clearly tracing the lines of demarcation with regard to the explication or deduction, in a logical and apologetic manner, of the possible ramifications developed by these systems in all their details. The approach, however, will not be able to re-orientate the gaze toward what religion intends to point at, through its very essence. In other words, instead of opening the path toward the ultimate principle-in order to enhance this connection, taking as a starting point only the manifestations reflected in texts, images, doctrines—the stress shifts, in the best case, toward the connection among systems.

The religious follower remains fastened to a system which thus confines the world and the viewpoint by cutting up and mutilating the path.

The connection pointed out by the authentic religious gesture forms a bridge between the interior viewpoint and the ultimate principle causing the viewpoint, regardless of the religious tradition taken into consideration (each tradition identifies, names and expresses in a different manner the two "heads" of the relation). Moreover, the etymology of the term "religion", as it is used in the Indo-European languages, points toward the same general meaning[7].

Gaze, Face, Authenticity

The level at which the "connection"—understood as (re)orientation of the gaze and the attention toward the ultimate principle—emerges and is fixed will also provide parameters for a better understanding of religious perception and experience. Whenever these parameters are inculcated by tradition or doctrine, the gaze does not belong to the one who looks. How and to what extent is it possible to see through the eyes of one system?

What we lack within the secularised frameworks of religious education in Europe is precisely this pedagogy of regaining one's own gaze. In fact, the aim of religious systems is not represented by the systems themselves, but by the guidance and re-orientation of one's own gaze along the way. If the system is or seems to be the same for everyone, the gaze of each person travelling along the way will be unique.

The refuse of uniqueness and thus authenticity nourishes systems and ideologies. The overestimation of differences and otherness, as well as unity and uniformity, without returning and restoring man's image and likeness in their uniqueness, constitutes a tool to promote, implement, and perpetuate the ideological.

A reconfiguration of the concept of community and authority, as well as the key-elements they circumscribe, proves necessary at this point.

How might a community be defined, understood and crystallised in the absence of any ideological influence? Which are the hierarchies implied and developed by such a community, and how is the principle of authority reflected within the boundaries of such a community? What, in general, is the sense of community? A critical analysis regarding the foundations of religious cohabitation today is not the goal of the present study, and consequently I shall confine myself to highlighting some possible interrogations deriving from the debate about the idea of religious community.

To return back to our argument, several levels expressing the emergence of "connection" within the horizon of religious experience might be uncovered and understood as forming a bridge between one's own gaze and the founding principle perceived as the ultimate way marker.

The different representations and embodiments of the ultimate principle reconfigure, in a mirror image, self-perception and self-identity, which are reshaped according to an apprehension of the ultimate reference point (functioning as a correlated and correlative term).

The multiple faces of the divine denote, implicitly and correspondently, different levels of perception, as well as different states of consciousness[8], discernible, at the same time, as interior steps toward self-configuration. The projection is dual: the concomitance between one's self(-representation) and the ultimate principle, in their essential relation, is amply approached. The impossibility of "figuring" and "imaging" the divine, or, even more so, the explicit interdiction to make a graven image or likeness, *i.e.* to materialise and embody the ultimate essence of the transcendent principle, is thematised in the same ample manner. Hence the impossibility of assigning a name to the "unnamed" principle stands for the impossibility of encompassing the divine or circumscribing and confining it to the earthly sphere. Unnamed itself, it bears all names, and faceless itself, it bears all faces.

The various reconfigurations of one's own face within the dynamic of the personal relationship with the ultimate principle are indicative of the corresponding levels of inner trans-figuration and thus of the perception of self-identity.

The authenticity of this relationship bears witness to the possibility of inner transfiguration.

Following this line of thought, any "borrowed" relation, acquired by uncritically adopting and assuming a "face" (with reference to one's own face or the "face" attributed to the divine), is the sign of an unauthentic, exterior belonging to one ideology or another. In short, non-authenticity gives rise to the ideological and proliferates it. Therefore, the more "depersonalised" and constrained is the individual relation, devoid of direct experience of the sacred (as a manifestation of the divine presence), the more powerful is the ideological "charge" of the respective religious tradition.

Whereas religiosity by definition implies a series of exterior signs, symbols and reference points relevant to a group, but also a series of practices, rites and ceremonies meant to bind together the community, in the case of spirituality, the lack of a secularised doctrine in the form of theology brings the personalised relationship (usually that of master/disciple) to the fore, and therefore the auroral gesture of inner (re-)birth resists exterior, uprooted petrifaction. In the spiritual realm, the steps of the divine hierarchy are inwardly reborn, this time at the level of individual perception, by recognising the pre-eminence of the inner and by accordingly re-signifying outer and visible manifestations, taken as expressions of interiority. In this way, interiority, considered in its subjective dimension or understood as intra-divine dynamic, represents (beyond any "spatial" inside/outside, here/there reference) the ineffable and diaphanous register—unnameable and indefinable. It designates, par excellence, the lack of the deceiving mask and the presence of the living face irreducible to any particular manifestation. As a consequence, the complement of embodied, multifaceted exteriority, clearly perceived from the very first sight, is the "imperceptible" interiority which, unforeseeably, gives birth to forms, shapes or bodies. The safety ensured by the apparent stability of the exterior is complemented by the uncertainty of entering a totally uncontrollable, but paradoxically guiding realm. The spiritual experience succeeds in rooting out the intermediating "faces" of religious doctrines from their exterior, sterile immobility, and in making them fluid, by naturally bringing them into harmony with fruitful interiority. This transition, once perceived, reinstitutes the world and repositions the person undergoing this experience of the sacred in the right place wherefrom he may grasp the connections of his world and understand through the authenticity of a personal experience capable of reinstating the "flow" of all things along their proper path, without striving to imprint a "graven image" upon the manifestations of the visible.

By renouncing the imposition of a specific "face", the gate opens onto the place where all faces come into being.

Whereas at the personal, individual level the imposition of a graven image represents an impediment and an obstacle (usually in the form of preconceived ideas or misconceptions petrified in more or less systematic visions), at the community level, the imposition of a graven image (by tradition or by adherence to one system or another) represents the grounds of ideology.

Faces carved in stone are recognisable in the obstinate will to convey a certain identity or a certain set of rules which are to be adopted and applied without requiring personal choice or conviction arising from critical thinking; they are merely transferred or imposed as the sole alternative, without offering any place for discussion of the hidden criteria of this specific choice, whose premises and goals usually remain unchallenged, since the message is transmitted without encouraging or allowing any prior exercise of the free will. This is why education within frameworks which do not allow or perpetuate critical thinking (as opposed to delivering data and "objective" knowledge) constitutes a form of manipulation and ideological indoctrination. Consequently, man's actions and conceptions may in this way be controlled and conducted according to artificial criteria in the service of alien goals. The impossibility of previously experiencing the state of inner freedom makes the bondage to one or another ideology appear "natural", as any value judgement has already been contaminated (even before it can be articulated).

The Cartesian method of doubt[9] is, in this respect, the critical attitude required for self-re-construction, as a reflex of inner freedom regained. Repositioning and re-location within a new horizon is a sign of an advance along the way. However, transforming one's own path into a theory of the path invested with "objective" legitimacy is the germ of the ideologisation and petrifaction of freedom under the guise of a message that should otherwise constitute only one step in the process of comprehending.

This is why, following the spiritual line of oral traditions, the spiritual master does not con-figure systems or coherent doctrines aimed at offering an ultimate image or understanding of reality. The spiritual master maintains a state of freedom and authenticity; in doing so, he avoids producing, imprinting or imposing counterfeit "faces", and always expresses, in a unique way, the uniqueness of a particular situation or state.

In this light, any endeavour to approach the divine nature by interposing an image, configu-ration or articulation with claims to explicative value is nothing but a deviation, in the form of a mental projection meant to replace the ultimate principle, by insinuating itself as the sole path and ultimate truth.

Therefore, knowledge acquired via initiation is never meant to become collective; it remains subjective and thus authentic, unique, inalienable. It in fact rejects political expression in the form of the many reduced to a multitude by following the same path. The perspective is reversed: the path takes its unique course for each and every follower.

Otherwise, we may talk about "series of followers". Whenever a path is clearly artic-ulated, described in detail, and imposed as a model or formula, the political dimension becomes manifest.

It is the same distinction we may make when talking, for example, about the different objects created by an artist and the same kind of objects produced in a series, which are seemingly identical because they have the same pattern. The former objects, made by the artist, are unique and individual, bearing a "personalised", authentic message, whereas the latter objects irritate due to the "power" of their message trying to impose and multiply the same "face"; each object in this second category gives the impression that it can at any time replace or be replaced by any other similar object from the same series, while the author himself usually remains unknown, since his imprint is neither personal nor personalised.

Man creates objects that claim to be identical. One cannot find, in nature, two perfectly identical objects or entities. The desire brutally and commercially to multiply and reproduce the same message and thus to impose it by sheer numbers is political in nature and points toward an understanding of a sense of community that distorts by obliging every follower to borrow the same unspecific, unnatural and unauthentic "face".

How then might uniqueness be regained in the communal (and political) context? In other words, what, in this case, would be the new "face" of authority, regarded not as an imposing power, but as a creative one, which would enable re-formation and re-orientation toward one's own path?

The answer formulated by political theories generally comes under the category of utopian visions.

Within the religious framework, the answer is offered by the oral traditions which propose the transmission of knowledge via initiation.

In Judaism, the highest and most suggestive formula to express this relation is "mouth to mouth" or "face to face" (with reference to God and Moses). The authenticity of oral culture, as well as its power, perceived as "invisible" authority, is easily recognisable in any religious tradition whenever it makes reference to its (auroral) "contexts" characterized by the oral. What does the written text change in the process of transmitting the message by using imprinted materials? The written text endangers the message itself, which borrows the same (graphic or graven) "face", being apparently available (and identical) to everyone in the community that tries to approach it. Moreover, the message is endangered a second time due to the potential for the imposition of a common understanding of the text, thus obliterating the original or authentic message. Whenever reference is made not to the text itself, but to a commonly accepted understanding of the text, the political dimension prevails. The text meant to bear witness to a unique and authentic message is abusively (and ideologically) replaced by a distorted, uniform interpretation.

Texts, the same as things and beings, are unique, not only in themselves, but also (and especially) in relation to the "reader". Uniqueness is manifest not only at the level of the essence (in that it is one particular thing rather than another), but especially at the level of the relation (as a being together). Any existence essentially rests under the sign of the relation. In this case, how could we impose on a text the way it should "face" (or relate to) its reader?

To accept uniqueness and allow it to be unveiled as a relation means to renounce ideology and propaganda, and to put forward a new "face" for authority.

More is different.[10] Many does not mean each is the same, but each is unique.

Through its highest message, spirituality offers a path without boundaries, a path which is built with every step while advancing, thus opening the way for the manifestation of the sacred, made possible only by reducing to silence any personal project or deflecting any intervention rooted in systems or articulations designed to substitute for reality. In other words, the world we live in and what we are depend on our mental projections. The reconfiguration of self-perception (and self-identity) will entail successive reconfigurations of the way we perceive the world (and vice versa).

The Religious and the Spiritual: A Necessary Distinction

Any message propagated at the level of the community will inevitably be contaminated by the risk of becoming ideological from the outset. If its authority is also imposed at the institutional level, then political contamination will be obvious.

The religious or spiritual experience, once transferred in an articulated manner, becomes theology, acquiring, by assuming authority, a political dimension as well.

At this point, a distinction is required in order adequately to approach the understanding of religious experience.

The methodological distinction I propose is that between "religious" and "spiritual". This differentiation is meant to distinguish between an ideologically contaminated message and one freed from doctrinal or systematic constraints.

The religious message belongs to a specific system described as religion, theology or religious tradition, whereas the spiritual message is personal and resists any systematic appropriation.[11] Buddha was not a Buddhist, Christ was not a Christian, Muhammad was not a Muslim, in the same way in which we cannot say that someone is born a carpenter, a journalist or a cook. All these "attributes", denoting a belonging to a specific system (be it religious, political or professional), appear on the scene *post factum*. Ideologies are the same: they intervene in an abusive way. The spiritual message is born as such, and it naturally emerges without being forged within the framework of any doctrinal or systematic approach. The spiritual message is not "added". It emerges from within. Imposition is present whenever one form suffocates the other. Ideology strangles and suffocates the pre-existent "strata", whereas the spiritual message transfigures, without remainder.

By its very nature, personal experience is never ideologically framed. It organically eludes any system. The natural follows "systems" other than the ideological, the counterfeit.

Religion, inasmuch as it institutes itself as a system to be imposed or embraced, comes under the reign of the ideological. Any structure, configuration or ideational system embodied within a predictable doctrine becomes, through instrumentation, an ideology. Freed from any political claim, these structures are the expression of a natural, disinterested phenomenality.

The ideological is founded on the obstinacy of incarceration, always insisting on imposing a form through aggression toward others.

Religion, taken as a system, is ideological in nature, whereas spirituality rejects any doctrinal framework and preserves what is unique, unrepeatable, authentic. Preaching authenticity means a programmatic renunciation of any "content" which might be transferred or adopted as such. This, for example, is the difference between giving someone a fish and teaching him how to fish.

The spiritual message is characterised by its gratuitousness. It emerges without any systematic "intent", as a purified expression of the transcendent principle, which can never be "captured" or enclosed within a system.

Spirituality supposes the unforeseen and perpetual spontaneity. Religion grants safety and stability, as if conferring "life insurance", or even "next life insurance", depending on the "system".

This is why we always say "spiritual master", but never "religious master".

Religion and Authority

Religious traditions display, according to the specific features and "imaginaire" of a particular culture, make manifest the relationship between man and ultimate principle (regardless of different means of describing, imagining or interpreting it) in different ways. Religious systems, however coherent they might be, are thus meant to provide a "vehicle" to preserve and transfer this relation through texts, techniques, practices or rites that have the power to reinstitute, perpetuate and reenhance the connection for oneself, as well as for others. This intermediating power should not confer grandness and authority upon the system, but rather it should point toward the grandeur and authority of the ultimate principle as it reveals itself and makes itself present and manifest through the system. The repeatability of ritual refreshes and nuances the relation, endowing it with rhythm and continuity.

Consequently, any petrifaction and imposition of a religious system in order to preserve and perpetuate the authority of that system, as higher than and a substitution for the ultimate principle, represents a deviation from the authentic relation, which is thus replaced by "idolatry". The founding principle is reduced to and identified with the system being proselytised.

In this light, several levels of interreligious communication are to be discerned, according to the emphasis placed on communication among religious systems themselves or between man and the ultimate principle through the intermediary of religious systems.

Schematically, I would represent these different layers as follows:

Reference points	Spiritual authority	Political authority
man	- spiritual master/leader - intermediary	- political leader - head
system	- liturgical value - to intermediate - presence of the principle	- ideological value - to manipulate - obnubilation of the principle
principle	- authenticity - non-system	- deviation, substitution - reversal of the principle-system

The "religious", as a category, might thus be situated between the "spiritual" and the "political", since it incorporates and is contaminated by both registers.

Consequently, religious communities will also bear a more spiritual or political imprint.

The stronger the ideological dimension, the less evident the possibility of regaining an authentic relationship, as the system gradually replaces the principle.

The stronger the liturgical dimension, the more evident the possibility of an authentic relationship emerging, as the system itself is receptive to intermediating the manifestation of the principle.

The two possible moves, if we take into consideration the methodological distinction between spiritual and political authority, are, metaphorically, the "descent" of the principle and the "ascent" of the system.

The consequences are in each and every case different:

The "descent" of the principle invigorates the system by strengthening its power to intermediate. In this way, the system does not become petrified or mere reflection of the human mind, but rather unites the different levels of the hierarchy in a creative manner, functioning as a ladder between man and the founding principle.

The "ascent" of the system implies the dethronement of the principle and its substitution with a "graven image" or idol. The system, separated from its founding principle, is no longer able to function as an intermediary and thus becomes a rigid structure, proliferating and striving to impose itself as the principle or the unique path leading to the principle.

Interreligious communication will develop differently, according to the pre-eminence granted to spiritual or, contrariwise, political authority.

Once these precautionary steps have been taken, we may move on to an outline of the different types and mechanisms of interreligious communication, making reference to the methodological distinctions put forward and explained in this study.

Political Authority and Ecumenism

Interreligious communication, as a political *desideratum* and consequently as a political programme, is instantiated in its weak form as religious tolerance and, in its stronger version, as ecumenism. The latter excludes any differentiation among religious systems or doctrines recurring to criteria that lead to any possible kind of discrimination (ethnical, political, religious etc.).

This understanding of interreligious (and interdenominational) dialogue recognises the intrinsic value of every religious system and promotes freedom of belief, placing the emphasis on religious cohabitation and avoidance of religious conflict.

Communication is not real, but desirable and encouraged. Ecumenism in fact programmatically proposes and provides arguments for non-violence and the equality of religions.

The higher dimension of ecumenism is developed by bringing together, within different frameworks and contexts, representatives of the cohabitant religions, in order to build a bridge between different doctrines and thus to enhance real dialogue.

The academic milieu might offer, in this respect, an adequate, neutral framework for discussion and research *sine ira et studio*.

In conclusion, the axis of ecumenism is represented by the communication of the systems, its stake being mainly political.

Spiritual Authority and "The Peace of Religions"

As a mirror image, spiritual communication among religions would no longer place at the forefront the problem of religious toleration and cohabitation, but would concentrate on bringing religious systems together in the (common) search for an approach to the ultimate principle, in order to reinstitute and deepen the human/divine relationship.

As a result, the axis is now represented by the man/ultimate principle relationship, the various systems, doctrines and theories brought into discussion being instrumental and secondary. I have called this *modus* of interreligious co-operation "the peace of religions", borrowing the suggestive formula introduced by Nicolaus Cusanus.

This understanding of the religious dialogue reveals the positive dimension of interreligious communication that is no longer placed under the sign of avoidance of conflicts and promotion of co-operation, but is reinstituted out of a desire to impart and share knowledge.

At this level, communication overcomes the reserved, cautious and timid attitude, since it takes as a premise familiarity to be pre-existent by the virtue of the ultimate principle that bestows unity in diversity. This unity, however, is not the unity of doctrine, but the unity that expresses itself through multiplicity[12]. The new stage shifts the attention from the unity of one's belief or doctrine to the unembodied unity of the ultimate principle unveiled in multiple forms, dimensions or attributes.

"Peace" is not instituted *between* or *among* systems, but emerges in the meantime through recognition of the principle.

This is the postulate formulated by Frithjof Schuon in terms of the "transcendent unity of religions"[13].

The solution is not to reduce a system to the matrix of the other or to reduce multiple systems to a general matrix for the sake of "peaceful" uniformity. Communication does not imply annulment of diversity or the particular features of the different systems, and it does not derive from the imposition and promotion of one doctrine or opinion over others. The peace of religions, as formulated here, is fundamentally correlated to the unity of the ultimate principle and does not derive from the imposition of one system as the principle of unity. By its status, every system belongs to the realm of created things, and thus, to the realm of multiplicity. Only the unity of the ultimate principle is absolute, since only the ultimate principle is the unlimited One.

Whereas René Guénon endeavoured to substantiate the communicability of the religious systems by highlighting common or complementary symbols, themes and meanings, Frithjof Schuon goes further, leaving the level of "system to system" communication behind, and pointing toward the communication of systems by virtue of the ultimate principle.

The "peace of religions" moves the stress from systems and theories to the personal authentic human/divine relation.

In this new light, development and evolution can no longer be conceived in terms of the elaboration and improvement of systems, but in terms of recovery of the human/divine person-alised relationship by means of personal development.

Education and Interreligious Communication

Such a significant reversal would implicitly lead to a substantial reform of the educational system.

The passage from a weak understanding of interreligious communication to educational systems that promote ecumenism in its highest version is already perceptible.

Taking into consideration, for example, the case of the educational systems in the post-com-munist countries, the precarious diversity of the denominational programmes (usually organised within theology faculties or departments) still preserves (or even recalls) the atmosphere of religious toleration. At the same time, interdenominational and nondenominational Religious Studies programmes are developed within official academic frameworks.

The further opening toward developing programmes unshackled to "disciplinarity" is to be found only in countries with a tradition of promoting ecumenism *de facto*. I refer to the development of new multiand meta-disciplinary frameworks and projects intended to unite specialists and researchers from different fields (including Theology and Religious Studies) in a common approach focused on issues relevant to the understanding of the "ultimate reality".

I would underline, in this respect, the endeavour to develop new fields and research areas such as the study of consciousness (bringing together specialists and researchers in the natural sciences: Neurobiology, Biochemistry, Microbiology, Brain Computer Interfaces, Theoretical Physics, Applied Mathematics, etc.) or contemplative sciences (initiated by Buddhist monks in cooperation with Western scientists).[14]

Multi-disciplinarity and meta-disciplinarity[15] are not meant to reduce the religious phenom-enon to a mere scientific experiment or ideology, but rather to foster educational paradigms able to develop new frameworks for emerging fields of research.

Religious Minorities and Ecumenism

In this new light, how might we reconfigure the debate about religious minorities and com-munication with them? What are the particular features of this debate in Central and Eastern Europe? A possible answer might be provided by a consideration of the concretisation of the relationship between political and religious authority in this particular context.

Terms such as "religion", "minority", "denomination", in their plural form ("religions", "minori-ties", "denominations"), refer to different groups and communities embracing a system, a doctrine or a set of beliefs and practices, which confer, by adherence to them, a group identity.

The denominations have distinguished themselves mainly based on their doctrine, whereas minorities are to be defined in their correlation with the (numerical or political) majority. Con-sequently, religious minorities are to be understood by reference to the correlative religious majority. In non-democratic countries, the religious majority is defined by its adherence to the "official religion" or "state-religion"; in this case, the religious minorities are subordinated and marginalized, functioning as a tolerated "periphery".

What does "religious minority" mean? The criterion for establishing a hierarchy is related either to the small number of adherents, without involving any other value judgement, or to the precarious political status of the respective community, in comparison with the officially favoured religion.

Thus, the only option left is value judgement, which supposes the hierarchy of the religions themselves; this perspective is rejected *de iure* in democratic countries, but accepted *de facto* in countries which promote the principles of democracy without succeeding in putting them into practice.

In communist and post-communist countries, for example, the Christian religion functioned and was "naturalised" as a state religion; for a long period of time, there was no religious education in terms of actually promoting tolerance or interreligious dialogue.

What are the effects of this situation today?

The majority, who embraced the official religion without necessarily practising it, also uncritically adopted the ideology that claimed the superiority of that religion as the sole depository of the truth.

Openness toward ecumenism, politically required by the shift from a dictatorial regime, has provoked in these countries several reactions that are difficult for neighbouring countries with longer democratic traditions to understand. To be more exact, the passage from the recognition of one religion to acceptance of the equality of all cohabitant denominations is slow and onerous, and comes up against the resistance of the erstwhile "first religion", which loses its political prerogatives.

In these circumstances, the "defeated" religion will nonetheless fight for authority, this time invoking numerical (non-political) superiority in order to preserve its supremacy. Maintaining and increasing the number of its followers becomes the instrument for preservation or recovery of (political) authority.

The new situation may be described as follows: officially, the "defeated" religion sustains and promotes ecumenism (in accordance with the official political requirements), whereas unofficially, in its own places of worship and before its adherents, it preaches, even more than before, its superiority, as well as the duty and need to be intolerant toward all the other denominations, which are regarded and presented as the incarnation of evil.

The demonisation of other religious traditions and the practice of superficial ecumenical tolerance, as a mere political interface, emerging in official contexts alone, lead, for the moment, to the impossibility of attaining any *de facto* the level of interreligious communication.

Any debate regarding religious minorities in a particular context will inevitably refer to political and geopolitical reference points, when the topic of spatial demarcation is touched upon. "Central and Eastern Europe", for example, would function, in the framework of such a debate, as part of a "map" which is politically defined, and delineated.[16] It is not an area we delimit and identify in purely geographical terms; on the contrary, "Central and Eastern Europe" is particularised as such according to criteria other than neutral geographical ones; it actually represents a geographical area delimitated by political boundaries on a political map.

From a religious perspective, "Central and Eastern Europe" is characterised by features deriving from the specific way this area has evolved historically and politically. We may, on the one hand, talk about the secularisation of religion in particular institutionalised forms, and, on the other, about the evolution and dynamic of these developed forms, according to the different political regimes which have regulated and imposed power (and authority) relations.

Ioan Petru Coulianu[17] proposes a binary model to explain the functioning and generation of the mind, showing that different systems of thought are produced by different combinations which cover a map of all the existing possibilities for the creation of combinations. These *mind games* generate diverse and diversified structures, which partly overlap and communicate. Each of the mind-generated systems has the same legitimacy, as value judgements, at this level, are pointless and superfluous. To the question of how it nevertheless comes about that in history some models and systems prevail and impose themselves over others, Ioan Petru Culianu answers by distinguishing between "mind games" and "power games". Since every single mind-generated model has the same value in the mind realm, the actualisation and imposition of one possibility chosen from among others is a matter of power. The mind game would thus imply absolute freedom in terms of the generation of models and constraining power in terms of the actualisation and imposition of systems in history.

In conclusion, the power play between spiritual and political authority reconfigures the map of religions and the framework of interreligious communication.

The political *desideratum* of interreligious communication finds its model in ecumenism, whereas the spiritual *desideratum* puts forward "the peace of religions".

Once taken to its final outcome, the accomplishment of the spiritual *desideratum* might be illustrated suggestively, from a Christian perspective, by the image of the messianic age.

Notes

1   Acknowledgements: This work was supported by the strategic grant POSDRU/89/1.5/S/62259, Project *Applied social, human and political sciences. Postdoctoral training and postdoctoral fellowships in social, human and political sciences* cofinanced by the European Social Fund with the Sectorial Operational Program *Human Resources Development 2007–2013.*

2   The formula *pax fidei* introduced by Nicolaus Cusanus in his treatise of the same name (*De pace fidei*) was translated by "peace of belief" (literal translation) or "peace of religion(s)" (figurative meaning).

3   Different perspectives and methods (historical, theological, philological, philosophical, sociological, anthropological, phenomenological, integrative etc.), stressing either the experiential dimension (practice, techniques, ritual) or the philosophical and hermeneutical approach (text, discourse, hermeneutical devices, interpretation) are used, most of the time independently, in the research area of Religious Studies. This is why, in the present study, special attention was paid, contextually speaking, to authors combining the applied analysis of the religious experience

and the philosophical interpretation using hermeneutical devices (e.g., Rudolf Otto, Mircea Eliade, Giuseppe Tucci, Henry Corbin, Gershom Scholem, Henri de Lubac, Frithjof Schuon, Vladimir Lossky, Roberte Hamayon, Moshe Idel, Jean-Luc Marion). Insofar as the interreligious perspective is concerned, the research conformed to the methodological concept of *perspectivism* as reformulated by Moshe Idel: "By this concept [perspectivism] I designate the possibility of interrogating a certain religious literature from the perspective of acquaintance with another religious literature. This is neither a matter of comparison [...], nor a case of historical filiation between two bodies of writing or thought. It is rather an attempt to better understand the logic of systems by comparing substantially different ones and learning about one from the other". Moshe Idel, *Ascensions on High in Jewish Mysticism: Pillars, Lines, Ladders*, (Budapest/New York: Central European University Press, 2005), 11.

4   For the different interpretations regarding the meanings and mechanisms of ideology and its relation to religion, see: Peter Scott, *Theology, Ideology and Liberation*, Series: *Cambridge Studies in Ideology and Religion* (Cambridge: Cambridge University Press, 1994), Karl Mannheim, *Ideology and Utopia* (London: Routledge, 1936), Michael Freeden, *Ideologies and Political Theory: A Conceptual Approach* (Oxford: Oxford University Press, 1996), David Hawkes, *Ideology* (London: Routledge, 2003), Slavoj Zizek, *The Sublime Object of Ideology* (New York: Verso, 1989), Terry Eagleton, *Ideology. An introduction*, (New York: Verso, 1991). For the ideological dimension in configuring and developing the Religious Studies area from the educational point of view, see: Timothy Fitzgerald, *The Ideology of Religious Studies. Contributors* (New York: Oxford University Press, 2000).

5   See Eric Voegelin, *Modernity Without Restraint*, *Collected Works*, Volume 5 (Columbia: University of Missouri Press, 2000), 19–74.

6   Spinoza, *Theological-Political Treatise*, trans. and ed. Samuel Shirley (Indianapolis: Hackett Publishing House, 2001).

7   See, for instance, Clara Auvray-Assayas, "Religio", in *Vocabulaire européen des philosophies* (Paris: Le Seuil/Le Robert, 2004).

8   For the relation between religion and the study of consciousness, see Philip Clayton et. al., *The Re-Emergence of Emergence. The Emergentist Hypothesis from Science to Religion*, ed. Philip Clayton and Paul Davies (Oxford: Oxford University Press, 2006), and Philip Clayton, *Mind and Emergence. From Quantum to Consciousness* (Oxford: Oxford University Press, 2004).

9   See René Descartes, *Discours de la méthode* (Paris: Librairie Philosophique J. Vrin -Bibliothèque des textes philosophiques, 1987).

10   The formula was introduced by P.W. Anderson in "More is different", *Science*, New Series 177, 4047 (1972): 393–396.

11   For the various definitions and interpretations of spirituality in its connectedness to religion, see: W. James, *The varieties of religious experience* (Cambridge, MA: Harvard University Press, 1985), Kees Waaijman, *Spirituality: forms, foundations, methods* (Leuven: Peeters, 2002), Dalai Lama, *Ethics for the New Millennium* (NY: Riverhead Books, 1999), Michael Hogan, *The Culture of Our Thinking in Relation to Spirituality* (New York: Nova Science Publishers, 2010), Matthew Alper, *The*

"God" Part of the Brain: A Scientific Interpretation of Human Spirituality and God (Naperville, Illinois: Sourcebooks, Inc., 2008).

12 For the dynamics between unity and multiplicity in religious and theological context, and the critical understanding of monotheism, see: Henry Corbin, *Le paradoxe du monothéisme* (Paris: L'Herne, 1981), T. W. Jennings, *Beyond Theism: A Grammar of God-Language* (New York: Oxford University Press, 1985), Laurel Schneider, *Beyond Monotheism: A theology of multiplicity* (New York: Routledge, 2008), M. Smith, *The Early History of God: Yahweh and Other Deities in Ancient Israel* (New York: Harper & Row, 1990) and *The Origins of Biblical Monotheism: Israel's Polytheistic Background and the Ugaritic Texts* (Oxford: Oxford University Press, 2001), J. Kirsch, *God Against the Gods: The History of the War Between Monotheism and Polytheism* (New York: Penguin, 2004), Loren Stuckenbruck and Wendy North, *Early Jewish and Christian monotheism* (London: T&T Clark, 2004), Harry A.Wolfson, *The Philosophy of the Church Fathers, Faith, Trinity, Incarnation* (Cambridge: Harvard University Press, 1956), Michael Taylor, *Theological Reflections: On the Trinity, Christology, and Monotheism* (Lanham: University Press of America, 2002).

13 Frithjof Schuon, *De l'Unité Transcendante des Religions* (Paris: Gallimard, 1948).

14 See, for example, http://www.cbs.mpg.de/index.html,
http://consciousness.arizona.edu/index.htm,
http://www.colorado.edu/research/,http://www.mindandlife.org/,
http://www.contemplativemind.org/,
http://www.brown.edu/Faculty/Contemplative_Studies_Initiative/etc.

15 For a meaning analysis with regard to the emerging features of metadisciplinarity, see: Michael Finkenthal, *Interdisciplinarity. Toward the Definition of a Metadiscipline?*, American University Studies, Series V, Philosophy, vol. 187 (New York: Peter Lang Publishing, 2001).

16 See Larry Wolff, *Inventing Eastern Europe: the Map of Civilisation on the Mind of the Enlightenment* (Stanford: Stanford University Press, 1994). For a complex analysis regarding the religious boundaries of Central and Eastern Europe, see Monica Neațu, "Ortodoxie şi catolicism în Europa sud-estică în prima jumătate a secolului al XIII-lea" (PhD diss., University of Bucharest, 2008).

17 See Ioan Petru Coulianu, *The Tree of Gnosis: Gnostic Mythology from Early Christianity to Modern Nihilism*, trans. Hilary Suzanne Wiesner and I.P. Coulianu (San Francisco: HarperSanFrancisco, 1992).

References

Alper, Matthew. *The "God" Part of the Brain: A Scientific Interpretation of Human Spirituality and God*. Naperville, Illinois: Sourcebooks, Inc., 2008.

Clayton, Philip, Paul C.W. Davies, Erich Joos, George F. R. Ellis, Terrence W. Deacon, Lynn J. Rothschild, Barbara Smuts, Jaegwon Kim, Michael Silberstein, Nancey Murphy, David J. Chalmers, Arthur Peacocke, and Niels Henrik Gregersen. *The Re-Emergence of Emergence. The Emergentist Hypothesis from Science to Religion*. Edited by Philip Clayton and Paul Davies. Oxford: Oxford University Press, 2006.

Clayton, Philip. *Mind and Emergence. From Quantum to Consciousness*. Oxford: Oxford University Press, 2004.

Corbin, Henry. *Le paradoxe du monothéisme*. Paris : L'Herne, 1981.

Corbin, Henry. Mundus imaginalis *or the Imaginary and the Imaginal*. Suffolk: Golgonooza Press, 1976.

Couliano, Ioan Petru. *The Tree of Gnosis: Gnostic Mythology from Early Christianity to Modern Nihilism*. Translated by Hilary Suzanne Wiesner and I.P. Coulianu. San Francisco: HarperSanFrancisco, 1992.

Cusanus, Nicolaus. De pace fidei *and* Cribratio Alkorani. Translated by Jasper Hopkins. Minneapolis: Arthur J. Banning Press, 1994.

Dalai Lama. *Ethics for the New Millennium*. NY: Riverhead Books, 1999.

Descartes, René. *Discours de la méthode*. Paris: Librairie Philosophique J. Vrin—Bibliothèque des textes philosophiques, 1987.

Eagleton, Terry. *Ideology. An introduction*. New York: Verso, 1991.

Eliade, Mircea. *Shamanism: Archaic Techniques of Ecstasy*. Translated by W.R. Trask. London: Routledge and Kegan Paul, 1964.

Eliade, Mircea. *The Sacred and the Profane: The Nature of Religion*. Translated by W.R. Trask. New York: Harvest/HBJ Publishers, 1957.

Finkenthal, Michael. *Interdisciplinarity. Toward the Definition of a Metadiscipline?*. American University Studies, Series V, Philosophy, vol. 187. New York: Peter Lang Publishing, 2001.

Fitzgerald, Timothy. *The Ideology of Religious Studies. Contributors*. New York: Oxford University Press, 2000.

Freeden, Michael. *Ideologies and Political Theory: A Conceptual Approach*. Oxford: Oxford University Press, 1996.

Frithjof, Schuon. *De l'Unité Transcendante des Religions*. Paris: Gallimard, 1948.

Hamayon, Roberte. *La chasse à l'âme. Equisse d'une théorie du chamanisme sibérien*. Nanterre: Société d'ethnologie, 1990.

Hawkes, David. *Ideology*. London: Routledge, 2003.

Hogan, Michael. *The Culture of Our Thinking in Relation to Spirituality*. New York: Nova Science Publishers, 2010.

Idel, Moshe. *Absorbing Perfections: Kabbalah and Interpretation*. New Haven&London: Yale University Press, 2002.

Idel, Moshe. *Ascensions on High in Jewish Mysticism: Pillars, Lines, Ladders*. Budapest/New York: Central European University Press, 2005.

Idel, Moshe. *The Mystical Experience in Abraham Abulafia*. Translated by Jonathan Chipman. Albany: SUNY Press, 1988.

James, W. *The varieties of religious experience*. Cambridge, MA: Harvard University Press, 1985.

Jennings, T. W. *Beyond Theism: A Grammar of God-Language*. New York: Oxford University Press, 1985.

Kirsch, J. *God Against the Gods: The History of the War Between Monotheism and Polytheism*. New York: Penguin, 2004.

Lossky, Vladimir. *The Mystical Theology of the Eastern Church*. New York: St. Vladimir's Seminar Press, 1976.

Mannheim, Karl. *Ideology and Utopia*. London: Routledge, 1936.

Marion, Jean-Luc. *L'Idole et la distance*. Paris: Livre de Poche, 1991.

Neațu, Monica. "Ortodoxie și catolicism în Europa sud-estică în prima jumătate a secolului al XIII-lea". PhD diss., University of Bucharest, 2008.

Otto, Rudolf. *The Idea of the Holy*. London: Oxford University Press, 1958.

Schneider, Laurel. *Beyond Monotheism: A theology of multiplicity*. New York: Routledge, 2008.

Scholem, Gershom. *On the Mystical Shape of the Godhead: Basic Concepts in the Kabbalah*. Translated by Joachin Neugroshel, Edited by Jonathan Chipman. New York: Schocken Books, 1991.

Scott, Peter. *Theology, Ideology and Liberation*, Series: *Cambridge Studies in Ideology and Religion*. Cambridge: Cambridge University Press, 1994.

Smith, M. *The Early History of God: Yahweh and Other Deities in Ancient Israel*. New York: Harper & Row, 1990.

Smith, M. *The Origins of Biblical Monotheism: Israel's Polytheistic Background and the Ugaritic Texts*. Oxford: Oxford University Press, 2001.

Spinoza. *Theological-Political Treatise*. Trans. and edited with Notes and Commentary by Samuel Shirley. Indianapolis: Hackett Publishing, 2001.

Stuckenbruck, Loren, and Wendy North. *Early Jewish and Christian monotheism*. London: T&T Clark, 2004.

Taylor, Michael. *Theological Reflections: On the Trinity, Christology, and Monotheism*. Lanham: University Press of America, 2002.

Tucci, Giuseppe. *The Religions of Tibet*. Translated by Geoffrey Samuel. London: Routledge & Kegan Paul, 2000.

Voegelin, Eric. *Modernity Without Restraint, Collected Works*, Volume 5. Columbia: University of Missouri Press, 2000.

Waaijman, Kees. *Spirituality: forms, foundations, methods*. Leuven: Peeters, 2002.

Wolff, Larry. *Inventing Eastern Europe: the Map of Civilisation on the Mind of the Enlightenment*. Stanford: Stanford University Press, 1994.

Wolfson, Harry A. *The Philosophy of the Church Fathers, Faith, Trinity, Incarnation*. Cambridge: Harvard University Press, 1956.

Zizek, Slavoj. *The Sublime Object of Ideology*. New York: Verso, 1989.

Activities for Further Exploration and Discussion

Assignment

For each of the following videos, blogs, and/or readings, have students complete the following:

> Based on what you learned in the video and the article you read, reflect on your new/revised understanding of religions, religious beliefs, and its potential effects.

Article

Read the article. Use the questions that follow to complete your reaction paper.

Article: Maller, "Are Jews a nation, a Religion or a Race?"

https://tinyurl.com/ybxyurrt

1. Jewish: Is it a race, religion, or ethnicity?
2. What does Muslim law say?
3. Can you become Jewish?
4. If you can become Jewish or Muslim, can it be a race?

Blog Post

Read the descriptions of each war. Use the questions that follow to complete your reaction paper.

Blog: "10 Biggest Religious Wars Ever Fought"

https://tinyurl.com/yaqqy4wq

Religion is one of the most sensitive issues, and although every religion encourages the idea of peace and tolerance, almost no one remains in peace or tolerates anything when it comes to others' religion. History is full of religious wars, and some of them have continued for years and killed many. Here is the list of 10 of the biggest wars that were fought over religious conflicts and differences counting down from number 10 to number 1.

10.   Second War of Kappel

9.   Lebanese Civil War

8.   The Crusades

7.   Second Sudanese Civil War

6.   First Sudanese Civil War

5.   German Peasants' War

4.   Nigerian Civil War

3.   French Wars of Religion

2.   Thirty Years' War

1.   Eighty Years' War

Suggestion: Have students form groups and answer the following questions or complete the reaction paper assignment on their own.

1.   What other religious wars are not included on the list?
2.   Which war stood out to the group the most? Why?

Reaction to 9/11 Article

Suggestion: Have students read this article before class and answer the question by writing a reflection paper. Use class time to facilitate discussion.

Article: Hope and Despair: Being Muslim in America After 9/11

https://tinyurl.com/zroutay

1.   How can you hold the religion accountable for its extremist fractions? Provide details to support your answers.

References

Anonymous. (2005). Hinduism. *Nursing Management, 12*(6), 8–10.

Barrett, D. A. (2001). *World Christian encyclopedia* (2nd ed.). Oxford University Press.

Beyers, J. (2017). Religion and culture: Revisiting a close relative. *HTS Theological Studies, 73*(1), 1–9.

Casares, A. M., & Delaigue, C. (2013). The evangelization of freed and slave Black Africans in Renaissance Spain: Baptism, marriage and ethnic brotherhoods. *History of Religions, 52*(3), 214–235.

Company, R. F. (2012). Religious repertoires and contestation: A case study on Buddhist miracle tales. *History of Religions, 52*(2), 99–141.

Fabricant, D. S. (1993). Thomas R. Gray and William Styron: Finally, a critical look at the 1831 "Confessions of Nat Turner." *American Journal of Legal History, 37*(3), 332–361.

Few-Demo, A. L., Humble, A. M., Curran, M. A., & Lloyd, S. A. (2016). Queer theory, intersectionality, and LGBT-parent families: Transformative critical pedagogy in family theory. *Journal of Family Theory & Review, 8*(1), 74–94.

Hacker, P. (2006). Dharma in Hinduism. *Journal of Indian Philosophy, 34*(5), 479–496.

Hackett, C. & McClendon, D. (2017, April 5). *Christians remain world's largest religious group, but they are declining in Europe.* Pew Research Center. https://www.pewresearch.org/fact-tank/2017/04/05/christians-remain-worlds-largest-religious-group-but-they-are-declining-in-europe/

Hayward, R. D., & Kemmelmeier, M. (2011). Weber revisited: A cross-national analysis of religiosity, religious culture, and economic attitudes. *Journal of Cross-Cultural Psychology, 42*(8), 1406–1420.

Presidential Proclamation 9645 and Presidential Proclamation 9983. (2018, June 26). Retrieved from https://travel.state.gov/content/travel/en/us-visas/visa-information-resources/presidential-proclamation-archive/presidential-proclamation9645.html?wcmmode=disabled

Kunka, A. J. (2011). Intertextuality of the historical graphic narrative: Kyle Baker's "Nat Turner" and the Styron controversy. *College Literature, 38*(3), 168–193.

McRae, J. R. (1995). Buddhism. *The Journal of Asian Studies, 54*(2), 354–371.

Mehta, P. B. (2004). World religions and democracy: Hinduism and self-rule. *Journal of Democracy, 15*(3), 108–121.

Merriam-Webster. (n.d.). *Animism.* https://www.merriamwebster.com/dictionary/animism

Pyysiäinen, I. (2003). Buddhism, religion, and the concept of "God." *Numen, 50*(2), 147–171.

Olsson, S., & Stenberg, L. (2015). Engaging the history of religions-from an Islamic studies perspective. *The Finnish Society for the Study of Religion, Temenos, 51*(2), 201–225.

Ristuccia, N. J. (2013). Eastern religions and the West: The making of an image. *History of Religions, 53*(2), 170–204.

Saroglou, V. (2011). Believing, bonding, behaving, and belonging: The big four dimensions and cultural variation. *Journal of Cross-Cultural Psychology, 42*(8), 1320–1340

Sharma, I., Pandit, B., Pathak, A., & Sharma, R. (2013). Hinduism, marriage and mental illness. *Indian Journal of Psychiatry, 55*(2), S243–S249. https://doi.org/10.4103/0019-5545.105544

CHAPTER 5

Ageism

A GEISM HAS GARNERED more attention in society and scholarly research in the last 20 years, yet the subject is still understudied (North & Fiske, 2012; Palmore, 1999). Traditionally, more attention has been given to racism and sexism, but the issue of age-based prejudices has come into focus as American society is aging more rapidly and experiencing an increase in life expectancy (International Longevity Center, 2006; Nelson, 2016). This creates a concern for Social Security, the welfare of elders, healthcare, retirement and disability benefits, and the political power of the elderly. The focus of this chapter is to highlight some of the issues related to ageism that are prevalent across these spectrums. These topics, as well as a historical perspective from the United States; an analysis of intersectionality and the ways ageism intersects with race, class, gender, and sexual orientation; and the detrimental effects of ageism, are provided in this text and the selected readings.

Ageism

Ageism is a complicated concept to understand due to its multifaceted nature. Although ageism is usually associated with the treatment of older adults, ageism can be directed to any person or group when age is the discriminatory factor (Butler, 1989; Palmore,1999). Elements of ageism were in existence before the term was coined (Anti-Ageism Taskforce at the International Longevity Center, 2006). Historically, the term was used to describe discrimination against seniors, which Butler modeled after sexism and racism (Butler, 1989). Butler (1989) originally defined ageism as "the systematic stereotyping of and discrimination against people because they are old, just as racism and sexism accomplish this with skin color and gender" (p. 139). Butler (1980) initially characterized ageism with these three interconnected elements:

1) Prejudicial attitudes toward the aged, toward older age, and toward the aging process including attitudes held by the elderly themselves; 2) discriminatory practices against the elderly, particularly in employment, but in other social roles as well; and 3) institutional practices and policies which, often without malice, perpetuate stereotypic beliefs about the elderly, reduce their opportunities for a satisfactory life and undermine their personal dignity (p. 8).

Because of the nature of ageism and its complexity, ageism is often overlooked and disregarded as a discriminatory practice comparable to other minoritized groups. In his research on ageism Palmore (1999) developed criteria to determine if the aged were a minority group using Streib's (1965) model. In this modified model, Palmore submits the following as criteria to determine if the aged are a minority group:

1. **Do elders have identifying characteristics with accompanying status-role expectations throughout the life cycle?** The answer is yes to the first part and no to the second. Yes, most persons older than age 65 possess the identifying characteristics of old age, such as gray hair and wrinkles (unless they are chemically or surgically hidden), and there are accompanying status-role expectations, such as retirement and increasing infirmity. But no, by definition, they do not possess this characteristic throughout life. The fact that they are not born with these characteristics make their problems and opportunities rather different from those of the usual minority groups, such as Black people and women.

2. **Does the majority group hold negative stereotypes about elders? Or, to put it more simply, is there prejudice against elders?** The answer is clearly yes. There are several common kinds of prejudice against the aged. Various studies have shown that most Americans believe that most aged are sick or disabled, senile, impotent, useless, lonely, miserable, and in poverty.

3. **Are the elderly discriminated against?** The answer appears to be no in the area of most civil rights and political power, but in other areas, such as employment, education, government services, and even in the family, the answer is yes.

4. **Are elders a deprived group?** Economically, the aged are no longer a deprived group. They now have less poverty than those under 65 and have a greater proportion of the national personal income than their proportion in the population. Also, there is little residential or institutional segregation of the kind encountered by racial minorities. The main area in which they could be considered deprived is the area of employment; despite laws to the contrary, many are pressured or forced to retire even though they are willing and able to keep working.

5. **Do elders have a sense of group identity or political unity?** The answer appears to be "some do, but the majority don't." Most deny that there is a chronological dividing line marking the beginning of old age (Harris, 1981). They tend to use functional criteria to

identify old age, such as retirement or poor health. As a result of discrimination, many are ashamed of their age, and most resist identification as old or elderly. Elders are at least as heterogeneous in their attitudes, behaviors, and politics as are younger people. There is little or no "aged vote" (Palmore, 1999).

With these criteria, Palmore (1999) suggests that the aged are like other marginalized groups because they are subject to prejudice, discrimination, and deprivation. The modified criteria are an essential springboard to clearly define whether the aged as a general group could be considered a minority group, but this version bears an update since its publication in 1999, particularly the ideas that elders are no longer a deprived group and the political power that the graying population possesses.

In 2016, the median income for older men was $31,618 and $18,380 for older women (Administration for Community Living, 2018). Poverty for individuals 65 and older also increased according to the Supplemental Poverty Measure (SPM) from the U.S. Census Bureau (Fox & Pacas, 2018). The SPM is an extended report that accounts for government assistance programs such as the Supplemental Nutritional Assistance Program (SNAP), school lunches, housing aid, home energy assistance programs, and refundable tax credits, which are programs designed to help low-income families but are not included in the official poverty measure (Fox & Pacas, 2018). In the analysis of the poverty increase, Fox and Pacas (2018) found that the overall population of individuals 65 and older grew slightly from 2015 to 2016 by 3.6%. Furthermore, compared to 2015, Social Security benefits helped fewer individuals 65 and older get out of poverty. Fox and Pacas (2018) attribute the rise in poverty to a "combination of more people remaining poor, fewer people exiting poverty, and/or more people entering poverty" (p. 14), considering that "a substantial part of the growth in poverty is due to the movements across the near-poor groups" (p. 16). However, according to the U.S. Census Bureau (2018), in general, those 65 and older still have a lower poverty rate than those under 65. Nevertheless, that does not negate the fact that millions of older adults struggle to meet monthly expenses.

Poverty is lacking enough money to meet basic needs. According to the Elder Economic Security Standard Index (also referred to as the Elder Index), on average, a retired single, elder homeowner without a mortgage requires $1,672 per month for basic needs; that number increases to $1,947 per month for an individual who rents one bedroom and to $2,581 for a single elder homeowner with a mortgage. For a retired elder couple who owns their home without a mortgage, the monthly required amount for basic needs is $2,548; that number increases to $2,843 if they rent a one-bedroom, and $3,457 if they are homeowners with a mortgage (Gerontology Institute at the University of Massachusetts Boston, 2019). With a rise in the cost of housing, health care, adequate nutrition, transportation, and daily living expenses, one major life event can have an adverse effect on the well-being of older adults.

The U.S. poverty guideline (also referred to as the federal poverty level [FPL]) is used to determine if one is eligible for certain federal programs and assistance. In 2019, the FPL was $12,490 per year for a single person and $16,910 per year for a couple (U.S. Department of

Health and Human Services, 2019). Another program that is offered is the Supplemental Security Income (SSI) program. This program is for disabled adults and children who have limited income, as well as those 65 and older without disabilities who meet financial restrictions. In 2019, those who are eligible can receive a monthly maximum amount of $771 as an individual and $1,157 for a couple (Social Security Administration, 2019).

These current figures revise Palmore's (1999) claim that the aged are no longer a deprived group. Although this group has a lower poverty rate than those under 65, this does not negate the fact that this group still demands attention. Many are not only pressured to retire from careers in which they have devoted decades of time but are also forced to reenter the workforce at lower-paying wages in order to meet the demands of their basic needs. While these poverty guidelines determine eligibility for assistance, poverty itself can have a detrimental effect on health and increase one's vulnerability for poorer social, financial, mental, and emotional well-being.

Without discussing specific political affiliations, but to address Palmore's (1999) fifth criteria, which asks, "Do elders have a sense of group identity or political unity?" (p. 5), the answer provided, and one in which is disagreed with is, "some do, but the majority don't," because there are a number of organizations, specifically for older people, that have astounding membership, which creates a sense of belonging and group identity. Additionally, the gray vote is becoming more powerful in elections in the United States. The critical issues being voted on and advocated for include Medicare, Social Security, prescription drugs healthcare and insurance, caregiving, retirement, and financial security, and taxes (Brown, 2018), to name a few. In fact, data collected for the U.S. Census since 1980 showed that the 2016 U.S. presidential election marked the first time voters 65 and older surpassed the voters who were 30 to 44 years old. The 65 and older age group were the second largest group, surpassed by the 45- to 64-year-old voters, in the 2016 U.S. presidential election (File, 2018). This validates not only the sense of group identity but also the unification of a group through politics, as older adults have come together to vote and advocate for issues that are important and directly affect their well-being. As a result, there is such a thing as an "aged vote."

Furthermore, although one may deny that there is a chronological dividing line marking the beginning of old age, as aforementioned and along with the functional criterion that Palmore offers, one also uses a subjective criterion (how young or old one feels), which has a bearing on perceptions of successful aging, well-being, and health (Kotter-Grühn et a;., 2016). The classification of "old age" is also different culturally and historically (Victor, 2013). Thus, to answer if the elderly is a minority group based on the aforementioned criteria, there is no definitive yes or no answer because there are elements that are similar to traditional minority groups, such as being subjected to prejudice and discrimination. However, unlike other traditional minority groups, an elder is not "born" into this group, and at one point every person will be a member of this group if they live long enough, regardless of if they want to be a member (Palmore, 1999, 2015).

Different Types of Ageism

There are various types of ageism. The Anti-Ageism Taskforce at the International Longevity Center (2006) has defined four types of ageism, the first is personal ageism, which are biased beliefs, attitudes, or ideas because of a person's old age. An example would include subjecting an elder to physical, social, mental, or psychological abuse; social isolation; and perpetuating stereotypes. Next, institutional ageism is the discrimination against older people because of their age that are perpetuated through guidelines, practices, and delegations. A common example is mandatory retirement. Then there is intentional and unintentional ageism. Intentional ageism is knowingly discriminating, taking advantage of, or victimizing an older person. Intentional ageism takes shape in one's attitudes, ideas, policies, and practices or comments. Examples may include financial exploitation, housing scams, or denying a right to work. On the other hand, unintentional ageism is unknowingly discriminating against older people. The contributors to the Anti-Ageism Taskforce at the International Longevity Center (2006) term this "inadvertent ageism" (p. 21). Examples of unintentional ageism may include how older people are portrayed and lack of accessibility concern in public or private spaces (i.e., consideration of the height of the tub/shower when hosting older visitors).

What is commonly presented in the literature is "negative ageism"; however, in addition to negative ageism, "positive ageism" is a type of ageism (Palmore, 1999). Positive ageism is "prejudice and discrimination in favor of the aged" (Palmore, 1999, p. 6). For example, to assume that one is wise because they are older is a form of positive ageism. Positive ageism also presents as much of a problem as negative ageism because it can present itself as an entitlement, a benefit regarding one's age. For example, people expect younger people to give up their seat for older people because of their perceived "frailty."

"Okay, Boomer"

There has been a cross-generational dialog between baby boomers and millennials that has boiled over into a quarrel about issues ranging from boomers criticizing millennials for acting entitled and expecting things to be handed to them without putting in the hard work to an intolerance of elders, to millennials being spaced out, thanks to the internet and technological devices, and having a "Peter Pan syndrome" by not wanting to "adult" or grow up. Millennials have criticized boomers for hoarding wealth, being out of touch by not embracing the changing world and voting to end social programs, and not understanding or empathizing with the worries of the high cost of education and student loan debt, general economic instability, uncertainty of health insurance, rent, or the effects of climate change. The frustration of millennials (those born roughly between 1980–1996) and Generation Z'ers (those born roughly between 1996–2015) has been the creation of the phrase "Okay, Boomer" to sarcastically disregard the narrow-minded and judging attitudes of people, specifically baby boomers. As was stated in the *New York Times* (Lorenz, 2019), "boomer" is having a certain attitude—one who doesn't like change or understand technology or equality. Therefore, anyone can be labeled a "boomer." The ideals of the past generations, such as the resistance to technological advances, denials of the effects of climate change, and the opposition and marginalization of minorities and younger generations have influenced the political, economic, and social sphere in the United States, and "Okay, Boomer" is a dismissal and rejection of the ideals in this unending debate (Romano, 2019). The backlash of the "Okay, Boomer" movement has been that boomers feel the saying is motivated by ageism, in which millennials and Gen Z'ers retort that they are missing the point, which is precisely the point of creating "Okay, Boomer": Boomers are missing the point of embracing the younger generations, failing to see beyond the yesteryears, and failing to acknowledge that the world is changing and that some of the increasing economic, social, and environmental concerns have been caused by the baby boomer generation, and the younger generation is left with the aftermath and cleanup.

Intersectionality of Ageism

The ideas and concepts of *intersectionality* have been discussed by Black activists, feminists, womanists, and Latina, queer, and indigenous scholars (Collins, 2003; Davis, 2008; hooks, 1981; Lorde, 1995) before the term was coined in 1989 by Crenshaw (1989). The idea of intersectionality grew out of race-based and gender-based research, which failed to acknowledge the effects other intersecting identities had on one's lived experiences (McCall, 2005). For example, not attending to the racialized component of a Black woman's life in research negates the intersection of race and gender, allowing for research conducted on Black women to be assessed with their White counterparts, although their experiences are not the same.

Intersectionality and its concepts span across many disciplines (i.e., social sciences, humanities, education, law) and are included in theoretical discussions, as well as taken into consideration in political and educational arenas (Davis, 2008). There are many scholars that have integrated intersectionality in their work as a lens to interrogate ageism and the labor market (Calasanti & King, 2015; McBride et al., 2015; Moore & Ghilarducci, 2018); race, class, and gender (Azulai, 2014; Chrisler et al., 2016; Douglas, 1999; Hankivsky, 2012; Warner, & Brown, 2011); sexual orientation (Cronin, & King, 2010; De Vries, 2014); and religion (McFadden, 1996; Nelson-Beker et al., 2006).

To further explicate intersectionality, Hankivsky (2014), suggests that it

> promotes an understanding of human beings as shaped by the interaction of different social locations (e.g., 'race'/ethnicity, Indigeneity, gender, class, sexuality, geography, age, disability/ability, migration, status, religion). These interactions occur within a context of connected systems and structures of power (e.g., laws, policies, state governments and other political and economic unions, religious institutions, media). Through

such processes, interdependent forms of privilege and oppression shaped by colonial-ism, imperialism, racism, homophobia, ableism, and patriarchy are created (p. 5).

The belief that one's identity must be viewed through the intersections of one's social identity is fundamental to intersectionality (Harrison, 2017). If one is not viewed in those terms, part of one's identity is likely to be diminished, resulting in similar aftermath that people who deal with racism and sexism encounter, such as internalizing abusive messages; anger and self-inflicted prejudice; reduced self-determination; lesser status in society; restriction to education oppor-tunities, employment prospects, and adequate healthcare; adverse health effects; and social and cultural cost of dismissing the wisdom, folk tales, and cultural resources (child care, multigener-ational family units, support, and mentorship) (Achenbaum, 2015; Palmore, 1999; Sue, 2010). This has far-reaching implications as racial and ethnic minority populations have increased and will continue to increase, older women outnumber older men, and more older men are married than older women (Administration for Community Living, 2018).

The Supplemental Security Income figures, poverty guidelines, and other general data that is often presented overlooks the intersectional aspects of the racialized and gendered aspect of poverty for the older adult. Structural forms of inequality exist on many levels and vary among many dimensions, particularly with regard to race, ethnicity, marital status, sexual orientation, income, ability, education, and if one has children (Griffin, 2012). These intersections are also a factor in elder housing and eldercare options.

Social Security is likely a primary source of income for an older person. Social Security is based on how much one has earned during their career. One's work history determines the eligi-bility for retirement or disability benefits (Borland, 2019). Many women choose (or sometimes are forced), in their adult years, when to enter and exit the workforce. Some of those deci-sions are influenced by rearing children and caring for parents or a spouse. Women play many roles while caregiving. In general, daughters provide more caregiving to elder parents than sons, which can lead to a struggle with balancing elder care and employment and with career sacri-fices, lower earnings, financial burdens, and negative mental and physical health consequences (Grigoryeva, 2017). While men do contribute to family and caregiving responsibilities, women are primarily responsible for caregiving duties. This puts women at a disadvantage. Although women have made significant strides, they are still likely to earn less over their lifetimes than men (Bureau of Labor Statistics, 2016; Gould et al., 2016). While women live longer than their male counterparts, they receive lower lifetime earnings and often smaller pensions and other assets upon retirement (Borland, 2019). Thus, the cost impact on women caregivers is approximately $40,000 more than men in lost wages and Social Security benefits (MetLife, 2011). They are also more likely than non-caregivers to live in poverty and receive SSI (Rice University, 2004). Couple that with race, age, socioeconomic status, ability, and marital status (never married, divorced, or widowed), and this may limit access to housing, resources, or elder care and lead to discrimination and displacement. Stereotypes and labels of older adults exacerbate these issues and can lead to residential and social isolation and inadequate care and assistance, which directly affects one's life and well-being, resulting in discrepancies in care, especially for women of color, poor women, lesbian, and older women (Griffin, 2012).

The Effects of Ageism and Microaggressions

Unlike the other "isms" (racism, sexism, and heterosexism), ageism is something that will likely affect everyone (North, 2015). Ageism is complex and sometimes difficult to detect. The subtleties of ageism, like racism, sexism, and homophobia, can appear unnoticed or undetected because many statements can be overlooked until one reflects on what has happened and feels as if they have been slighted or victimized. Moreover, the perpetrator may not realize they are advancing these slights because they can be well-intended behaviors or remarks and the person advancing the discriminatory practice may not be aware of their actions (Sue, 2010). One example would be implying that something that is old is defective or inferior and something that is new, young, or fresh as good (Gendron et al., 2016). Also similar to the other "isms," ageism can persist ingroup as well, as people discriminate against others because of age, which perpetuates internalized ageism (Gendron et al., 2016). These subtle (unintended or intended) statements or actions that debase people are microaggressions (Sue, 2010). Given the nature of intersectionality, older people can encounter microaggressions multiple times throughout the day and in various ways. Microaggressions reach beyond the traditional biases and prejudices against those of different races, classes, and genders. Microaggressions can apply to other marginalized groups (Sue, 2010). Microaggressions "reflect attitudes and beliefs about inclusion/exclusion, superiority/inferiority, healthiness/unhealthiness, and normality/abnormality between groups," and because of this microaggressions can be recognized in nearly all "socially devalued groups" (Sue, 2010, p. vii). They communicate verbal, behavioral, and environmental offenses to marginalized groups (Sue, 2010).

These slights can happen in various contexts such as within the family or at a doctor's office visit. For example, older people generally are not given as much time and care as their younger counterparts by a physician because they are near the end of life (Butler, 1989). When they are seen, older people are often treated as children when visiting the doctor's office with an adult child. This is often illustrated as a conversation ensues about the older patient, but does not include the older patient, inferring that the older person is incoherent or incapable of understanding the doctor's instructions (North & Fiske, 2012).

Furthering this notion is elderspeak (North, 2015), the tone of voice that is used when speaking to older people, which may mimic what is called "motherese" or infant-directed speech in child development. It is the higher-pitched, slower speech rate using shorter and more simplified words (North, 2015). In these instances, this tone of voice may be patronizing and demeaning to the older adult, as it is assumed they cannot comprehend the message that is being conveyed to them.

Ageism and negative stereotypes impact older people's lives (Chrisler et al., 2016). Their effects are similar to other racist, sexist, or homophobic microaggressions, and these subtleties can be seen in all areas of life (Gendron et al., 2016; Sue, 2010). For example, assuming that older people are computer illiterate, not tech-savvy, or unable to connect with younger colleagues or clients may result in them being passed on for opportunities and having lower self-esteem. Another example that is often overlooked is the joke at the expense of older people engaging in sexual relations or companion relationships as if older people are unable to be affectionate or engage in romantic relationships because of their age.

Conclusions

Ageism is the systematic stereotyping of and discrimination against people because of their age. Some people will not understand, nor see the value in discussing the topic because they do not want to interrogate their beliefs, attitudes, or ideas, but it is a complex topic that merits dialogue as the population continues to age. The implications of ageism are far reaching and affect matters such as Social Security, the welfare of elders, healthcare, retirement and disability benefits, and the political power of the elderly. Although the discussion on ageism may be uncomfortable, these conversations are important because at some point every person will be a member of this group if they live long enough, regardless of if they want to be a member. Also, it is important to remember that this population plays a significant role in the family as a holder or disseminator of a family's history and/or traditions.

Implications for Family Life Educators

Traditionally, old age was valued as elders taught survival and ways of adapting to younger members of society, but as the population of frail and diseased older people increased, they were seen as a burden, and the value of the older person began to diminish (Anti-Ageism Taskforce at the International Longevity Center, 2006). The decrease in value magnified the generational differences and the stereotypes of older people, which increased the dispensability of the elder. Stereotypes of older people include them being too old and senile to function in society, unable to comprehend or keep up with technical or job-related duties, incapable of managing their own affairs (doctor's appointments, financial affairs, etc.), cranky, set in their ways, disagreeable, irritated, prone to injury, bored and lonely, unwilling to listen, out of touch with reality, and unattractive (Palmore, 1999; Robinson et al., 2008). These stereotypes of older people are inaccurate (Palmore, 2015). Just as with any other group there are "rich and poor, wise and foolish, strong and weak, nice and mean" and stereotypes cannot adequately capture the essence of an entire group (Palmore, 2015, p. viii). The process of aging and the mental and physical progression may be different for an older person, but that does not mean they are unable to contribute to society. Aging is natural and inevitable and one aspect that every person can relate to since we will all grow older.

Education, knowledge, and understanding can alter perceptions and stereotypes. Professionals and students in the helping fields often perpetuate ageism in their practice and work unintentionally by not reflecting on and challenging their own predispositions. Oftentimes people refuse to discuss controversial topics because they do not want to unearth their own biases and prejudices, and they feel uncomfortable confronting friends, family, colleagues, and so on because they also would rather turn a blind eye than confront someone who is essentially "a good person." When one is silent on such issues, it not only gives a subtle affirmation to the perpetrator but makes the bystander complicit in silencing those who are the target of such comments, jokes, or slights, thus perpetuating oppression (Palmore, 2015). Generational differences can also create a distance, both physically and psychologically (North & Fiske, 2012). Unless they are intentionally being discriminatory, people are often unaware that they are perpetuating ageism (Boswell, 2012).

Since the contemporary family has evolved from traditional family forms to include a variety of definitions for what constitutes a "family," aging parents, extended kinship relationships, and elders who serve as proxy grandparents to the community all contribute to this definition of family. Students learning about diverse families in their distinctive context adds value to any program and constructs a more culturally sensitive student. Students who engage in gerontology education decrease ageism and aging anxiety and increase their knowledge base and interest in working with older adults (Boswell, 2012). Additionally, having contact with older people, trying to understand and get to know others, identifying ageist attitudes, and increasing one's awareness of others generates empathy and less negative attitudes toward people we come in contact with (North & Fiske, 2012). It also matters how families engage with older family members and the behavior that is modeled for younger generations (Nelson, 2016). Positive family relations and interactions convey a message of solidarity and family support. Changing the language we use and allow others to use around us can create a more positive environment. Words matter and they construct a reality around us. If one uses negative language, they are likely to believe the negative talk. If one changes their mind-set and language, their perception may also change, which can contribute to a family environment that accepts aging as natural and inevitable.

Other considerations for family life educators to avoid jeopardizing the integrity of the profession and promote dignity in growing old (Azulai, 2014) are to avoid using stereotypes and inappropriate labels and learn about the aging process. Get to know a person by actively engaging in conversation; ask questions for areas of mentorship or advice and to bridge the generation gap. Listen to their concerns and encourage positive attitudes. As with any group, a person should be judged on their own merit and not the stereotypes or the basis of a group, whether that is race, sexual preference, gender, or age.

Additional Readings

The selected readings examine concepts related to ageism in the United States. The first reading, "A History of Ageism Since 1969," by W. Andrew Achenbaum (2015) describes how "ageism" came to be a term that defined discrimination and injustices against older people. Achenbaum (2015) describes that Robert Butler (the first director of the National Institute of Aging) coined the term *ageism* as he challenged the opposition of some residents of a wealthy Washington DC, suburb who opposed developing a housing community for the elderly poor (including African Americans). Butler saw how the interplay of race, class, and aging could affect a person's well-being. He was disgusted with how people despise those who were not aging gracefully and questioned if it was because of racism (Achenbaum, 2015). In this article, Achenbaum also delivers a brief history of ageism and specifies how age bigotry will develop into a larger issue in the future and parallel racism, classism, and sexism. Additionally, in an effort to define and measure ageism, Achenbaum presents scholars who study ageism and its effects.

Concluding, Achenbaum gives us much to think about by framing the history of ageism before and after 1969 and how it intersects with racism, classism, and sexism. In a way, he also asks the reader to consider that as one lives longer, they should also have further opportunities to explore and discover what life has to offer and not be regarded as one who should disengage and diminish their contributions to society.

The second reading, "Ageism Stakes Its Claim in the Social Sciences," by Michael S. North (2015) trails the first reading by presenting ageism in a social sciences context. North offers theoretical perspectives (death anxiety, sociocultural trends, and generational tensions) and how they assist in explaining how ageism is ingrained in U.S. culture and society, like racism and sexism. North highlights the negative effects ageism can have on a person.

A History of Ageism Since 1969

By W. Andrew Achenbaum

Ageism predated Robert Butler, and remains in effect to this day.

The term "ageism" was coined in 1969 by Robert N. Butler, M.D., then a 42-year-old psychiatrist who (among his other civic and age-focused advocacy responsibilities) headed the District of Columbia Advisory Committee on Aging. In partnership with the National Capital Housing Authority (NCHA), Butler used the term "age-ism" during a *Washington Post* interview conducted by then cub reporter Carl Bernstein. The *Post* story, "Age and race fears seen in housing opposition," described the apprehension of homeowners in Chevy Chase, Maryland, an affluent Washington, D.C., suburb, who were distressed by the NCHA's decision to turn an apartment complex into public housing (Bernstein, 1969). The project was intended to offer residences for the elderly poor—including African Americans—and was opposed by residents who feared Chevy Chase would never be the same.

"People talk about aging gracefully, which is what they want to do of course. So, naturally, they don't want to look at people who may be palsied, can't eat well... who may sit on the curb and clutter up the neighborhood with canes," Butler told Bernstein. "Until our society builds [a] more balanced perspective about age groups, this lends to embittered withdrawal by old people" (Bernstein, 1969).

Ageism: The Greater Prejudice?

In Butler's opinion, long-standing racial prejudices and palpable class biases fueled an animus against age, a stigma that few Americans at the time acknowledged. "In the course of a *Washington Post* interview, I was asked if this negativism was a function of racism," Butler recalled (Butler, 1989). "In this instance, I thought it more a function of ageism."

Anger about age-driven injustices impelled Butler to engage in political activism on behalf of the old (and the young). As a delegate to the 1968 Democratic National Convention, Butler had witnessed clashes on the Chicago streets between age groups. This mayhem, to his mind, underscored a generation gap fomenting "in the political year 1968 [with] the elements of a counterrevolution by the middle-aged against both the young and the old" (Butler, 1969).

Elaborating upon his insights into ageism in *The Gerontologist*, he predicted that age bigotry would not soon fade. "Aging is the great sleeper in American life," he declared, noting that ageism permeated programs and resources meant to serve older Americans, such as Medicare, Social Security, and public housing, marginalizing older adults. "Age-ism might parallel (it might be wishful thinking to say *replace*) racism as the great issue of the next 20 to 30 years," he wrote (Butler, 1969).

Contempt, Down Through the Ages

Butler was not the first to identify a seemingly universal, widespread contempt for old people. Negative attitudes toward age and aging have been, and remain, deeply rooted in global history. Men and women who no longer could contribute to communal survival in Neolithic cultures were cast aside, often left to die. "*Senectus morbidus est*" ("Old age is a disease"), the philosopher Seneca (4 BC–AD 65) said.

Robert Butler declared that 'aging is the great sleeper in American life.'

By associating late life with disease and death, generations down the ages have justified the futility of granting the aged access to care (Achenbaum, 1978; Haber, 1983; Cole, 1992). Ageism is ubiquitous—evident in places as far-flung and with differing cultures as Japan (Gerlock, 2005) and east Africa (Ogonda, 2006)—and embedded in Western culture. The Roman poet Juvenal's *Satires* mock impotent and priapic septuagenarian satyrs alike; other classical authors disparaged mature women's disfigured grace and beauty. Unflattering imagery, like that in Keats' poem,

"Ode to a Nightingale," permeates more modern works (de Beauvoir, 1971; Wyatt-Brown and Rossen, 1993). It is no wonder that post–World War II researchers, sampling respondents' attitudes about old people, reported stereotypically negative responses to age and aging (Barron, 1953; Rosow, 1962; Tuckman and Lorge, 1953).

Robert Butler's achievement was to give meaning to ageism as an affliction. (In 1969, "ageism" appeared in the *Oxford English Dictionary*; in 2003, "new ageism" showed up in the dictionary's electronic version.) For the rest of his career, Butler's critiques of ageism repeated themes enunciated when he had first introduced the subject:

> Ageism can be seen as a systematic stereotyping of and discrimination against people because they are old, just as racism and sexism accomplish this with skin color and gender... I see ageism manifested in a wide range of phenomena, on both individual and institutional levels—stereotypes and myths, outright disdain and dislike, simple subtle avoidance of contact, and discriminatory practices in housing, employment, and services of all kinds (Butler, 1989; Butler, 2005).

Whether working with the Veterans Administration, serving as founding director of the National Institute on Aging, and, subsequently, as the (first U.S.) chair of geriatrics at New York's Mount Sinai Hospital and Medical School, Butler constantly sought ways to rid eldercare of ageism. A top priority was training healthcare professionals to treat older patients with dignity and compassion (Butler, 1980; Achenbaum, 2013).

Combating ageism was the frequent goal of the publications and workshops of the New York-based International Longevity Center (ILC), which Butler founded and led during his last two decades of life. *Media Takes: On Aging*, an influential ILC report (Dahmen and Cozma, 2009), documented that much remained to be done to counter the insidious effects of age-based prejudice. The report claimed that 80 percent of Americans were subjected to ageism. A year before his death in 2010, Butler wrote:

> The advent of possible means to delay aging and extend longevity is a great intellectual and social as well as medical achievement... The very words we use to describe people are undergoing greater scrutiny. It is ironic, then, that at the same time Americans are beginning to see an unfolding of the entire life cycle for a majority, we continue to have embedded in our culture a fear of growing old, manifest by negative stereotypes and language that belittles the very nature of growing old, its complexities and tremendous variability (Butler, 2008).

Efforts to Define and Measure Ageism

The United States has always been an age-graded society. Its segmented age groups do not necessarily unify the populace, although most citizens claim to agree with Robert Wohl (1979) when he says, "the truest community to which one can belong is that defined by age and experience."

Intergenerational tensions flamed ageist rhetoric in the 1980s and 1990s, however. *The New Republic* depicted older people as "greedy geezers" who squandered their life savings and depleted Social Security funds (Fairlie, 1988). Younger Americans, struggling to obtain an education, a home, or a decent job blamed older Americans.

Debates over generational equity abated over time, without uprooting the perception that different age groups compete for diminishing resources in a zero-sum world. "Age-based social divisions, particularly in the current economic environment of budget deficits and fiscal tightening, threaten the sustainability of the American social compact" (Network on an Aging Society, 2012).

Scores of researchers have since followed Butler's lead in defining and measuring ageism. And scholars have deployed knowledge-building and consciousness-raising to mitigate, if not eradicate, the stigma. A fair number of investigators merit attention here.

The Researchers Go to Work

Donald McTavish (1971) prepared an exhaustive review of research methodologies and cumulative findings concerning perceptions of old people; he found the literature at hand mixed in terms of validity and usefulness.

Ageism became the cornerstone of Erdman Palmore's research while he was a graduate student in the 1950s. With Kenneth Manton, Palmore published the first systematic comparison of age-based inequality to racism (the pair reported small but significant gains at the time) and sexism (they claimed that women's inferior status was barely maintained). "Few people recognize the magnitude of age inequality in our society," they reported (Palmore and Manton, 1973).

In 1976, Palmore developed, and subsequently maintained, a twenty-five-point "Facts on Aging" quiz to help the public recognize the extent of their misinformation about older people's qualities—a bias that contributed to age discrimination (Bennett, 2004). In a guest editorial, Palmore (2000) offered usage guidelines for avoiding ageism in gerontological language. At age 82, he co-edited the *Encyclopedia of Ageism* (2005), wherein sixty authors reviewed 125 aspects of ageism, ranging from mapping elder abuse to assessing ageism among children.

Emerging Scholars Take Their Turn

A rising generation of scholars contributed to fresh understandings of ageism. Some validated insights by Butler and Palmore, while presenting novel approaches (McGuire, Klein, and Chen, 2008). Becca Levy (2001), for example, demonstrated how *implicit* ageism generated adverse health effects. Stereotypes previously aimed at African Americans or women were internalized by aging Americans, eliciting self-inflicted prejudice.

> **'Class still matters: Disenfranchised older people have less access to power, prestige, or property.'**

Todd Nelson, in a collection of essays on ageism (2002) and a handbook on *The Psychology of Prejudice* (2005), sought to contextualize the syndrome by documenting the extent to which Americans' derogation of aging clashed with their views concerning youth, mobility, change, and fear of death. In *Agewise*, Margaret Morganroth Gullette (2010), in her analysis of the Fourth

Age, provided a devastating critique of the "culture of decline" and the "systems of decline" (including those fostered by healthcare professionals and pharmaceutical firms) that distort how we view passages through the life course.

Other investigators tracked policies undermining ageism, such as changes in employment discrimination legislation, noting limitations in our country's landmark Age Discrimination in Employment Act of 1967, which abolished mandatory retirement (Pampel and Williamson, 1992; Burchett, 2005).

International researchers—especially those in the United Kingdom—enriched the literature on ageism. Bill Bytheway (1995) surveyed the settings in which age biases compromised medical care, among other senior services. John Macnicol, who published a historical and contemporary analysis of age discrimination (2006) and also presented a think piece to the ILC (2010), argued that the British government took steps (not replicated in the United States) to encourage—even to force—older workers back into paid employment. Robin Blackburn claimed that poor public responses to older adults' vulnerabilities posed a societal risk (2006).

Exploring the nature of spirituality in the Fourth Age, Malcolm Johnson and Keith Albans (2013) recounted and interpreted stories of people's anxieties over declining capacities and fears of dying. Their treatment of ageism in late, late life recalled efforts by Nobel Laureate Elie Metchnikoff (1908) and psychologist G. Stanley Hall (1922), who linked gerontology and thanatology—a connection rarely pursued by investigators that is dedicated to probing "successful aging."

Parsing the Evolution (or Devolution) of Ageism

As ageism studies progressed, unresolved debates over definitional matters gave rise to measurement issues about ageism. Palmore acknowledged that his pioneering Equality Index was a useful but insufficient basis for such comparisons (Palmore, 1999). Synthesis is difficult (Aosved, Long, and Voller, 2009; Dittmann, 2003) because few researchers investigate intolerant beliefs simultaneously. Furthermore, as much survey data on ageism are self-reported; the negativity is likely to be implicit or unnoticed (as Becca Levy has shown). Ageism, after all, takes on various and nuanced forms, each with unique impacts: Making jokes at an older person's expense is vastly different from hitting one's grandparents or stealing their assets and resources.

And, times change: "Racism, sexism, homophobia, and other forms of discrimination don't look the way they used to" (Covert, 2014). Jim Crow laws may be history, but entrenched signs of disenfranchisement in African American communities remain—poverty, homelessness, incarceration, and violence. The status of women has improved due to greater opportunities in higher education and professional advancement, yet women are expected to interrupt their careers to be caregivers; and income disparities have not dissipated much since the passage of the Equal Pay Act of 1963, or with its amendment in 1974.

'We no longer limit comparisons of ageism to racism and sexism.'

Though few Americans gave much thought to the presence of Spanish-speaking immigrants in America in the late 1960s, this now burgeoning, diverse segment of our society has become a potent force in contemporary life and culture. The same might be said of immigrants from Asia and the subcontinent. And, since the Stonewall Riots of 1969, there has been a radical transformation of attitudes and public policies that support and affirm the rights of gays, lesbians, bisexuals, transgender individuals, and self-identified queers to participate in everyday affairs.

Much since 1969 remains the same about ageism. Then, as now, older Americans were a variegated group; their circumstances remain divergent in terms of financial resources and employment opportunities, mental and physical health, educational attainments, cultural diversity, marital status, religion, and region. Class still matters: Disenfranchised older people have less access to power, prestige, or property.

Ageism continues to bedevil segments of the older population in distressing ways. Most older African American women still embody a triple jeopardy (being female, African American, and old), which public agencies cannot fully ameliorate. Older Americans remain under-represented in the media. And gerontology's great irony persists—whereas most of us now live long enough to become old, ageism is the only prejudice that can diminish *everyone's* quality of life.

That said, ageism itself has taken on four new forms since Butler identified the prejudice:

- Older Americans benefit from age-based discounts and entitlements, which is a positive development, but the benefits still convey a scent of ageism. Many of these perquisites originated in the pervasive notion that older people, uniformly, were poor. That is no longer the case. As a group, the old, on average, have more income at their disposal than younger cohorts.

- The Baby Boom Generation has seen both sides of ageism. In their youth, they mocked people older than age 30. Now, they face job discrimination and competition from younger generations. And, they are taunted for their obesity and improvidence. Their very numbers fan worries that they might bankrupt Social Security and Medicare.

- We no longer limit comparisons of ageism to racism and sexism. New dyads have emerged, notably ones associated with the disabled and with lesbian, gay, bisexual, transgender, and queer (LGBTQ) individuals. Conjoining age with Alzheimer's Disease and related disorders, or recognizing the risk of HIV infections after age 60 arouses fears of loss of control and independence in late life and despair over prospects for a meaningful existence. Rates of dementia, sexually transmitted diseases, and drug use and abuse underscore the need to invest more in mental health and to provide greater access to older Americans to public health education and interventions.

- Elderly men and women who are feverishly committed to extending careers well into what had been considered retirement years rarely notice how ageism cripples peers. This is one reason Americans can postpone the 1960s version of age 65.

Ageism preys on vulnerability—fragility, frailty, and dependency at advancing ages—especially as dread of dying and death mounts.

Conclusion

Two ironies frame the history of ageism, both before and after 1969. First, ageism predates Butler's naming of a syndrome endemic over time and across space. Vulnerable elders feared physical and psychological abuse, regardless of their cohort's proportionate numbers in a given population. Second, ageism remains virulent amidst "the longevity revolution" (Butler, 2008).

The gift of extra years should afford time and opportunities to grow, to cherish bonds, to review life's meaning. Instead, older people often find themselves marginalized, which diminishes their capacities to contribute—and to matter.

References

Achenbaum, W. A. 1978. *Old Age in the New Land*. Baltimore, MD: The Johns Hopkins University Press.

Achenbaum, W. A. 2013. *Robert N. Butler, MD: Visionary of Healthy Aging*. New York: Columbia University Press.

Aosved, A. C., Long, P. J., and Voller, E. K. 2009. "Measuring Sexism, Racism, Sexual Prejudice, Ageism, Classism and Religious Intolerance." *Journal of Applied Social Psychology* 39(10): 2321–54.

Barron, M. L. 1953. "Minority Group Characteristics of the Aged in American Society." *Journal of Gerontology* 8(4): 477–82.

Bennett, R. 2004. "Professor Palmore's Amazing Facts on Aging Quiz." www.timegoesby.net/weblog/2004/09/dr_erdmans_amaz.html. Retrieved May 6, 2015.

Bernstein, C. 1969. "Age and Race Fears Seen in Housing Opposition." *The Washington Post*, March 7.

Blackburn, R. 2006. *Age Shock: How Finance Is Failing Us*. London, UK: Verso.

Burchett, B. M. 2005. "Employment Discrimination." In E. B. Palmore et al., eds., *Encyclopedia of Ageism*. Binghamton, NY: Haworth Press.

Butler, R. N. 1969. "Age-ism: Another Form of Bigotry." *The Gerontologist* 9(4, Part 1): 243–6.

Butler, R. N. 1980. "Ageism: A Foreword." *Journal of Social Issues* 36(2): 8–11.

Butler, R. N. 1989. "Dispelling Ageism: The Cross-cutting Intervention." *Annals of the American Academy of Political and Social Science* 503: 138–47.

Butler, R. N. 2005. "Ageism." *Generations* 29(3): 84–6.

Butler, R. N. 2008. *The Longevity Revolution: The Benefits and Challenges of Living a Long Life*. New York: PublicAffairs.

Bytheway, B. 1995. *Ageism*. New York: McGraw-Hill.

Cole, T. R. 1992. *The Journey of Life*. New York: Cambridge University Press.

Covert, B. 2014. "Racism and Sexism Look Different Than You Think." *ThinkProgress*, May 21. http://thinkprogress.org/economy/2014/05/21/3440209/discrimination-favoritism/. Retrieved May 8, 2015.

Dahmen, N. S., and Cozma, R., eds. 2009. *Media Takes: On Aging*. New York: International Longevity Center; San Francisco: Aging Services of California.

deBeauvoir, S. 1971. *The Coming of Age*. New York: G. P. Putnam's Sons.

Dittmann, M. 2003. "Fighting Ageism." *American Psychological Association Monitor on Psychology* 34(5) 50.

Fairlie, H. 1988. "Talkin' 'bout My Generation." *The New Republic*, March 28.

Gerlock, E. 2006. "Discrimination of Older People in Asia." Paper presented at the International Federation on Aging Conference, May 30–June 2, Copenhagen.

Gullette, M. M. 2010. *Agewise: Fighting the New Ageism in America*. Chicago: University of Chicago Press.

Haber, C. 1983. *Beyond Sixty-Five: The Dilemma of Old Age in America's Past*. Cambridge, UK: Cambridge University Press.

Hall, G. S. 1922. *Senescence: The Last Half of Life*. New York: D. Appelton & Co.

Johnson, M. L., and Albans, K. 2013. *God, Me and Being Very Old: Stories and Spirituality in Later Life*. London, UK: SCM Press.

Levy, B. 2001. "Eradication of Ageism Requires Addressing the Enemy Within." *The Gerontologist* 41(5): 578–79.

Macnicol, J. 2006. *Age Discrimination*. Cambridge, UK: Cambridge University Press.

Macnicol, J. 2010. *Ageism and Age Discrimination*. London, UK: International Longevity Center-UK.

McGuire, S. L., Klein, D. A., and Chen, S. L. 2008. "Ageism Revisited." *Nursing and Health Sciences* 10(1): 11–16.

McTavish, D. G. 1971. "Perceptions of Old People: A Review of Research Methodologies and Findings." *The Gerontologist* 11 (Supp.): 90–108.

Metchnikoff, E. 1908. *The Prolongation of Life: Optimistic Studies*. New York: G. P. Putnam's Sons.

Nelson, T. D., ed. 2002. *Ageism: Stereotyping and Prejudice Against Older Persons*. Cambridge, MA: The MIT Press.

Nelson, T. 2006. *The Psychology of Prejudice*. Boston: Pearson.

Network on an Aging Society. 2012. *Intergenerational Cohesion and the Social Compact*. Chicago: Mac-Arthur Foundation. www.agingsocietynetwork.org/sites/default/files/files/generational%20cohesion%20brief%20.pdf. Retrieved June 22, 2015.

Ogonda, J. 2006. "Age Discrimination in Africa." Paper presented at the International Federation on Aging Conference, May 30–June 2, Copenhagen.

Palmore, E. B., and Manton, K. 1973. "Ageism Compared to Racism and Sexism." *Journal of Gerontology* 28(3): 363–9.

Palmore, E. B., ed. 1999. *Ageism* (2nd ed.). New York: Springer.

Palmore, E. B. 2000. "Guest Editorial: Ageism in Gerontological Language." *The Gerontologist* 40(6): 645.

Palmore, E. B., Branch, L., and Harris, D. K., eds. 2005. *Encyclopedia of Ageism*. Binghamton, NY: Haworth Press.

Pampel, F. C., and Williamson, J. B. 1992. *Age, Class, Politics, and the Welfare State*. New York: Cambridge University Press.

Rosow, I. 1962. "Old Age." *The Gerontologist* 2: 182–91.

Tuckman, J., and Lorge. I. 1953. "'When Aging Begins' and Stereo types about Aging." *Journal of Gerontology* 8: 489–92.

Wohl, R. 1979. *The Generation of 1914*. Cambridge, MA: Harvard University Press.

Wyatt-Brown, A. M., and Rossen, J., eds. 1993. *Aging and Gender in Literature: Studies in Creativity*. Charlottesville, VA: University Press of Virginia.

Ageism Stakes Its Claim in the Social Sciences

By Michael S. North

Perhaps because of its complexity and self-perpetuating nature, ageism is finally piquing the interest of science, advocacy movements, and society in general.

Tom is not just a typical baby boomer; he has always been one of the hipper ones. A regular participant in Civil Rights marches, a Woodstock attendee, an open proponent of free love, and a career-long jazz bassist, Tom has always managed to stay at the epicenter of cool.

But as the years pass, Tom has noticed subtle changes in the way people view him. On the street, complete strangers have begun to smile at him, almost apologetically. When he sports his historically popular leather jacket, people today don't praise his fashion sense. When he goes out to eat, he feels ever-so-subtly that the wait staff doesn't pay as much attention to him as they do to other customers—and when they do, they often talk to him in an exaggerated, slow, high pitch, as if he were a child. Sure, people are polite, but Tom can't help but feel less relevant, less connected to the mainstream. The change has been so gradual, yet palpable, that he wonders exactly how and when things got to be this way.

Age, Aging, and Ageism Are Under the Radar

Tom's perplexity can be chalked up to a number of issues. One is that the aging process sneaks up on everyone, and any subtle treatment might also go largely unnoticed, by perpetrators and recipients alike. Indeed, save for annual (usually derogatory) birthday-related jokes, people rarely acknowledge getting older as they go about their everyday lives. Despite the fact that everyone is aging, the subject remains largely—and sometimes surprisingly—taboo.

> **Per the 'terror management' theoretical perspective, older adults are pushed aside, as a coping mechanism.**

Similarly, the study of ageism—the systematic stereotyping of and discriminating against people on the basis of their age—also has been relatively neglected in the social sciences. This might be for practical reasons: Until recently, national-level, systematic research initiatives for studying the issue have been relatively scant (Carstensen and Hartel, 2006). A different meta-explanation is that ignoring the study of ageism might represent a bias in and of itself, where researchers are either in denial of their own aging, or guilty of overlooking ageism as a prejudice, due to its unusually socially condoned nature (Nelson, 2005; North and Fiske, 2012).

Nevertheless, the importance of understanding ageism is undeniable, for reasons that go well beyond the practical realities of an aging population. For one thing, it is widely known that the three fundamental categories of social perception are age, race, and gender (Fiske, 1998). Moreover, age is the only category composed of groups that every living person eventually joins, provided sufficient life span. Nevertheless, when it comes to understanding forms of discrimination, the latter two categories have enjoyed greater research attention—not to mention greater social movement momentum. Age has remained below the radar, and ageism is mostly a "second-class civil rights issue" (Cohen, 2009). Fortunately, this is changing—albeit slowly.

Why Does Ageism Persist?

Given the universality of aging, that ageism persists at all is perplexing at first glance. Although the topic is generally understudied, the following scholarly theories/perspectives may help explain its rootedness in our culture and society:

Death anxiety. A common theory is that aging is uniquely threatening, deriving from people's anxieties surrounding their own mortality. Per this "terror management" theoretical perspective, older adults are pushed aside, physically and psychologically, as a coping mechanism (Greenberg, Schimel, and Mertens, 2004), thereby spurring ageism. The threat of getting older is so closely linked with death anxiety that older adults themselves often dis-identify as "old" (Weiss and Freund, 2012).

Sociocultural trends. Other explanations derive from a variety of historical events, which gradually devalued the roles of elders in society as primary sources of storytelling and wisdom. Such trends include the introduction of the printing press and increased literacy (improving record-keeping and de-emphasizing verbal narratives) and the Industrial Revolution (emphasizing youth-oriented manual labor; Nelson, 2005). These trends have relegated older adults to a generally noncompetitive, low-status position in society—generating interpersonal perceptions of benevolence, but low competence (Cuddy and Fiske, 2004).

Generational tensions. A different theory de-emphasizes mortality and focuses more on practical assets (jobs, healthcare) and symbolic ones ("coolness"). This standpoint conceptualizes ageism as deriving from generational tensions over resources, and argues that a uniquely intergenerational form of ageism derives from expectations for older generations to make way for new ones, literally and figuratively—including explicit expectations to provide financial support and to transfer wealth (North and Fiske, 2013a, 2013b).

Ageism in Relation to Other "isms"

Ageism shares parallels with other prejudices, such as racism and sexism. Like any form of bias, ageism effectively reduces individuals to broad, stereotypical categories—often unfairly. In the case of older adults, common ageist stereotypes might suggest that any individual older than age 65 is mentally and physically incapacitated, even though the overwhelming majority of older adults are not (Plassman et al., 2007). Much like sexism—in which good intentions can result in the subjugation of women (e.g., believing that women "should be cherished and protected by men"; Glick and Fiske, 1996)—ageism often takes a benevolent form, such as when people (including health practitioners) communicate in well-intentioned but demeaning "elderspeak," resembling baby talk (Kemper, 1994).

In a psychological process of 'stereotype threat,' older adults performed worse on a reading task when it was framed as indicative of memory.

Also, like other forms of prejudice, ageism's targets are at risk of internalizing negative expectations and prejudicing themselves. In a psychological process known as "stereotype threat," older adults performed worse on a reading task framed as indicative of memory, as compared to a comparable group of older adults who performed the same task under the guise of reading comprehension (Kang and Chasteen, 2009). The same internalization-based under-performance pattern has applied to women in math-focused domains and ethnic minorities within standardized testing contexts (Steele, Spencer, and Aronson, 2002).

An increased presence of older adults should bring about enhanced respect, provided they are not seen as directly impeding younger generations.

Nevertheless, ageism is unique in a variety of respects. One is its noted status of being more socially condoned than other forms of bias—to the point of people overlooking it as an extant form of prejudice. This obliviousness leads to alarming consequences: In healthcare, doctors might dismissively undertreat certain symptoms as part of the "natural aging process," and medical schools spend comparatively little time on geriatric training (North and Fiske, 2012). More broadly, many believe ageism to be based on greater truth than other stereotypes, given the "inevitability" of age-based decline—though research increasingly shows that perceptions of declines in domains such as memory (Salthouse, 2011) and work performance (McEvoy and Cascio, 1989) are largely overblown.

Another important distinction is that, as noted, every person (if living long enough) eventually joins each age group—rendering ageism the only prejudice that eventually targets everyone. This also makes ageism self-contradictory, as virtually everyone strives to live a long time, while simultaneously moving toward joining a (mostly) undesirable social group. Perhaps as a result of this—and adding to ageism's complexity—older people are ageist, often holding negative attitudes toward "the elderly" (Nosek, Banaji, and Greenwald, 2002) and psychologically dis-identifying from their own chronological age group (Weiss and Lang, 2012). Ageism is unique in being actively perpetuated by its most at-risk population—older adults.

Can Ageism Change?

All of this might paint a pessimistic and seemingly inevitable picture. After all, if older adults are ageist, then who is not? Some elements of the issue present significant challenges, as negative attitudes toward aging appear largely automatic and resistant to change.

Nevertheless, there are reasons for optimism, which include the following:

A pressing societal need to accommodate the older population. Demographic trends are making the issue of ageism virtually impossible to ignore, as societies around the world undergo unprecedented population aging. In the United States, already more than

13percent of the population is older than 65 years of age, and, by 2030, that number will increase to at least 20 percent (Ortman, Velkoff, and Hogan, 2014). Meanwhile, a corresponding steady rise in laborforce participation among older age groups (Copeland, 2014) has coincided with a spike in age discrimination charges (increasing 66 percent from 1999 to 2011; Kreamer, 2012).

Society is thus being forced to accommodate the growing older population—considered by some to be world's primary growing natural resource. According to a "contact hypothesis" prediction, an increased presence of older adults should bring about enhanced respect, provided they are not seen as directly impeding younger generations (Dovidio and Gaertner, 1999).

A growing body of research. Taking note of these demographic trends, a rising number of social science researchers are enhancing scholarly knowledge on ageism, in fields like psychology, sociology, anthropology, political science, and economics (North and Fiske, 2012). Such work not only covers the social policy implications of the issue, but also indirectly helps to combat it by identifying the positive qualities that come with age (e.g., wisdom and perspective-taking; Grossmann et al., 2010). All of this helps elucidate the ways in which older adults might be best utilized and properly valued in the modern world. This is a key ingredient for reducing prejudice, given perceptions of older adults as societal non-contributors (Cottrell and Neuberg, 2005).

A growing advocacy movement. Meanwhile, a community of writers and activists also are raising awareness about ageism's existence and potential interventions (as described elsewhere in this issue of *Generations*). Grassroots movements, such as The Radical Age Movement (http://theradicalagemovement. com), are working to generate and change the conversation around aging and ageism, much as those who protest to and speak out against racism, sexism, and gay bigotry have accomplished success in their respective movements.

Conclusion

Although scholarly focus on ageism has been comparatively sparse, demographic, economic, and political trends are beginning to change this. This increased amount of attention has begun to uncover the similarities, as well as surprising differences, of ageism compared with other forms of bias. Social scientific identification of exaggerated, negative age-based perceptions and positive aspects of aging—combined with growing advocacy movements—promise to rectify this emergent and uniquely universal social concern.

References

Carstensen, L. L., and Hartel, C. R., eds. 2006. *When I'm 64*. Washington, DC: The National Academies Press.

Cohen, A. 2009. "Age Bias Gets Second-class Treatment." *The New York Times*, November 7.

Copeland, C. 2014. "Labor-force Participation Rates of the Population Ages 55 and Older, 2013." *EBRI Notes* 35(4). www.ebri.org/pdf/notespdf/ebri_notes_04_apr-14_lbrpart.pdf. Retrieved June 24, 2015.

Cottrell, C. A., and Neuberg, S. L. 2005. "Different Emotional Reactions to Different Groups: A Sociofunctional Threat-based Approach to 'Prejudice.'" *Journal of Personality and Social Psychology* 88(5): 770–89.

Cuddy, A. J., and Fiske, S. T. 2004. "Doddering, but Dear: Process, Content, and Function in Stereotyping of Older Persons." In T. D. Nelson, ed., *Ageism: Stereotyping and Prejudice Against Older Persons.* Cambridge, MA: The MIT Press.

Dovidio, J. F., and Gaertner, S. L. 1999. "Reducing Prejudice: Combating Intergroup Biases." *Current Directions in Psychological Science* 8(4): 101–4.

Fiske, S. T. 1998. "Stereotyping, Prejudice, and Discrimination." In D. T. Gilbert, S. T. Fiske, and G. Lindzey, eds. *The Handbook of Social Psychology* (4th ed.). New York: McGraw-Hill.

Glick, P., and Fiske, S. T. 1996. "The Ambivalent Sexism Inventory: Differentiating Hostile and Benevolent Sexism." *Journal of Personality and Social Psychology* 70(3): 491–512.

Greenberg, J., Schimel, J., and Mertens, A. 2004. "Ageism: Denying the Face of the Future." In T. D. Nelson, ed. *Ageism: Stereotyping and Prejudice Against Older Persons.* Cambridge, MA: The MIT Press.

Grossmann, I., et al. 2010. "Reasoning About Social Conflicts Improves into Old Age." *Proceedings of the National Academy of Sciences* 107(16): 7246–50.

Kang, S. K., and Chasteen, A. L. 2009. "The Moderating Role of Age-group Identification and Perceived Threat on Stereotype Threat Among Older Adults." *The International Journal of Aging and Human Development* 69(3): 201–20.

Kemper, S. 1994. "Elderspeak: Speech Accommodations to Older Adults." *Aging and Cognition* 1(1): 17–28.

Kreamer, A. 2012. "Looking For a Job When You're No Longer Young." *Harvard Business Review,* March 12. https://hbr.org/2012/03/looking-for-a-job-when-youre. Retrieved June 24, 2015.

McEvoy, G. M., and Cascio, W. F. 1989. "Cumulative Evidence of the Relationship Between Employee Age and Job Performance." *Journal of Applied Psychology* 74(1): 11–17.

Nelson, T. D. 2005. "Ageism: Prejudice Against Our Feared Future Self." *Journal of Social Issues* 61: 207–21.

North, M. S., and Fiske, S. T. 2012. "An Inconvenienced Youth? Ageism and Its Potential Intergenerational Roots." *Psychological Bulletin* 138(5): 982–97.

North, M. S., and Fiske, S. T. 2013a. "Act Your (Old) Age: Prescriptive, Ageist Biases Over Succession, Consumption, and Identity." *Personality and Social Psychology Bulletin* 39(6): 720–34.

North, M. S., and Fiske, S. T. 2013b. "A Prescriptive Intergenerationaltension Ageism Scale: Succession, Identity, and Consumption (SIC)." *Psychological Assessment* 25(3): 706–13.

Nosek, B. A., Banaji, M. R., and Greenwald, A. G. 2002. "Harvesting Implicit Group Attitudes and Beliefs from a Demonstration Web Site." *Group Dynamics: Theory, Research, and Practice* 6: 101–15.

Ortman, J. M., Velkoff, V. A., and Hogan, H. 2014. "An Aging Nation: The Older Population in the United States." Washington, DC: U.S. Department of Commerce, Economics and Statistics Administration. www.census.gov/prod/2014pubs/p25-1140.pdf. Retrieved June 24, 2015.

Plassman, B. L., et al. 2007. "Prevalence of Dementia in the United States: The Aging, Demographics, and Memory Study." *Neuroepidemiology* 29(1–2): 125–32.

Salthouse, T. A. 2011. "Neuroanatomical Substrates of Age-related Cognitive Decline." *Psychological Bulletin* 137: 753–84.

Steele, C. M., Spencer, S. J., and Aronson, J. 2002. "Contending with Group Image: The Psychology of Stereotype and Social Identity Threat." *Advances in Experimental Social Psychology* 34: 379–440.

Weiss, D., and Freund, A. M. 2012. "Still Young at Heart: Negative Age-related Information Motivates Distancing from Same-aged People." *Psychology and Aging* 27(1): 173–80.

Weiss, D., and Lang, F. R. 2012. "'They' Are Old but 'I' Feel Younger: Age-group Dissociation as a Self-protective Strategy in Old Age." *Psychology and Aging* 27(1): 153–63.

Activities for Further Exploration and Discussion

Questions for Discussion

1. As you review the articles think about your stance on ageism. Is it really a big deal? If not, why not? If so, what are some of the ramifications of ageism?

2. Is ageism really a social construct? What is the relevance of ageism, or is it irrelevant?

3. Is there an area of aging research that interests you? Conduct preliminary research to find more about the field.

4. As you review the articles, think about ageism from a family life educator or social scientists' lens. How can a family life educator or social scientist change the perception of ageism?

5. How might one go about advocating for interventions or advancing the conversation about ageism?

6. How are older people who are marginalized (by racism, sexism, or heterosexism) affected by ageism and ageist practices? How are these concepts linked through intersectionality? How might they differ? Explain and cite relevant sources to support your position.

7. How is ageism taught or perpetuated? What roles may family members play? Are discriminatory or prejudiced views acquired from our environment or is discrimination and prejudice an active process that we play a part in? Explain?

8. Achenbaum (2015) states, "Whereas most of us now live long enough to become old, ageism is the only prejudice that can diminish *everyone's* quality of life" (p. 14). What might this mean?

9. If ageism is having a negative attitude, prejudice, discrimination, or stereotyping against or in favor of an age group, can ageism apply to young people? Explain your position and cite scholarly literature to support your claim.

10. Based on the criteria presented by Palmore (1999), when the intersections of race and gender are included with age would a person then be considered a minority? Explain and provide a citation to support your stance.

Movie Analysis

The Intern (2015) PG-13

A recent retiree (Robert DeNiro) finds that retirement isn't as fulfilling as he thought it would be, so he ventures back into the work world as a "senior" intern at an online clothing website founded and run by a young Jules Ostin (Anne Hathaway).

5 Flights Up (2014) PG-13
Ruth (Diane Keaton) and Alex (Morgan Freeman) are an older married couple living in New York. In this film, they discover how different their neighborhood has become—hipper and more contemporary—a big difference from when they first bought their home. Through a series of events that mirror the chaos in their own lives, they learn how different it is to buy and sell a home as an older couple versus a younger couple and how the real estate market can make buying and selling a home a feat for older people.

Still Alice (2014) PG-13
In this sentimental film, Alice (Julianne Moore) is a linguistics professor who begins to forget words. As she is diagnosed with early-onset Alzheimer's, Alice and her family have to make some important and unpleasant decisions. Throughout the film, we journey with Alice as she fights to remain bonded to who she is and her family.

Ageless

https://agelessthemovie.com/purchase/

A documentary about the world from various women's eyes. Throughout the documentary women of various ages discuss ageism and sexism and how finding one's voice can be empowering.

The Age of Love

http://theageoflovemovie.com/#

A documentary about the adventures of older single adults "in Rochester, NY who sign up for a first-of-its-kind speed dating event for 70- to 90-year-olds. Forced to take stock of life-worn bodies and still-hopeful hearts, they find themselves confronted by the startling realities of seeking new relationships at an unexpected time in life."

Guiding Questions for the Films

1. What are the ways ageism is demonstrated in the film?
2. What intergenerational or cross-generational connections are made?

3. As people live longer, we will see the need for the workplace and society to accommodate the older person. What can you glean as the value and a potential drawback of a multi-generational workplace?
4. How can the concepts of ageism be applied to the film(s)?
5. What are your cohorts' attitudes regarding aging and how is that different from previous or later cohorts?
6. What major world events have impacted your cohort, and in what way(s) has this same event impacted older cohorts? Discuss the similarities and differences in the impact.

Adulthood Interview

Interview someone who is 60 or older, and in the summary of the interview, discuss the following. Cite relevant literature and theories or theoretical concepts to support the information in the interview.

1. Provide a brief biological summary of the interviewee. Some questions to consider are the following:
   a. How would the interviewee describe the culture in which they grew up? What similarities and differences do they see in that culture and the culture of today?
   b. What type of work do (did) you do?
2. The aging process:
   a. In their mind, what age are they? What does that mean to them?
   b. Does age affect the way they think and feel about their body?
   c. Do they think they look younger/older than their peers?
   d. What do they like/dislike about being their age?
   e. What does the person consider successful aging?
   f. Do they think they have aged successfully based on their criteria?
   g. What changes has the interviewee experienced as a result of aging (attitudes, interests, views)?
   h. Do people treat them differently due to their age?
   i. What, if anything, are they looking forward to in the next 5 years? 10 years?
   j. Do you see value in living to be very old? (What would very old look like to you?)
   k. How do you think aging differs for men and for women?
   l. What do you fear about getting older?
   m. What's surprising about getting older?
   n. Do you have friends of all ages or mostly in your peer group? What do you think about cross-generational friendships?
   o. Has getting older influenced your perception about sex or romantic relationships?
   p. Have you personally experienced ageism?
   q. What challenges related to age, race, class, or gender did you encounter and overcome growing up?

r. How has ageism played a part in you concept of self?

s. Do you think their analysis is from an ageist perspective? Why or why not?

3. Family life education application:

a. How might the information you gathered impact you as a professional?

b. As a family professional, what should you consider when working with older adults?

c. What suggestions could you provide to family professionals when working with older adults?

References

Achenbaum, W. A. (2015). History of ageism since 1969. *Journal of the American Society on Aging, 39*(3), 10–16

Administration for Community Living. (2018). *2017 profile of older Americans.* https://acl.gov/sites/default/files/Aging%20and%20Disability%20in%20America/2017OlderAmericansProfile.pdf

Anti-Ageism Taskforce at the International Longevity Center. (2006). *Ageism in America.* https://aging.columbia.edu/sites/default/files/Ageism_in_America.pdf

Azulai, A. (2014). Ageism and future cohorts of elderly: Implications for social work. *Journal of Social Work Values and Ethics, 11*(2), 1–12.

Borland, J. (2019). *Why Social Security retirement is important to women.* https://blog.ssa.gov/why-social-security-retirement-is-important-to-woman/

Boswell, S. S. (2012). "Old people are cranky": Helping professional trainees' knowledge, attitudes, aging anxiety, and interest in working with older adults. *Educational Gerontology, 38*(7), 465–472.

Brown, S. (2018, October 16). *AARP's 'Be the difference vote' stresses the importance of voting in this year's midterms.* National Council on Aging. https://www.phillytrib.com/news/across_america/aarp-s-be-the-difference-vote-stresses-the-importance-of/article_54ea283b-20a9-5b1b-bc0b-a5d92e9f52ae.html

Bureau of Labor Statistics. (2016). *The economics daily.* https://www.bls.gov/opub/ted/2016/womens-earnings-83-percent-of-mens-but-vary-by-occupation.htm

Butler, R. (1989). Dispelling ageism: The cross-cutting intervention. *Annals of the American Academy of Political and Social Science, 503*(1), 138–147.

Butler, R. N. (1980). Ageism: A foreword. *Journal of Social Issues, 36*(2), 8–11.

Calasanti, T., & King, N. (2015). Intersectionality and age. In J. Twigg & W. Martin (Eds.), *Routledge handbook of cultural gerontology* (pp. 193–200). Routeldge.

Chrisler, J., Barney, A., & Palatino, B. (2016) Ageism can be hazardous to women's health: Ageism, sexism, and stereotypes of older women in the healthcare system. *Journal of Social Issues, 72*(1), 86–104.

Collins, P. H. (2003). Some group matters: Intersectionality, situated standpoints, and Black feminist thought. In T. L. Lott & J. P. Pittman (Eds.), *A companion to African American philosophy* (pp. 205–229). Blackwell.

Crenshaw, K. (1989). Demarginalizing the intersection of race and sex: A Black feminist critique of antidiscrimination doctrine, feminist theory and antiracist politics. *University of Chicago Legal Forum: 1989*(1). https://chicagounbound.uchicago.edu/uclf/vol1989/iss1/8/

Cronin, A., & King, A. (2010). Power, inequality and identification: Exploring diversity and intersectionality amongst older LGB adults. *Sociology, 44*(5), 876–892.

Davis, K. (2008). Intersectionality as buzzword: A sociology of science perspective on what makes a feminist theory successful. *Feminist Theory, 9*(1), 67–85. https://doi.org/10.1177/1464700108086364

De Vries, B. (2014). LG (BT) persons in the second half of life: The intersectional influences of stigma and cohort. *LGBT Health, 1*(1), 18–23.

Douglas, K. B. (1999). *Sexuality and the Black church: A womanist perspective.* Orbis Books.

File, T. (2018). *Characteristics of voters in the presidential election of 2016* (Current Population Reports P20–582) https://www.census.gov/content/dam/Census/library/publications/2018/demo/P20-582.pdf

Fox, L., & Pacas, J. (2018). *Deconstructing poverty rates among the 65 and older population: Why has poverty increased since 2015?* U.S. Census Bureau [SEHSD Working Paper #2018–13]. https://www.census.gov/content/dam/Census/library/working-papers/2018/demo/SEHSD-WP2018-13.pdf

Gendron, T., Welleford, E., Inker, J., & White, J. (2016). The language of ageism: Why we need to use words carefully. *The Gerontologist, 56*(6), 997–1006.

Gerontology Institute at the University of Massachusetts Boston (2019). *Elder Index results.* http://www.basiceconomicsecurity.org/EI/locations.aspx

Gould, E., Schieder, J., & Geier, K. (2016). *What is the gender pay gap and is it real?: The complete guide to how women are paid less than men and why it can't be explained away.* Economic Policy Institute. https://www.epi.org/publication/what-is-the-gender-pay-gap-and-is-it-real/

Griffin, S. (2012). *What does gender have to do with housing?* https://bridgethegulfproject.org/blog/2012/what-does-gender-have-do-housing%E2%80%A8

Grigoryeva, A. (2017). Own gender, sibling's gender, parent's gender: The division of elderly parent care among adult children. *American Sociological Review, 82*(1), 116–146.

Hankivsky, O. (2012). Women's health, men's health, and gender and health: implications of intersectionality. *Social Science & Medicine, 74*(11), 1712–1720.

Hankivsky, O. (2014). Intersectionality 101. *Institute for Intersectionality Research & Policy*, 1–34.

Harris, L. (1981). *Aging in the eighties: America in transition.* National Council on the Aging.

Harrison, L. (2017). Redefining intersectionality theory through the lens of African American young adolescent girls' racialized experiences. *Youth & Society, 49*(8), 1023–1039. http://doi.org/10.1177/0044118X15569216

hooks, b. (1981). *Ain't I a woman: Black women and feminism.* South End.

Kotter-Grühn, D., Kornadt, A. E., & Stephan, Y. (2016). Looking beyond chronological age: Current knowledge and future directions in the study of subjective age. *Gerontology, 62*(1), 86–93.

Lorde, A. (1995). Age, race, class, and sex: Women redefining difference. In B. Guy-Sheftall (Ed.), *Words of fire: An Anthology of African American feminist thought* (pp. 284–291). New York: The New York Press.

Lorenz, T. (2019, October 29). "OK Boomer marks the end of friendly generational relations. *New York Times.* https://www.nytimes.com/2019/10/29/style/ok-boomer.html

McBride, A., Hebson, G., & Holgate, J. (2015). Intersectionality: Are we taking enough notice in the field of work and employment relations? *Work, Employment and Society, 29*(2), 331–341.

McCall, L. (2005). The complexity of intersectionality. *Signs, 30*(3), 1771–1800.

McFadden, S. H. (1996). Religion, spirituality, and aging. In J. E. Birren & K.W. Schaie (Eds.), *Handbook of the psychology of aging* (4th ed.) (pp. 365–382). Academic Press.

MetLife. (2011). The MetLife study of caregiving costs to caregivers: Double jeopardy for baby boomers caring for their parents. https://www.caregiving.org/wp-content/uploads/2011/06/mmi-caregiving-costs-working-caregivers.pdf

Moore, K., & Ghilarducci, T. (2018). Intersectionality and stratification in the labor market. *Generations, 42*(2), 34–40.

Nelson-Beker, H., Nakashima, M. & Canda, E. R. (2006). Spiritual assessment in aging. *Journal of Gerontological Social Work, 48*(3–4), 331–347. https://doi.org/10.1300/J083v48n03_04

Nelson, T. (2016). The age of ageism. *Journal of Social Issues, 72*(1), 191–198.

North, M. (2015). Ageism stakes its claim in the social sciences. *Journal of the American Society on Aging, 39*(3), 720–734.

North, M., & Fiske, S. (2012). An inconvenienced youth? Ageism and its potential intergenerational roots. *Psychological Bulletin, 138*(5), 982–997.

Palmore, E. (1999). *Ageism: Negative and positive.* Springer.

Palmore, E. (2015). Ageism comes of age. *Journals of Gerontology: Social Sciences, 70*(6), 873–875.

Rice University. (2004). *Rice University sociologists calculate caregivers' risk of living in poverty.* https://news.rice.edu/2004/08/16/rice-university-sociologists-calculate-caregivers-risk-of-living-in-poverty/

Robinson, T., Gustafson, B., & Popovich, M. (2008). Perceptions of negative stereotypes of older people in magazine advertisements: Comparing the perceptions of older adults and college students. *Ageing & Society, 28*(2), 233–251.

Romano, A. (2019, November 19). *OK Boomer isn't just about the past. It's about out apocalyptic future.* Vox. https://www.vox.com/2019/11/19/20963757/what-is-ok-boomer meme-about-meaning-gen-z-millennials

Social Security Administration. (2019). *SSI federal payment amounts for 2019.* https://www.ssa.gov/oact/COLA/SSI.html

Streib, G. (1965). Are the aged a minority group? In A. Gouldner & S. Miller (Eds.), *Applied sociology* (pp.311–328). Free Press.

Sue, D. W. (2010). *Microaggressions and marginality: Manifestation, dynamics, and impact.* Wiley.

U.S. Census Bureau. (2018). Current population survey: 1960 to 2018 annual social economic supplements. https://www.census.gov/programs-surveys/sahie/technical-documentation/model-input-data/cpsasec.html

U.S. Department of Health and Human Services. (2019). *Poverty guidelines.* https://aspe.hhs.gov/2019-poverty-guidelines

Victor, C. R. (2013). *Old age in modern society: A textbook of social gerontology.* Springer.

Warner, D. F., & Brown, T. H. (2011). Understanding how race/ethnicity and gender define age trajectories of disability: An intersectionality approach. *Social Science & Medicine, 72*(8), 1236–1248.

CHAPTER 6

Fathers, Fathering, and Fatherhood

THROUGHOUT THE TEXT, we have discussed the significance of understanding family life and the various ways life intersects. Our hope is that the material and information contained within this text will be utilized to advance the work that is done with families. Specifically, this chapter seeks, not to diminish the strength of mother-headed households or to provide a deleterious view of other family systems, but to illuminate the importance of fathers and the changing culture regarding the essential role fathers play in the lives of children, communities, families, and society.

It would take more than a chapter to adequately address all of the factors that influence the male experience, given that the intersections of race, class, religious upbringing and beliefs, systemic oppression (ableism, child support, custody battles, incarceration, wrongful convictions, economic pitfalls, poverty, etc.), and many others that have a powerful impact on how men navigate the terrains of fatherhood, family, and other related factors. It is not the intention of the authors to disregard the lived experiences or to overly generalize the male experience and transition to fatherhood, but to help students transition from the classroom to the field, armed with information that assists in shaping their worldview and work with diverse populations.

Perspectives of Fatherhood

North America's historical-cultural view of fathering[1] and fatherhood[2] has created an ambiguous terrain for understanding fathering (Pleck, 1998). Since the 18th and 19th centuries, men were thought to be more rational than women. Therefore, only men were able to successfully lead the children and the family. Consequently, the emotional caring for infants and toddlers

---

1   Fathering implies to act or serve as a father or in a father role.
2   Fatherhood is the responsibility of being a father.

was primarily the mother's responsibility, while the father held a significant responsibility to guide sons to understand their plight as young men. They were also responsible for the arrangements of courtship prospects for their daughters, to guide children through moral and religious teaching, and to assist them with understanding worldly beliefs (Pleck, 1998). To some extent, these responsibilities were central to the father-child relationship because as the children worked near the father farming or in other trades, these lessons were taking place (Pleck, 1998; Rabun & Oswald, 2009). Although father-son relationships were highly regarded and emotionally close, fathers often displayed their affection through approval and disapproval, seldom through emotion (Rotundo, 1982). Furthermore, since the father was viewed as a more rational and intellectual being, and the mother more emotional, the father was often granted custody rights if the family dissolved as a unit during this time period. Nevertheless, the significance of the father's role lessened, and the father-child relationship began to shift in the late 19th century.

In the late 19th century, a new ideology about gender emerged. This new dogma prescribed nurturing, selflessness, and purity as feminine characteristics, and these characteristics were thought to be better suited to rear children (Demos, 1982). The parent-child roles changed as the mother was the leading caretaker, involved in the mate selection of the children, and more emotionally involved in the children's lives. Moreover, as infant and early childhood education began to gain popularity and female teachers in elementary school emerged, mothers were thought to have a greater influence on the child through birth and early childhood rearing (Demos, 1982). Thus, if the family as a unit dissolved, it became the mother who received custody of the child because it was believed that the child needed the mother more than their father (Grossberg, 1983).

While the shift to maternal validation advanced, the paternal influence was minimized. The Industrial Revolution (the mid-1800s) took the men away from the home and created a new depiction of fatherhood—one who works in factories farther from the home to care for the family. As fathers spent more time away from the home, their reach as a key figure also lessened, turning the women into consumers and managers of the household. All the while, fathers became producers and breadwinners and served as disciplinarians (Demos, 1982). Consequently, with the mother as the manager of the household and the father the breadwinner, the "traditional nuclear family" emerged and became the culturally dominant perspective.

People are socially constructed to accept mothers as competent, instinctive, and natural caregivers and fathers as awkward, cautious, and peculiar when around children. These stereotypes position fathers as the helper and not the primary caregiver (Morison, 2015). The American standard family as positioned by Smith (1993) is a working adult male who is married to an adult female who may earn an income, but her sole responsibility is to care for her husband and children, relegating the male role to the provider of economic stability for the family. Although Smith's research focused on women, this ideology has influenced research and policy and the formation of the ideals of the American family. This position is consistent with the notion of a married man and woman, living in the suburbs with 2.5 children.

Following WWII (1939–1945), the absence of the father brought awareness to the role of the father in the father-child relationship (Pleck, 1998). Many men had not returned from the war, thus leaving women to care for the family without husbands and fathers and forcing them into the workforce (Pleck, 1998), which once again changed the social structure of the family.

The roles and composition of U.S. households also changed from the 1960s to the 2000s. For instance, although the majority of children live in a two-parent household, there was an increase in the number of children who did not live in two-parent households and a rise and acceptance of single fathers raising children (U.S. Census Bureau, 2016). Furthermore, more women are working outside of the home, while fathers are taking on more of the responsibilities surrounding child care for various reasons such as being unemployed and not able to find work, unable to work due to disability status, or wanting to stay home to care for the family (U.S. Census Bureau, 2016).

Intersectionality of Fathers, Fathering, and Fatherhood

As defined in the text, intersectionality, as a theoretical framework, requires us to examine the different processes that individuals use to "negotiate competing and harmonious social identities" (Few-Demo et al., 2016, p. 76). The standpoint of fathering, fatherhood, and traditional family contexts, attitudes, and perceptions of family life vary due to racial and ethnic differences, multicultural variances, social status, and religious association. Since research has been conducted mostly by middle- and upper-class White researchers with mostly middle- and upper-class White male participants, children and families of color are often mis- and underrepresented in research. These factors create a Euro-American bias perpetuating an "otherness" and causing families of color to be seen as abnormal or inept and to confuse cultural differences with developmental deficits (Graham, 1992; Wittmer et al., 2016). The dominant cultural values and cultural systems of kinship and gender impact the views society has of what fatherhood entails. For many it includes what Townsend (2002) refers to as the "package deal": marriage, fatherhood, employment, and homeownership, thus, perpetuating a standardized vision of what successful fatherhood looks like. In the United States, there are cultural variations and several sets of values that compete and compliment, but dominant values, beliefs, norms, and behaviors shape the overall perception of fatherhood for society (Townsend, 2002). Men who do not share the values or concerns of the dominant culture, nor achieve or measure success by the dominant culture's standards, are often excluded and oppressed and often judge themselves for failing to meet the dominant expectation (Townsend, 2002).

The nature of fatherhood is constantly evolving and the discussion surrounding fathering (including but not limited to father involvement, absent fathers, new fathers, stay-at-home fathers, stepfathers, divorced and noncustodial fathers, gay fathers) and their roles are happening more in academic and contemporary mediums. The traditional views of fathering and fatherhood are narrow and static and may imply fatherhood simply encompasses emotionally distant patriarchs, providing and protecting the family. Generally, fatherhood is more complex than sometimes assumed by the models family scholars use, which may lead one to think that fatherhood is primarily the direct father-child interaction (Goodsell et al., 2010). Fatherhood consists of more than the conventional presumed societal mores and expectations.

Since not all fathers have biological children and not all men are biological fathers, the meanings of fatherhood vary. Although this chapter focuses on fatherhood and fathering, males who are not fathers are also important to consider when discussing this topic and how the interactions with their fathers or father figures shape their standpoint. Fathers of color, especially African American fathers, are oftentimes classified as absent, without taking into account or crediting father figures: "men who are not biological fathers but assume some of the roles and responsibilities of the father in the African American family" (Rentie, 2011, p. 77). Father figures may include family friends, relatives (e.g., brothers, uncles, cousins), neighbors, or step-fathers who fulfill the role of the father and can include the wider kinship network or extended family (Connor & White, 2006).

These interactions range from casual to close and span from single exchanges to decade-long relationships. These bonds are influenced by psychological health and resiliency; social factors (e.g., economic wealth, institutionalized and perceived racism, family dynamics and systems, environmental hardships); ecosystems, their communities, and the wider society (e.g., family, school, and religious institutions and friendships); and cultural systems, which may vary by geographic location, socioeconomic status, and ethnicity. Cultural influences also evolve from generation to generation. These elements can influence development, shape the expectations about fatherhood, and influence behavior and the relationships one nurtures over time (Townsend, 2002). The prevailing dialogue among men and fathers unsettles the traditional ideas of what fathering looks like or should be and includes nurturing and emotional connection as part of the gender socialization for men.

Additionally, this discourse encourages paternal involvement, embraces discussions surrounding being a provider, as well as health and self-care, which includes mental and physical well-being. Also, healthy relational functioning, such as how to treat significant others and women, respect for others and themselves, as well as the importance of religion and faith, have become standard practice while fathering. Now, the approval of being vulnerable and the need for healthy emotional expression are beginning to become emphasized. These views are often passed down through informal learning, consciously but oftentimes subconsciously through culture, socialization, conversations, and interactions with and between other men, fathers, and father figures.

Cabrera et al. (2014) observed that research has not been presented to describe the routes that may move boys to the practice of fathering, nor has there been research to develop a theory that explains the dynamic developmental processes that shape fatherhood (Hildreth et al., 2018). Feminist theory explores the relationship within and between gender, social institutions, and families and their communities and contexts (Doucet, 2016). Therefore, it is due, in part, to feminist theory and research on mothers and motherhood that research on men as gendered beings, masculinity, manhood, and fatherhood has evolved (Townsend, 2002).

Many men have to create their own ways of being fathers, especially if they come from a background where a father is not present in their lives. Likewise, many fathers are taking on various roles in parenting and family, some by choice and others out of necessity. Men usually become stay-at-home fathers by circumstance, not by choice (e.g., losing a job, laid off, relocation, etc.) and may see it as a temporary adjustment. Since paid employment is still assumed for fathers, many fathers feel the impact of the conflicting roles of caregiving as the central component of fathering, although breadwinning is just as important (Solomon, 2014). Some find themselves in a dilemma, as they are expected to be present and love their family but also provide and work, oftentimes away from the home and family. To adapt to the new designation of stay-at-home father, oftentimes they will work part time to contribute financially to the family or take on other roles, such as home repairs or coaching sports, to compensate and build a community, which may connect to their masculinity (Chesley, 2011; Doucet, 2004).

Research suggests that fathers have the capacity for caregiving and children benefit from the father's contributions (Cabrera et al., 2014). Although a man's approach may vary from a woman's, they are capable of loving and being warm, caring, and playful. What is more, there is a rise and acceptance of single fathers raising children (U.S. Census Bureau, 2016). According to the U.S. Census Bureau (2017), in the United States, there were 2 million single fathers in 2016. Men such as Dwayne Wade (a former NBA player) have shared their narratives on how difficult it is to seek full custody in order to see their children when the relationship with the children's mother is turbulent. It is often difficult because there are not many examples from other men about the legal, financial, emotional, and/or social process of being a single father but may be a necessary decision if a man wants to be in his children's lives. The transition from the children visiting on the weekends to living with the father full time is a transition for all of them, potentially changing roles from being a fun weekend parent to the disciplinarian and the one who teaches them how to navigate life. This decision is complicated and complex and emphasizes the significance of fatherhood and fathers in society.

Conversely, there are a number of reasons for a father to be absent in the family structure, including, but not limited to, divorce, lack of commitment, limitation of (community, economic, emotional) resources, choices and legal ramifications and custody battles, communication and social challenges, and death. The effects of absent fathers have been the subject of many discussions. Father absence is reported to have an influence on psychosocial, cognitive, and personality development; educational attainment; and future parenting behaviors. The absence may also lead to negative emotional, social, academic, and behavioral outcomes and contribute to higher rates of crime, poverty, marital conflict, and substance abuse (Adams, 2004; Baer,1999).

However, researchers (Harris, 2002) challenge the notion of negative effects on children when fathers are not present. Men who grow up without fathers are capable of being good fathers, and the long-standing history of resilience and in(ter)dependence of Black and Brown families has moderated the negative effects of detached families, allowing one to move from a deficiency model to a strengths-based perspective and provide a nuanced narrative of fathers of color.

Although research is forthcoming on gay parenting, gay fathers contribute to the expansion of the normative nuclear family ideal (Rabun & Oswald, 2009). Through their relationships with friends and loved ones, gay men consider parenting and are further concerned about the barriers to parenting (e.g., political, economic, alternative routes to parenting). Gay men have become parents by way of previous heterosexual relationships, stepparenting, surrogacy, adoption and fostering, semen donation to heterosexual or lesbian women, and co-parenting arrangements with heterosexual women (Barrett & Tasker, 2001; Carnerio et al., 2017).

Gay men's visions of fatherhood may consist of "conscious parenting," in which having children is consciously planned for (Morison, 2015). Just like other families, gay families range in form and often explore their kinship networks beyond biological ties, but tend to divide childcare more equitably (Morison, 2015). This arrangement may operate outside of traditional gender roles. Gay couples are often judged more harshly and less accepted than lesbian and heterosexual couples because of the traditional model of masculinity and the prescribed gender norms (Connell, 2005; Rabun, & Oswald, 2009). As with the aforementioned stereotype of fathers as awkward, cautious, and peculiar when around children, gay men are also charged with being less emotionally stable, incompetent, and incapable of creating an established environment for children (Crawford & Solliday, 1996). However, when compared to heterosexual parents, children of gay fathers demonstrate less internalizing and externalizing problems (Miller et al., 2017). Similar to heterosexual men, many homosexual men yearn for fatherhood but are aware that becoming a father may require them to postpone their life goals. Also, they may want to be in a committed relationship with a significant other and want to be involved in their children's lives (Hutchinson, Marsiglio, & Cohan, 2002; Rabun & Oswald, 2009).

Conclusions

Fathering and fatherhood can be complicated and complex topics because the vision of what successful fatherhood looks like varies culturally and socially. There is significant research that considers and emphasizes the significance of fatherhood and the roles fathers play in society. Additionally, there are many aspects that have a powerful impact on how men navigate the terrains of fatherhood, family, and other related factors. Therefore, it is important to illuminate the importance of fathers and the changing culture regarding the essential role fathers play in the lives of children, communities, families, and society.

Implications for Family Life Education

Society has taught us to play certain roles, and many times that gets in the way of progressive philosophy, research, and policy. Gatekeeping, deciding what information is disseminated and who receives that information, is a powerful phenomenon that has affected family systems and functioning. Media images, research, and lexis have a great impact on the perceptions of people. This is especially true for people who may have never interacted with others of different races, ethnicities, religions, sexualities, and so on in their own communities, thus causing marginalized people to become victims of perception. These perceptions can lead one to believe in stereotypical thoughts and ideas, which may lead to harsher judgments, less empathy and understanding, less attainable economic resources (e.g., jobs, bank loans, affordable housing, etc.), and disproportionate opportunities.

Life experiences and environmental factors can have negative and positive effects on a person and the family system. It is imperative for family life educators to understand and respect the effects the intergenerational transmission of trauma can have on one's mental, physical, emotional, and social well-being. Trauma can occur in various forms such as death or loss of a loved one, social trauma, enslavement, poverty, homelessness, and many others. Researchers (Solomon, 2014; Wade, 1998) have documented the ramifications when fathers are not present and have shown that when a father or father figure is absent from a child's life they are more likely to perform poorly in academics, have poor mental health (anxiety and mood disorders), abuse substances, and attempt suicide. There is no disputing the effect fatherlessness has on children's lives. By supporting fathers and families, we ultimately increase healthy families and communities. Although there are often barriers to accessing care, it is imperative the mental health concerns be identified and addressed. Essentially, this means that family life educators need to be knowledgeable about mental health problems to reduce stigma, understand the illness, and provide appropriate ways to respond with available resources.

Fathers today spend more time with their children than the fathers in previous generations, but many times the assumption is made that they are forced into this relationship. What is more is that oftentimes when we discuss fatherhood, men of color are not part of the conversation or are a part of the negative discourse on absentee fathers and dead-beat dads, largely because that is the narrative that is perpetuated and continually advanced (Hamer, 2001). The fact is that there is always a narrative behind and beyond the numbers. Despite what is chronicled, African American fathers spend more time in their children's day-to-day lives than any other racial group (Jones & Mosher, 2013). Although Black fathers are more likely to live outside of the home, there is no significant difference to White fathers (Jones & Mosher, 2013). As family life educators it is imperative that we examine our assumptions, decrease the invisible barriers, and work to connect fathers with resources to thrive in a society that has demeaned their role. To effectively promote responsible fatherhood and make resources available, family life educators need to adopt a strengths-based mind-set and understand the strengths of the father and family members. Programs such as Head Start have supported and strengthened parent-child relationships for more than 50 years. Whether parents are cohabitating or living separately, custodial or noncustodial, Head Start and many of the other programs that are mentioned in the chapter appreciate the essential role that positively engaged fathers can play in support of children, families, and their communities. Following this practice, practitioners should help fathers connect with their children in developmentally appropriate ways while encouraging and recognizing engaged fathers and their contributions to their children's behavior. Furthermore, soliciting and respecting the input of the father to address barriers that may impede their active engagement can strengthen the interconnected relationships (e.g., father/child, father/mother, father/family system, father/ecological system) and set the tone for a healthy family functioning.

Essentially, advocating for communication and skills building within the family (e.g., father-child, couples, co-parenting, stepfamilies), workplace and other social interactions provide an opportunity to restore relationships, acquire communication skills, and establish healthy family systems and subsystems. Each community is unique. Communicating with fathers in a healthy and respectful way may provide the opportunity to know how one can best partner with and support the families. Additional ways to advocate and advance the conversation regarding fathers and fatherhood is to become involved in professional organizations, create effective community partnerships with faith-based organizations, mentoring groups, community networks, and boy's and girl's clubs. Additionally, continue to search for resources and have conversations about what fathers really think about fatherhood, the gendered differences in expectations, and the importance of the relationship between fathers and their children, so we can better understand men as fathers. These will not only challenge fathers to unpack their biases, values, and expectations but also the practitioner in understanding the populations we may serve.

Additional Readings

The readings that have been included in this chapter include a broad look at father-related policies in the United States, as well as an ethnographic account detailing how life events have influenced one father to begin reciprocating love while learning to love himself. The implications for both of the readings are significant when conceptualizing fathering from a wide-ranging perspective. The narrative and roles of fathering and fatherhood are shifting, and the selected readings will provide information related to policies that have affected fathering; the importance of understanding men's health (mental, physical, relational, and spiritual), specifically related to their role as fathers; the importance of knowing their family history and how it impacts one's trajectory; and the importance of passing down wisdom and learning from others accounts.

Fatherhood and Family Policies

By Scott Coltrane and Andrew Behnke

Introduction

Although all modern industrialized nations have policies and programs designed to fulfill specific family-related goals, most legislation affecting families in the United States does not explicitly spell out its goals for fathers or families (Bogenschneider, 2000; Kamerman & Kahn, 2001). Just two decades ago, researchers were arguing that family policy does not really exist in the United States, because there is no set of laws or administrative orders labeled *family policy* and because there are no high level offices in federal or state governments that are responsible for directly overseeing policies that affect families (Bane & Jargowsky, 1989). Although most concede that things have changed, a recent decade review (Bogenschneider & Corbett, 2010b, p. 783) begins by stating "*family policy* is still not a term that is widely used by knowledge consumers, such as policymakers, journalists, or the public. It has not yet achieved the status of economic or environmental policy, nor is it even recognized in its own right as a subfield of social policy."

Nevertheless, a huge range of government policies and programs at the federal, state, and local levels have had dramatic impacts on family well-being and have shaped the roles of men and women as partners and as parents (Coltrane & Adams, 2008; Gornick & Meyers, 2003; Moen & Coltrane, 2004). In this chapter, we define family policy as the state's deliberate shaping of laws and programs intended to help families and children. Such a definition limits family policy to programs consciously undertaken to affect families in a positive way, making it easier to study recent policy initiatives, especially those aimed at fathers, though it leaves unexamined other important effects on families of less targeted programs and policies. As Cabrera (2010) points out, the mid-1990s was a turning point because the Clinton administration established the Fatherhood Research Initiative aimed at promoting research and policy development relating to fathers' involvement with their children, followed by the Bush administration's Healthy Marriage Initiative which focused on keeping low-income men connected to the mothers of their children (see also Cabrera, Brooks-Gunn, Moore, West, & Boller, 2002; Coltrane, 2001; Mincy, Garfinkel, & Nepomnyaschy, 2005). In this chapter we build on this earlier scholarship by discussing federal and state level policies, bridges to other disciplines, and future directions for research on father-related policy.

Brief Historical and Theoretical Overview

Many social scientists and child advocates have defined family policies in terms of the well-being of children (Hernandez, 1993). For example, Marian Wright Edelman (2003), founder of the Children's Defense Fund, suggested that instead of formulating something called family policy, we should fund health, nutrition, education, and housing programs aimed at directly benefiting children (virtually all of whom live in some sort of family), and others have suggested we should focus on job training or poverty reduction to benefit at-risk youth (Lerman, 2010). A large number of researchers and policy makers have focused on the plight of children living in single parent families, most of whom live at or near the poverty level, with special attention to African American and Latino children, whose life chances have been declining. When compared to White children, African American children are much more likely to be poor, lack health insurance, and live with one or no parents in the household (Edelman, 2003; Haskins, 2009). Similar declining life chances are evident for Latino youth (Eamon, 2005; Lieb & Thistle, 2005).

Studies comparing child poverty in the United States to other industrialized countries show that things may be getting worse for American children (Adamson, 2010). Children living in single-mother homes worldwide are at particular risk for being poor, although, in most nations, government assistance is more effective than in the United States at lifting poor families and children out of poverty (Barrientos & DeJong, 2006; Rainwater & Smeeding, 2003). The tendency to spend so little on children and to avoid creating explicit family policies in the United States stems from the common assumption that families are private and separate from the government (or the church, schools, economy, or any other social institution), a conclusion that is challenged by most recent social science research (Coltrane & Adams, 2008).

Sometimes child or family policies can influence family form, such as with the American Aid to Families with Dependent Children (AFDC) program, the federal welfare effort phased out in 1996 to become TANF (Temporary Assistance to Needy Families). One of the problems with AFDC, designed to help single mothers with children, was that it actually discouraged fathers from living with their children. Early-on in the AFDC program, mothers and children were denied benefits if a social worker visited the home and found a man's clothes or other belongings in the house. Following historical patterns and in conjunction with low wages and systemic patterns of job discrimination, this discouraged low-income African American fathers from marrying the mother and living in the child's home. By the late 1990s, less than half of African American children were living with two parents, compared to over three-fourths of White children (Haskins, 2009; McLanahan, 2009). An unintended consequence of AFDC, this provision was changed when AFDC was replaced by TANF in conjunction with the 1996 overhaul of welfare known as PRWORA (Personal Responsibility and Work Opportunity Reconciliation Act) as discussed below. Unlike AFDC, which provided cash payments to single-parent families, TANF gives block grants to states. The states are then guided by the federal government to use the funds primarily to provide basic assistance with food (Supplemental Nutrition Assistance Program [SNAP]), child care, and transportation with the stated aim of aiding families in producing healthy and productive citizens.

Today, some government programs aimed at low-income children are designed to bring men (and their limited incomes) back into the family by encouraging them to sign paternity declarations at the child's birth, by performing blood tests to determine paternity, and by directly withholding child support payments from their pay checks (Sorensen, 2010). For example, the Paternity Opportunity Program (POP) in many states works through hospitals, prenatal clinics, county welfare offices, local vital records offices, and courts to increase paternity declarations and conduct paternity blood tests. Additionally, programs like Support Has A Rewarding Effect (SHARE) helped some noncustodial parents to work more, earn more, and pay more child support after their involvement in the program (Perez-Johnson, Kauff, & Hershey, 2003). Head Start and Early Head Start have encouraged increased father involvement through the Male and Father-Involvement Initiative. As discussed below, recent initiatives changed focus from encouraging poor men to pay up or to marry the mother of their children, to instead focus on helping provide fathers with education, job training, and access to jobs so they can be the dads they want to be (Haskins, 2009; Lerman, 2010; Sorensen, 2010; Waller, 2009).

During most of the 20th century, both researchers and policy makers assumed that pre-school children's well-being was largely determined by mothers' contributions to parenting and fathers financial contributions to families, with state level contributions focused on serving populations with special needs (poor families, single-parent families, orphans and foster children, children with health problems or developmental disabilities). With men's and women's patterns of labor force participation converging in the late 20th century, governments in developed countries have focused on ways to aid both mothers and fathers with parenting, as well as providing child care, educational and health services directly to children.

Several decades of accumulated social and behavioral science research affirms that investments in the early years of children's lives can "pay off" in terms of the reduction of future social costs associated with criminality, employability, and mental and physical health (Featherstone, 2010; Wagmiller & Adelman, 2010). Recent research (Leidy, Schofield, & Parke, this volume) finds that enhancing father involvement can also have beneficial influence on child development and social efficacy in middle childhood. Across the globe, governments are investing in paternal involvement schemes to support the healthy development of infants and children. Scandinavian countries first offered innovative leave programs for employed fathers as well as employed mothers in the 1970s, with the pace of adoption in other nations accelerating in the mid-1990s (Liera, 2002; Moss & Deven, 2006; O'Brien, 2009). By 2007, 66 nations had enacted policies that included fathers' entitlement to paid parental leave, typically adopted in the context of more general work-family reconciliation frameworks geared toward both women and men (Gornick & Meyers, 2003; Heyman, Earle, & Hayes, 2007). Most of these father-friendly policies now exist in European Union countries, though many new initiatives also came from Australia and Canada (Lero, Ashbourne, & Whitehead, 2006; O'Brien, 2009; Sullivan, Coltrane, McAnnally, & Altintas, 2009). Although the United States lags behind many nations in promoting child well-being and father involvement, U.S. efforts have increased recently, as researchers and policy makers have focused on fathers.

In this chapter we briefly review such efforts drawing on a multidisciplinary life course perspective (Elder, 1998). We explore how such policies are seen as influencing the lives of fathers and children over time depending on their circumstances and stages in life. This framework helps us to understand how policies influence the linked lives of fathers and their children, and how policies can impact the life course trajectories on which these men and their children embark (Coltrane & Galt, 2000; Doherty, Kouneski, & Erickson, 1998).

Current Research Questions

Several overarching sets of research questions are crucial to exploring how policies and father involvement are related, including (a) What are the implicit and explicit goals of specific policies? (b) What are the conditions under which different policies are developed, adopted, and implemented? (c) What influence do these policies have on women, men, children, families, and society? As discussed below, the first question is typically seen as self-evident, although some research does focus on specifying more directly why we should worry about promoting father involvement. The second set of research questions is most often addressed in comparative perspective with historical data. Such studies often focus on the importance of differing political cultures and processes, as well as social structural conditions, with theoretical emphasis on nation states and differences among policy regimes. In contrast, the more plentiful research on the third set of questions about the consequences of various policies takes many forms and ranges from assessing individual psychological outcomes to studies focused on how various policies are associated with different demographic and economic indicators. Assessing the specific consequences of individual policies, or of clusters of policies, is not an easy matter, even when a specific target population is identified. Researchers must always consider the possibility of endogeneity and spurious associations, as well as facing the difficult task of determining causal order. As Kelly (2008) notes and as we discuss below, the best research uses sophisticated methodologies to address these challenges, but also acknowledges the limitations of any chosen method.

Finally, it is important to note that despite our best efforts, there seems to be a tenuous relationship between academic research and social policy. Not only is there often a weak and indirect relationship between societal needs and the passage of policies designed to address those needs, but the influence of academic research on the creation and implementation of policy is typically much less than assumed. For example, in a chapter titled "Exploring the Disconnect between Research and Policy," two prominent distinguished professors from one of the leading American research universities comment,

> It is hard to shake the impression that we may be functioning in a policy environment that operates, ironically enough, according to an inverse relationship between science and politics the more and better research we produce, the less effect it has on the policymaking process. With increasing amounts of data and analysis emerging from our universities and research/evaluation firms, the likelihood that even the most studious of public officials can sort through and make sense of the science available to them is not very high. (Bogenschneider & Corbett, 2010a, p. 3)

As these scholars point out, the relationship between social science and public policy is complex, ambiguous, and very contextual. Sometimes social science research influences policy making and sometimes it does not. Even when research does inform a specific policy or influence a specific piece of legislation, the researchers themselves typically admit that their work carried far less weight than they wanted and was viewed with far more skepticism than they expected (Danzinger, 2001). And in those instances when policy based on social science evidence is implemented, the results are so hard to attribute to individual programs that the true cause of the trend or outcome remains unclear. Most policies are the result of many years of work by diverse coalitions of advocates and policymakers, and resulting programs often reflect competing understandings from lengthy processes of legislative drafting, executive rulemaking, judicial interpretation, and legislative modification (Feldblum & Appleberry, 2008). Finally, given the cyclical nature of influence in American politics, policies, and programs are often abandoned before they have a chance to accomplish their goals.

Coupled with an academic environment at most top U.S. research universities that is assumed to give only bland support and no real encouragement to policy-related research (Bogenschneider & Corbett, 2010a), why should researchers even care about conducting research on fatherhood policy? In our view, this is a question with a simple answer. As fathers and sons we know on a personal level that fathers matter to their children, and as the chapters in this volume attest, the social and behavioral science evidence from the last several decades is helping us to understand how and why father involvement influences child development and family well-being. Despite the complexity of the task, we advocate for parallel research into how and why policies might help men become better partners and parents.

Research Measurement and Methodology

Among the many approaches taken to the study of family and fatherhood policies, some research focuses on the purposes of specific policies or the political processes that produce them, whereas other researchers evaluate the impact of policies and programs on the lives of fathers and their families. First, policy researchers often assess the explicit goals of specific policies by studying their written narratives and background materials, and then attempt to understand the reasoning and underlying goals of these policies by interviewing and surveying policy makers and those that influence their decisions. Second, large-scale national studies (e.g., ECLS-K) and census data are often used to understand and contextualize how and why these policies are developed, adopted, and implemented in the lives of fathers and their families. Third, these same large-scale studies, as well as numerous qualitative and mixed method studies (e.g., Fragile Families, FCI) provide considerable important descriptive information to assess the influence of these policies on women, men, children, families, and society. These studies can take years to be adequately assessed and interpreted, causing some lag between implementation and outcomes. However, these studies can influence conversations about the effectiveness of public and private policies and programs. A detailed methodological critique is beyond the scope of this review, but we provide some basic information on research methods related to various family and fatherhood policies of the last decade.

Empirical Findings
Exploring Implicit and Explicit Goals of Fatherhood Policies

Before reviewing how policies related to fathers are framed or adopted and before evaluating how effective they are at accomplishing their objectives, it is important to ask more fundamental questions. Why should we target special policies and programs toward fathers? On what basis do researchers claim that promoting father involvement will be beneficial for men, women, and children? These are the sorts of questions that are left implicit in most research, but they are important for scholars to explore in more depth than has been done in the past.

Although research on fatherhood is becoming more prevalent, it still represents only a tiny fraction of research on families and child development (Goldberg, Tan, & Thorson, 2009). For most of the 20th century, practitioners and academics either focused on fathers as symbolic heads of families and/or assumed that fathers were relatively unimportant figures in terms of child development outcomes (Coltrane, 1996; Parke, 1996). Although many have been concerned that father absence might have deleterious effects on children and mothers, most studies did not collect information on what fathers actually did with and for children and families (Coltrane & Galt, 2000; Griswold, 1993; Pleck & Pleck, 1997). Not only did most family and child development studies in the twentieth century ignore fathers, but family-related policies focused almost exclusively on mothers and children.

With the rise of female labor force participation in the late twentieth century, a critique of stereotyped separate public and private spheres for men and women emerged, and the cultural contradictions of motherhood and fatherhood became a topic for scholarly exploration (e.g., Bernard, 1981; Hays, 1996). Part of this dialog concerned the extent to which public policies were designed to protect men's privileged position in the family, including a "family wage" and the rights and opportunities to enjoy the domestic services of wives and mothers (Coltrane & Adams, 2008; Thorne, 1992). In the late twentieth century, these debates highlighted the well-being of mothers and children versus the rights and obligations of fathers, sometimes framed in the context of campaigns to limit divorce, promote marriage, or defend paternal custody rights (e.g., Adams, 2006; Coltrane, 2001; Doherty, 1991; Hays, 2003).

A new father ideal gained prominence in American popular culture during the 1980s (Coltrane, 1996; Griswold, 1993; Pruett, 1987). According to Furstenberg (1988), "[T]elevision, magazines, and movies herald the coming of the modern father—the nurturant, caring, and emotionally attuned parent…. Today's father is at least as adept at changing diapers as changing tires" (p. 193). No longer limited to being protectors and providers, at least some fathers came to be seen as intimately involved in family life. Fatherhood proponents focused on the potential of the new ideals and practices (Biller, 1976), but many researchers reported that fathers resisted assuming responsibility for daily housework or child care (Thompson & Walker, 1989). Some researchers claimed that popular images far exceeded men's actual behaviors (LaRossa, 1988), and others suggested that men were less committed to families than they had been in the past (Ehrenreich, 1984). In contrast, some claimed that the sensitive or androgynous parenting styles of new fathers might lead to gender identity confusion in sons (Blankenhorn, 1995; Popenoe, 1996) and others questioned whether the symbolic importance granted to fathers was supported by available empirical evidence (Stacey, 1996; Silverstein & Auerbach, 1999). The debates of the 1980s and 1990s thus seemed to focus on a contrast between old-style breadwinner fathers and new-style nurturing fathers, though in reality most of the empirical evidence showed that the two were intimately linked in the everyday lives of average Americans (e.g., Coltrane, 1996; Pleck & Masciadrelli, 2004; Townsend, 2002).

In contrast to earlier eras, there now seems to be an emerging consensus that fathers matter to the well-being of children and families, and this view has made its way into policy formulations and political rhetoric. It is difficult to attribute priority to a specific cause, but whether propelled by women's increasing ability to command economic, political and personal resources, or the recognition of the intrinsic importance of men to family life and child development, the late twentieth century witnessed a remarkable transformation in family policy justifications. The Department of Health and Human Services' policies on fathers are now shaped by five principles (see Cabrera, 2010, p. 530): (a) All fathers can be important contributors to the well-being of their children; (b) Parents are partners in raising their children, even when they do not live in the same household; (c) The role fathers play in families is diverse and related to cultural and community norms; (d) Men should receive the education and support necessary to prepare them for the responsibility of parenthood; (e) Government can encourage and promote father involvement through its programs and through its workforce policies.

Despite these principles, most public policies in America are still primarily shaped by a focus on fathers' provision of financial support to mothers and children. On the one hand, we have cultural and legal traditions that treat fathers as financial providers and family heads, but on the other, we have an emerging view that treats fathers as equal partners to their wives and equal parents to their children. Not surprisingly, the dilemmas and contradictions inherent in the tensions between these views of fatherhood underlie most policy efforts to promote men's involvement in families (Coltrane & Adams, 2008; Hays, 2003).

Although typically taken for granted, we believe that research is still needed to address the first question of why we would want to promote father involvement in marriages and families, and further, what types and what level of involvement we should expect from men. Studies designed to address these questions typically lack sophisticated empirical data, but usually raise provocative issues about ethics, family values and gender equity (Coltrane, 2001; Nock, 1998; Stacey, 1996; Wilcox, 2004). For example, research on domestic violence (e.g., Johnson, 2006; Stark, 2007) tends to take a different view of the influence of masculinity on family dynamics than that offered by fatherhood advocates who champion male family headship and masculine role models (Blankenhorn, 1995) or men's rights advocates who argue for paternal custody on the basis of parental alienation syndrome (Adams, 2006). We need more studies that delineate the specific objectives of various constituencies related to men and fathers, and research methods that can trace their impact on the legislative initiatives that garner support.

The promotion of father involvement policies and the funding of fatherhood research efforts have been the product of very different political constituencies. For example, Democratic Vice President Al Gore was one of the first top-ranking officials to promote the study of fathers and to advocate for policies designed to encourage father involvement, especially among disadvantaged groups (Marsiglio et al., 1998). Republican George W. Bush defeated Gore in his 2000 presidential bid. President Bush, through appointment of fatherhood advocates such as Wade Horn, maintained an emphasis on the importance of fathers, but changed the policy focus to family values and marriage-related media campaigns, provision of faith-based counseling and services, and promotion of (heterosexual) couple relationship education (Coltrane, 2001). The passage of new policy initiatives frequently depends on forging coalitions among ideologically competing constituencies, and fatherhood and marriage policies are a prime example of this, though few would have predicted this based on the history of policy development around issues of child support, child custody, and divorce reform in the previous decade (Coltrane & Adams, 2008). Research in this area should highlight which aspects of father involvement the policies are trying to advance and which family and social goals are being promoted (e.g. compare Hays, 2003 or Stacey, 1996 with Popenoe, 1996 or Wilcox, 2004).

What Predicts How Different Policies Are Developed, Adopted, and Implemented?

Studies designed to address how and why specific policies arise and are implemented in different contexts exemplify the second set of research questions noted above. Over the past several decades, scholars have provided many theories and empirical studies to illuminate how changes in state policies and programs are related to the organization of paid labor and family life, with related implications for fatherhood and gender relations (Fraser, 1994; Gornick & Meyers, 2003; Hobson & Morgan, 2002; O'Brien, 2009). Gornick and Meyers (2007) suggest that researchers and policy makers have been engaged in at least three overlapping but nonintersecting conversations about work and family life focused on child well-being, work-family conflict, and gender equality (see Coltrane, 2009). The *Child Well-Being* conversation focuses on maternal care during the child's first months and on the quality of care throughout childhood. A major concern in this conversation is the lack of availability of parents to their children and a secondary concern is the quality of both parental and substitute child care provision. The *Work-Family* conversation focuses on the problems of working parents (especially mothers) whose conflicting responsibilities leave them penalized at work and overburdened at home. This conversation, motivated by women's rapid entry into the paid labor force, tends to focus on how to "balance" work and family obligations. The *Gender Equality* conversation uses feminist insights to highlight gender equity issues in the workplace and in the home, including historically lower wages and a disproportionate expectation that women will do the domestic work associated with raising children and maintaining homes.

Gornick and Meyers (2007) suggest that these conversations produce very different policy proposals. A *Child Well-Being* approach suggests the need for policies like child tax credits and maternity leaves so that mothers can drop out of the labor market, at least temporarily. A *Work-Family* approach also tends to locate the major conflict in the lives of mothers, suggesting policies such as part-time work, job sharing, telecommuting and flextime that allow for individual women (and sometimes men) to balance their work and family commitments. A *Gender Equality* perspective views inequities as stemming from women's weak and intermittent connection to employment and the assumption that they should perform the unpaid family work. Policies suggested by this approach focus on reducing employment barriers, raising women's wages, and providing alternatives to maternal care through the provision of child care centers or subsidies.

As Gornick and Meyers point out (2007, p. 15), although they differ in naming the problem and in the solutions they propose, the conversations they identify have two things in common (see Coltrane, 2009). They all focus on women and do little to question assumptions about the organization of men's employment and caregiving activities. These conversations also suggest that the interests of men, women, and children are essentially in conflict. Children can have more time with their parents only if women reduce their employment commitments and career prospects; women and men can achieve greater equality in their employment only by reducing their time and commitment to caring for their children. In contrast to these approaches, Gornick and Meyers (2003, 2007) assume that the interests of women, men, and children are only "apparently" competing. They suggest that the real culprit, and the cause of the putative competition between interests, is the failure of social, market, and policy institutions to adequately address the care of children in high-employment societies. They propose (following others such as Crompton, 1999; Fraser, 1994; Hobson & Morgan, 2002; Knijn & Kremer, 1997) that the solution must involve men as well as women, and the state as well as the family. They envision a dual-earner/dual-caregiver society, one that supports equal opportunities for men and women in employment, equal contributions from mothers and fathers at home, and high quality care for children provided both by parents and by well-qualified and well-paid non-parental caregivers.

Just as the state facilitated and even encouraged women to become workers, it is reasonable to expect that states, through different political processes and social policies, can also facilitate and encourage fathers to become caregivers. However, as Hobson and Morgan (2002) demonstrate, there is no neat fit between the welfare regimes of industrialized countries and their fatherhood policy regimes (defined as fatherhood obligations and fatherhood rights). Because of wide variation in political, economic, social, and cultural context, and because historical events and institutional forces have shaped many different, sometimes conflicting, policies related to fathers and families, it has often proved difficult to categorize countries using such typologies. In the area of parental leave, for example, O'Brien (2009) presents a typology of national policy contexts specifically focused on what she terms "father-care sensitive" policies, in which the major classifying dimensions are (a) the length of paternal leave and men's access to parental leave and (b) the level of income replacement available during such leave. This kind of typology, explicitly designed to address children's access to men's parental resources, provides a framework sensitive to differences in policies affecting men's caregiving. There have been some recent studies focused on such complexities with promising results (Folbre, 2008; Fuwa & Cohen, 2007; Gornick & Meyers, 2003; Hook, 2006; Smith & Williams, 2007). We need more research on such questions incorporating the local complexity of multiple policies and their adoption in specific national contexts.

What Influence Do Fatherhood Policies Have on Women, Men, Children, Families, and Society?

Research questions focused on the consequences of policies promoting father involvement are likely to have great influence on scholarship and legislation in the coming decade. As noted above, the social and policy contexts in which fathers parent has changed dramatically over the past several decades. Because research on the Healthy Marriages Initiative is only now making its way into the published literature in sufficient volume to assess it, we can begin to identify a new set of questions about the consequences of these specific policies on fathers and families. For example, Cabrera (2010, p. 525) reminds us that issues of poverty, non-marital fertility, cohabitation, and nonresidential parenting pose a challenge for fathers who want to support their children and for policies designed to protect child welfare: "The Healthy Marriage Initiative created a policy context that may be untenable for some families and may be inconsistent with how families are organized and do not offer the help these families need to provide a healthy and stimulating environment for their children. The question is under what conditions and for whom is marriage good?" And the situation is complicated by the fact that the Obama administration is promoting only some aspects of the previous emphasis on healthy marriages. If we hope to fulfill the promise of evidence-based policy making, we need to document how different policies and programs have affected the lives of men, women, and children who have been touched by them (Bogenschneider & Corbett, 2010a).

Some emerging questions that come out of our own and others' recent research agendas include identifying the conditions under which it is best to (a) involve nonresidential fathers in the lives of their children; (b) value fathers for their contribution to families outside of the provider role; and (c) encourage healthy relationships regardless of marital status or living situation. These questions are not independent from the political situations that give rise to specific policy agendas, but we have faith that scientific inquiry can indeed shed light on when and how we should invest in the well-being of future generations through family programs. We are confident that research will begin to address these sorts of questions in the coming decade, along with continuing to address the ones that came out of the last 20 years of scholarship during which attention to fathers increased dramatically (Goldberg et al., 2009).

Bridges to Other Disciplines

Policy oriented research is necessarily multi-disciplinary and typically spans several social science fields, including sociology, psychology, political science, history, anthropology, and economics as exemplified by the studies noted above. In this section we further highlight potential bridges to other disciplines by investigating one realm of fatherhood policy; father provisioning, which has a relatively long and contentious history in sociology, economics, law enforcement, political science, and legal circles. Fathers are often seen by policy makers as primarily, if not solely, providers for their families. Commentators have observed that policy in the United States focuses primarily on a father's financial support role, as compared to the nurturing and care aspects of fathering (Vann, 2007). Indeed research continues to show that fathers agree that they are the providers, or at least that they should be (Bianchi & Milkie, 2010; Townsend, 2002). Providing monetary support might facilitate more nurturing aspects of fathering, and Bianchi and Milkie (2010) note that fathers who are earning more income are more likely to live with their children, and non-resident fathers are more likely to have closer ties to active parenting when they contribute monetarily as in child support. The impact of non-resident fathers' monetary contribution on engagement with children depends on other factors such as relationship with mother, which differ by race and ethnicity (e.g., Cabrera, Ryan, Jolley, Shannon, & Tamis-Lemonda, 2008; Tach, Mincy, & Edin, 2010).

Though the emphasis of fatherhood policy may be changing somewhat, most government programs aimed at fathers continue to be seen by many as punitive in nature, because they are focused primarily on child support enforcement. Child support is essential for many single-parents raising families with limited incomes. In fact, some of these families receive support that amounts to more than one-quarter of their typical yearly salaries (Sorensen & Zibman, 2001). Each state designs its own child support enforcement program, typically enforcing punishments for those in arrears without regard for ability to pay, including garnishing wages, seizing of bank accounts or other assets, and suspension of driving or professional licenses.

Studies show that state initiated child support enforcement policies for low-income parents have discouraged payments and led fathers to participate in the underground economy, have fewer contacts with children, and develop less healthy coparenting arrangements (e.g., Jarrett, Roy, & Burton, 2002). Low-income non-resident fathers often face significant barriers to acquiring employment such as criminal histories, limited schooling or job experience, few employable skills, lack of transportation, and limited social skills (Tach, Mincy, & Edin, 2010). Ethnographic studies show how this situation is often exacerbated by mounting child support payments that spiral out of control, with fathers becoming less able and willing to pay.

Indeed, single mothers play a role in a resulting situation that has been termed "low-disregards." This refers to the phenomenon where women on government assistance choose not to cooperate in filing for child support because they realize the risk of losing some or all of their benefits (Jarrett et al., 2002). Mothers recognize that complying with state laws and filing for child support will likely reduce their assistance benefits, because child support is inconsistent and the state takes a percentage off the top to recoup its costs. In this system, fathers often feel that it would be easier to pay the mothers of their children outside of the welfare system even if it means they face potential future legal action. Sometimes parents get caught playing both sides, leading to negative repercussions for the father-child relationship and the mother-father relationship (Furstenberg & Featherstone, 2010; Roy, 1999, 2006).

Policy Implications

In this section we briefly review five major policies of the last decade designed—at least in part—to influence how fathers connect with their children. The recession of 2007–10 has been one of the most significant influences on families during this period. Effects felt by many families include increased difficulty in finding employment, heightened unemployment, plummeting real estate values, increasing foreclosure rates, as well as diminished retirement resources. One of the most salient repercussions of the recession is the nearly doubled rate of unemployment and its impact on families. Children in these families are hit hard in the short-term (e.g., nutrition, housing, school changes), but also face negative long-term effects (e.g., health, future education and employment opportunities, risky behaviors, substance abuse; Conger & Elder, 1994; Holzer, Schanzenbach, Duncan, & Ludwig, 2008). As with studies of the depression of the 1930s, it will take considerable time before researchers can document the multiple effects of the recent economic recession on children and families (Elder, 1998).

Early Childhood Education

Enacted in 2009, the American Recovery and Reinvestment Act (ARRA) included increased federal funding of programs that benefit children with an infusion of more than $2.1 billion to enhance Head Start and Early Head Start to provide child care, education, and parent classes for low-income families. Research on early childhood education (ECE; e.g., Head Start, Early Head Start, Smart Start) and measurement of the impacts on early learning in children has expanded and grown in the past 15 years. For example, Head Start programming has increased the availability of, and access to, quality child care centers and school readiness programming for low-income families and their children, success for children is both mediated and moderated by several factors, ranging from parental involvement, to level of parent education, to the relationship between both parents (Fagan, Newash, & Schloesser, 2000; Palm & Fagan, 2008).

In their overview, Palm and Fagan (2008) examined factors influencing fatherhood involvement in ECE. Overall, there is relatively low father involvement at Head Start centers, fathers tend to be more involved with their child's education when more educated and less depressed, and fathers are more likely to engage in the learning process with their children when they have more social support at large or by the mothers and teachers (Palm & Fagan, 2008). Research shows that while mothers *and* fathers may express interest in their children's early learning experiences and practice this in the home, fathers may not opt to become involved with Head

Start or other ECE type programming due to work-family conflict, feeling discouraged by mothers, and lack of encouragement from child care teachers (Fagan et al., 2000). Fathers are less likely to engage with teachers, visit children in school settings, and co-parent regarding school issues due to their feelings about paternal role expectations, gatekeeping experiences with mothers, and discouragement from teachers.

Making Work Pay

In 2009, the ARRA legislated various provisions to help "make work pay" for low-income families. It included the creation of the Child Care Development Fund (CCDF) to help low-income parents find work and participate in programs which provide them with the necessary skills to retool for new employment. Laws making work pay have historically been largely focused on low-income women and their families; when in fact men also need incentives or supports to encourage employment. However this current legislation takes a different approach supporting any and all low-income parents.

For example, provisions within the Act expand the child tax credit for low-income working families. These tax incentives "make work pay" by providing a $400–$800 tax credit for lower and mid-income families. Other such financial benefits include the Child Tax Credit, the Child Care Credit, and the Earned Income Tax Credit. The credits are not linked to gender; single fathers as well as single mothers can obtain tax breaks. Research has shown that these incentives are promising in terms of their economic and social impact (e.g., Immervoll & Pearson, 2009). Families that participate in these programs appear to have more stable employment, improved financial standing, and reduced reliance on social services. However, only a few impact studies have measured the long-term influence of such programs (for one exception see Holt, 2006). And there are downsides to these policies; for example, some individuals have learned to "play the system," claiming to have custody of children in order to receive unlawful tax breaks. Some parents justify their actions by declaring that parenting is much more than claiming one's children on court documents, and that if they care for a child physically, emotionally, and financially, they should be eligible to claim such tax incentives.

Health Care Supports

In 2009 President Obama signed a reauthorization of State Children's Health Insurance Program (SCHIP) which expanded its reach across the nation to help families and single parents who did not meet requirements for Medicaid to access public health insurance at very low costs. The SCHIP program has been widely successful insofar as it is an effective means for poor and low-income families' children to access routine and urgent care, prevent serious illnesses, and reduce hospitalizations (Johnson, Rimsza, & Johnson, 2006). However, as the economy has worsened, more and more families have become eligible for Medicaid, while states' tax revenues have decreased. The resulting financial burden has forced most states to make changes to their SCHIP programming in order to decrease enrollment, such as: raising premiums, adding co-payments, and even reducing benefits (Johnson et al., 2006). In 2010 President Obama signed into law sweeping healthcare reform legislation which is projected to provide health care to more than 11 million children, which will have implications for eligible fathers as they attempt to care for the health of their children.

TANF and Welfare Programs

The welfare reform legislation of 1996 was intended to reduce single motherhood, increase family self-sufficiency, and increase monetary support for children by their non-resident fathers (Bronte-Tinkew et al., 2007). However, since TANF was aimed at encouraging employment for mothers, it did little to help fathers stay in the lives of their children, nor did it improve father's employability (Cabrera, 2010). Some argue that both past and present welfare systems lack support and programming for poor fathers of children (other than SNAP—previously food stamps, and in some cases Medicaid). Because of the focus on employment at any cost, and lack of focus on education and skills, welfare today appears to favor work over family well-being in the first years of children's lives (Hays, 2003). TANF still has rigid requirements such as the maximum benefit clock of 60 months, strict guidelines on documentation and proof of job searches and employment, and requiring employment within a year of a child's birth. The latter requirement is noteworthy; this means a mother and/or father must work and obtain child care, even in a home with two parents. Following the birth of a child, poor fathers and mothers who lack education or work skills often find themselves working minimum wage jobs, taking unpredictable work shifts, and trying to arrange child care (much less survive downturns, health problems, or other family issues) just to complete this requirement of TANF. In addition, job loss plagues many of these families due to schedule changes, child illness, or loss of hours and lay-offs; approximately 20% of those who leave welfare return within one to two years (Brodkin, 2003).

Family Medical Leave

Prior to the Family and Medical Leave Act of 1993 (FMLA) mothers and fathers' jobs were not protected if they took new parent leave, had a long-term illness, or ill family members. The FMLA allows for *parents* (including fathers) of biologically related newborns or adopted children to take unpaid leave of up to 12 weeks without penalty (Wisensale, 2003). There has been legislative movement to strengthen unpaid leave under the FMLA in recent years. More than 10 states have improved and expanded the unpaid FMLA policies, including more time off, flexibility regarding the minimum size of employer requirement, and permitting intermittent leave (Appelbaum & Milkman, 2011). Unfortunately, there remain some drawbacks to the FMLA that prevent it from being utilized by the poor yet employed, and by under-employed workers. First, part-time employees are not eligible to receive it; second, companies with less than 50 employees are not required to provide it unless mandated in certain states; and, third, workers must be employed for at least a year before taking the leave. FMLA guidelines and implementation details will continue to be adjusted providing a good example of the complex and sometimes contradictory legislative, implementation, and legal processes producing family policy (see Feldblum & Apple-berry, 2008). California pioneered the first *paid* family leave expansion program for employers and four other states have followed suit and approved paid leave (Appelbaum & Milkman, 2011).

Future Directions

There are many opportunities for improved policy and programming for fathers and children, and we briefly review a few key areas below.

Early Child Education

In the realm of Early Childhood Education programming such as Head Start and subsidized quality daycare, there is great need to better engage both parents (fathers and mothers) in children's early learning experiences. First, ECEC center/school policies and staff should reflect an expectation of—and support of—fathers' involvement in their child's education, such as classroom volunteering, meetings with teachers, and special school programming just for fathers. Often times, fathers are an afterthought, encouraged to come to father nights once a year, or seen as lacking competence in the realm of child education. Second, more research is needed to document the impact that fathers do have on children when involved at this level. From a legislative perspective, policies should stress that father involvement in early children's development is more than financial support. Third, policy makers and program developers are encouraged to explore what specific types of programming will help fathers to engage with children and stay engaged when they encounter hardship. To accomplish this, a multi-pronged approach is warranted, whereby providers and relevant communities are educated about the impact fathers can have on child development, along with program offerings that are easily accessible, salient, and interesting to non-resident and resident fathers alike.

Non-Resident Fatherhood

Support for non-resident fathers is a ripe area for policy enhancements. Although research shows most non-resident fathers have high interest levels in coparenting and supporting their children, poor non-resident fathers are in need of additional programmatic supports in order to fulfill their roles and responsibilities (Raikes & Belloti, 2007; Roy, 1999, 2006). In response to this need, programs have emerged in various regions of the country that focus on providing poor fathers job training and parenting advice. Responsible Fatherhood initiatives have made grants available to public and private groups, including religious organizations, to promote healthy couple relationships, educate men about good parenting practices, and build career skills. It appears that policy makers are beginning to realize that fatherhood is more than contributing dollars each month to support a family. The hypothesis is that fathers who are encouraged through programmatic efforts and incentives to be committed partners and parents will be more likely to remain involved in their children's lives and to have positive influence on their development. We lack systematic studies to support the validity of such policies and practices, however, and future research is needed to evaluate their merits.

Moreover, non-resident fathers report difficulties staying close to their children due to issues with finding employment, criminal backgrounds, and troubled relationships with the mothers of their children (Tach, Mincy, & Edin, 2010). It is not difficult to imagine a father's apprehension and frustration when he is informed by a case worker that he must obtain employment, perhaps seek some vocational training, and pay child support, yet be offered few incentives or support to succeed. Some call attention to the negative effects of a pervasive assumption in the welfare system that a non-resident father will *not* want to work or be involved with his children (Roy, 1999). Indeed, a shift in thinking and behavior can be supported by policy, program adjustments, and research into the relationships among them, as demonstrated by changes in Headstart, where federal regulations required programmatic activities specifically for fathers (Cabrera, 2010; Raikes, Summers, & Roggman, 2005).

Researchers point to the importance of broad policy change impacting fathers because the current welfare-to-work programming is not wholly effective. We suggest evaluation of policies and legislation that attempt to provide fathers with employment programs similar to those for single mothers, increase fatherhood/parenting programming, and continue to provide support for fathers involved with programs such as Head Start or other forms of child development/parenting programming (Raikes & Belloti, 2007). We envision a time when non-resident fathers would receive "credit" from welfare programs for visiting with, providing in-kind support, coparenting, and nurturing their children (Roy, 2006). However significant questions remain: How would this work in practice and what unintended consequences might result? Under this type of programming, non-resident fathers might be allowed to receive some financial benefits such as Medicaid and potentially a portion of TANF type programming if they complied with the program and provided proof of their efforts. With such a programmatic shift, fathers might be more responsible as caregivers, yet would still receive support to obtain work, increase education opportunities, and make earnest efforts in supporting themselves and their children.

According to Ron Haskins (2009), a former White House and congressional advisor on welfare issues, in order to make such programs work for men, an enticing incentive must be created. Such an incentive may entail utilizing the child support system. For example, upon gaining employment fathers' back-pay/pay toward child support might be suspended or a tax credit could be introduced. Other ideas include mandatory work programs to promote job-skills and relationship/parenting skills. Such programs would help provide individuals with not only the skills to obtain or keep jobs but the actual incentives to continue because they could receive a tax credit, or their child support payments could be reduced/suspended.

One example of this approach is the multi-site Fathers to Work program launched in 2001 which attempted to bridge the gap between public and private programming for fathers. Studies of such programs have shown consistently positive results for fathers and their children (Spaulding, Grossman, & Wallace, 2009). By offering fathers a unique combination of services, training, access to resources, and support, the programs promote significant increases in fathers' employment rates and wages, level of engagement and involvement with their children, and increased child support payments. More research is needed to examine the impact of job training combined with paid work for fathers (and for mothers). In addition, further research is needed to understand how to help fathers retain employment, and how to increase actual financial support received by children (Spaulding et al., 2009).

Fatherhood Programming

Across the nation fatherhood programs are targeting areas where social services have historically provided little support to fathers: supports for financial stability, coparenting, and effective communication (Bronte-Tinkew et al., 2007; Roy & Dyson, 2010). The Administration for Children and Families (ACF) has actively supported efforts to integrate fathers into other funded services through grants, policies, and promotion of best practices, however, impact evaluation reports show that they have had limited measurable benefits for participants (Bronte-Tinkew et al., 2007). Further research is needed.

Because fatherhood and family policies have received so little attention in the academic literature, we have limited our review to introducing a few key questions in this chapter and highlighting the need for more focused research. We hope that with more research on why various constituencies advocate for specific policies; the circumstances under which various policies are adopted, implemented, and changed through legal challenges; and a more thorough assessment of the impacts such policies have on fathers, mothers, children, and society; researchers will be in a better position to make valid contributions to the policy process. If we can answer these questions, researchers will be better able to work with advocates and legislators to produce real and lasting impact on the laws and policies that shape the everyday lives of American fathers, mothers, and children.

References

Adams, M. (2006). Framing contests in child custody disputes: Parental alienation syndrome, child abuse, gender, and fathers' rights. *Family Law Quarterly, 40,* 315–338.

Adamson, P. (2010). *The children left behind.* Florence, Italy: Innocenti Research Center. Retrieved January 15, 2011, from http://www.unicef-irc.org/publications/619

Appelbaum, E., & Milkman, R. (2011). *Leaves that Pay.* Report by the Center for Economic and Policy Research. Retrieved May 20, 2011, from http://www.cepr.net/documents/publications/paid-family-leave-1-2011.pdf

Bane, M. J., & Jargowsky, P. (1989). The links between government policy and family structure: What matters and what doesn't. In A. J. Cherlin (Ed.), *The changing American family and public policy* (pp. 219–262). Washington, DC: Urban Institute.

Barrientos, A., & DeJong, J. (2006). Reducing child poverty with cash transfers: A sure thing? *Development Policy Review, 24,* 537–552.

Bernard, J. (1981). The good provider role: Its rise and fall. *American Psychologist, 36,* 1–12.

Bianchi, S., & Milkie, M. (2010). Work and family research in the first decade of the 21st Century. *Journal of Marriage and Family, 72,* 705–725.

Biller, H. B. (1976). The father and personality development. In M. E. Lamb (Ed.), *The role of the father in child development.* New York: Wiley.

Blankenhorn, D. (1995). *Fatherless America.* New York: Basic Books.

Bogenschneider, K. (2000). Has family policy come of age? A decade review of the state of U.S. family policy in the 1990s. *Journal of Marriage and the Family, 62,* 1136–1159.

Bogenschneider, K., & Corbett, T. J. (2010a). *Evidence-based policymaking.* New York: Taylor & Francis.

Bogenschneider, K., & Corbett, T. (2010b). Family policy: Becoming a field of inquiry and subfield of social policy. *Journal of Marriage and the Family, 72,* 783–803.

Brodkin, E. Z. (2003). Requiem for Welfare. *Dissent, 50*(1), 29–36.

Bronte-Tinkew, J., Carrano, J., Allen, T., Bowie, L., Mbwana, K., & Matthews, G. (2007). *Elements of promising practice for fatherhood programs.* Washington, DC: Child Trends.

Cabrera, N. (2010). Father Involvement and Public Policies. In M. E. Lamb (Ed.), *The role of the father in child development* (pp. 517–550). Hoboken, NJ: Wiley.

Cabrera, N., Brooks-Gunn, J., Moore, K., West, J., & Boller, K. (2002). Bridging research and policy. In C. S. Tamis-Le-Monda & N. J. Cabrera (Eds.), *Handbook of father involvement* (pp. 489–523). Mahwah, NJ: Erlbaum.

Cabrera, N., Ryan, R., Jolley, S., Shannon, J., & Tamis-Lemonda, C. (2008). Nonresident father engagement with and responsibility to their toddlers. *Journal of Family Psychology, 22,* 643–647.

Coltrane, S. (1996). *Family man.* New York: Oxford University Press.

Coltrane, S. (2001). Marketing the marriage 'solution'. *Sociological Perspectives, 44,* 387–418.

Coltrane, S. (2009). Fatherhood, Gender and Work-Family Policies. In J. C. Gornick, M. K. Meyers, & E. O. Wright (Eds.), *Gender Equality* (pp. 385–409), New York: Verso.

Coltrane, S. & Adams, M. (2008). *Gender and families.* Lanham, MD: Rowman & Littlefield.

Coltrane, S., & Galt, J. (2000). The history of men's caring. In M. H. Meyer (Ed.), *Care work: Gender, labor, and welfare states* (pp. 15 36). New York: Routledge.

Conger, R. D., & Elder, G. H., Jr. (1994). *Families in troubled times.* New York: DeGruyter.

Crompton, R. (1999). *Restructuring gender relations and employment.* Oxford, UK: Oxford University Press.

Danzinger, S. (2001). Welfare reform policy from Nixon to Clinton. In D. Featherman & M. Vinovskis (Eds.), *Social science and policy making* (pp. 137–164). Ann Arbor: University of Michigan Press.

Doherty, W. J. (1991). Beyond reactivity and the deficit model of manhood. *Journal of Marital and Family Therapy, 17,* 29–32.

Doherty, W. J., Kouneski, E. F., & Erickson, M. F. (1998). Responsible fathering: An overview and conceptual framework. *Journal of Marriage and the Family, 6,* 227–292.

Eamon, M. K. (2005). Social-demographic, school, neighborhood, and parenting influences on the academic achievement of Latino young adolescents. *Journal of Youth and Adolescence, 34,* 163–174.

Edelman, M. W. (2003). Why don't we have the will to end child poverty. *Georgetown Journal on Poverty Law & Policy, 10,* 273–277.

Ehrenreich, B. (1984). *The hearts of men.* Garden City, NY: Anchor Press/Doubleday.

Elder, G. H. (1998). The life course and human development. In R. Lerner (Ed.), *Handbook of child psychology, vol 1* (pp. 939–991). New York: Wiley.

Fagan, J., Newash, N., & Schloesser, A. (2000). Female caregivers' perceptions of fathers' and significant adult males' involvement with their Head Start children. *Families in Society, 81,* 186–196.

Featherstone, B. (2010). Writing fathers in but mothers out. *Critical Social Policy, 30,* 208–224.

Feldblum, C., & Appleberry, R. (2008). Legislatures, agencies, courts, and advocates: How laws are made, interpreted, and modified. In M. Pitt-Catsouphes, E. E. Kossek, & S. Sweet (Eds.), *The work and family handbook* (pp. 627–650). New York: Psychology Press.

Furstenberg, F. F., Jr., & Featherstone, B. (2010). Writing fathers in but mothers out! *Critical Social Policy, 30,* 208–224.

Folbre, N. (2008). *Valuing children.* Cambridge, MA: Harvard University Press.

Fraser, N. (1994). After the family wage. *Political Theory, 22,* 591–618.

Furstenberg, F. F. (1988). Good dads—bad dads. In A. Cherlin (Ed.), *The changing American* family and public policy (pp. 193 218). Washington, DC: Urban Institute Press.

Fuwa, M., & Cohen, P. (2007). Housework and social policy. *Social Science Research, 36,* 512–530.

Goldberg, W. A., Tan, E. T., & Thorsnn, K. L. (2009). Trends in academic attention to fathers, 1930–2006. *Fathering, 7,* 159–179.

Gornick, J., & Meyers, M. (2003). *Families that work.* New York: Russell Sage Foundation.

Gornick, J., & Meyers, M. (2007). Institutions for gender egalitarianism. New York: Verso.

Griswold, R. L. (1993). *Fatherhood in America: A history.* New York: Basic Books.

Haskins, R. (2009). Moynihan was right: Now what? *The Annals of the American Academy of Political and Social Science, 621,* 281–314.

Hays, S. (1996). *The cultural contradictions of motherhood.* New Haven, CT: Yale University Press.

Hays, S. (2003). *Flat broke with children.* New York: Oxford University Press.

Hernandez, D. J. (1993). *America's children.* New York: Russell Sage Foundation.

Heyman, J., Earle, A., & Hayes, J. (2007). *The work, family and equity index: How does the United States measure up?* Montreal, Quebec: Institute for Health and Social Policy.

Hobson, B., & Morgan, D. (2002). *Making men into fathers.* UK: Cambridge University Press.

Holt, S. (2006). *The earned income tax credit at age 30: What we know.* Washington, DC: The Brookings Institution.

Holzer, H., J., Schanzenbach, D. W., Duncan, G. J., & Ludwig, J. (2008). The economic costs of childhood poverty in the United States. *Journal of Children and Poverty, 14,* 41–61.

Hook, J. (2006). Care in context. *American Sociological Review, 71,* 639–660.

Immervoll, H., & Pearson, M. (2009). *A dood time for making work pay?* OECD Social, Employment, and Migration Working Paper No. 81. Retrieved on March 12, 2011, from www.iza.org/en/webcontent/publications/policypapers

Jarrett, R., Roy, K., & Burton, L. (2002). Fathers in the 'hood: Qualitative research on African American men. In C. Tamis-LeMonda & N. Cabrera (Eds.), *Handbook of father involvement: Multidisciplinary perspectives* (pp. 211–248). Hillsdale, NJ: Erlbaum.

Johnson, M. P. (2006). Conflict and control gender symmetry and asymmetry in domestic violence. *Violence Against Women, 12,* 1003–1018.

Johnson, T., Rimsza, M., Johnson, W. (2006). The effects of cost-shifting in the state children's heath insurance program. *American Journal of Public Health, 96,* 709–715.

Kamerman, S. B., & Kahn, A. J. (2001). Child and family policies in an era of social policy retrenchment and restructuring. In K. Vleminckx & T. M. Smeeding (Eds.), *Child well-being, child poverty and child policy in modern nations: What do we know?* (pp. 501–525). Bristol, UK: Policy Press.

Kelly, E. L. (2008). Work-family policies: The United States in international perspective. In M. Pitt-Catsouphes, E. Kossek, & S. Sweet (Eds.), *The work and family handbook* (pp. 99–123). New York: Psychology Press.

Knijn, T., & Kremer, M. (1997). Gender and the caring dimension of welfare states: Toward inclusive citizenship. *Social Politics, 4,* 328–361.

LaRossa, R. (1988). Fatherhood and social change. *Family Relations, 37,* 451–458.

Lerman, R. I. (2010). Capabilities and contributions of unwed fathers. *The Future of Children, 20,* 63–85.

Lero, D., Ashbourne, L., & Whitehead, D. (2006). *Inventory of policies and policy areas influencing father involvement.* Guelph, Canada: Father Involvement Research Alliance.

Lieb, H., & Thistle, S. (2005). The changing impact of marriage, motherhood and work on women's poverty. *Journal of Women, Politics & Policy, 27,* 5–22.

Liera, A. (2002). *Working parents and the welfare state.* Cambridge, UK: Cambridge University Press.

Marsiglio, W. R., Day, J., Evans, M., Lamb, M., Braver, S., & Peters, E. (1998). Report of the Working Group on Conceptualizing Male Parenting. In *Nurturing fatherhood.* Washington DC: Federal Interagency Forum on Child and Family Statistics.

McLanahan, S. (2009). Fragile families and the reproduction of poverty. *The Annals of the American Academy of Political and Social Science, 621,* 111–131.

Mincy, R. B., Garfinkel, I., & Nepomnyaschy, L. (2005). In-hospital paternity establishment and father involvement in fragile families. *Journal of Marriage and Family, 67,* 611–626.

Moen, P., & Coltrane, S. (2004). Families, theories, and social policy. In V. Bengtson, D. Klein, A. Acock, K. Allen, & P. Dilworth-Anderson (Eds.), *Sourcebook of family theory and research* (pp. 534–556). Thousand Oaks, CA: Sage.

Moss, P., & Deven, F. (2006). Leave policies and research: A cross-national perspective. *Marriage and Family Review, 39,* 255–285.

Nock, S. L. (1998). *Marriage in men's lives.* New York: Oxford University Press.

O'Brien, M. (2009). Fathers, parental leave policies, and infant quality of life. *The Annals of the American Academy of Political and Social Science, 624,* 190–212.

Palm, G., & Fagan, J. (2008). Father involvement in early childhood programs: Review of the literature. *Early Child Development and Care, 178,* 745–759.

Parke, R. D. (1996). *Fatherhood.* Cambridge, MA: Harvard University Press.

Perez-Johnson, I., Kauff, J., & Hershey, A. (2003). *Giving Noncustodial Parents Options.* Washington, DC: Mathematica Policy Research, Inc.

Pleck, J. H., & Masciadrelli, B. P. (2004). Paternal involvement. In M. E. Lamb (Ed.), *The role of the father in child development* (4th ed., pp. 222–271). New York: Wiley.

Pleck, E. H., & Pleck, J. H. (1997). Fatherhood ideals in the United States. In M. E. Lamb (Ed.), *The role of the father in child development* (3rd ed., pp. 33 48). New York: Wiley.

Popenoe, D. (1996). *Life without father.* New York: Free Press.

Pruett, K. D. (1987). *The nurturing father.* New York: Warner Books.

Raikes, H., & Belloti, J. (2007). Policies and programmatic efforts pertaining to fatherhood: Commentary. *Applied Development Science, 11*(4), 271–272.

Raikes, H., Summers, J. A., & Roggman, L. A., (2005). Father involvement in EHS programs. *Fathering 3,* 29–58.

Rainwater, L., & Smeeding, T. M. (2003). *Poor kids in a rich country.* New York: Russell Sage.

Roy, K. (1999). Low-income single fathers in an African American community and the requirements of welfare reform. *Journal of Family Issues, 20,* 432–457.

Roy, K. (2006). Father stories: A life course examination of paternal identity among low-income African American men. *Journal of Family Issues, 27,* 31–54.

Roy, K., & Dyson, O. (2010). Making daddies into fathers. *American Journal of Community Psychology, 45,* 139–154.

Silverstein, L. B., & Auerbach, C. F. (1999). Deconstructing the essential father. *American Psychologist, 54,* 397–407.

Smith, A., & Williams, D. R. (2007). Father-friendly legislation and paternal time across Western Europe. *Journal of Comparative Policy Analysis, 9,* 175–192.

Sorensen, E. (2010). Rethinking public policy toward low-income fathers in the child support program. *Journal of Policy Analysis and Management, 29,* 604–610.

Sorensen, E., & Zibman, C. (2001). *Poor dads who don't pay child support: Deadbeats or disadvantaged?* Research Report B-30. Washington, DC: Urban Institute.

Spaulding, S., Grossman, J., & Wallace, D. (2009). *Working dads.* Retrieved March 12, 2011, from http://www.ppv.org/ppv/publications/assets/310_publication.pdf

Stacey, J. (1996). *In the name of the family.* Boston: Beacon.

Stark, E. (2007). *Coercive control.* New York: Oxford University Press.

Sullivan, O., Coltrane, S., McAnnally, L., & Altintas, E. (2009). Father-friendly policies and time use data in a cross-national context: Potential and prospects for future research. *The Annals of the American Academy of Political and Social Science, 624,* 234–257.

Tach, L., Mincy, R. B., & Edin, K. (2010). Parenting as a "package deal". *Demography, 47,* 181–204.

Thompson, L., & Walker, A. (1989). Gender in families: Women and men in marriage, work, and parenthood. *Journal of Marriage and the Family, 51,* 845–871.

Thorne, B. (Ed.). (1992). *Rethinking the family.* Boston: Northeastern University Press.

Townsend, N. W. (2002). *The package deal.* Philadelphia, PA: Temple University Press.

Vann, N. (2007). Reflections on the development of fatherhood work. *Applied Developmental Science, 11*(4), 266–268.

Wagmiller, R. L., & Adelman, R. M. (2010). Childhood and intergenerational poverty. National Center for Children in Poverty, Columbia University, Mailman School of Public Health. Retrieved January 15, 2011, from http://www.nccp.org/publications/pub_909.html

Waller, M. (2009). Viewing low-income fathers' ties to families through a cultural lens. *The Annals of the American Academy of Political and Social Science, 629,* 102–124.

Wilcox, W. B. (2004). *Soft patriarchs, new men.* Chicago, IL: University of Chicago Press

Wisensale, S. (2003). Two steps forward, one step back: The Family and Medical Leave Act as retrenchment policy. *Review of Policy Research, 20*(1), 135.

Fatherhood Love

By Gerald Green

In the 1950s Mother and I lived with her parents because Dad often travelled in the navy. My grandparents Charlie and Cornelia Patillo migrated from Norlina, North Carolina, and they watched over my youthful play within the boundaries of Chesapeake Gardens, one of Norfolk's colored communities. They shepherded me through the intricacies of a separate and unequal society, typical of the segregated South. Mother was the youngest of five daughters, and she loved taking me to her grandfather's two-story white farmhouse surrounded by green crops and red soil. My mother's grandparents and five other families purchased land in 1879 and built Chapel on the Hill Baptist Church about a mile from their house. Those founding families instituted homecoming on the third Sunday in July, and over time, the small church grew. Many families that had migrated north returned to their agrarian roots for homecoming and made large annual donations to support church projects. As a young boy, I would sit still on pews in sweltering heat next to my great-aunts fanning their perspiration-dotted faces. Watching their arms move back and forth reminded me of times when they whipped sweet potatoes into smooth pie fillings. I listened to the choir and preacher, rocking my head in cadence with the spirit, until time to feast on home-grown fried chicken and smoked ham, fresh greens from the garden, rice and gravy, and of course, sweet homemade pies with cake on the side—the type of cuisine *Dr. Gavin's Health Guide for African Americans* (Gavin & Landrum, 2004) recommends that people eat in moderation.

Granddaddy owned a janitorial company, and I helped him clean White people's churches. "Does we pray to the same God?" I asked. Charlie's majestic Black face smiled. "Yes." This strong proud Black man taught me humility and showed me how to line up chairs in rows. My grandmother on the other hand tempered my defiance with fresh green switches. We lived for a better future by day and at night filled our lungs with sentinel spirits from Norlina's red clay. Granddaddy died when he was 68 and returned to the red-clay plot at the Chapel on the Hill. His spirit still helps me in my time of need.

Kids at the "colored" elementary school pushed in their noses while looking at me and shouted "snub-nosed .38," and others laughed when I stammered, "Uh ... uh ... sqr ... eet," for the word *street*. Some called me Gappy Hayes because of the gap between my front teeth. My immediate family called me Jerry, and other relatives called me Cousin Jerry. This youthful preteen banter lowered my self-esteem, before I started high school in Lexington Park, Maryland, where White students called me "nigger."

On cold Maryland nights, Dad taught me the strategic sacrificial role of pawns in chess, a similar role a disproportionate number of African Americans soldiers played in the Vietnam War. In the spring of 1966 when the war was escalating, we relocated to San Diego. The name-calling taunts didn't stop. I was late for class one day when a Black high school student shouted, "Look at that nigga walking like a tinman." Some students imitated my knock-kneed walk while others called each other names like Zit-face, Monkey-man, and Foe-head. Foe-head's real name was Paul. He was my best friend and he had a big smile, overshadowed by his Rock of Gibraltar-sized forehead, crowned with black kinky hair combed into a pompadour. Foe-head started calling me Tin-head because I would drink more than my share of liquor when the bottle was passed around in the car en route to parties. Foe-head was drafted and died in Vietnam a few years after graduating from high school.

Although I had good college prep grades, my test scores were weak—except on the civil service exam. Immediately after high school, I went to Mesa Community College in San Diego to evade the draft. I partied more than I studied data processing and wrecked my white convertible returning home late one night. Many times my father had told me, "As long as you live in my house, you will obey my rules. And I don't care how late you stay out, you're going to church." I struggled getting up in time for church and felt like a hypocrite sitting in the pew with a hangover. When Dad returned from 6 months at sea, he sought solace on the golf course—no more chess games. His absences caused marital tension and emotionally wounded me and my brothers, pain I thought moving out would help heal.

I was determined not to become a pawn in the Vietnam War after graduating from high school in 1967; however, I dropped out of college and accepted a civil service job where my strong math skills helped me learn two jobs in less time than most people took to learn one. I worked in a production control unit that managed repairs and overhauls on air-planes from aircraft carriers deployed in Vietnam. In the summer of 1969, I moved to the Bay Area to attend a dental technology school, not knowing at the time the Bay Area harbored cancer clusters in some of its heavy industrial communities.

By that fall, many college students had protested the Vietnam War. Shortly thereafter, the government made everyone's chance of being drafted equal by using birthdays instead of local draft boards; the lower one's number was the greater the probability was that one would be drafted. My number was 363 out of 366, which assured me that I would never be drafted. I dropped out of school, started partying more and slipped into the Bay Area's blissful subculture. I introduced myself as Tinman because that persona wasn't afraid of rejection and was immune to those hurtful words that made Jerry and Gerald feel inadequate. I eventually lost my job. I slept on a friend's floor, where rat traps snapped continuously, and I foraged for burned meaty dog scraps my friend brought home from local barbeque joints. Things improved when I started working for Chevron, but I soon discovered that I worked long odds hours, compared to those with a college education. So I returned to college in 1975 when I was 25, and 7 years later I graduated with a degree in mechanical engineering—cancer wasn't in my lexicon.

I was a newly hired design engineer at PG&E (Pacific Gas and Electric Company) in the fall of 1982, and I had the great fortune of meeting Mr. Owen Davis. I'm 6'2" and he towered over me, and corporate cuisine challenged both of our waistlines. His intense work load didn't stop his regal smile or hinder him from sharing friendly words of encouragement. He was a big supporter of employees volunteering on company time to serve community-based organizations. He once said, "Everybody wants a problem solver on their team," and he became PG&E's first African American vice president. Mayor Diane Feinstein appointed him police commissioner, and everyone was shocked when this Renaissance man died from pancreatic cancer.

PG&E allowed me to volunteer at the San Francisco African American Cultural Society (SFAACS), while on probation for my first 6 months of employment. I arrived early for a meeting and surprised Monica Scott, the executive director. I stammered, "Hello, my name is Gerald, isn't there a meeting here?" "Yes," she hesitantly answered. She then cracked the door open a little, exposing her bright smile. My eyes ventured beyond her radiant face, before reuniting with hers. "I'm Monica, please come in." The butterflies in my stomach fluttered, when she welcomed me into her apartment with its expansive view of Lake Merritt and Oakland's downtown skyline. I enjoyed playful flirting with her that spring when I volunteered at the SFAACS. We completed a book, *Contemporary African American Scientists and Inventors From 1920 to the Present*, in late October, and PG&E published it in time for Black History Month (February 1984). And in time, I became more than a volunteer in Monica's life.

My pneumatic gas well control design set the stage for a promotion to a gas engineer in the spring of 1984. I developed and managed projects to drill gas storage wells, became PG&E's expert on subsurface safety valves, and played a key role in converting analog well controls into digital. I often travelled to southern California to test equipment in Ventura, where a very large confederate flag at a truck stop reminded me of the old segregated South. Sometimes while testing, a White inspector would attempt to tell me jokes about "colored people." When I returned to northern California, I supervised the removal and installation of safety valves on work-over rigs that employed predominantly White crews. Many had never worked with a Black engineer and their questions suggested a distrust in my ability, and their demeanor brought back memories of my Maryland high school classmates who called me "nigger."

In 1978, PG&E had a Blow Off Prevention Equipment failure. It was similar to BP's 2010 experience in the Gulf of Mexico, except PG&E's gas wells are on land. A major fire resulted and burned for weeks before a relief well was drilled to kill it.

Afterward, safety became the number one priority on the rig. It was shut down for repairs when equipment failed, and many times operations took longer because a procedure failed a test. Consequently, I spent many cold nights sleeping in the back of a station wagon, waiting to remove or install subsurface safety valves. Thoughts of Monica kept me warm.

We were married in October 1991, and at our reception her father, Mr. Scott, tapped rhythms as he sauntered and danced to the Calvin Keys Trio. He had that big father-of-the-bride smile, waving his white table napkin above his head in traditional New Orleans steps called the second line: a partying dance step congregations did during burial rituals in New Orleans. The trio recognized his gesture and started playing "When the Saints Go Marching In." Mr. Scott had started playing drums in elementary school and had learned New Orleans-style music, which was influenced by African slaves' drumbeats and guttural chants from the Crescent City's past—the blue note tones. Monica's mother joined in and everyone danced the second line around tables in La Casa de la Vista, located on Treasure Island in the middle of the San Francisco Bay.

Four years later, my life changed during a routine dental visit to see Dr. Curtis Perry. Dr. Perry became a dentist like his father and uncle, and he loved electronic devices. He offered me special glasses to watch him work on my teeth. I declined the offer and listened to music instead. Dr. Perry told me how he had started a jazz band called Schedule II, which is the script name for state-controlled drugs. He played the bass guitar and had a weakness for chocolate. I, on the other hand, loved playing the phantom bass with Jimi Hendrix. Music stitched our fabric together. He discovered a lesion on my tongue that I thought was a simple tongue bite, and he recommended a follow-up visit with Dr. William R. Murphy, a specialist in oral and maxillofacial surgery. Dr. Perry had used Dr. Murphy's services before. He specialized in sedating patients to pull difficult teeth, and his office was walking distance from Dr. Perry's office. After a couple of visits to see Dr. Murphy, he requested permission to conduct a biopsy.

I tried to imagine a dentist cutting out a portion of my tongue, but the thought of cold hard steel against my tongue ignited my fear. How could I allow a medical inquisition into my most intimate muscle, designed from birth to nurture my body and articulate thoughts from my soul? Later that week, Monica and I celebrated Charles's first birthday. Charles crawled, smiled, and laughed as he played with other children. I enjoyed watching them. His antics helped me release suppressed thoughts of those unpleasant visits to Dr. Murphy. I ate Monica's delicious spaghetti dinner. My tongue cramped with spasms, but I was determined nothing would interfere with Charles's birthday, not even my slipping partials.

One week after Charles's birthday, Monica went on a business trip to Washington, D.C. She returned through New Orleans to check on her mother, who was recuperating from a heart attack. I called and talked about everything but never mentioned my growing anguish. The last thing she needed was more melancholy news. That night I tried to ignore the syncopated throbbing, which became more frequent and intense. My original decision to delay the biopsy haunted me. I surrendered to pain's grip and called Dr. Murphy the next morning for an appointment. It was time for a biopsy; time to confirm what these two men of medicine believed was going on inside me.

"Relax your tongue," he said. He waited. It seemed like an eternity. He then eased a long needle into my gum, reloaded his elixir, and injected various nerves throughout my tongue and mouth. Those injections didn't numb me, so he repeated and we waited. Ten minutes later, I lost all sensation and feeling. I closed my eyes as Dr. Murphy began snipping at my tongue. I could hear him cutting, and my mind told me it should hurt, but I felt no pain. Dr. Murphy scooped and gouged my tongue, and my mind felt like a fish with the hook torn from its mouth, while I listened to the soothing sound of Grover Washington blowing "Winelight" on his tenor saxophone in the background. Periodically, Dr. Murphy interrupted the melody with the clicking sound of his instrument cutting and stitching as he sewed my bleeding tongue, *click, click, click, click.*

Dr. Murphy warned me not to eat anything until the anesthesia wore off because I could mistakenly bite my tongue and not know it. His staff provided me some gauze and a prescription for some painkillers. I drove past Lake Merritt on the way home and thought about the first time I met Monica, which pushed aside my pain and hunger. Twelve years earlier, I had ridden a bus from San Francisco to the Lake Merritt area and met with members from various organizations to develop a book about the contributions of African American scientists and inventors. No thoughts of cancer then.

"Good morning, Mr. and Mrs. Green, please be seated," Dr. Murphy said. He was a slight man with a polite smile, not like some of those champion Walmart greeters. We sat in front of his desk flanked by family pictures of fishing trips and other vacations. Seeing those pictures brought back glum memories of Dad and me baking in the sun, fishing from a rowboat—we seldom caught anything. I felt trapped and hid suspicion of bad news from Monica. She relaxed in her chair, and we engaged Dr. Murphy in conversation. Our eyes were drawn to a manila folder. He picked it up from a pile, and the room became quiet.

"Mr. Green, I have your pathology report," he said. Our nervous energy warmed the room. We held hands and peered at the messenger. "Mr. Green, I'm sorry to tell you, but your report showed malignant cells. You have squamous cell carcinoma, cancer of the tongue."

Our hands broke apart. I choked, then gasped for air, and moisture escaped my mouth. I looked at Monica crying and wanted to say something comforting but sat speechless. Dr. Murphy's words—*cancer of the tongue*—continued to reverberate. Monica's face pleaded for help, and I did nothing. Her tears spilled to the floor, and her gut-wrenching sobs echoed in my ears. I wanted to hold her tight but didn't and retreated to my youthful safe harbor; and when I opened my eyes, I saw strained, uncomforting lines on Dr. Murphy's face.

He stood and pointed to the restroom. Monica didn't see my quivering hand. She ran into the restroom. I felt lost. The walls swallowed me. Cancer digested my energy. My soul sang, *Gerald, you must live, live for your son, live for your wife, live for yourself, just live!* I licked my lips and sang quietly to myself until Monica returned. "Baby, don't cry, we'll make it through this," I said. We hugged. Her crying slowed, but she still hadn't said a word. Silence heightened my anxieties, and my fears grew worse.

Similar to my grandparents, my core health providers were African American, but unlike them I had a choice. I was fortunate to live in a medical community where sons followed in their dad's footsteps, like my personal physician Dr. Geoffrey Watson. He inherited his father's good looks, taste for expensive shirts, and bedside manner, although he was a decade my junior. His father was one of three African American physicians who founded the Arlington Medical Group in 1956 in North Oakland and provided the predominantly African American community excellent medical services for over 30 years. He grew up in Norfolk, Virginia, and graduated, as my mother and her sisters did, from segregated Booker T. Washington High School.

Dr. Geoffrey Watson helped me navigate through numerous treatment decisions necessary to survive tongue cancer and, later, neck and prostate cancer. I trusted him because he had invested years in helping me understand what caused my health to change. He regularly prescribed diagnostic tests while treating my hypertension. He believed African Americans are more receptive to hypertension, because during the middle passage, slaves' bodies had to learn how to retain water in order to survive. Now that water retention serves as a potential source of hypertension.

My team of oncologists recommended two forms of radiation treatment for my tongue cancer in the summer of 1995. First, I had implant therapy, where my tongue was sewed to the floor of my mouth and 35 catheters were inserted through my cheek and circled the tumor in my tongue. A radioactive isotope was positioned in the catheters at various locations for short periods of time for eight separate treatments. Second, I had external beam therapy, where I was exposed to a gamma ray source for weeks at a time. Each treatment was painless; however, over time my neck and face were burned and blackened. It became painful to swallow water and food, and I lost all taste and most of my strength. I dropped from 235 pounds to 185, and spent many hours reading while in bed. Colin Powell's book, *My American Journey* (1995), lifted my spirits. It brought me some comfort to learn that he, too, thought that the deaths of many poor and less educated men drafted during the Vietnam War was unfortunate. An expendable "economic cannon fodder" considered by some policy makers.

Dr. Watson threatened me with an intravenous feeding tube if I continued to lose weight. I increased my consumption of Ensure Plus® from two cans a day to four. They wanted me to drink six. My strength slowly returned after I started adding ice cream to it. I started walking a few minutes a day on the treadmill, and thoughts about helping Monica raise Charles gave me hope for another day's breath. I gained enough strength to walk in the neighborhood where visions of Charles attending school motivated me to walk further and those thoughts helped me heal. Sometimes I prayed.

Oh, God, please help me through this crisis. Charles needs me. Give me time in his early years of life to nurture his soul with love and prevent self-hatred. God, let me extend my hand to him, as my grandfather did when I was a little boy in need of guidance during my parents' temporary separation. Please allow me time with Monica to help Charles through his rites of passage and introduce him to African rituals and Kwanzaa celebrations so he may become a positive contributor and not dream of ways to escape responsibilities. Please make me whole, Lord, and allow me the privilege of growing older and wiser so I may share fatherhood life experiences with my loves, Monica and Charles.

Charles was born on June 6, 1994, and he was abandoned by his biological father. His mother decided she couldn't raise a baby alone. Her faith that Monica and I would give her newborn a better home led us to become first-time parents even though we were both in our mid-40s. His preschool teachers and other parents thought we were grandparents. That age differential forced us to exercise daily. We walked in open space within an eyeshot from our backyard, and occasionally, an off-leash dog startled Charles. One evening, we sat with him in front of the fire-place, and the red glow reflected off Monica's smile as she read aloud a children's book about adoption. His big brown eyes wandered before his attention focused on the fire. He didn't seem to care about the animal characters in the story. Monica gave me a perplexed look and then told him that just like Fuzzy Bear, he was adopted.

"I would have carried that secret to my grave," my mother told me later. Her forceful voice reminded me of arguments she had with Dad when he returned home after 6 months at sea. He eventually replaced us with golf, and my relationship with him all but ended after he deserted Mother and had two sons by his mistress in the Philippines. He later retired from the navy, moved back to Oklahoma all alone, and married a woman not much older than me. Hesitantly, I called him after I became ill, but neither of us shared the small talk gene. Our words got lost over the telephone line, and cramps rolled up my neck. My hands sweated, and I stammered, "I was diagnosed with cancer." Our conversation continued. I told him we adopted Charles. That was the longest we had talked in years, without me getting upset about something—until …

"Jerry, I adopted you," he said. I dropped the phone. "You did?" "I thought your mother told you," he said, and my wounded heart quickened. Silent tears tumbled into a world I once knew.

Mother and I had an awkward conversation the summer before she took Monica, Charles, and me to visit my deceased biological father's sister. I was told that he had been in poor health before he died. I was in my mid-50s and I felt angry and cheated when I carefully examined a picture of his face. I wondered what traits I had inherited from him. Was one of them desertion? Mother died 5 days before Christmas that year. She almost achieved her goal of taking her secret to her grave. My discovery helps me understand Charles's pain when he asks questions about why his biological parents gave him up for adoption.

In the spring of 1996, fifteen pairs of hands took turns feeling my tongue at the tumor board, where Dr. Michael Kaplan was the lead oncologist. Unlike the other doctors, he didn't believe my cancer had metastasized. But in his matter-of-fact tone, he explained that if it was cancer, his surgical team would have to reconstruct my jawbone, using a small bone from my lower leg, and remove a portion of my tongue before they woke me from the biopsy procedure.

"You're lucky; it's just radiation necrosis. Your pain comes from internal scarring, a by-product of radiation therapy," Dr. Kaplan said after the procedure. Happy tears rolled down the right side of my burned-black face. A smile larger than his small frame illuminated the room, and from that moment on, Monica and I looked forward to his medical counsel. I would later receive 4 weeks of 90 minutes per day of hyperbaric oxygen therapy sessions for pain relief.

At my first treatment for pain, a technician greeted me with a Southern drawl. "Howdy. Are you ready?" he asked. His voice reminded me of the not-so-good old boys from my 1950s childhood. My anxiety soared when he opened what looked like a blue-frame iron lung with a submarine hatch-like cover.

"Here, take this. It'll relax you," he said in his gatekeeper's voice. "You should feel your ears … tightening." The pressure increased, and the glass walls hugged me tight like slaves packed in the hull of a ship. My eyes flickered. I looked up at the television through the convex glass, and the background music slowly relaxed me. I fell asleep and recalled one of my favorite childhood memories of skipping down gravel-covered Workwood Road in Chesapeake Gardens with cousins to Grandmother's house. It was when I felt most secure—kicking stones in one of Norfolk's 1950s segregated communities. I remembered looking up at them as they teased me while we walked. They constantly tried to avoid swarms of gnats that I simply walked under. I wanted to keep up with them, but their legs were almost as long as I was tall. They would run off and leave me alone to skip to Grandmother's house. Sometimes, when the weak part of my shoes hit sharp-edged stones not worn down by cars, I jumped because those sharp hot stones cut my foot. I felt relieved upon arriving at Grandmother's house because she had a smooth concrete walkway from the street to her front door, flanked on both sides by roses, which I saw from their bottoms. Usually, I ran up to the porch, next to those thorny sweet-smelling giant roses abuzz with big black bumblebees. Best of all was opening the storm door with the capital *P*, which stood for Patillo, before entering a little kid's paradise.

Grandmother's living room had three tables with lots of whatnot figurines for a kid to play with, although her rule was, "Don't touch." All the grandkids played with the brightly painted opaque figurines, and Grandmother spanked those she caught. Playing with them was fun, and what I remembered most about those whatnots was licking their sour-tasting bottoms; it must have been the lead—a taste I hope Charles never experiences.

Charles and I would, years later, return to Workwood Road on the Fourth of July to celebrate colored people's 50th anniversary of home ownership in Chesapeake Gardens' enclave protection from White Southern brutality. My old haven, the woods and marsh, had been replaced with highways and sound walls that failed to keep the neighborhood quiet. Many houses still boasted green front yards full of roses and bumblebees; however, 860 Workwood Road no longer had a capital *P*. Mother and her sisters had sold the house. And like rhythmic singing cicadas rising from the ground to feed, we sampled cuisines in front yards. I later saw Charles sitting with a group of children on the grass listening attentively in a crisscross applesauce position that he hated in kindergarten. An elder called out names of the founding families of Workwood Road from a quilt. Tears and sweat clung to my cheeks as she read, "Charlie and Cornelia Patillo." I heard them whisper, "Present." In time, many families ventured from this safe harbor in pursuit of the American dream, only to live through decades of turbulent transition. Some have returned.

I emerged from the blue chamber with Monica in my heart. I wore thin light blue static-proof clothing with matching booties to reduce the potential of a spark and fire while I was inside the chamber's oxygen environment. The technician helped me stand on weak knees, and I meandered across the cold floor into the changing room. My tongue's pain ebbed at the end of my first treatment. Monica drove home. As I sat in the passenger seat, the lingering effect of the blue chamber continued to bring back old memories. I recalled how love had compromised our resolve not to socialize at the SFAACS while we worked and how we spent our honeymoon on Paradise Island in the Bahamas.

I had surgery in December 1997 to remove a tumor on the right side of my neck. A tendon was cut. Now my right arm droops, which makes my weak jump shot even weaker. I can't raise my arm above my head in one continuous move, and I have constant neck pain. But joy continues in simple pleasures like tasting good food and talking to family and friends. I'm privileged with breath and life's experiences that I may offer to those caught in cancer's grip. I'm living proof that time heals emotional and physical scars.

My first scar is hidden within my tongue, where external gamma-beam treatment killed the tumor but left scar tissue where it had once thrived. This invisible scar sapped my life's pleasure. Two years after tongue cancer, I washed my face and smiled in the mirror at the new scar on my neck, a constant reminder of my second cancer surgery. It is the source of great pleasure and sometimes throbs. I get joy looking at it and thinking how fortunate I am it was discovered before it metastasized. What's a little daily pain in exchange for years of life? I've been told an amputee has phantom pains. Who am I to complain about background soreness on a body part that still functions?

Between the two scars, which one would I trade in? Neither. I have grown with these pains; they are a part of who I am. To trade them in would be to deny me—a survivor—cancer free and ready for life.

> A life filled of joy and love of family,
> A life that gives back to my community,
> A life struggling to be the best father,
> A life with love,
> A life with Monica,
> A life with dancing memories,
> A life with scars, the scars that blessed me with another day.

Another day to observe a predawn duckling swimming alone on placid Lake Merritt with his breast leaning forward in the thick brackish water, where a V-shaped pattern trails. A group of ducks flies above in the same pattern. Their innate ability to travel in such patterns strengthens their survival during migration. Monica and I toiled to introduce Charles to his "V" survival pattern. We decided to ground him in the seven principles of Kwanzaa *nguzo saba*, as we prepared him for his flight in a turbulent world that sees little Black boys as an ugly gateway to manhood, not worthy of freedom. We pumped him full of *nia* (purpose) and *imani* (faith), in hopes a shield of Teflon would protect him from constant assault by a society blind to his humanity. We clothed him in *kujihagulia* (self-determination) as we pushed him further out on branches of his decisions until his wings either spread like the giant raptor that catches a gust of wind and carries him away on prosperity's breeze or like a homing pigeon that returns him home to surrogate parents, who would in turn pray that he accomplishes *ujima* (collective work and responsibility). We prayed that he would return to Workwood Road in time to celebrate its 100th anniversary. Maybe by then, it will reflect America's hue, and God will have touched homes with his blessings of *umoja* (unity) of faith, family, and friends.

I tried to hide my illness from Charles, but as he grew, my neck scar became a constant reminder. He didn't understand that he was one of the lucky ones. At least he had a father who loved him daily. I prayed that Charles wouldn't become an absentee father. Let him exercise *kuumba* (creativity) and improve our community's quality of life while practicing *ujamaa* (cooperative economics).

Monica and I prayed that our love coupled with the seven principles of Kwanzaa, Charles's "V" pattern, would guide him, but that didn't stop him from acting out in kindergarten. He began hitting little girls. A child psychologist encouraged us to enroll him in a martial arts class to curb his aggression. He seemed so excited when he took tests for his belts, and watching him perform gave my heart joy. In the third grade, Charles started taking Djembe (an African drum) lessons. He joined a chess club while in the fourth grade, which met in a local pizza shop on Fridays. When I played chess with him, it was hard for him to focus on the various moves, and he complained the pace was too slow. Monica and I played other board games with Charles, but he was impatient and hated losing. We took turns ferrying him to his different activities. I loved interacting with the other parents. They helped me smile. I wasn't surprised when Charles told us he didn't want to continue with the chess club. I guess the pizza lost its attraction.

However, he continued practicing his drumming, and his drum troop had the privilege of representing South Africa in a parade at the 2006 Beijing International Cultural Tourism Festival. They accompanied thousands of other representatives from around the world. They played at cultural events and at a school where all of the children in the auditorium spoke some English. I tried to help Charles understand that he was competing with kids not only in America but around the world. We were treated like dignitaries and toured the Great Wall of China, the Forbidden City, and other cultural sites. Charles currently plays his Djembe for the church choir and he plays behind me at public readings from my book *Life Constricted* (Green, 2010).

Monica and I were disappointed when he quit martial arts while studying for his black belt. He said it was because of a verbal disagreement with his Sifu (martial arts instructor). His teen-age testosterone levels were rising and he repeatedly challenged authority. He had become more rebellious—nothing wrong was his fault. "That's not fair," Charles constantly says, and he is right. Life isn't fair, but as parents, we must teach our children fairness and—to our boys especially—that no means no. My grandfather and my son's namesake, Mr. Charles Patillo, a generation removed from slavery and an entrepreneur from North Carolina, overcame racism and taught me fairness, humility, and self-reliance in segregated Virginia. I hope to pass on his wisdom to Charles in post–civil rights America, while surviving cancer. Unfortunately, today's teenagers are digitally connected, and their peer pressure is ubiquitous. It challenges our skill set rooted in an analog world, although Monica and I are early adapters.

Charles constantly tells me how he isn't interested in boring school and how he doesn't want to be like me. I understand him not wanting to be like me. At his age, I didn't want to be like my dad either, but I'm concerned about his academic performance. We have tried numerous incentive-based systems to help improve his academics and behavior with minimum success. We told him if he improved his grades, we would consider getting him a puppy. His last marking period was his best to date in high school. Charles wanted to name his puppy "Catfish" after the name his cousins called him in New Orleans, the Crescent City. We suggested he consider another name. He searched the Internet and found a 7-week-old black and white cocker spaniel and settled on the name "Crescent."

Crescent, Charles, and I all share a common trait: We don't know our biological fathers' medical histories, and that ignorance could potentially be fatal. Crescent's unexpected bathroom slips are teaching Charles what it means to raise a child. He is learning it requires a mountain of patience and an ocean of love to motivate and encourage a youngster to behave and learn new social skills. Monica and I have given Charles our core values to help him cross the threshold to manhood, but that's not enough. We have asked our community of elders to help guide him on his journey to achieve self-truth so he may be responsible for his children and community. Hopefully, he and future fathers can build communities where our youth stop becoming "economic cannon fodder" in the local killing fields we call home.

I discovered a few weeks before our 2008 summer vacation that my prostate-specific antigen (PSA) score had jumped from 2.2 to 3.15. A PSA test is a common way to screen for prostate cancer. Although it was within the lab report's good reference range from 0.0 to 4.0, two things stuck in my mind. First, my previous PSA scores had moved up in small increments, and this one was up almost an entire point. And second, my neighbor who has survived prostate cancer for over 9 years had told me many times when a Black man's PSA score goes over 2.5, he should be concerned. Well, I was, but not enough to have a biopsy before my vacation.

We arrived in Raleigh, North Carolina, two days before the reunion. Charles, now 14, spent most of the time with his teenage cousins playing video games, and Monica and I settled into a quiet routine of morning walks. On Friday, the first day of the reunion, I greeted family members arriving for check-in. Relatives from all five Patillo sisters came, and two of the three surviving sisters were present. Charles and his cousins splashed in the swimming pool while adults sipped refreshing drinks. We looked at old pictures and videos from previous reunions that sparked intense dialogue about who remembered what. Everyone enjoyed the home-cooked and catered cuisine on Saturday, and we played bid whist, dominoes, and other board games. Budding family poets read on Sunday, the last day of the reunion, and we said blessings for the deceased. Everyone clung to precious memories, and I remembered how Mother thought my brothers and I were sick if we didn't eat seconds at dinner. And now we struggle against mid-ridge bulge.

As we drove away from the reunion, sheets of rain flushed away views of trees' green canopies, and darkening clouds hid daylight. The car hydroplaned, and lightning lit up the sky, but that didn't faze Charles. He stayed glued to his electronic game's flashing screen. Monica's voice crackled, and I pulled off the road. Unlike our first trip, we had no grapes to share as rain pelted the car. Our breath fogged the windows, and a crescendo of thunderclaps finally scared Charles. He dropped his electronic device.

Eventually, the sun came out and bake-dried sides of trees whose inner growth rings had witnessed runaway slaves escaping through the thicket. Unfortunately, some were trapped, returned, and hanged from local branches. My great-grandfather survived that American tragedy and pooled his resources with several families to purchase land, after the Civil War, on which they built the Chapel on the Hill Baptist Church. He and his descendants, and members of those other families, are buried adjacent to the building, and my mother rests a few rows down a gentle slope from them, a stone's throw from creeks that once nourished crops. Charles, Monica, and I held hands, bowed our heads, and said a prayer at her grave, and fond childhood memories visited me.

Every summer, Mother would bring me to a big white house, surrounded by corn and tobacco, where her father grew up with his 10 brothers and sisters, about a mile down a dusty road from the church. The elders would get up before dawn, eat a big breakfast, and go to work, many in the fields. I shared breakfast with them, but instead of working, I chased chickens and ran through the fields' red soil. Mother's thin lips would smile at me while we swung in the porch swing on those cool evenings drinking fresh lemonade.

None of the circuitous, mazelike dirt roads had names then, but Mother navigated them with ease. Now they are paved, and many carry her relatives' last names, and during a recent visit, we saw my 92-year-old great-aunt. My granddaddy's sister outlived all of her siblings and unlike them she never moved from Norlina. While visiting, one of Mother's cousins saw the resemblance in my face. "That's Rotelia's boy," she said. Those words made me feel loved. I want that kind of love for Charles too.

Déjà vu, I heard *click, click.*

The doctor removed his staple gun-like instrument from my hemorrhaging rectum. I whimpered like a wounded animal, and my muffled cries escaped from the tiny room. He carefully placed the sample on the tray before reloading a fresh needle and reinserting. *Click, click,* he snatched another piece of my prostate. At 60, I have survived tongue and neck cancer for 14 years with no guarantees, just daily opportunities to share love. Now prostate cancer has provided yet another thread to weave into my life's fabric and binds me with 192,000 American men who were diagnosed with prostate cancer in 2009.

Prostate cancer affects more African American men than men of other races. The legacy of segregation may play a part in the mistrust that hampers many Black men from going in for early screening; consequently twice as many Black men die from prostate cancer when compared to White men. A study published by the National Cancer Institute in 2000 suggests that environmental and nutritional factors may play an important role. Blacks in Africa do not have the same high rate of prostate cancer and mortality as Blacks in the United States. A genetic difference and lower levels of vitamin D may contribute to the higher rates of prostate cancer in African American men. It also states that less access to health care, including lack of insurance, may mean that African American men don't always get the preventive care they need. And that distrust or negative attitudes toward screening tests and health care may mean that prostate cancer is diagnosed when it is more advanced in African American men.

Because of my previous experiences with cancer, I aggressively pursue personal health matters. For example, even though my digital rectal exam was inconclusive and my PSA score of 3.15 was considered within the norm, I chose to get a biopsy. It revealed cancerous cells in the right apex of my prostate with benign results in all other sampled areas. My Gleason score was 6, where a score of 7 through 10 usually indicate a more serious prognosis. Again, I agreed with an aggressive treatment recommendation of a radical prostatectomy (removal of the prostate) by my urologist and Dr. Watson.

My brother-in-law had been diagnosed with prostate cancer a few years earlier and opted for brachytherapy, where radioactive seeds are planted in the prostate. A close family friend opted for external beam treatment. Both radiation therapies had acceptable long-term outcomes but not as good as a radical prostatectomy. I selected the robotic-assisted laparoscopic prostatectomy, where the surgeon sits at the console of the da Vinci® Surgical System. He or she views 3-D images and the system translates their hand, wrist, and finger movements into precise, real-time movements of surgical instruments inside the patient. I spent less time in the hospital, experienced less bleeding, and endured fewer days with a catheter in my penis, when compared to traditional surgery. I had surgery on a Friday morning and I was released the next day before noon. I started walking in my neighborhood that Monday, with my catheter and waste bag strapped to my leg.

Unfortunately, while writing this chapter, I learned that a family member died from advanced prostate cancer. Early detection and treatment could have potentially saved this 61-year-old father's life and spared his family and community a tragic loss.

New cars come with a manual, with a list of instructions for the owner to follow. Charles's pediatrician gave us such a manual in the form of an infant and child care handbook. It contained an infant care schedule through young adulthood. It started at Week 1, with the collection of medical history; regrettably we could not offer any information about Charles's biological parents, and the appointment concluded with a physical examination. The schedule progressed to Week 2, then Month 1 through 18 and then each year thereafter until age 20. All visits included a physical examination, a basic requirement for good health, and this is especially true for men with incomplete family medical records.

Our bodies and automobiles are similar in that they work, consume fuel, and require maintenance. The car was originally designed to transport passengers from point A to point B; however, over time they have morphed into something else—a fashion statement for some who adorn them with 26-inch rims and treat them like kings. Some drivers (fathers) take their cars in for maintenance checkups, but fail to get annual physical exams. It's a matter of priority. Which is king—the car or the driver (father)?

I remember when a gallon of gas cost less than 25 cents. Then American cars came equipped with big engines and few were concerned about gas mileage. The American diet for cars changed when gas prices climbed above 50 cents a gallon. Fuel-efficient imports stole the lion's share of purchases, and Japan replaced Detroit as auto king. The American auto failure isn't lost on the food industry. Now corn is king, and its pervasive calories invade our meals and drinks, accompanied by meat growth hormones. Our children's waistlines have ballooned and their health has plummeted. In *Dr. Gavin's Health Guide for African Americans* (Gavin & Landrum, 2004), he says if a man's waist exceeds 40 inches and if a woman's waist exceeds 35 inches then they have what is referred to as central obesity. They are at risk for heart attack, heart disease, diabetes, and death, because their vital organs and insulin could fail to function properly.

Fathers, get on your job and get a physical exam and learn your blood pressure, glucose, and cholesterol numbers! Understanding those three vital statistics could save your life. Start treating yourselves like kings instead of pawns—potential casualties of war (foreign and/or domestic). Your family and community need your wisdom to guide new generations.

> Are you ready for Fatherhood Love?
> Your children are.
> Don't disappoint them,
> Or, your family, and community.
> Get a check up,
> Don't check out!
> We need you, Dad
> Alive!!

Conclusion

I'm living proof that early medical intervention works; however, it's my loving family's strength that sustains me. And the challenge was learning how to reciprocate their love, because I didn't know how to love myself. I had bought into years of a false manhood doctrine—be a strong and courageous individual; real men don't cry or show weakness—a belief system that's incongruent with making sound medical decisions. Before I could break out of my cocoon of medical ignorance, I had to peel back years of loneliness, those selfish bachelor years before I developed a loving and understanding relationship with my wife, Monica. And then, I had to learn how to accept her love and acknowledge her needs, including the need for my unconditional love. She needed me to help her raise our son, Charles. Monica helped facilitate my transformation, and that change prepared me for my destiny, to become a multiple cancer survivor. We were shepherded by caring medical professionals and graced with excellent medical coverage that didn't bankrupt us.

My transition to fatherhood love requires men to answer the following questions:

1. What will cause me to love myself so that I will make good health care decisions?
2. How can I overcome societal distractions that prevent me from seeking early medical attention?
3. What will stop me from practicing emergency room medicine and take myself and my children in for routine and regular checkups?
4. How do I go about establishing a healthy medical baseline that includes knowing my blood pressure, glucose, and cholesterol levels and PSA score?

Our wives and families deserve answers to these questions, which support our sons' decisions to build strong healthy communities—a legacy of longevity.

Reflective Questions

1. Many African American males are hesitant to seek medical advice in their youth, particularly as relates to prostate health. What issues are involved and what can be done to correct the situation?
2. A major area of concern and support is that offered by one's mate. What is reflected in the author's story about this issue?
3. Adoption is a topic of concern. What should children be told and when? What are the cultural issues?

References

Gavin, J., & Landrum, S. (2004). *Dr. Gavin's health guide for African Americans*. Alexandria, VA: Small Step.

Green, G. (2010). *Life constricted: To love, hugs and laughter*. N.p.: Xlibris.

Green, G., & Scott, M. (1984). *Contemporary African American scientists and inventors 1920-present*. San Francisco: Unpublished manuscript.

Powell, C. (1995). *My American journey*. New York: Random House.

Fatherhood Initiatives, Programs, and Resources

The following is a list of programs and initiatives related to fathering and fatherhood. This is not an exhaustive list, and others should be added as you see fit, but for further information or ideas on programming and resources, these are a good place to start.

24/7 Dad

https://www.depelchin.org/fatherhood/

This site offers tools and workshops to fathers and father figures on a range of topics, including balancing work and family, dealing with children and behaviors, and co-parenting, among others.

Boot Camp for New Dads

https://www.bootcampfornewdads.org/

This program was developed by the New Fathers Foundation. It focuses on father involvement in pregnancy, birth, and parenting.

Bringing Baby Home

https://www.gottman.com/professionals/training/bringing-baby-home/

This program was developed by the Gottman Institute to prepare couples for life with a baby and learn to strengthen their relationship.

California Social Work Education Center

https://calswec.berkeley.edu/toolkits/father-engagement-and-father-involvement-toolkit

The father engagement and father involvement toolkit assists in putting a new practice, program, or intervention in place to advance the importance of father engagement in communities to positively impact fathers, children, and families. The toolkits aid professionals in implementing and evaluating the practice, program, or intervention.

Dad Info

https://www.dad.info/

Dad Info was established as a "new generation men's lifestyle channel and the leading voice for Dads." The site boasts a celebration of the changing role of dads by offering engaging, helpful, practical, entertaining resources and content for every stage of their journey through a community of active, involved dads and peer-to-peer support and advice.

Fatherly: The Science of Dad and the "Father Effect"

https://www.fatherly.com/

Fatherly is dedicated to empowering men to raise their children and lead fulfilling adult lives. The site offers original reporting, expert parenting advice, and insights into fatherhood.

Good Men Project

https://goodmenproject.com/

The Good Men Project advances a conversation about changing roles and the modern lifestyle of men and fathers. They examine wide-ranging issues such as fatherhood, family, sex, ethics, war, gender, politics, sports, pornography, and aging.

National Fatherhood Initiative: Educating and Equipping Communities to Engage Fathers

https://www.fatherhood.org/

National Fatherhood Initiative (NFI) is a nonprofit organization whose mission is to end father absence and lack of father involvement in their children's lives. NFI works within the community, corrections, military organizations, and government agencies to create fatherhood programs.

National Responsible Fatherhood Clearinghouse (NRFC)

https://www.fatherhood.gov/

The National Responsible Fatherhood Clearinghouse is a national resource for fathers, practitioners, programs/federal grantees, states, and the public at large who are serving or interested in supporting strong fathers and families. The site offers research for policymakers, information to get fatherhood programs started or expanded, and information for fathers on managing family life.

The Fatherhood Institute

http://www.fatherhoodinstitute.org/

The work of the Fatherhood Institute focuses on policy, research, and practice. They offer a variety of resources for fathers, father figures, and their families to create strong, positive relationships. The institute also lobbies for legal and policy changes, helps public services and employers become more father inclusive, and participates in disseminating research.

The Fatherhood Project

http://www.thefatherhoodproject.org/

The Fatherhood Project is a nonprofit fatherhood organization in the Department of Psychiatry at Massachusetts General Hospital (MGH) in Boston. Their mission is to improve the health and well-being of children by empowering fathers to be active, informed, and emotionally engaged with their children and families.

True Dads

http://truedads.com/

TRUE Dads is a nonprofit based in Oklahoma City and equips fathers with resources and skills to support and parent children, build healthy relationships, and get help with employment. They offer a series of free workshops and a network of other fathers and local services.

Tuning in to Kids

http://www.tuningintokids.org.au/

This is a parenting program that helps kids learn to understand and regulate their emotions through education on emotional intelligence, emotion coaching, and effective communication.

Activities for Further Exploration and Discussion

Questions for Reflecting and Discussion

1. After reading the article, "Fatherhood and Family Policies" (Coltrane & Behnke, 2014), discuss the following:
   a. What are your main takeaways?
   b. What have you learned or what new insights have you gained?
2. What influence do these policies have on women, men, children, families, and society?
3. Are the policies reflective of the changes in society?
4. What should be considered when discussing fatherhood and family policies?
5. Who are the essential groups included in the discussion on fatherhood and family policy? Is anyone excluded? How might this exclusion impact conversation and future policies?
6. What lessons can we learn from the past?
7. There is much to unpack in the article "Fatherhood Love" (Green, 2011), from adoption and family secrets to dealing with illness and death. What are your takeaways from the article? Has this had an impact on your views?
8. At the end of the article, Green provides questions for reflection. Meditate on these questions and provide a brief answer to each.
9. Examine the initiatives, programs, and resources section. What information did you find?
10. What direct examples of effective parenting did you witness growing up?
11. What is one thing you would like to change in your personal relationship with your father?
12. Do biological relationships make a difference when considering the impact fathers have on children?
13. How does the Eurocentric framework for definitions, customs, and norms affect one's perspectives of families and the nature of fathering?

14. What principles, norms, values and worldviews inform your responses and reactions? (Think about the absences of these as well.)

15. What assumptions do you make about fathers, single fathers, and absent fathers? How do your assumptions play out when encountering or serving this population?

16. How does your commitment to family science legitimate and respect fathers' cultural experiences?

Teaching With Media

Suggested Videos and Films

The Fatherhood Project
A series that explores what it means to be a good father and the role dads play in our lives.

What Does It Mean to Be a Dad?

https://tinyurl.com/y784dj46

Committing to Hard Work and Perseverance

https://tinyurl.com/y7l3bqts

Don't Wait Until You Have It All Figured Out

https://tinyurl.com/y9dbj5co

How This 19-Year-Old Took on Fatherhood Is Inspiring

https://tinyurl.com/ydfolswo

Visiting a Gay Dad Family

https://tinyurl.com/yaatz989

Kramer vs. Kramer **(1979)**

A classic movie about a dissolving marriage and a mother and father choosing what is right for themselves and their family. It is a tale of divorce and a fight for child custody.

Mrs. Doubtfire **(1993)**

A divorced actor impersonates a nanny to spend time with his children.

John Q. **(2002)**

This movie is an example of a father who will do anything for his son who is on the edge of death.

The Pursuit of Happyness **(2005)**

This movie is based on a true story of a homeless scientist trying to raise a young boy while trying to get a job.

Fathers and Daughters **(2015)** *Adult content

A man grapples with being a widower and a father after a mental breakdown. This exemplifies how childhood experiences help shape your relationships.

Daddy's Little Girls **(2007)**

This is the story of a father trying to make ends meet to care for his three daughters.

Guiding Questions for the Films

1. How does fatherhood change a man?
2. How does a father become a man?
3. Sexism can be displayed both ways—discrimination against men as well as women. What are ways sexism is demonstrated in any of the films?
4. Does a father's influence or presence leave once he is gone (through death, abandonment, exile)?
5. From the film(s), provide examples of how childhood experiences help shape your relationship with yourself and others.
6. How important are friendship and supportive relationships in learning to be a father and a man?
7. What narrative do you think is important to change about men and fatherhood?

Father Biography

Write a short biography of your father or a father figure (e.g., coach, teacher, friend's father, cousin, uncle, brother, etc.). Following are suggestions to get you started.

Birth and childhood:

1. Place and significant historical events or relationships
2. Family life
3. What family gatherings and traditions you remember as a child?
4. What direct examples of parenting did you witness?

Adult Life and Legacy:

1. Is there a difference between being a father and being a dad? Explain.
2. Who were your fathering role models?
3. What is one thing your mom or dad always used to tell you growing up that turned out to be true?
4. What does it mean to be a good father?
5. How does one become a good father if there was not a father in the home?
6. What influence did your father have on your ideals about fathering?
7. What kind of father or dad are you? Are you the type of father you want(ed) to be?
8. What do (will) you enjoy most about being a dad?
9. In hindsight, is there a time you did not stand up for someone or something (a person, a cause) but wish you did? What prevented you from standing up?
10. How has (will) fatherhood change(d) you?
11. How has your idea of what it means to be a man changed over the span of your life?
12. What is your role in the family?

13. How do you care for yourself? Annual physicals and exams?
14. What is one underrated but important skill a person should possess?
15. What advice or wisdom would you like to pass down?
16. What legacy would you like to leave behind? How do you want to be remembered?

Ask any other questions you think are relevant to provide a complete picture of your father or father figure.

References

Adams, K. R. (2004). Influences of childhood/adolescence paternal relationships on African American women's expectations and needs for adult emotional (heterosexual) intimacy [Doctoral dissertation]. *Dissertation Abstracts International, 65*(3-A), 1112.

Baer, J. (1999). The effects of family structure and SES on family process in early adolescence. *Journal of Adolescence, 22*(3), 341–354.

Barrett H., & Tasker F. (2001). Gay fathers and their children: What we know and what we need to know. *Lesbian Gay Psychology Review, 3*, 3–10.

Cabrera, N. J. Fitzgerald, H. E., Bradley, R. H., & Roggman, L. (2014). The ecology of father child relationships: An expanded model. *Journal of Family Theory & Review, 6*(4), 336–354.

Carneiro, F. A., Tasker, F., Salinas-Quiroz, F., Leal, I., & Costa, P. A. (2017). Are the fathers alright? A systematic and critical review of studies on gay and bisexual fatherhood. *Frontiers in Psychology, 8*, 1636.

Chesley, N. (2011). Stay-at-home fathers and breadwinning mothers. Gender, couple dynamics, and social change. *Gender & Society, 25*(5), 642–664.

Coltrane, S. & Behnke, A. (2014). Fatherhood and family policies. In N. J. Cabrera & C. S. Tamis-LeMonda (Eds.), *Handbook of father involvement: Multidisciplinary perspectives* (pp. 419–437), Routledge.

Connor, M. E., & White, J. L. (2006). *Black fathers, an invisible presence in America.* Erlbaum.

Connell, R. W. (2005). *Masculinities.* University of California Press.

Crawford I., & Solliday E. J. (1996). The attitudes of undergraduate college students toward gay parenting. *Homosexuality, 30*(4), 63–77.

Demos, J. (1982). The changing faces of fatherhood: A new exploration in American family history. *Father and child: Developmental and clinical perspectives,* 425–445.

Doucet, A. (2004). It's almost like I have a job, but I don't get paid: Fathers at home reconfiguring work, care, and masculinity. *Fathering, 2*(3), 277–303.

Doucet, A. (2016). Is the stay-at-home dad (SAHD) a feminist concept? A genealogical, relational, and feminist critique. *Sex Roles, 75*(1–2), 4–14

Few-Demo, A. L., Humble, A. M., Curran, M. A., & Lloyd, S. A. (2016). Queer theory, intersectionality, and LGBT-parent families: Transformative critical pedagogy in family theory. *Journal of Family Theory & Review, 8*(1), 74–94.

Goodsell, T. L., Barrus, R. J., Meldrum, J. T., & Vargo, D. W. (2010). Fatherhood harmony: Polyphony, movement, and subjectivity. *Fathering, 8*(1), 3.

Graham, S. (1992). "Most of the subjects were White and middle class": Trends in published research on African Americans in selected APA journals, 1970–1989. *American Psychologist, 47*(5), 629–639. https://doi.org/10.1037/0003-066X.47.5.629

Green, G. (2011). Fatherhood love. In M. E. Conner & J. White (Eds.), *Black fathers: An invisible presence in America* (pp. 199–217). Routledge.

Grossberg, M. (1983). Who gets the child? Custody, guardianship, and the rise of a judicial patriarchy in nineteenth-century America. *Feminist Studies, 9*(2), 235–260.

Hamer, J. (2001). *What it means to be daddy: Fatherhood for Black men living away from their children.* Columbia University Press.

Harris, S. M. (2002). Father absence in the African American community: Towards a new paradigm. *Race, Gender, and Class, 9*(4), 111–133.

Hildreth, E., Jr., Hildreth, G., & Combes, B. (2018) Overcoming father absence through extended family engagement. *National Council on Family Relations, 31*(1), 20–23.

Hutchinson, S., Marsiglio, W., & Cohan, M. (2002). Interviewing young men about sex and procreation: Methodological issues. *Qualitative Health Research, 12*(1), 42–60.

Jones, J., & Mosher, W. D. (2013). Fathers' involvement with their children: United States, 2006–2010. *National Health Statistics Report, 71.* https://www.cdc.gov/nchs/data/nhsr/nhsr071.pdf

Miller, B. G., Kors S., & Macfie, J. (2017). No differences? Meta-analytic comparisons of psychological adjustment in children of gay fathers and heterosexual parents. *Psychology of Sexual Orientation and Gender Diversity, 4*(1), 14–22. https://doi.org/10.1037/sgd0000203

Morison, T. (2015). *What gay fathers can teach us about feminism and parenthood.* The Conversation. http://theconversation.com/what-gay-fathers-can-teach-us about-feminism-and-parenthood-47489

Pleck, J. H. (1998). American fathering in his historical perspective. In K. V. Hansen & A. I. Garey (Eds.), *Families in the US: Kinship and domestic politics* (pp. 351–361). Temple University Press.

Rabun, C., & Oswald, R. (2009). Upholding and expanding the normal family: Future fatherhood through the eyes of gay male emerging adults. *Fathering, 7*(3), 269–285.

Rentie, R. (2011). Debunking the myth: Understanding fathering in the Black community. In M. E. Connor & J. White (Eds.), *Black fathers: An invisible presence in America* (2nd ed.) (pp.84–97). Routledge.

Rotundo, E. A. (1982). Manhood in America: The Northern middle class, 1770–1920.

Smith, D. E. (1993). The standard North American family: SNAF as an ideological code. *Sage Journals, 14*(1), 50–65.

Solomon, C. (2014). I feel like a rock star: Fatherhood for stay-at-home fathers. *Fathering, 12*(1), 52–70.

Townsend, N. W. (2002). *The package deal: Marriage, work, and fatherhood in men's lives.* Temple University Press.

U.S. Census Bureau. (2016, November 17). *The majority of children live with two parents.* https://www.prnewswire.com/news-releases/the-majority-of-children-live-with-two-parents-census-bureau-reports-300365509.html#

U.S. Census Bureau (2017, June 28). *Fathers in the United States.* https://www.census.gov/schools/resources/news/fathers.html

Wade, M. (1998). Father presence: An enhancement of a child's well-being. *Journal of Men's Studies, 6*(2), 227–243.

Wittmer, D. S., Petersen, S. H., & Puckett, M. B. (2016). *The young child. Development from prebirth through age eight.* (7th ed.). Pearson.

Printed in the USA
CPSIA information can be obtained
at www.ICGtesting.com
LVHW070834291123
765201LV00008B/23